THE HANDBOOK OF
INTELLIGENT POLICING

THE HANDBOOK OF INTELLIGENT POLICING

CONSILIENCE, CRIME CONTROL, AND COMMUNITY SAFETY

EDITED BY

DR CLIVE HARFIELD
PROFESSOR ALLYSON MACVEAN
PROFESSOR JOHN GD GRIEVE
SIR DAVID PHILLIPS

OXFORD
UNIVERSITY PRESS

OXFORD

UNIVERSITY PRESS

Great Clarendon Street, Oxford OX2 6DP

Oxford University Press is a department of the University of Oxford.
It furthers the University's objective of excellence in research, scholarship,
and education by publishing worldwide in

Oxford New York

Auckland Cape Town Dar es Salaam Hong Kong Karachi
Kuala Lumpur Madrid Melbourne Mexico City Nairobi
New Delhi Shanghai Taipei Toronto

With offices in

Argentina Austria Brazil Chile Czech Republic France Greece
Guatemala Hungary Italy Japan Poland Portugal Singapore
South Korea Switzerland Thailand Turkey Ukraine Vietnam

Oxford is a registered trade mark of Oxford University Press
in the UK and in certain other countries

Published in the United States
by Oxford University Press Inc., New York

British Library Cataloguing in Publication Data

Data available

Library of Congress Cataloging-in-Publication Data
The handbook of intelligent policing / edited by Clive Harfield ... [et al.].
    p. cm.
Includes bibliographical references and index.
ISBN 978-0-19-953313-8 (hardback : alk. paper)— ISBN 978-0-19-953312-1 (pbk. :
alk. paper) 1. Police—Great Britain—Handbooks, manuals, etc. 2. Intelligence
service—Great Britain. I. Harfield, Clive.
    HV8195.H26 2008
    363.2'30941—dc22

2008019805

Typeset by Laserwords Private Ltd, Chennai, India
Printed in Great Britain
on acid-free paper by
Biddles Ltd., King's Lynn

ISBN 978–0–19–953313–8
ISBN 978–0–19–953312–1 (Pbk.)

1 3 5 7 9 10 8 6 4 2

ACKNOWLEDGEMENTS

This present volume is the culmination of a long-term project. Its impetus can be traced to a sequence of events fostered at the John Grieve Centre for Policing and Community Safety, culminating in a series of practitioner lectures informed by a number of senior female officials who operate in the world of intelligence.

The inspiration for a book to record emerging thinking was a series of conversations between Lord Imbert, previously Commissioner of the Metropolitan Police Service, and Professors Grieve and MacVean. In this regard we would also like to record our gratitude to Anil Patani, Assistant Chief Constable West Midlands Police, who has been steadfast in his support for the work of the John Grieve Centre. His encouragement has been unwaveringly energetic and steadfast.

Further inspiration was derived from Steven Johnson who, in his book *The Ghost Map*, interweaves an extraordinary story about two very different men, Dr John Snow, a teetotaller anaesthesiologist, and Reverend Henry Whitehead, an affable clergyman living in Soho. A man of God and a man of science, resorting to different methodologies and philosophical foundations, they came to discover through a combination of research, map-making, local knowledge, analysis, and logic, that cholera was spread by water and not borne on the air as most authorities at the time believed. Both Snow and Whitehead were consilient thinkers, building bridges between different disciplines, some of which barely existed as functional sciences in their day. This book, we hope, follows in that vein, representing a consilient approach towards intelligent policing. For that we are indebted to all our colleagues in academia, local government, and law enforcement who have given so generously of their time and effort in contributing to this volume and, in doing so, have produced unique and insightful contributions of research, map-making, and local knowledge in the disciplines which inform and invigorate intelligent policing.

Finally, our thanks go to Lindsey Davis, Jodi Towler, and Peter Daniell at Oxford University Press who steered the development of the book with gentle understanding and skill.

Dr Clive Harfield
Professor Allyson MacVean
Professor John GD Grieve CBE QPM
Sir David Phillips

SUMMARY CONTENTS

PART III CASE STUDIES—INTELLIGENCE AND PARTNERSHIP

PART IV BENCHMARKING THE WAY FORWARD

CONTENTS

PART II THE ROLE OF ANALYSIS

CONTRIBUTORS

Adrian Bhatti Community and Diversity Officer, Thames Valley Police.

Ludo Block Manager, IRS Forensic Services and Investigations, Rotterdam; former Netherlands Police International Liaison Officer, stationed in Moscow.

Adrian Bowers Recently retired West Midlands Detective Superintendent whose police service included work developing the National Intelligence Model and Knowledge Management. He continues to work in intelligence, knowledge management, and business process at <www.kis-c.com>, in partnership with the National Improvement Agency.

R Mark Evans OBE Director, Analytical Services, Police Service of Northern Ireland, currently seconded as National Manager: Intelligence, New Zealand Police.

Professor Frank Gregory Professor of European Security and Jean Monnet Chair in European Political Integration, University of Southampton.

Professor John GD Grieve CBE QPM Chair of the John Grieve Centre for Policing and Community Safety, London Metropolitan University; Independent Monitoring Commissioner, Northern Ireland; former Director of Intelligence, Metropolitan Police Service; former Independent Chair of the Greater London Alcohol and Drug Alliance.

Dr Clive Harfield Reader, John Grieve Centre for Policing and Community Safety, London Metropolitan University.

Federal Agent Michael Hawley Federal Agent, Australian Federal Police.

Laura Juett Senior Policy Officer, Greater London Authority.

Catherine Kelly Senior Lecturer in Information and Knowledge Management, London Metropolitan University.

Richard J Kerr Former Deputy Director, Central Intelligence Agency, USA. Recipient of the William J Barker award for lifetime achievement in intelligence.

Maren Eline Kleiven Politioverbetjent, Politihøgsklen, The Norwegian Police University College.

Sarah Lewis Manager, Greater Manchester Community Safety Partnership Team.

Professor Allyson MacVean University of Cumbria; founder and former Director of the John Grieve Centre for Policing and Community Safety, London Metropolitan University.

Esther Martin Head of Profession for Analysis, Intelligence Department, West Midlands Police.

Professor Ken Pease OBE Visiting Professor, UCL, Jill Dando Institute of Crime Science.

Sir David Phillips Former Chief Constable, Kent County Constabulary; former President of the Association of Chief Police Officers.

Dr Nick Ridley Senior Lecturer, John Grieve Centre for Policing and Community Safety, London Metropolitan University.

Sir Paul Scott-Lee Chief Constable, West Midlands Police.

Andrew Shipman Chief Inspector, West Midlands Police.

Jacqueline Sissens Senior Strategic Analyst, West Yorkshire Police; former intelligence analyst with Kent Country Constabulary, the Security Industry Authority, and the Special Anti-Crime Unit, Trinidad and Tobago. She undertook the research discussed in this chapter whilst studying at the Institute of Criminal Justice Studies, University of Portsmouth.

Rebecca Smith Senior Policy Officer, Greater London Authority.

Kalbir Sohi Research student, Department of Philosophy, Kings College London.

Professor Betsy Stanko Senior Advisor, Strategic Analysis, Directorate of Strategic Development, Metropolitan Police Service; Visiting Professor, Royal Holloway, University of London.

TABLE OF LEGISLATION

INTRODUCTION:
INTELLIGENT POLICING

Dr Clive Harfield

'If ever you believe only intelligence then you are lost.'

(Powell, 2008)

Why 'intelligent policing' when the prevailing and emerging mantras are 'intelligence-led policing' and 'knowledge-based policing'? For precisely the reason implicit in Sir Colin Powell's observation quoted above: intelligence has to be gathered, analysed, and used in context.[1] This collection of essays seeks to illustrate contexts of intelligent policing within which the technicalities of intelligence-led policing and knowledge-based policing might operate.

The 'profession' of intelligence is not self-contained. That is to say its constituent elements, information, interpretation, and implementation are rarely solely undertaken by intelligence professionals. Raw information may be generated by intelligence professionals but it will more often come from third parties and its accuracy therefore cannot be guaranteed. Intelligence professionals will then interpret the information gleaned, sometimes within given parameters that could include erroneous preconceptions held by those commissioning the intelligence analysis. In the next stage of the process decisions will be taken and actions will be implemented by the customers or users of the intelligence. They may or may not apply their own additional interpretations and their response to the intelligence may or may not be constrained by other factors that define how the analysed intelligence can, or cannot, be used. In other words the so-called second-oldest 'profession' (Knightley, 1986) is vulnerable to the variable vagaries of both professional and non-professional participation. There is a perceptual danger that the increasing use of science in seeking evidential certainty in the trial process has created the same public expectation of forensic certainty in intelligence work—within which context a fourth emerging constituent element of the intelligence profession might be suggested in the light of recent events: inquiry into what went wrong. Doubts about the intelligence that informed the decision to go to war in Iraq and confusion of the terrorist threat assessment immediately preceding the London bombing attacks of July 2005 (Butler, 2004; Hutton, 2004) arguably have eroded public confidence in 'intelligence' and its use.

Has any of this doubt and reduced confidence translated across from the security arena to the law enforcement arena? Given the increasing overlap between the two arenas in the issue of counterterrorism such a translation is perhaps inevitable, but

[1] Sir Colin Powell was Foreign Policy Advisor to former British Prime Minister, Margaret Thatcher.

even before the 'war on terror' in Britain domestic law enforcement episodes had significant intelligence-management implications not only for the police but also for partner agencies within the wider criminal justice system. There is much to be learnt from the circumstances leading up to, and in some cases following, the murders of Stephen Lawrence, Victoria Climbié, Jessica Chapman and Holly Wells, and Naomi Bryant (MacPherson,1999; Laming, 2003; Bichard, 2004; HMIP, 2006). Although no substitute for reading the original sources, for an introductory summary of these lessons together with a literature review of recent relevant HMIC thematic inspections see Harfield and Harfield, 2008.

At a strategic level, the evolution of intelligence learning catalogued in the cases above demonstrates the expanding expectations of intelligence within policing in its widest sense: from a historical focus on the proactive investigation of crimes and criminals (HMIC, 1997) to the preventative and, increasingly, pre-emptive demands now expressed in the continuum of community safety that is neighbourhood policing, public protection, and national security (Tilley, 2003; Home Office, 2004; HMIC, 2005). All this sits under the umbrella philosophy of risk management (Ericson and Haggerty, 1997; Nash, 1997) within the imperative of trying to meet ever-increasing demand for services from resources that could not exponentially increase in parallel to the demand: such is the political context and driver for intelligent policing in the twenty-first century.

The response to this drive for intelligent policing was the concept of intelligence-led policing which has widespread currency and almost as widespread interpretation (Ratcliffe, 2003). The interpretation in vogue in the UK found articulation in the National Intelligence Model (NIM) developed by the police service (Flood, 2004), and which, on the face of it, added some substance to the rhetoric of intelligence-led policing. Whether the outcome has been what the originators of the NIM intended is a moot point.

Seen as a mechanism for standardizing responses amongst the forty-three police forces of England and Wales, implementation of the NIM by 1 April 2004 was a requirement of the then National Policing Plan. This was achieved to varying degrees with neither interpretation nor implementation being standardized (John and Maguire, 2004a; John and Maguire, 2004b). Police practitioners have suggested that the label 'National Intelligence Model' is a misnomer and as such gives a misleading impression of what the NIM actually does (Kleiven, 2007: 269). Its focus is on business processes with defined meeting schedules and products—features that are easily quantifiable in a performance measurement-oriented culture. In part its purpose is to assign responsibility for those regional crime issues that sit outside the current local and national policing provision infrastructure. The NIM does not, in and of itself, facilitate the acquisition, collation, and management of intelligence. It requires intelligence units to be in place with prescribed roles but it does nothing to ensure these units are properly resourced or skilled. The greatest vulnerability of the NIM is its exposure to the possibility that the processes could be followed and the various tick-boxes achieved without intelligence-led policing actually happening.

A second weakness is that strict adherence to and focus on business processes fosters formulaic approaches that constrain lateral thinking and innovation. This injects particular vulnerability into partnership working because partner agencies can be excluded simply because the NIM is seen as a 'Police' tool, rather than a tool for policing in its widest sense. Ideas for potential resolutions and interventions that partners might seek to introduce may be rejected because they do not conform to 'Police' interpretations of the NIM.

Thus, a situation has been created in which expectations of 'intelligence' in policing are high; there are defined intelligence professionals who do not have control over the use of intelligence but are likely to be singled out for criticism in identified intelligence failings at a time when public confidence in intelligence has been shaken; and a defined structure which includes 'intelligence' in its title but is in fact a business model used to direct activity towards achieving performance management targets rather than necessarily responding to the prevailing crime and community safety environment. This context is the domestic policing and community safety equivalent of the 'fog of war' that so bedevils military intelligence.

There has been an expanding academic literature on the subject of intelligence in policing (Ratcliffe, 2002, 2003, 2004; Cope, 2004; Innes and Sheptycki, 2004; John and Maguire, 2004a and b; Innes, Fielding et al, 2005; Brodeur and Dupont, 2006; Maguire and John, 2006; Kleiven, 2007), together with an increase in official doctrinal and practice guidance (ACPO, 2005; ACPO/NCPE, 2005; Home Office, 2005; ACPO/NCPE, 2006) to set alongside the official inquiry literature already alluded to. Juxtaposed against this emerging literature is the already established literature on military intelligence (Gudgin, 1989; Hughes-Wilson, 1999; Moffat, 2002), on national security now repositioned within the context of global security post-9/11 (Andrew, 1985; Jeffreys-Jones, 2002; Innes, 2006; Brodeur, 2007; Johnson, 2007; Northcott, 2007; Wilkinson, 2007), on commercial competitive intelligence (West, 2001), and on private intelligence and its increasing interface with public security (Lippert and O'Connor, 2006; Dorn and Levi, 2007). This arena, too, has its own inquiry literature (Intelligence and Security Committee, 2002; Intelligence and Security Committee, 2003; Butler, 2004; Hutton, 2004).

So what, then, does this present volume add? What contribution does it seek to make? The collection of essays that follow illustrates various aspects of intelligent policing, rather than 'intelligence' per se. This is not a volume that purports to assert how intelligence should be 'done'. The variety of material herein illustrates that there is no one way of 'doing' intelligence for policing: precisely the point the reader is called to reflect upon. The material is arranged in four sections starting with some historical and theoretical considerations which provide a context for thinking about the development of and influences on police intelligence. There follows an examination of the use of analysis by law enforcement intelligence professionals which is intended to highlight part of the intelligence profession too often overlooked or taken for granted but which is a key to understanding intelligence material in context. The third part comprises five case studies on intelligence and partnership which illustrate current innovations seeking to bridge the gap between police and partner agencies in community safety. Finally a number of reflections on possible developments in intelligent policing are presented. Some of the contributors are established academics or commentators but many of them are practitioners with law enforcement and central or local government policy-making experience and as such represent new voices in the published discourse.

Intelligence-led policing has been defined as the gathering of information designed for action (Grieve, 2004: 25). Intelligent policing might be described as raising the discourse above the tactical operational level to consideration of policing in its widest sense. At this level there is no monopoly on good ideas and every reason to spread the net far and wide when seeking suitable and appropriate interventions. As the adage goes, if the only tool one has is a hammer, every problem looks like a nail. Partnership is an expression of intelligent policing rather than intelligence-led policing. Partnership, spreading the risk and the resource implications, is much in vogue at present (Home Office, 2004), and it was a partnership in Victorian England that inspired the editors of this volume to invite new voices amongst the contributors.

In 1854 a cholera epidemic, leading to 50,000 deaths, began in Soho, London, and spread across the country. As the authorities of the day laboured under the conventional wisdom that cholera was an air-borne disease, individually and for different reasons, in Soho a local doctor, John Snow, and the parish priest, Henry Whitehead, began their own investigations into the cause of the outbreak. Their independent analyses of different data led to the cumulative insight that cholera was a water-borne disease: a discovery that revolutionized medical and public health responses. It challenged prevailing conventional wisdom and earned neither Snow nor Whitehead any plaudits from the medical establishment. But methodical research and analysis, and the eventual pooling of disparate approaches, meant that together and in collaboration they arrived at a solution which neither would have arrived at alone. Success depended upon 'reconciling seemingly contradictory facts; recognising the significance of both particulars and patterns; recognising when correlation had been mistaken for causation; and above all drawing together different knowledge from a variety of contexts in order to look at a conventional wisdom from a different perspective' (Harfield and Harfield, 2008: 189).

It is a classic case study of consilient thinking, 'when an induction, obtained from one class of facts, coincides with an induction obtained from another class' (nineteenth-century Cambridge philosopher William Wherwell, quoted in Johnson, 2006: 67), thus illuminating ground-breaking insight. The misconceived prevailing medical wisdom in Victorian England ensured that 'the first defining act of a modern, centralized public-health authority was to poison an entire urban population' (Johnson, 2006: 120). In November 1983 preconception and failure to appreciate the influence of context on perceptions on the part of Cold War protagonists brought the world to the eve of nuclear Armageddon without US and UK military and intelligence communities having any idea that the Russians had deployed 300 intercontinental ballistic missiles in retaliatory readiness and the mistaken belief that President Ronald Reagan was about to rid the world of its 'evil empire' with a pre-emptive nuclear strike (*1983: The Brink of Apocalypse*, Flashback Television Ltd, Channel 4, 5 January 2008). Reagan's reflections on what nearly happened prompted him to recant his own prejudices, start talking with the Russians, and so bring about the end of the Cold War through dialogue.

It is the drawing together of different ideas and reflections with their potential for new insight that inspired this present collection. It is offered as a step away from technical discussions on the mechanics of the new conventional wisdom of intelligence-led policing and the emerging elaboration of knowledge-based policing towards an exploration of what intelligent policing might look like, with the ever present caveat from history that context is all: 'it's not just that the authorities of the day were wrong . . .; it's the tenacious, unquestioning way they went on being wrong' (Johnson, 2006: 125).

REFERENCES

ACPO, *The Recording and Dissemination of Intelligence Material: Code of Practice* (London: Association of Chief Police Officers, 2005).

——/NCPE, *Guidance on the National Intelligence Model* (Wyboston: National Centre of Policing Excellence, 2005).

——/——, *Guidance on the Management of Police Information* (Wyboston: Centrex, 2006).

ANDREW, C, *Secret Service: The Making of the British Intelligence Community* (London: Heinemann, 1985).

BICHARD, M, *The Bichard Inquiry Report* (House of Commons, London: TSO, 2004).

BRODEUR, J-P, 'High and Low Policing in Post 9/11 Times' *Policing: A Journal of Policy and Practice* 1/1 (2007) 25–37.

—— and DUPONT, B, 'Knowledge Workers or "Knowledge" Workers?' *Policing and Society* 16/1 (2006) 7–26.

BUTLER, Lord, *Review of Intelligence on Weapons of Mass Destruction* (London: TSO, 2004).

COPE, N, 'Intelligence Led Policing or Policing Led Intelligence?' *British Journal of Criminology* 44/2 (2004) 188–203.

DORN, N and LEVI, M, 'European Private Security, Corporate Investigation and Military Services: Collective security, market regulation and structuring the public sphere' *Policing and Society* 17/3 (2007) 213–238.

ERICSON, R and HAGGERTY, K, *Policing the Risk Society* (Oxford: Clarendon Press, 1997).

FLOOD, B, 'Strategic aspects of the UK national Intelligence Model' in Ratcliffe, J, ed, *Strategic Thinking in Criminal Intelligence* (Sydney: The Federation Press, 2004) 37–52.

GRIEVE, J, 'Developments in UK Criminal Intelligence' in Ratcliffe, J, ed, *Strategic Thinking in Criminal Intelligence* (Sydney: The Federation Press, 2004) 25–36.

GUDGIN, P, *Military Intelligence: The British Story* (London: Arms and Armour, 1989).

HARFIELD, C and HARFIELD, K, *Intelligence: Investigation, Community, and Partnership* (Oxford: Oxford University Press, 2008).

HMIC, *Policing with Intelligence: Criminal Intelligence—A Thematic Inspection of Good Practice* (London: HM Inspector of Constabulary, 1997).

——, *Closing the Gap: A Review of the 'Fitness for Purpose' of the Current Structure of Policing in England and Wales* (London: HM Inspector of Constabulary, 2005).

HMIP, *An Independent Review of a Serious Further Offence Case: Anthony Rice* (London: HM Inspectorate of Probation, 2006).

HOME OFFICE, *Building Communities, Beating Crime: A Better Police Service for the 21st Century* (London: TSO, 2004).

——, *Code of Practice on the Management of Police Information* (London: TSO, 2005).

HUGHES-WILSON, J, *Military Intelligence Blunders* (London: Robinson, 1999).

HUTTON, Lord, *Report of the Inquiry into the Circumstances Surrounding the Death of Dr David Kelly CMG* (London: TSO, 2004).

INNES, M, 'Policing Uncertainty: Countering terror through community intelligence and democratic policing' *Annals of the American Academy* 605 (May 2006) 1–20.

——, Fielding, N, et al, 'The Appliance of Science? The Theory and Practice of Crime Intelligence Analysis' *British Journal of Criminology* 45/1 (2005) 39–57.

—— and SHEPTYCKI, J, 'From Detection to Disruption: Intelligence and the changing logic of police crime control in the United Kingdom', *International Criminal Justice Review* 14 (2004) 1–24.

INTELLIGENCE AND SECURITY COMMITTEE, *Inquiry into Intelligence, Assessments and Advice Prior to the Terrorist Bombings on Bali* 12 October 2002 (London: TSO, 2002).

——, *Iraqi Weapons of Mass Destruction—Intelligence and Assessments* (London: TSO, 2003).

JEFFREYS-JONES, R, *Cloak and Dollar: A History of American Secret Intelligence* (New Haven: Yale University Press, 2002).

JOHN, T and MAGUIRE, M, (2004a) *The National Intelligence Model: Key Lessons From Early Research* (London: Home Office, 2004).

—— and ——, (2004b) *The National Intelligence Model: Early Implementation Experience in Three Police Force Areas* (Cardiff: School of Social Sciences, Cardiff University, 2004).

JOHNSON, L, ed, *Handbook of Intelligence Studies* (London: Routledge, 2006).

KLEIVEN, M, 'Where's the Intelligence in the National Intelligence Model' *International Journal of Police Science and Management* 9/3 (2007) 257–273.

KNIGHTLEY, P, *The Second Oldest Profession: The Spy as Bureaucrat, Patriot, Fantasist and Whore* (London: Andre Deutsch, 1986).

LAMING, L, *The Victoria Climbié Inquiry* (London: TSO, 2003) 427.

LIPPERT, R and O'CONNOR, D, 'Security Intelligence Networks and the Transformation of Contract Private Security' *Policing and Society* 16/1 (2006) 50–66.

MACPHERSON, W, *The Stephen Lawrence Inquiry: Report of an Inquiry by Sir William MacPherson of Cluny* (London: TSO, 1999).

MAGUIRE, M and JOHN, T, 'Intelligence Led Policing, Managerialism and Community Engagement: Competing priorities and the role of the National Intelligence Model in the UK' *Policing and Society* 16/1 (2006) 67–85.

MOFFAT, J, *Command and Control in the Information Age: Representing its Impact* (London: TSO, 2002).

NASH, M, *Police, Probation and Protecting the Public* (London: Blackstone Press, 1997).

NORTHCOTT, C, 'The Role, Organization and Methods of MI5' *International Journal of Intelligence and CounterIntelligence* 20/3 (2007) 453–479.

POWELL, C, Interviewed for *1983: The Brink of Apocalypse* (Flashback Television Ltd, broadcast Channel 4, 7.30pm, 5 January 2008).

RATCLIFFE, J, 'Intelligence-Led Policing and the Problems of Turning Rhetoric into Practice' *Policing and Society* 12/1 (2002) 53–66.

——, 'Intelligence-Led Policing' *Trends and Issues in Crime and Criminal Justice No 248* (Australian Institute of Criminology, 2003).

——, ed, *Strategic Thinking in Criminal Intelligence* (Sydney: The Federation Press, 2004).

TILLEY, N, 'Community policing, problem-oriented policing and intelligence-led policing' in Newburn, T, ed, *Handbook of Policing* (Devon: Willan Publishing, 2003) 311–339.

WEST, C, *Competitive Intelligence* (Basingstoke: Palgrave, 2001).

WILKINSON, P, ed, *Homeland Security in the UK: Future Preparedness for Terrorist Attack since 9/11* (London: Routledge, 2007).

PART I

THINKING ABOUT INTELLIGENCE

INTRODUCTION TO PART I:
IDEAS IN POLICE
INTELLIGENCE

Professor John GD Grieve CBE QPM

For a subject that has dominated much of the theoretical rhetoric about policing in the UK since the 1990s (encapsulated in the sound-bite 'intelligence-led policing'), there has been surprisingly little literature that attempts to collate and collect ideas about the profession of intelligence in policing, Ratcliffe's edited collection on *Strategic Thinking in Criminal Intelligence* being a notable exception (Ratcliffe, 2004). The essays gathered here in Part I explore different aspects of ideas and theories in police intelligence work and, in doing so, set the scene for the remainder of the volume. For the practitioner audience a literature review of significant official inquiries and studies of the National Intelligence Model (NIM) will be found elsewhere (Harfield and Harfield, 2008). Here the editors have drawn together thoughts from various perspectives to provide a conceptual context.

In the absence of a significant body of literature devoted to intelligence work in policing, it is hardly surprising that the military and national security arena have influenced key thinkers. The later parts of this volume seek to redress the balance by calling upon policing and community safety practitioners to present their own approaches and so contribute to the wider discourse. In this part, however, some of the contributions draw upon the parallel worlds of military and security intelligence. The section begins with contributions from two of the architects of intelligence-led police thinking in England and Wales: former Metropolitan Police Service Deputy Assistant Commissioner John Grieve and former Kent County Constabulary Chief Constable, Sir David Phillips, both of whom have active interests in military intelligence history.

The conceptual silver thread running through this whole collection is the concept of consilience: the examination of ideas in other disciplines to see if they offer insights into the problem currently under examination. Grieve's chapter is, in many respects, an exploration of consilience in action, drawing upon his personal reflections and experiential learning together with the thinking of Victorian writers on policing, military intelligence historians, the literature of the British empire, modern philosophy, and security lessons from Northern Ireland. He notes how responses to project and organized crime in London in the 1970s and performance management in the 1980s began to shape modern police thinking about the role of intelligence and the importance of understanding communities that provide both intelligence and the context for the practical application of intelligence.

Sir David Phillips does not necessarily agree. For him the essence of intelligence-led policing is fighting crime and convicting the criminals; community- or neighbourhood policing and performance management are seen as potential intelligence diversions from the primary function. Indeed, he suggests that neighbourhood policing 'may in fact provide a presence that at best might address some of the low-level but significant problems outside the effective grasp of intelligence work!' (see page 30 below). Community intelligence, which fuelled the consilient thinking of Dr John Snow and the Rev Henry Whitehead and that of William Farr and Edmund Cooper, whose work informed Snow (Johnson, 2006), and which in turn inspired this handbook, is presented almost as the antithesis of intelligence-led policing.

There follow the career reflections of former CIA Deputy Director, Dick Kerr, now a member of the Independent Monitoring Commission for the Northern Ireland peace process. The chapter highlights, in many respects, the different worlds in which national security/military intelligence and policing operate. It reminds us that intelligence is far more imprecise than evidence in the criminal justice system, and challenges us to reflect on why it is, why political pundits operating overtly cannot accurately predict the outcome of the democratic electoral process, why we the public expect the intelligence community and police analysts to be able accurately to predict and forestall terrorist atrocities and bring the offenders to justice.

Frank Gregory's paper then injects original research into the exploration of ideas about how intelligence is practised. He examines the dynamic relationship between UK national security intelligence and British policing, a relationship that has found (sometimes rapidly) evolving expression since the terrorist crimes perpetrated in New York and Washington DC in September 2001. At a time when partnership is promoted as the means to effective government (Home Office, 2004), Gregory observes a lack of clarity in mutual expectation between the police and intelligence communities, complicated by different organizational purposes, hierarchies and structures, and concerns about inter-agency rivalry and empire-building.

This inter-agency relationship gives rise to significant issues of governance in intelligence which are considered by Allyson MacVean. Highlighting the different governance traditions in the intelligence community and in policing, she questions the extent to which policing should draw on the intelligence community when managing its own intelligence profession. By looking to the lessons of the Butler and Hutton inquiries into the way in which intelligence was managed and portrayed in preparation for the invasion of Iraq, she argues that police intelligence must be protected from undue politicization.

Finally, and perhaps from left field but then that is the value and contribution of consilient thinking, Kalbir Sohi and Clive Harfield take a theoretical linguistic perspective on the language of intelligence as it relates to policing, and in doing so provide a caveat about the need for common understanding in debates that have recourse to labels widely employed but variously understood, despite the illusionary perception of consensus.

REFERENCES

HARFIELD, C and HARFIELD, K, *Intelligence: Investigation, Community, and Partnership* (Oxford: Oxford University Press, 2008).

HOME OFFICE, *Building Communities, Beating Crime* (Cm 6360, London: TSO, 2004).

JOHNSON, S, *The Ghost Map* (London: Allen Lane, 2006).

RATCLIFFE, J, ed, *Strategic Thinking in Criminal Intelligence* (Sydney: The Federation Press, 2004).

1

LAWFULLY AUDACIOUS: A REFLECTIVE JOURNEY

Professor John GD Grieve CBE QPM

> Police work is impossible without information, and every good officer will do his best to obtain reliable intelligence, taking care at the same time not to be led away on false issues. Information must not be treasured up, until opportunity offers for action by the officer who obtains it, but should be promptly communicated to a superior, and those who are in a position to act upon it. Not only is this the proper course of action to take, in the public interest, but it will be certainly recognised, both by authorities and comrades, promoting esteem and confidence, which will bring their own reward.
>
> (Vincent, 1881: 202)

This chapter provides an account of my journey as a police officer, who had the privilege of contributing towards the development of intelligence-led policing, and particularly the exploitation of intelligence for detectives. As Howard Vincent noted in the nineteenth century, 'every good officer will do his (sic) best to obtain reliable intelligence' (Vincent, 1881: 202) and this remains true in the twenty-first-century where intelligence is required for an ever increasing range of activities from counter-terrorism to neighbourhood policing. What follows is a contribution to an account of police intelligence as 'fragmentary; the pieces have yet to be put together, and the full jigsaw puzzle revealed.' (Porter, 2000: 13).

My thinking on intelligence falls broadly into two categories: first, theories of intelligence, originally military then individuals who have motivated and contributed to the philosophy of police intelligence; and second 'intelligence in action' through participating and reflecting on police operations This a limited, subjective overview of operations and strategies, I have not dealt with the important role of the interception of communications, nor with Special Branch, both of which have nevertheless contributed to and influenced my thinking but are still secret.

For the purposes of this chapter I accept John and Maguire's (2007: 201) definition of 'intelligence-led' as being the acceptance of proactive policing methods beyond the remit of specialist squads. My considerations provide a narrative from historical influences which precede that of John and Maguire, as is apparent from Howard Vincent's (1881) instruction quoted above. For that reason I do not deal here with specialized force intelligence branches like C11, some Home Office initiatives, nor generally with ACPO directives from the 1970s.

THEORIES AND PHILOSOPHIES OF INTELLIGENCE

SUN TZU: CONCEPTS 'FOREKNOWLEDGE AND ESTIMATES'

The *Art of War* is about leadership in statecraft and waging war. It is both strategic and tactical. Sun Tzu did not summarize his basic principles but many commentators have done since earliest times. Cleary (1991) notes that there were at least eleven Chinese commentators interpreting his work between the second and twelfth centuries. It is widely accepted that Sun Tzu's core tenets are 'know yourself, know your opposition and know the environment'. These still hold value today (McNeilly, 2001; Krause, 1996).

The Art of War defines foreknowledge as intelligence from human sources but significantly it also highlights that the enlightened and wise also know that intelligence can come from alliances such as with people with knowledge of the terrain and native guides (Griffith, 1963: 104, 138). Sawyer translates these alliances as 'advance knowledge' (1996: 118). McNeilly (2001) takes forward the work of Griffith and argues for the wider nature of the information now available for foreknowledge.

Consider for a moment the Chinese character that represents the title for Chapter 13 in *The Art of War*. This character has been identified as 'Secret Agents' (Griffith, 1963; McNeilly, 2001), but as Griffith records in a footnote (1963: 144) the character denotes: '"the space between two objects" (such as the "crack between two doors"), and thus "cleavage", "division" or to "divide". It also means "spies", "spying" or "espionage".'

The resonance for me is beyond agents, CHISs[1] or undercover officers; it goes to listening at doors, eavesdropping, collecting useful information, or as Jennifer Sims asserts 'information designed for action' (Sims, 1993). In addition, the advance knowledge from alliances further represents partnerships, local knowledge, and local guides, thus introducing independent advice in analysis. Nonetheless, as Sun Tzu shrewdly observed, 'He who is not sagacious and wise, humane and just cannot use secret agents. He who is not delicate and subtle cannot get the truth out of them.' (Griffith, 1963: 147, 149).

In 1997 the HMIC published a report, *Policing with Intelligence*, which summarized Sun Tzu:

Hence in the work of the entire force: Nothing should be regarded as favourably as Intelligence: nothing should be as generously rewarded as Intelligence: nothing should be as confidential as the work of Intelligence. Subtly, very subtly, nowhere neglect the use of Intelligence. It is called the Divine Web. It is the treasure of the Ruler. Sun Tzu c490 BC.

The report argued for a triple-track policing approach, using information from reactive, proactive, and prevention sources. These sources were to include the targeting

---

[1] Covert Human Intelligence Sources—a term applied to informants and police agents who use their position to obtain information from another without their knowing the true reason for the association.

of specific criminally active individuals and the monitoring of activities to obtain evidence for successful prosecution (HMIC, 1997). The model they proposed included:

- analysis of *all available information*[2] (author's italics) on crime and criminals;
- preparation of collection plan;
- execution;
- continuous feedback loop;
- problem-solving policing.

The report provided the basis for the work of Brian Flood and Roger Gaspar, which was to develop the National Intelligence Model (NIM)(Flood, 2004). The NIM is a business model comprising information around five key indicators: an accurate picture of the business, what is actually happening on the ground, the nature and extent of the problems, the trends, and where the main threats lie (NCIS, 2000: 11). The NIM takes account of local, cross-border, national, and international crime. In terms of the intelligence process, Canadians described it as a cyclical process involving a series of stages, including:

- collection of intelligence/information;
- evaluation;
- development;
- analysis/assessment;
- further development;
- dissemination;
- judgement;
- action—which may be an operational intervention or a return for further collection, thus creating an intelligence cycle (Canada, 1986 and 1995).

SIR JOHN KEEGAN (2003)—MODELS OF INTELLIGENCE IN A WORLD WHERE CRIME MEETS TERRORISM AND WARFARE

Describing military intelligence in war, the historian Sir John Keegan (2003:28) describes intelligence as a necessary but not sufficient ingredient in military success. He identifies a slightly different fundamental sequence for the intelligence process:

- acquisition—information has to be found;
- delivery—intelligence has to be sent to user at a time and place to be useful;
- acceptance—it has to be believed;
- interpretation—information comes in scraps, sometimes described as jigsaw (kaleidocope might be better—from Keegan's account it is about the piecing together of a whole cloth from scraps; it requires many experts and alliances);
- implementation—the intelligence has to be acted on by others.

Keegan explores with approval Rudyard Kipling's novel, *Kim* (Kipling, 1901). For many years I have asked myself how can what is widely perceived as a children's book

---

[2] This is relevant to the human rights model that says all interference by the state (and hence, by analogy, anyone) should amongst other considerations, be proportionate to the problem, legal, accountable, necessary and act upon the *best information*. See Neyroud and Beckley (2001).

help ease the pressure of managing the twenty-first-century risks for policing as Keegan now argues? In 1993 when dealing with street crime and the issues of juvenile CHISs we had turned to *Kim*. A former high ranking USAF intelligence specialist told me the model was as relevant today as in the nineteenth century in the border tribal areas where he had worked. Can *Kim*, a novel of empire, really help us avoid or resolve twenty-first-century problems in Stockwell or Forest Gate? An unlikely alliance seems to agree it might. Edward Said (2000: 12), once considered a philosopher for terrorists, described *Kim* as a 'racialist' book yet still hugely important for adults. Sir John Keegan agrees on the book's importance and says it might be a model for counterterrorist intelligence operations. It provides a novel and innovative way of looking at the difficult problems in understanding and managing the risks. *Kim* is about a boy with his feet in several cultures and communities in nineteenth century India. He is growing to manhood surrounded by threats and risks. The book reflects on Kim's growing sensitivity to the world he inhabits, his education, his mentors, his love for his fellow men and women, and his recruitment and training as an intelligence officer.

However, in the twenty-first-century, the police officer not only has to seek out the best available intelligence; he or she also has to act in ways that are proportionate, legal, accountable, and necessary in managing the risks. As a senior police officer said to me recently:

... the communities and people who populate the most diverse cities correctly expect us to get it right every time. But as we learnt with PIRA [Provisional IRA] attacks, the terrorists have only to get it right once; the consequences of the police getting it wrong in a terrorist attack, just the once, are now magnified a thousand-fold.

How do we start to understand the complexity of intelligence? What is it we need to understand or appreciate about the task of policing and the demands on police officers? The increasing speed and trajectory of intelligence about possible attacks arriving on their and their colleagues' desks; the variety of enemies and allies; the sheer volume of terrorist cases stacking up in the courts; the questions of intelligence shared or not between international allies; contradicting accounts in press and legal commentary; allegations of police blunders and cover-ups.

Is there some unifying theme throughout these complex and competing demands? Part of the current debates about policing in time of extreme terrorist threats has revolved around decisions and choices made based on intelligence. Yet, as the same senior police officer acknowledged,

The final part of the intelligence cycle is taking action, when and where to find the evidence, when to disrupt. As time goes by the risks can begin to escalate, to become unacceptable...

As the first Director of Intelligence for New Scotland Yard and as National Coordinator for Counter Terrorism Investigations I have experienced criticisms of police intelligence operations and fatal police shootings. My Commissioners had to answer for my decisions and choices, the information I had received, the assessments and analyses carried out, the operational deployments, and the resources employed.

Keegan argues that intelligence, even the best intelligence—even that of 'superlative tactical value' (Keegan, 1982: 151)—'while generally necessary is not a sufficient means to victory' (Keegan, 2003: 28). Adapting Moltke, Keegan has argued 'no intelligence assessment, however solid its foundation, fully survives the test of action' (Keegan, 2003: 4). The great intelligence analyst George W Allen (2001) who trained Dick Kerr (see Chapter 3 below) wrote that in the ideal intelligence assessment there was 'no substitute for thorough, conscientious, objective analysis of all the factors bearing on a decision, of alternative courses of action, and of weighing the consequences of all the options available' (Allen, 2001: 282).

In exploring his hypothesis that intelligence is a necessary but not sufficient ingredient in success, Keegan goes on to illustrate how no intelligence is so pure it will resolve all doubts; that no intelligence assessment, however solid its foundations, fully survives the test of action; and that local knowledge is always required to make successful use of real-time intelligence (Keegan, 2003: 89 and 399). This last is a rare product for the military, he argues but, I would argue, not rare, but core business, for police. His former students on Operation Banner in Northern Ireland concluded that information was more vital than firepower (MOD, 2006: 5–1). I argue that analysed intelligence is more potent than coercive force for policing.

HOFSTADTER (1980)—A PHILOSOPHICAL APPROACH

Douglas Hofstadter (1980: 29) offered the reform programme for intelligence in the late 1990s a wider use of the word 'intelligence' for educated customers. As a philosopher creating an account of mind and identity through discussion of artificial intelligence, he takes us into the intelligent use of intelligence. He maintains that it is essential to:

- respond to situations flexibly
- take advantage of fortuitous circumstances
- make sense of ambiguous or contradictory information
- recognize the relative importance of different elements, finding similarities between situations despite differing elements and drawing distinctions despite similarities
- synthesize new concepts from old
- assimilate material and information together in new ways
- advance solutions and ideas that are novel.

These theoretical approaches should now be applied to some milestones in policing with intelligence.

THE RESPONSES TO THE RISE OF PROJECT AND ORGANIZED CRIME

The last three elements from Hofstadter are evident in the changing roles of the Flying Squad, Robbery and Pickpocket (Dip) Squads, Street Robbery, Drugs and Regional Crime Squads as part of the response to what Mary McIntosh (1971) called 'Changes in the Organisation of Thieving'. She records that the police strategy changed as crimes developed from craft to project crimes of growing volume. Of particular relevance is the opportunity for police intelligence-gathering during the planning and preparatory efforts for project crimes. Volume project crimes for McIntosh include organized car crime (stolen car squads—1960s), burglary (for example, Operation Bumblebee—1980s), street theft and street robbery (Operation Eagle Eye, Operation Strongbox—1990s) and other urban volume crimes as well as the 1963 Great Train Robbery (McIntosh, 1971: 116–130). The intelligence-led responses operated in real-time at both the tactical and strategic level, allowing the exploitation of dedicated surveillance teams. Being intelligence-led enabled operations to be considered and directed in a multi-layered approach, thus allowing a more effective response at policy, co-ordination and tasking, case law, and legal requirements, including the increased use of undercover officers and informants (later to be classified as Covert Human Intelligent Sources, CHIS).

THE INTELLIGENCE RESPONSE TO DRUGS TRAFFICKING

The police response to drug-trafficking illustrates multiple layers of intelligence-led policing and neatly encapsulated John and Maguire's (2007: 201) definition as the intelligence-led approach of highly specialized squads rapidly permeated down to local and street level. It also illustrates the growth of individual, local, and specialized responses to national policy. Policing drug-trafficking also needs to consider the complex interaction of volume/project crimes, the growth of highly organized crime, money-laundering, and corruption (Dorn, Murji and South, 1992; Clutterbuck, 1995), the intelligence role of informants who were traffickers themselves (Clark, 2001), and techniques like the first international specialist liaison officers from the USA (Honeycombe, 1974) and their proliferation in many other countries.

A notable event in intelligence was the development of the police self-created and Home Office Indices from the 1920s which were transformed into the CI Drugs Index in the 1960s at New Scotland Yard, and which then further evolved to become the foundations for the Central Drugs Illegal Immigrants Intelligence Unit 1972 and finally the NCIS and SOCA (Grieve, 2004b).

Here lay the foundation of open-source intelligence. Abram Shulsky (1993) has written that one role of an intelligence officer is to educate their customers. One task of intelligence is to inform policymakers and to provide strategic information. Another is to provide tactical or operational information at a local level, thus providing the 'information base' for partnerships in giving advice on best practice. This shift towards sharing intelligence with partners was a move towards some aspects of police intelligence becoming open. A far-reaching development from the 1960s onwards in open source or wider intelligence-led drugs policing involved policing roles in policy formation, assessing the scale of drug use, supervision of licensing, prescription, research, and training (Bean, 2002; Grieve, 1998 and 2004b). This initiative was the beginning of the development of local indicators, and one in which the police showed considerable interest as the concept of local solutions to local problems emerged. Later, during the late 1990s, the same concept was to be applied to the policing of racist attacks (Metropolitan Police and Home Office, 2002).

By the end of the 1970s, police drug strategy primarily focused on enforcement, the supervision of licit supply, the pursuit of dealers, and was becoming nationally and internationally increasingly intelligence led. However, the 1980s were to mark another decade of intelligence change. This included changed structures, changed tactical and strategic intelligence, changes in the nature of dealers, changes to the nature of drug-trafficking, and of course major statements of changes in policy (Bean and Billingsley, 2001; Bean, 2002).

The report of the Home Affairs Committee on the Misuse of Hard Drugs (1982) advocated a raft of recommendations in respect of intensified intelligence-led law enforcement efforts. These included the role of armed services, the seizure and forfeiture of assets, a strategy to undermine international banking secrecy, the laundering of cash, an increase in penalties for trafficking to life, trial in UK for UK-related offences committed abroad, and crop eradication and substitution policies. These recommendations were enhanced further by the Confiscation of the Proceeds of Drug-Trafficking Act, which received royal assent in 1986. The strategy was now to link drugs, money, and prisoners; the nucleus being intelligence. The legislation identified new offences, powers, restraint orders, confiscatory fines, and international dimensions.

In addition to legislation, the web to gather intelligence was extended when in the 1980s the UK posted a National Drugs Intelligence Unit Officer to Amsterdam; a Customs Officer was also posted to Karachi, thus being the first two of the UK Drug Liaison Officers, and a world intelligence structure began to emerge. Two European initiatives in the 1990s were to illustrate the further development for multi-agency open-source intelligence. The Institute for the Study of Drug Dependence is the UK operational end of the European Monitoring Centre on Drugs and Drug Abuse (the Home Office is the policy end for the UK). The other is the European Association for the Treatment of Addiction. Both provide Europe-wide analysis and comparative data on an open database to any customers.

As I argued in 1998, open intelligence on drugs as education (Grieve, 1998: 4) has to be even-handed otherwise it tends towards dogma, propaganda, censorship of the unwelcome, or indoctrination. Education must not be just for teachers, parents, peers, and governors but also for the customers of intelligence, as Shulsky (1993) argued.

INFORMANTS AND ETHICS

Informants were at the heart of both successful and unsuccessful anti-drugs operations. Sun Tzu acknowledges five categories of informers:

- the 'Natives' who provide a source of intelligence from the enemy country's own people;
- the 'Insiders' who are employed enemy officials;
- the 'Doubled' who are enemy spies that are employed and turned;
- the 'Expendable' who are given fabricated information;
- the 'Living' are those who return with information.

(Griffith, 1963: 145)

These five categories of CHISs comprise the 'Divine Skein' and provide the finest of insider, up to the minute, real-time operational information. Griffith (1963) explains the concept of the 'Divine Skein' as '... information may be gathered in as fish are by pulling on a single cord and so drawing together the various threads of a net.' He identifies the importance of these information sources as 'of all those in the army close to the commander none is more intimate than the secret agent; of all rewards none more liberal than those given to secret agents; of all matters none is more confidential than those relating to secret operations' (Griffith, 1963: 145).

Though not identical to the needs of post-modern policing, these are useful analogies. The Home Office Guidance of 1969 and 1986 referred to CHISs as 'informers who participate in crime' and said they 'should not counsel incite or procure the commission of an offence'(see also Clarke, 2001).

One of the challenges of using CHISs as a source of intelligence is to ensure that the system operates within an ethical and principled environment. Powis (1977) was instrumental in the progress to an ethical informants system (Metropolitan Police, 1998; Clarke, 2001). He reviewed and increased the 'rewards' from public funds and set out clear audit trails for rewards from outside bodies, particularly from banks and insurance companies. However, it was in the field of 'participation in crime' that he left his greatest mark, both at the participation in crimes yet to be and in the super-grass system (Kelland, 1986: 217).

TERRORISM, INTELLIGENCE, AND THE LESSONS FROM NORTHERN IRELAND

Terrorism, intelligence, and the lessons from Northern Ireland blend military intelligence theories with those of police intelligence thinking. The British Army's closing report on Operation Banner during their 38-year-long deployment in Northern Ireland concludes that it is hard to understate the importance of intelligence: 'in peace support or counter-insurgency operations, information is the currency, not firepower' (MOD, 2006: para 8–5, page 818). The expansion and increased effectiveness of both the Army and Police intelligence-gathering operations, from close observation covert surveillance platoons to stop and search, led to a massive increase in accurate information flow: 'There was a huge expansion in the numbers employed in intelligence collection, collation, analysis, and dissemination, with the greatest qualitative emphasis being on collection' (MOD, 2006: 5–1).

At one point, one in eight regular soldiers in Northern Ireland were engaged in intelligence operations and, during the course of two months, one hundred and six PIRA senior figures were arrested. The lessons of these operations were incorporated into wider policing practices, not least by Sir Kenneth Newman. Newman had worked in Palestine and Northern Ireland and returned to the Metropolitan Police via the Police Staff College (Savage, 2007). He brought with him thinking, not just about intelligence lessons, but about many other disciplines, most notably twentieth-century business models of planning and performance—Problem-Oriented Policing and Policing by Objectives. As a consilient thinker, Newman had been in community relations before he went to Northern Ireland and his consideration of the impact on the community from certain kinds of crimes and policing responses to them was innovative. This led to collection plans for intelligence and action, allocation of resources, coordination, and tasking groups at the local borough level (Savage, 2007).

THE RISE OF INTELLIGENCE-LED SYSTEMS

During the 1990s, Kent Constabulary were pioneering a range of intelligence processes and tools. These included dissemination of intelligence using dedicated permanent briefing officers and from prisoner interviews. At the same time, systems to record and process the intelligence so that it could be 'developed for policy and operations, strategy and tactics' (Sims, 1993) were being developed. The System for Investigation and Detection (SID) was the first pan-London system. The system was able to identify minimum staffing levels for local borough-based intelligence cells (the roles included analysts and researchers) responsibilities for senior officers and authority levels, procedures and commonality of reporting, including evaluation criteria and confidence levels. The SID project encompassed every level—local, area and force—and included education of both intelligence staff and customers. It developed three kinds of subjects:

- Promnoms: active criminals who were the subject of local activity to arrest;
- Devnoms: those who were the subject of research or collection either locally or in partnership with others;
- Agencynoms: those who were the subject of interest to other teams, for example, Regional Crime Squads or Drugs Squads (Metropolitan Police).

Stephen Lawrence's ghastly racist murder on 22 April 1993 led to many important and fundamental changes to policing, particularly in intelligence systems (Grieve, 2007: 50 ff). The ensuing inquiry provided the driver for more changes in local intelligence gathering through the implementation of community impact assessments. Michael Mansfield QC, a critic of police intelligence gathering on human rights grounds was an unlikely advocate, but advocate he is of the proposition to make intelligence community-friendly. In his closing speech at the Inquiry (1999), he stated:

Where the offence occurs in the hours of darkness over a short space of time and the perpetrators disappear on foot into the locality, it then behoves investigating officers to act with speed and intelligence. Time is of the essence. With every passing hour . . . (Steven Lawrence Inquiry, 1999, Transcript Michael Mansfield QC closing speech, p 11063, lines 20–25).

He further asserted:

In summary, there plainly has to be a compendious and effective local intelligence gathering operation in existence that can be accessed quickly by officers at any time, day or night, especially when those officers may not be familiar with the locality. The information itself should be categorised in such a way that it can be called up by reference to name, or description, or address, or offence, or modus operandi, or vehicle or associates. Computerisation must clearly have made this possible for the future (Stephen Lawrence Inquiry, 1999, Transcript Michael Mansfield QC closing speech, p 11055, lines 2–12).

Three simultaneous developments at the millenium—the Intelligence Cell Analytic System (ICAS) to provide leadership for community-impact-driven imperatives (Metropolitan Police), the introduction of the Regulation of Investigatory Powers Act (2000), and the business model NIM (NCIS, 2000) formalized many existing systems so that they could be controlled (Harfield and Harfield, 2005).

CONCLUSION

I have used three of many models and five of the milestones that record my journey. It is worth reflecting on the potential for intelligence systems whether these overlapping models have led to an over-concern with control, regulation, and compliance to the cost of innovation. I introduced this chapter with Sun Tzu and Howard Vincent. 'Police work is impossible without information, and every good officer will do his best to obtain reliable intelligence, taking care at the same time not to be lead away on false issues' (Vincent, 1881: 202).

Intelligence is a system which operates in a non linear world; there are a vast number of complex diverse communications, interconnections, and multiple feedback operations. There is a real risk that the system—its analysis and assessment—may be spread too thinly and hence fail broadly (Chapman, 2003). There is also a real danger that parochial (by which I mean unjustified) failure to allow access could mean that vital connections may be missed as they have in the past. There is the risk that a system adds to the pathologies some have identified (for example Sheptycki, 2004). Contrary to some accounts or interpretations, intelligence-led policing is not just derived from volume-crime investigative failure nor from a negative response to other ineffectiveness or failures (Lowe, 2001; Audit Commission, 1994 and 1996), but is a positive evolution of street tactics that followed Vincent's lead.

Some of the most powerful learning for me came from Lord Laming in his Victoria Climbié Inquiry Report (2003: 14.73) where he and John Fox examined the risks posed to Victoria and the inability to achieve safe resolution through missed opportunities, not least from the failure to share or use information intelligently. They specifically consider the failure to probe, question, and challenge when information was partial. They were also concerned with the blurred lines of accountability, not least in respect of that information held by different agencies on different systems, which contributed to the failures. They further wrote that the unquestioning acceptance of information, which was undesirable in a social worker, was unacceptable in a police officer and they should bring to an inquiry three dimensions:

• healthy scepticism;
• an open mind;
• an investigative approach.

There is no finer guidance for police intelligence officers nor greater tribute to Howard Vincent's leadership.

REFERENCES

ALLEN, GW, *None So Blind*: *A Personal Account of Intelligence Failure in Vietnam* (Chicago: Ivan R Dee, 2001).

AMIR, M and EINSTEIN, S, *Police Corruption: Challenges for Developed Countries—Comparative Issues and Commissions of Inquiry* (Huntsville Texas USA: Sam Houston University, 2004).

AUDIT COMMISSION, *Tackling Crime Effectively* (London: Audit Commission, 1994).

——, *Tackling Crime Effectively Part 2* (London: Audit Commission, 1996).

BAGGINI, J and STRANGROOM, J, *New British Philosophy: The Interviews* (London: Routledge, 2002).

BEAN, P, *Drugs and Crime* (Devon: Willan Publishing, 2002).

—— and BILLINGSLEY, R, 'Drugs, Crime and Informers' in Billingsley, R, Nemitz, T and Bean, P, eds, *Informers, Policing, Policy, Practice* (Devon: Willan Publishing, 2001) 25–37.

BILLINGSLEY, R, NEMITZ, T and BEAN, P, eds, *Informers, Policing, Policy, Practice* (Devon: Willan Publishing, 2001).

BEVERIDGE, P, *Inside the CID* (London: Pan, 1947).

Canada (1986 and 1995), Presentations during Metropolitan Police Research into Asset Seizure Legislation and the SID Project, unpublished.

CHAPMAN, J, *System Failure* (London: Demos, 2003).

CLARKE, R, 'Informers and Corruption' in Billingsley, R, Nemitz, T and Bean, P, eds, *Informers, Policing, Policy, Practice* (Devon: Willan Publishing, 2001) 38–49.

CARSON, D, MILNE, B, PAKES, F, SHALEV, K and SHAWYER, A, *Applying Psychology to Criminal Justice* (Sussex: Wiley, 2007) 39–64.

CLEARY, T, trans, Sun Tzu, *The Art of War* (Boston and London: Shambala, 1991).

——, *Mastering the Art of War: Commentaries on Sun Tzu's Classic* (Boston and London: Shambala, 1995).

CLUTTERBUCK, R, *Drugs, Crime and Corruption* (London: Macmillan, 1995).

COHEN, S, ed, *Images of Deviance* (Middlesex: Pelican Special for Penguin, 1971).

DORN, N, Murji, K and South, N, *Traffickers, Drug Markets and Law Enforcement* (London: Routledge, 1992).

FLOOD, B, in Ratcliffe, J, ed, *Strategic Thinking in Criminal Intelligence* (Sydney: Federation Press, 2004) 37–53, and personal communication 9 September 2004.

FRICKER, M, 'Power Knowledge and Injustice' in Baggini, J and Strangroom, J, *New British Philosophy: The Interviews* (London: Routledge, 2002) eds, 57–76.

GRIEVE, J, 'Sitting on the Lid' *Policing Today* 1/1 (1994).

——, 'Intelligence as Education for All' in O'Connor, L, O'Connor, D, Best, R, *Drugs: Partnerships for Policy, Prevention and Education* (London: Cassell, 1998) 3–10.

——, (2004a) 'Developments in UK Criminal Intelligence' in Ratcliffe, J, ed, *Strategic Thinking in Criminal Intelligence* (Sydney: Federation Press, 2004) 25–36.

——, (2004b) 'From Medical Contagion to Police Corruption' in Amir, M and Einstein, S, *Police Corruption: Challenges for Developed Countries—Comparative Issues and Commissions of Inquiry* (Huntsville, Texas: Sam Houston University, 2004) 251–266.

——, 'Behavioural Science and the Law: Investigation' in Carson, D, Milne, B, Pakes, F, Shalev, K and Shawyer, A, *Applying Psychology to Criminal Justice* (Sussex: Wiley, 2007) 39–64.

GRIFFITH, SB, trans, Sun Tzu, *The Art of War* (Oxford: Clarendon Press, 1963).

HARFIELD, C and HARFIELD, K, *Covert Investigation* (Oxford: Oxford University Press, 2005).

HMIC (Her Majesty's Inspectorate of Constabulary) *Policing With Intelligence, Criminal Intelligence—A Thematic Inspection of Good Practice* (Home Office, 1997).

HOFSTADTER, DF, *Godel, Escher, Bach: An Eternal Golden Braid* (London: Penquin, 1980).

HONEYCOMBE, G, *Adam's Tale* (London: Hutchinson and Co, 1974).

JOHN, T and MAGUIRE, M, 'Criminal Intelligence and the National Intelligence Model' in Newburn, T, Williamson, T and Wright, A, eds, *Handbook of Criminal Investigation* (Devon: Willan Publishing, 2007) 199–224.

KEEGAN, J, *Six Armies in Normandy* (Middlesex: Penguin, 1982).

——, *Intelligence in War* (London: Hutchinson, 2003).

KELLAND, *Crime in London* (London: Bodley Head, 1986).

KIPLING, R, *Kim* (London: Penguin Classic Edition, 1901).

KRAUSE, DG, *The Art of War for Executives* (London: Nicholas Brealey Publishing, 1996).

LAMING, Lord, *The Victoria Climbie Inquiry* (Cm 5730, London: TSO, 2003).

LOWE, D, 'Shifting Focus' in *Police Review* (30 March 2001).

MACINTOSH, M, 'Changes in the Organization of Thieving' in Cohen, S, ed, *Images of Deviance* (Middlesex: Pelican Special for Penguin, 1971) 98–133.

MCNEILLY, M, *Sun Tzu and the Art of Modern Warfare* (Oxford: Oxford University Press, 2001).

METROPOLITAN POLICE, *Informant Working Group Report. Informing the Community: Developing Informant Risk Assessment to Reflect Community Concerns* (London: MPS, 1998).

—— and HOME OFFICE, *Targeted Policing Initiative Joint Project. Understanding and Responding to Hate Crime—Fact Sheets (1) Domestic Violence, (2) Racial Violence, (3) Homophobic Violence* (London: MPS and Home Office, 2002).

MINISTRY OF DEFENCE (MOD), *Operation Banner: Report for Chief of General Staff* (London, 2006).

NCIS (National Criminal Intelligence Service) *The National Intelligence Model* (London, 2000).

NEWBURN, T, WILLIAMSON, T and WRIGHT, A, eds, *Handbook of Criminal Investigation* (Devon: Willan Publishing, 2007).

NEYROUD, P and BECKLEY, A, *Policing, Ethics and Human Rights* (Devon: Willan Publishing, 2001).

O'CONNOR, L, O'CONNOR D and BEST, R, *Drugs: Partnerships for Policy, Prevention and Education* (London: Cassell, 1998).

PORTER, R, *Enlightenment: Britain and the Creation of the Modern World* (London: Peguin Books, 2000).

POWIS, D, *The Signs of Crime* (McGraw-Hill, 1977).

RATCLIFFE, J, ed, *Strategic Thinking in Criminal Intelligence* (Sydney: Federation Press, 2004).

SAID, EW, in Kipling, R, *Kim*, Introduction and Notes (London: Penguin Classic Edition, 2000).

SAWYER, RD, *The Complete Art of War: Sun Tzu and Sun Pin* (Colorado: Westview Press, 1996).

SAVAGE, S, *Police Reform* (Oxford: Oxford University Press, 2007).

SHEPTYCKI, J, 'Organizational pathologies in police intelligence: Some contributions to the lexicon of intelligence-led policing' *European Journal of Criminology* 1/3 (July 2004).

SHULSKY, A, *Silent Warfare: Understanding the World of Intelligence* (Washington DC: Brassey's Inc., 1993).

SIMS, J, 'What is intelligence?' (paper 1) in Shulsky, A and Sims, J, *What is Intelligence?* (Working Group on Intelligence Reform, Washington. Consortium for the Study of Intelligence, Georgetown University, 1993).

TSO (HMSO), *The Stephen Lawrence Inquiry Report* (Appendices and Daily Transcripts, London: HMSO, 1999).

VINCENT, CEH, *Police Code: Manual of the Criminal Law* (London: Cassell, Petter, Galpin and Co, 1881).

2

POLICE INTELLIGENCE SYSTEMS AS A STRATEGIC RESPONSE

Sir David Phillips

The police, although a strong case can be made that it should be so, have never quite established 'professional' status. A consequence has been that the police service approach to 'doctrine' has been fragmentary. Doctrine is the establishment of good operational practice against published and evidence-based research. A professional is not bound by doctrine; rather he or she is expected to be able to use knowledge with discretion. But doctrine does imply a rational, methodical, and empirical approach and the contribution of experience to a shared corpus of knowledge. Over the last decade and a half the Association of Chief Police Officers (ACPO) has sought to bring more authority to its deliberations as a national policy lead and more recently government has financed its own agency to achieve the same ends. Nonetheless a proper 'corpus of knowledge' has been slow to develop. In the absence of credible doctrine in any organization good practice tends to be based upon vague craft values, ambitious clichés, and nostalgic if not atavistic instincts. Indeed there are present dangers that policy formation will, in the current climate of risk aversion, replace initiative founded on 'doctrine' with 'doctrinaire' rigidity.

The adoption of 'intelligence' as a method is entirely devoid of sentiment (except when it is misused). It does not allude to desired ends nor prescribe, nor indeed proscribe, any particular style of policing or scheme of deployment. It is merely rational. It applies a dispassionate measure to the problems faced *and* the methods used. In this sense it is a 'discipline' demanding knowledge against which informed choices can be made by thinking professionals. As such, and although initially conceived as a *tactical response* against difficult targets, the idea of 'intelligence' can be seen as a *strategic response* to many of the problems outlined earlier: a counter to sentimental policing mythologies and a solution to the problems of demand management, the changing criminal environment, and the inadequacy of the existing criminal justice framework. This chapter explores intelligence as a strategic professional response within the work of the police service.

INTELLIGENCE AS A DISCIPLINE

The first thing to be said about 'intelligence' as an idea is that it is to be distinguished from 'information'. Policing generates great quantities of information stored as voluminous records of crime and incidents. Much of it is situationally specific. The police can access information from other public agencies having an interest in the same people and of course can access open sources. Items of information in a technical sense stand alone as facts or presumptions: the details of a crime, an observation of a criminal target, the location of an arrest, the identity of a suspect—the list is endless. Dealing with information and recording it accurately is a necessary part of the policing routine. And although reports of crimes, incidents and cases for prosecution involve clusters of information, their association is specific to the case in hand. Voluminous files of information have a value as a point of reference but users tend not to generalize from them other than anecdotally or in a casual way.

Intelligence by contrast is about generalizing from information not merely identifying it as a reference (although the system may do that as well). It is the product of studying information to provide interpretive models and explanations (synthesizing connectable data) from which we can extract predictions (by analysis and assessment). At a formal level it is a discipline and a process; at a functional level it is descriptive and speculative. Crime and disorder present themselves in a random way; intelligence seeks to reduce that uncertainty by identifying patterns. Successful prediction based on 'models' creates the opportunity for intervention as a counterstroke. In this sense intelligence is not just a commodity (distilled information); it is a theory of crime control. Within it are sub-theories—the 'synthetic' models of particular criminal methodologies and conspiracies at various levels of generality.

Intellectually the constituents of intelligence (the collection, collation, evaluation and analysis of information) must be separated from the processes of dissemination and deployment (its practical application). The former represents a set of skills disciplines and obligations in the supply of intelligence both by professional intelligence staff such as analysts and across the broad chapel of 'collectors' and 'users'. The latter represents how intelligence as a commodity is employed within policing. The National Intelligence Model (NIM) is of the second order and might best be described as a 'knowledge-based deployment model'. It is decidedly not a policing style or method. Commanders should set a requirement to determine the broad picture (levels of crime and disorder, trends, patterns, risk and threat assessments, etc.) and then prioritize the issues that might be attended to in a way that offered problem resolution, not merely efficient servicing. Having identified what was important the next stage would focus intelligence effort to identify critical problem features that might be tackled. This process involves analysis and planning and should lead to the selection of options for deployment, particularly of tactical resources. The process is presumed to be iterative: review of results should lead to a fresh appraisal of problems and renewed focus in the light of outcomes.

There are valid criticisms of this formula. Suffice to say at this stage that, as a theory for getting the best out of scarce resources, it offered a good deal more than what it sought to replace—ie random events begetting random responses with occasional task forces mounted against problems that one way or another caused enough affront that something special had to be seen to be done. The NIM also fundamentally questions the 'neighbourhood' approach with its eponymous emphasis on locality—logically locality may be a function of the problem or not as the case may be.

In fact, although not particularly by design, the police idea of 'intelligence' very much followed the Sherman Kent tradition of the 'intelligence cycle'. First there is a requirement to set out an objective and determine what is in issue. Next is a requirement for *'collection'*, the purposeful recording and selection of data pertinent to the problem in hand. The process should move on to the *validation and assessment* of the material and then to the *analysis* of relevant material. Analysis is not merely 'presentation'; it is more accurately 'revelation'. It is about discovering patterns and linkages, often not obvious, and explaining how things work, identifying the critical players and locations, and eliminating the non-essential. The product of analysis leads to *interpretation* of its operational relevance, sometimes called *assessment,* and *dissemination*—passing on the product of assessments for operational staff to act upon. The last stage involves appraisal of outcomes or *impact assessment* leading to a reformulation of objectives.

It can be argued that the 'cycle' was a misnomer and that 'national intelligence' agencies tend to operate in a linear not cyclical way, absorbing information upwards from a broad base and disseminating the 'product' narrowly. In particular this paradigm is seen to be out of date for dealing with modern-day terrorism—a 'virtual jihad' with no obvious hierarchy, using Internet sites as operating bases, impelling the energies of disparate fanatics often submerged in diaspora communities and offering at best fleeting opportunities for intervention.

NETWORKS

The modern approach, inherent in the nature of modern technology, is for networks not hierarchies and best exemplified by Robert M Clark (2004) who presents an intelligence framework in which the actors (for example, tactical specialists, collectors, routine operatives, analysts), would all be on the same virtual network, contemporaneously contributing to both the intelligence picture (ie the current synthesis of information characterizing the 'target') and all capable of using analytical tools to extract relevant information for their purposes. This somewhat anarchic formulation is how modern information systems work and resembles the theory of 'network centricity' currently favoured within the military (for example Lambert and Scholz, 2005). By this formulation 'battlefield' *awareness* is shared across the network and operatives make instant but temporary local alliances to combine their assets to maximize strike power within the fragmentary time frames the speed of modern weaponry allows. The shift in paradigm is actually substantial. Instead of slow-moving information limping up the hierarchy and the subsequent transmission of outdated information to the front line, networks bring intelligence into real time, missing out the hierarchical steps and localizing and democratizing target selection and resource allocation.

There is probably much to incorporate from the Clark idea of 'target modelling' and from the idea of 'network centricity'. In fact of course the traditional approach and the network approach are not mutually exclusive except in the battlefield scenario. There is a proper place for measured intelligence analysis allowing commanders to make deployment decisions both at the tactical and strategic level in slower time. Some target operations and most preventive strategies take time and patience and need central direction (at least to prioritize the resources). The great benefit of the network-centric approach is to extend the realm of intelligence to support routine police activity. By extending 'awareness' and allowing staff engaged on routine duties to cross-reference their enquiries with corporate intelligence holdings, we offer the prospect of exploiting 'targets of opportunity'. Clark's idea of 'target models'—dynamic network diagrams illustrating how the target operates and linking related persons, locations and events—indicates the way in which both dedicated operations and chance encounters (routine police interventions) can both profit from core intelligence products which are, as a result, enhanced by contemporaneous update.

UNDERSTANDING THE CORE ELEMENTS OF INTELLIGENCE

Setting the intelligence requirement sounds straightforward enough but is more fundamental than merely being the starting point in a cycle. And albeit likely to be based upon some initial work by intelligence officers by way of scanning the horizon and taking stock of the most pressing problems, the task is deeply strategic; its objective is to prioritize the intelligence effort and set the operational course. Strategic choices are rarely made with the luxury of unfettered discretion: what is a vital necessity, what is merely important, and what is good to do but not critical must be distinguished at the outset. These are the questions that have to be settled before more detailed work can begin. Whilst this sounds clear enough, success is contingent upon both upon the quality of the initial assessment on which the requirement is based and even more on the strategic sense of the commander.

All too often in situations of conflict, and policing is about conflict in a general sense (like military operations and foreign policy where intelligence has its origins), commanders have a strong and sometimes sorry record of relying on their preconceptions rather than a current and measured appraisal of the problem in hand. Strong leaders can be personally effective and strategically weak. Indifferent commanders vacillate or, by making no decisions, decide to do nothing. The discipline of 'intelligence' is a direct challenge to preconception and inaction. But instincts are not a bad guide and, if the intelligence assessment points in a different direction, individuals are entitled to ask more questions. Simply dismissing unwelcome messages, however, leads inexorably to the pursuit of folly.

Directing strategy and tactics often calls for the combination of both intuition and systematic research. When dealing with problems that are pitched in obscurity or when confronting opponents who deliberately mask their intentions (which, of course, most criminals do), the strategist has to combine his or her experience with a demand for intelligence to help confirm or deny uncertainties. Unless commanders value and understand 'intelligence', recognizing its strengths and weaknesses, and feel confident enough to use it, they are unlikely to set clear requirements.

This observation is made because almost every review of intelligence failure, from Pearl Harbour to modern day Iraq, illustrates that the technical failures of intelligence collection and analysis are generally less to blame than the faulty perceptions of those taking the decisions (see MacVean, Chapter 5 below, also Hughes-Wilson, 1999). Strategy is about making the best use of resource, time, and space. It is also about recognizing the contingencies on the wider canvas and identifying a winning formula in the prevailing context; successful operations within a losing formula avail nothing. Indeed, therein lies one of the great dangers of intelligence. In providing actionable golden nuggets of information, the intelligence community can encourage commanders to supersede their own strategy by dissipating their resources. Strategic aims are all too easily set aside for short-term advantages. Strategic oversight is therefore an ongoing responsibility.

Commanders also have a responsibility to prioritize the resources necessary for effective intelligence work itself. Willing the ends and not the means is self-defeating. A weak intelligence component will lead to unimpressive and possibly inaccurate assessments resulting in its demise. Untrained and inexperienced intelligence operatives are just as likely as operational staff to be seduced by actionable information of passing significance. Quality analysis and assessment does not come without investing in good people and good technology, and effective covert operations depend entirely on developing skilled professionals.

It is not simply commanders that need to grasp the logic and scope of intelligence. Indeed the idea has to be understood throughout the organization. To the uninitiated intelligence means secret pieces of information that lead to raids and exciting interceptions. Whilst it is true that such outcomes are a proper function of intelligence work, they are only a small part of the picture. Such simplicity leads to negative perceptions and the tacit assumption that those in the front line are rarely if ever the recipients of anything useful. Just as damaging is the provision of vague, out of date, general briefings urging high levels of interest in unlikely opportunities.

Intelligence at the simplest level is the collation and analysis of various sources of information to infer additional meaning. It is about explaining what is otherwise obscure; about making explicit what is otherwise implicit or deliberately concealed. Explanation and description are fundamental to problem solution. This depiction of the intelligence idea has to be roundly understood. It is not easily grasped in an organization accustomed to routine response and the pre-eminence of cynicism about management targets as against criminal ones. Where it does flourish is in a learning culture that fosters both innovation and the sharing of knowledge. The introduction of the NIM to infertile territory by simply changing the names on doors to meet the formal model requirements without embracing the cultural shift to problem resolution based upon the search for understanding, achieves little and serves to undermine the very idea of intelligence.

Once the 'requirement' is set, a 'collection plan' should follow: essentially, what needs to be known in order to dominate the issue? A collection plan should involve direction and, as knowledge of the 'target' refines, it will be ever more specific. Encouraging intelligence collection without a coherent explanation of the requirement and some indication of the 'criminal paradigm' (for example a model and outline of the prevailing local drugs market) about which information is being gathered, is largely futile—although, sadly, many policing operations regard random intelligence collection by volume as an end it itself. Collection is rightly seen as a universal responsibility but all too often in practice it falls unequally on uniform patrols for whom it is counted as an artificial 'performance indicator'. Few detectives are active contributors, yet they are dealing daily with the most likely sources of relevant information. In general collection is wrongly assumed to be random: alert patrols registering what might be significant within the broad parameters of the 'requirement', often so broad that almost anything of police interest would fit. This formulation leads to the impression that intelligence collection is a sort of voluntary occupation alongside other work and particularly suitable for novices and enthusiasts. Just exactly what is grist to the intelligence mill needs to be clarified.

The data required is, of course, a function of the problem defined. And it might be worth noting that one danger in expectations of intelligence is that, whilst it can contribute to solving most problems, it does not do so equally. Road accident figures might identify hot-spots but road engineers rather than police officers make best use of the information. Casting the net too widely both in terms of targets and data is not helpful and can breed cynicism. The 'neighbourhood policing scheme' for example implies 'intelligence' is an end in itself and that provided the collectors are local they will naturally (almost organically) define the requirement and be best placed to meet it. Ironically the 'neighbourhood policing' scheme may in fact provide a presence that at best might address some of the low-level but significant problems outside the effective grasp of intelligence work!

Nonetheless there are some basics. First of all, the proper recording of crimes and incidents, by express public demand the heartland of police business, including the recording of all relevant material revealed in the enquiry, provides the backcloth to most analysis. A complete and accurate picture of recorded crimes and incidents is a fairly good reflection of the policing requirement and where there are high standards of data quality we have a good starting point. What is reported however is only part of the full picture of crime and incident and other sources of data can supplement what we know. In today's world there are huge amounts of open-source data that can be added to the mix and, theoretically at least, other public agencies are bound to assist in sharing relevant information. Broadly speaking, collating this information represents the *demand side* of the equation.

Information on the *supply side*, the activities of criminals, is much more difficult to fill in. There are number of core elements. First there is detected crime and what can be gleaned from successful cases including confessions and descriptions of individual styles of behaviour, and of criminal associations and their markets. Second is what we can reasonably suspect from previous patterns of offending, forensic links and other similarities, and what can be gleaned from suspicious or interesting information that police officers come by in the course of their duties. Lastly is the police equivalent to espionage—covert intelligence-gathering (the deployment of informants, agents, undercover operatives, and physical and technical surveillance).

In a sense the task of the analyst is to match the demand side with the supply side—to link visible criminality with criminal networks and criminal methodologies. Given that knowledge of the supply side is generally sketchy the task is not easy. In the national security arena intelligence agencies have found it necessary, as required, to bring together all the information for 'all source' analysis. The problem is that 'collection' in the national security world is often by 'single source' agencies (signals interception, images obtained by satellites, and agent handling). Experience has taught national security agencies that the system fails to work properly when raw information acquired on the covert side or by specialist collection agencies becomes a direct source of tasking. Information needs to be contextualized, checked against other operations, and augmented by other relevant material in the system. This is a fundamental proposition for all intelligence systems established in principle following the findings of the Roberts Commission in the United States (declassified document held by the Interagency Working Group (IWG) <http://www.archives.gov/iwg/declassified-records/rg-239-monuments-salvage-commission>), which led to the National Security Act and the creation of the Central Intelligence Agency. Although history has shown there has been a frequent tendency to deviate from it, the principle is still sound and reiterated after each new 'intelligence failure'. And so it should hold in police intelligence work—trusted analysts must have access to the full range of data and sources.

Their initial collation is likely to show where the gaps are. Indeed *gap analysis* perhaps should be considered as one of the stages in the process. It is at this point that the collection effort should be mandated. Intelligence collection is not a passive responsibility. Intelligence gaps should be the subject of specific *collection plans* that may well—and probably will—reach beyond the professional intelligence community.

The general idea of analysis has already been explained. Historically in the intelligence world there has been a certain looseness of language and usually the term 'intelligence' itself implies both the 'product' and the 'means'. 'Intelligence' logically must mean the 'product' of intelligence collection and the term 'analysis' too stands to be clarified. Strictly speaking, four theoretical stages should be separated: validation, research, analysis, and assessment. Checking the validity and indeed grading the value of uncertain material is a necessary function of quality control. Research is about searching for relevant material for the engine of analysis to work upon, and analysis involves applying standard techniques and some imagination in revealing links and meaning. The word 'meaning' is used because the analyst has always to be aware of the possibility of innocent association and false correlations. That two things are associated does not mean they are causally related and therefore analysis is not simply a technical exercise. Making a sensible connection often depends on being able to attribute meaning, which is why knowledge and experience of the subject under scrutiny is important. It is why some security services have preferred terms like 'desk officer', signifying ownership of the problem and knowledge of its nuances.

A debatable issue is the extent to which analysts should be located discretely. The Sherman Kent thesis was that 'all source' analysts should rely absolutely on their objectivity, a cardinal asset that regular communion with specialist collectors and operational staff (or policymakers) tends to subvert. The alternative view is that so important is the search for meaning that the analyst needs to imbibe operational understanding and can gain enormously from dialogue. Sherman Kent however was a liberal academic of his time, seeking to bring the disciplines of the social sciences, then enjoying higher prestige than at present, to the relatively new realm of formal intelligence management. Certainly as far as police intelligence systems are concerned dialogue between analysts and enforcers is often the difference between relevance and superfluity. The 'ivory tower' syndrome isolates the analyst from necessary criticism and diminishes their influence.

Assessment is the most refined stage of the process. Assuming the analyst has identified the parameters of the problem under study or, at a tactical level, the critical associations around the target under observation, the task of the 'assessor' is to put a value on the information. Specifically what is the level of threat and what are the risks of collateral damage; how does this opportunity rank against other options; and, in the case of more tactical options what is the *capability and intent* of the target under observation? It is about putting the problem in its proper context and about estimating the value of the operation in the context of other policing responsibilities. Good assessments make clear recommendations and, if they cannot, will provide warnings with the caveat that obtaining better intelligence is a priority.

THE INTELLIGENCE MODEL AS A THEORY

A theory is speculative thought affording explanation by applying a set of principles independent of the phenomenon to be explained. The definition of intelligence has been essayed by many different writers but there is a broad consensus that it is not about the possession of information itself but rather the distillation of information to reveal associations that, one way or another, allow us to be predictive. As the definition of 'research' could have more or less the same meaning this formulation is however incomplete. The missing ingredient that makes 'intelligence' specific to diplomacy, foreign policy, military affairs, police work, and perhaps other similar responsibilities of the State, is that, in the words of Abram Shulsky, (2002) 'intelligence' is often based on information expressly denied. Hostile powers, foreign armies, terrorists, and criminals not only deny access to their secrets but also take active steps to guard them and to deceive would be trespassers.

Governments approve of espionage to safeguard their national interests and they license deception and trespass against suspected terrorists and active criminals to protect their citizenry. In effect some intelligence collectors are licensed to do things which in another context would be unethical and illegal. Supervising clandestine departments is extremely difficult, as writers like Drexel Godfrey, an ex-CIA agent, have pointed out (Godfrey, 2000). Acting unethically and illegally, however, discredits intelligence in the public and political mind and usually brings calls for reform and tighter control. But transparency too is counterproductive and so one of the foremost principles of a successful intelligence system is that it retains public and political confidence by scrupulous legality.

The troubling dilemma of doing bad things in a good cause has caused many intelligence theorists to emphasise the open-source opportunities available to intelligence and minimize the use of human intelligence sources and schemes involving trespass and theft. When clandestine work has to be sanctioned in the face of national interests seriously at hazard, *technical intrusion*, satellites, and signals interception is preferred to agents and spies. At a less dramatic level, police intelligence work entails similar dilemmas.

The open-source approach is legitimate and less problematic but closing in on targets in the criminal and terrorist world usually requires some use of undercover work or informants (in English law, 'covert human intelligence sources'). Thus, exactly because intelligence work entails unmasking defended secrets, it begets ethical dilemmas. The first principle is that intelligence regimes can be both robust (even audacious) in their purpose but simultaneously respectful of the legal and ethical limits surrounding covert operations. The second principle is a corollary: an intelligence service and those who use it must keep its secrets. This applies not only in general terms but in the courtroom where there is an established legal doctrine that material that has 'public interest immunity' must, not may, be kept secret (the leavening in this doctrine is that the trial judge must have sufficient sight to act as honest broker). Maintaining confidentiality is therefore a legal as well as an ethical duty.

Defining intelligence helps identify its core essentials but perhaps the essence of 'intelligence' is more clearly made manifest in its use. As Robert Clark (2004) puts it, intelligence has the purpose of reducing uncertainty in conflict situations. To this end it sets out to be predictive albeit that there are few certainties and intelligence forecasts, essentially inductive, at every level are to some degree speculative. There is a deal of difference, however, between calculated and information-based speculation and 'seat of the pants' estimates. Whatever its limitations, intelligence serves to forewarn decision-makers of risks and opportunities. This means it must be more than a reference library; it must have *products* and it must be in a position to *influence* the decision-makers. This rather obvious point is made because many police intelligence systems operate mainly as criminal research facilities supplemented by regular but often banal summaries of their subject matter. It is not that providing information back-up is not a function of intelligence, rather it is that the theory of intelligence argued here is based upon it having a much greater role in setting operational strategy and tactics.

Another way of explaining its use is by reference to its iterative and progressive nature. Whilst the concept of an 'intelligence cycle' as such might be in question, there is some sequence to the intelligence process. Thinking outside the formal steps of the NIM, five progressive levels of activity can be envisaged that reflect the strategic, operational, and tactical levels of problem solving, shifting by degrees from a panoramic view and gradually focusing down to a sharp image.

First is the strategic level: obtaining a wide perspective of the operating environment, identifying problems, assessing risks, recognizing trends, and calculating resource availability and opportunity. The purpose of high-level assessment (strategic assessments and problem profiles) is to allow a judgement to be made about *priorities*—aside from 'business as usual', what problems will be addressed on a 'proactive' basis?

Having decided the focus, the subject must be understood. In the early days of 'intelligence-led policing' this was termed 'criminal business analysis'. Understanding criminality as a process not only illuminates where to look for evidence and information; it reveals the vulnerabilities inherent in the criminal enterprise and therefore where effort might be concentrated.

The third stage of intelligence explanation is to discover who the players are and identify associations, locations, vehicles, roles, and linkages. This network analysis provides 'operational' oversight of the problem and facilitates target selection. Whether it is concentration on 'peripherals' to create human intelligence sources, or to arrest 'kingpins' to paralyse the organization, choices are made with more than the immediate target in mind—the purpose is problem resolution in the longer term.

Once appropriate targets have been decided (knowing the what, the how, the who, and the where), it is necessary to discover the 'when'. One of the great misconceptions about intelligence is that it is enough to know who commits crime. Knowing at a general level whom the 'bad guys' are is not difficult information to obtain; most police officers on the ground already know, in general terms. Successful strikes to gain evidence or catch offenders in the act depend upon knowing when to strike! This is a key benefit of covert investigation (penetration and infiltration): getting close enough to the target by stealth to become privy to their plans and schedule.

Earlier it was asserted that successful intelligence collection and use depended upon organizational culture. There are few fixed positions in the volatile arena of crime and disorder (even less so in terrorism) and, both in terms of local knowledge and tactical skills, practitioners have to be constantly learning. Reviewing what has happened and what might be learnt can be a captious and negative experience but, if the organization is tuned to the process as part of routine business, review presents a golden opportunity to refine tactical thinking and enhance intelligence holdings. The fifth stage then is 'review'; its purpose is to learn from experience and redefine the problem in the light of reflection.

CONCLUSION

In summary, 'intelligence' is a process of information analysis providing a disciplined methodology for identifying critical problems, researching their characteristics to identify weak points and develop tactics, identifying the networks and assets in play to facilitate considered target selections, and eventually penetrating the network to give enough advance information to select the timing of operational strikes. As each operation unfolds, it should be reviewed to learn about both criminal targets and investigation methodology.

Properly employed intelligence can confer benefits at the levels of tactics, operations, and strategy. Employing skilled intelligence staff to identify targets brings obvious tactical advantages. Making an operational impact by generalizing good practice takes things a stage further. But strategical change is about changing the context within which conflicts are resolved. If the idea of 'intelligence' is fully embraced and its regime properly implemented, 'intelligence' becomes a natural requirement before any operation is undertaken whereby each operation is planned within the overall context. Perhaps the best analogy might be the way that radar was used in the Battle of Britain to provide not merely information about incoming attacks but an integrated defence system, marshalling resources, husbanding their use, and integrating the information system with command and control. 'Intelligence' could be used by policing to provide a strategic response to the otherwise unregulated demands of crime and disorder.

There are some pre-conditions. First is the inculcation of a learning culture wherein the natural response to problems is to define them by seeking out all relevant information and a relish for innovation in identifying solutions—to be contrasted with its antitheses: bureaucracy, risk aversion (usually termed risk assessment) and statistical performance regimes. There are risks in the nature of intelligence work but they are better addressed by knowledge of the law and an appreciation of ethics. Secondly, intelligence work is skilled and complex; without the investment in the right people and the right training it is best not undertaken at all. Finally, information technology, abundant in most people's daily lives, remains obscure and antique in the public services and needs to be improved. Today the problem is often not so much obtaining information as retrieving what is relevant from the blizzards of digitalized data now readily accessible across vast networks. If that hurdle is crossed the ultimate prospect exists that information and intelligence can be so mobilized across networks of users that targets of opportunity may be exploited alongside planned operations. Properly employed, the theory enables us to wrest back initiative from the chaos of unfolding events.

REFERENCES

CLARK, RM: *Intelligence Analysis: A Target-Centric Approach* (Washington DC: CQ Press, 2004).

GODFREY, DE, 'Ethics and intelligence' in Goldman, J, ed, *The Ethics of Spying* (Maryland: The Scarecrow Press Inc., 2005).

HUGHES-WILSON, J, *Military Intelligence Blunders* (London: Robinson, 1999).

KENT, S, *Strategic Intelligence for American World Policy* (Princeton NY: Princeton University Press, 1949).

LAMBERT, D and SCHOLZ, J, *A Dialectic for Network Centric Warfare*, 10th ICCRTS, Maclean, VA, June 13–16 2005.

SHULSKY, A and SCHMITT, G, *Silent Warfare: Understanding the World of Intelligence* (Potomac Books Inc. 2002).

3

THE PERFECT ENEMY: REFLECTIONS OF AN INTELLIGENCE OFFICER ON THE COLD WAR AND TODAY'S CHALLENGES

Richard J Kerr

INTRODUCTION

In the late 1940s and 1950s, there was an 'iron curtain' around the Soviet Union. Russian Communism was on the march, expanding its control over neighbouring countries and supporting nationalist causes throughout the world. Most important from the perspective of the US and its Western allies, the Soviets presented a major strategic threat to Western Europe and the United States' homeland. Its military forces, missile test facilities and nuclear production plants were hidden behind a barrier of secrecy and, moreover, spread throughout a sizeable country that was largely inaccessible. Developing confident judgments about the size, capability and location of Soviet forces became the primary goal of US and Allied intelligence. This challenge played to the strength of the US—technology, innovation, industrial know-how and resources. Although easier to say in hindsight and with contemporary eyes—the Soviet Union was the perfect enemy at least compared to the intelligence challenges faced by the US today.

The targets of US intelligence in today's world can hardly be characterized as 'perfect enemies'. Radical Islam is not confined to specific countries that can be confronted directly but is dispersed throughout the Islamic world in small groups or schools, and operates in cells not in divisions. Its objectives are to destroy not reform. In fact, nearly all the regimes in the Middle East are targets of Jihadist as well as Western countries. The US is in a conflict of cultures, religions, and ideas where its very presence is the issue. The process of compromise and negotiation, trust and 'good faith' are not part of the Jihadist lexicon. Whilst terrorism and the 'clash of civilizations' is not the only challenge of US intelligence, it is the most immediate and the most complex.

RELEVANCE OF FOREIGN INTELLIGENCE ANALYSIS TO POLICE INTELLIGENCE SYSTEMS

Much can be learned by comparing the disciplines of foreign intelligence analysis and police criminal intelligence. It can be a useful way of developing consilient thinking as our work in Northern Ireland for the Independent Monitoring Commission (IMC) has shown. Nearly all of the processes involved in Foreign Intelligence Analysis (FIA) also are present in policing. The similarity is less direct when the full range of policing activity including supporting prosecution is addressed, but this is changing.

Perhaps the most useful comparison between intelligence analysis and policing is to use the example from the work of the IMC set up by the Irish and UK governments to assess paramilitary activity in Northern Ireland. The IMC process for attributing violent incidents or significant criminal activity to a particular paramilitary organization relied heavily on the techniques used in the analysis of foreign intelligence. It collected information from a wide variety of sources including intelligence, the police, media, and others. It did not conduct detailed interviews of witnesses, those attacked, or those arrested in incidents. The IMC was not in the position of trying to collect information that would stand the test of a trial or meet the full standard of evidence before a court. It came to judgements where the information appeared strong enough to support a logical conclusion but did not attempt to advance or develop the kind of 'evidence' necessary to support a prosecution. The key is 'information' rather than 'evidence'. For example, a train is photographed going into a tunnel in a mountain but there is no photograph of it coming out on the other side of the mountain. It is a reasonable conclusion that the train did come out. But can it be proved? Intelligence analysts would argue that the train did emerge, but a criminal investigator might need to interview people on the train or observers on the other side of the mountain.

The objective of FIA is to come to conclusions even when information is neither comprehensive nor could it support a prosecution in a court of law. It often does not have the luxury of waiting for more information before weighing in to support policy formulation. It often cannot deal directly with the human sources of information it relies on and is nearly always dealing with an uncooperative target.

When police are dealing with the plans and intentions of a hostile group such as terrorists, they are placed very much in the same position as FIA. After a terrorist attack the situation changes into collecting evidence for prosecution. Intelligence is interested in who the terrorists were and how to stop them from further acts of terrorism.

The current trend is for intelligence to become more involved in the use of investigatory techniques, particularly on issues involving technical collection and analysis such as development or support of Weapons of Mass Destruction. Pressure to publicly present the intelligence analysis supporting judgements and therefore government policy, is growing. This often puts FIA in the position of trying to explain how rather subtle information/trends and unconfirmed reporting can be utilized to reach critical conclusions.

At the same time, police are more and more involved in analysis of trends, capabilities, and intentions. This is particularly true in the attempt to prevent terrorism and not merely prosecute those involved. Both groups have much to learn from the other.

THE SOVIET THREAT

It did not take long after the Second World War ended for the US administration and the American people to conclude that the Soviet Union was a major political and military threat to the West. While not characterized as the 'evil empire' until Ronald Reagan deployed the phrase,[1] there was broad consensus that the Soviet Union was a strategic, long-term threat that required full mobilization of the US and its allies. Over the nearly 50 years of the Cold War all administrations, politicians from around the world, the media, and the American people were united in their fear of the Soviet Union, the need for a strong defence and the requirement for aggressive intelligence collection and analysis. No event in US history with the exception of the Second World War provoked such consensus and none even approached the length of time this view of real danger was sustained.

THE PERFECT ENEMY—GROWTH OF US INTELLIGENCE

At the beginning of the Cold War, US intelligence consisted of the national organizations including the State Department, the Federal Bureau of Investigation (FBI), the Office of Strategic Services (OSS—the forerunner to the CIA), and the intelligence components of the military services. Immediately after the Second World War there was a struggle between General Donovan, the head of OSS, and Secretary of War Stimson over whether an intelligence organization that reported directly to the president and not through the Secretary of Defence was advisable or needed. As might be expected Secretary Stimson presented a strong argument that national intelligence was a job for the military. A letter from the Secretary of War to Major General Donovan on 1 May 1945 was direct in making the argument.[2] But growing concern about the Soviet Union, the surprise invasion of South Korea by the North in 1949, and the strong views of President Truman led to the establishment in 1949 of the Central Intelligence Agency, an independent organization that reported to directly to the president.

Creating such an organization was a first step, but getting information, particularly information about the secretive Soviet Union, presented a daunting challenge. Little was known about the country and other than signals intelligence, some military reconnaissance along the borders including aircraft imagery taken by the Germans during the Second World War, outposts in Europe, legal travellers, radio broadcasts,

[1] March 1983 speech.
[2] Declassified letter from Stimson to Donovan May 1945.

and some German POWs returning from Russia, there were few sources of good information on any aspect of Soviet life.

The US response to the lack of information on the strategic threat posed by the Soviets was impressive. The CIA began an effort to penetrate the Russian military, intelligence, and diplomatic services through clandestine means. But the analytic elements working on the Soviet Union were largely working on secondary data and there was little direct insight into Russia. For example, we only knew for certain about the Russian nuclear weapons programme when they detonated their first device in August 1949.

TECHNOLOGY, AMERICAN KNOW-HOW, AND MONEY TO THE RESCUE

The size, organization, and capability of the Soviet military were unknown quantities in the early 1950s. However, within a few years, scientists, engineers, and industry, under the leadership of CIA and Department of Defence (DoD) programme managers, created a significant technical collection capability that notably included the U-2, an impressive signals intelligence collection system and aircraft that sampled the atmosphere after nuclear tests. This led to the development of space collection, with a wide array of satellites that collected optical and radar imagery, communications and telemetry. The US Navy developed a major set of capabilities to track Soviet submarines and the US Air Force put in place a radar system that blanketed the work.

The analytic community grew rapidly. Utilizing this data and information put together probably the most comprehensive library of facts and analysis that existed on a single subject. As a result, by the late 1970s and early 1980s the US had a clear understanding of the Soviet strategic and conventional forces, their size, capabilities, strengths, and weaknesses. It also had a comprehensive overview of the strategies and tactics that the Soviets would exploit in war. All the strategic weapons had been identified such as missiles, bombers, and ballistic missile submarines. Consequently, when the Soviet empire collapsed there were few surprises. In fact, many of the conventional weapons had already been acquired and assessed including aircraft, tanks, and air defence systems.

The CIA's role in this endeavor was critical. Its unique authorities to contract with the private sector, engage with the finest programme managers, and willingness to take risks were crucial in rapidly advancing US knowledge of the Soviet Union. It had strengths in collection and analysis, and the ability to rapidly make and carry out decisions. It reported to the president and had the strong support of Congress thus providing the CIA with a number of unique advantages over traditional government organizations.

STAFFING 'THE COMPANY'

The veterans of OSS and the stream of people returning to civilian life after the Second World War offered the initial manpower for the CIA. Veterans returning to education were encouraged to join the 'Agency' by professors who had been in intelligence during the war. Initially, recruits came from the Ivy League schools, but veterans from other colleges and engineers from the national weapons laboratories and missile development centres like Redstone Arsenal became important sources. Many veterans were drawn to the organization because of their experiences in the Second World War, others were motivated by the threat of communism and some were looking for careers that had a real and meaningful purpose. There was a significant expansion of recruitment in the late 1950s and through the 1960s resulting from a conscious effort to recruit nationwide with some emphasis on universities in the Midwest and West Coast. The recruitment process for the CIA was very selective and carefully screened-out people using extensive testing, aptitude tests, and the polygraph.

The Heroes

Every organization has its heroes, those who make a difference and set the standards for the organization. The CIA was no exception. When I entered the CIA in 1960, the structure and mission of the organization had been established however many of the original members of staff were still employed. Their achievements and successes were impressive. The senior analysts I worked with had been involved in developing the first US nuclear weapons, radars, the submarine underwater detection system, and the first US missiles.

Like many young officers, I had a mentor that made a difference in my career. His name was Bruce Clarke. During the first 10 years of my service in the CIA, he provided strong direction and training in the 'art' of intelligence analysis; but more important, he taught me to be a professional intelligence officer. He sent me to support the Director of Central Intelligence during briefings, gave me an assignment to travel to Iran to brief the Shah, and to South Asia to brief the president of Pakistan, and offered increasingly challenging projects.[3]

ANALYTIC TRAINING

There was an introductory CIA training programme but it was intended primarily for operations officers, not analysts. Most analysts learned their craft through on-the-job experience. There were few formal mentors, although many models and people offered and provided constructive critiques and advice. Although there was a systematic process for identifying what should be included in the current intelligence products or what was required in order to respond to policymakers' questions, much of the initiative for analysis came from the branch chiefs or senior analysts. In my particular case I was fortunate to have access to supervisors who were able to provide me with the experiences and advice needed to advance in the organization. Nonetheless, more generally it did tend to be a sink or swim experience.

Critiques of draft products were ruthless and the organization had limited patience—analytical reports of a reasonably good product were demanded. The analysts performed a peer-review system and critically evaluated each other's reports: 'I would not have done it that way,' 'You missed the key point,' 'Why didn't you refer

---

[3] I was fortunate to have other mentors such as John McMahon and ultimately William Webster who had confidence in my abilities or knew how to develop those abilities.

to an earlier report on this subject?' In this environment, those who did not develop quickly were asked either to leave or would be moved to less demanding jobs. It was an uncompromising meritocracy. Analysts had to be able to write quickly and clearly, brief senior officials, and coordinate their articles with some very demanding people and organizations that were not all that enthusiastic about CIA writing on subjects they considered their area of responsibility. At one point a senior US Army general indicated that he saw no reason for the CIA to be involved in assessing the performance of Soviet tanks; that was an Army responsibility.

One of the most difficult jobs in the CIA was that of branch chief—managing a small group of people working on a particular subject or country. Providing constructive comments on analytic pieces, guiding production, protecting people who were learning but not there yet, and being productive yourself, was a major challenge that, if not met, left little chance of advancement.

THE ANALYTIC PROCESS

Intelligence products came in a variety of forms—short items reporting a single uncomplicated event and longer pieces assessing a complex situation and the implications for the future. There were a number of specialized products including what amounts to a daily newspaper, memoranda addressing specific questions raised by customers or senior management, formal intelligence reports, and national intelligence estimates that look to the future.

The process is much the same as that used by journalists, political scientists, or historians to produce articles and books. **Who, what, why, where** and **when** are the key questions for all analysts. However, intelligence analysts also need to address the relevance of what is being reported. Another way of characterizing the task of intelligence after describing the issue is to assess problems in a more activist manner:

- What is the desired outcome?
- What is a realistic outcome?
- What are the constraints and variable factors?
- What leverage does the US have to change the situation?
- What are the weaknesses and strengths of an opponent?
- What are the implications of different policy options?

William Casey, the Director of Central Intelligence in the first two Reagan administrations, challenged the assumption that reporting the facts and the implications of those facts was enough. Intelligence products and outcomes should be designed for action. He was convinced that every aggressive action by the Soviets should to be countered. It took some time for the CIA to comprehend and understand Casey's impulse toward action. Consequently, a new set of guidelines that assessed the desired outcome, a realistic outcome, constraints, and leverage was developed. The problem for analysts at this stage was to avoid being policy prescriptive while describing what opportunities or dangers might exist for various policy options. Policymakers were often not enthused by what they believed were CIA critiques of US policy.

CONTRARIAN AND COMPETITIVE ANALYSIS

Some of the limitations of US intelligence are discussed below; however, it is important to establish the point that debate in the CIA and the rest of the intelligence community was thriving during the Cold War as well as today. Controversial issues were keenly discussed and the deliberations generated arguments swirling around inside the CIA. One of the best examples was the insistence of Director William Casey and his deputy Robert Gates that analysts carefully examine evidence that might support a conclusion that the Soviets were involved in the attempted assassination of Pope Paul VI.[4] The first analytic work on the assassination attempt largely discounted this possibility. Even though subsequent efforts did not substantiate or refute the claim, the process was invaluable even though it led to claims by some that intelligence was becoming politicized. During the Vietnam War, CIA analysts were irritatingly consistent in their negative assessments. At one point, Director Richard Helms stopped sending what he considered the CIA's pessimistic reports to the White House because they were becoming so counterproductive.[5] In 1989, as the Deputy Director for Intelligence, I took a dissenting footnote to the principal conclusion of National Intelligence Estimate on the future course of Russia.[6] That document represented the formal position of the Director of Central Intelligence. It is interesting to note that there are few organizations that would let a subordinate formally dissent. There are many more examples where analysts were able to express their differing views and in fact were encouraged to do so by the leadership.

One area that needs additional attention is greater emphasis on how the US is perceived by both its friends and adversaries. Too often analysts do not place themselves in the camp of the opposition and look at US presences, actions, and statements from that perspective.

THE REST OF THE WORLD DURING THE COLD WAR

The CIA had worldwide coverage during the Cold War but the emphasis was on the struggle between the US and Russia to gain influence and access. Many of the conflicts in the Third World were between surrogates of either the US or Russia. Even though the two superpowers did not fight during that period there were a large number of bush fires that were caused or at least supported by one side or the other. The CIA had knowledgeable and experienced country and regional experts who assessed events in areas from Afghanistan to Zaire. Most of the Third World coverage focused on general military, political, and economic issues and were not directed at establishing any depth of understanding of the countries and their cultures. Generally, analysts were recruited for their general expertise in political, military, and economic issues and not because of their in-depth knowledge or experience in specific countries or areas.

---

[4] Gates, R, *From the Shadows* (New York: Simon & Schuster, 1996) 354–356.

[5] Helms, R, *A Look Over My Shoulder: A Life in the Central Intelligence Agency* (New York: Random House, 2003) 311.

[6] A Cold War's End—NIE, The Soviet System in Crisis. Prospects for the Next Two Years, published in November 1989 (Declassified).

THE NEW WORLD—LESS THAN PERFECT ENEMIES

The predictability of the Soviet Union in developing military hardware, training, and acting on the world scene is not a characteristic of the actors the US sees as its principal adversaries in the twenty-first century. The Soviets had a large empire to run and a significant military establishment to arm and operate. Consequently it operated by a comprehensive set of rules and procedures. Weapons development followed a very predictable set of processes: design, research and development, testing, deployment, and training of troops to use the weapons. Each of these processes were successfully monitored by intelligence systems. Political decisions were not as easy to follow but did tend to follow a set of predictable patterns. These decisions were not made by a single person but by a rather considerable group that included politicians, military leaders, and defence and economic planners: a protracted, deliberated, and often ponderous process not unlike our own. The process was opaque but not fully hidden.

The bipolar world described above no longer exists. The issues that held the Western alliances together have changed. The Warsaw Pact broke apart as Eastern European countries gained their freedom from Russian domination. NATO continues to exist but the commitment of European countries to a military alliance they must fund is weak. There are no common threats to bind them together.

Russia and China probably should be viewed less as military threats than political and economic competitors, although some countries do see China in particular as a military threat. China is trying to establish itself as a major player through aid and assistance in Latin America, Africa, and Asia, while Russia is financially prospering through oil sales and the provision of arms to old clients. It would be unwise to consider either country an 'enemy' in the traditional sense but they are competitors for influence and commerce.

Perhaps the greatest change is the emergence of organized groups who champion particular causes or values and who may not necessarily be supported by the States in which they exisit. The radical Islamic groups are the best example of these new actors and although they resemble organized crime or narcotics cartels, they have a radical ideology that attracts a fanatical following, which can radicalize the process.

The war in Iraq and the continuing threat of terrorism present the most serious challenge to the US and Western democracies. Yet there is no real consensus in the US, and even less among our 'allies', on these issues. There appears to be little agreement between various populations about identifying the threats and the potential resolutions. The US has been divided by the continuing war in Iraq and the loss of lives. The challenge of radical Islam and the threat of terrorism stills remain intensely debated. The continuing tensions between Israel and its neighbours also present major challenges for the US. Yet the spiral of violence that is emerging from these new world threats is different.

These new problems present unique challenges for the US. Historically, the US is good at using technology to build strategic and general-purpose military forces. It does well when operating and negotiating from a position of strength with an opponent it believes it understands and where there is some common ground. It functions best when it is clearly in charge of a problem and not dependent on others. However, nation building and other expertise that is now required is not necessarily a strength of the US. Post-war Japan and Germany were exceptions but they were countries totally defeated and in ruinsand which had no internal opposition elements.

Some of the shortcomings—or intelligence failures—in US national security that were encountered during the Cold War are similar to the problems we face today. The fall of the Shah of Iran in 1979, the attempt to overthrow Castro in 1960, the 1973 Arab-Israeli War, the 9/11 tragedy, the Indian-Pakistani nuclear weapons tests, the Weapons of Mass Destruction issue in Iraq, and strife in Iraq were problems that presented unique challenges to the US intelligence and US policymakers. Often the assumptions about the situations were wrong, our knowledge of different cultures too limited, our technological advantages ineffective, and in some cases, the events were just outside our experience—issues that have or are being experienced in policing.

There have been many Third World situations where intelligence did a competent job of supporting the policymakers, and it can be argued that the overall record on these issues are rather impressive. However, more recent events including 9/11 and Iraq WMD have seriously damaged the reputation of intelligence and the CIA in particular. The CIA and the intelligence community are working aggressively to improve performance against current and future threats. Analytic training, country expertise, and knowledge about collection are being emphasized. Nonetheless, change is slow and is made more difficult when administrations, Congress, and the public demand instant solutions.

EXPECTATIONS FOR INTELLIGENCE

The expectations of consumers of intelligence are quite often unrealistic. Intelligence organizations and departments often deal with countries, groups, and situations that have no 'plan or strategy' that can be stolen, uncovered, and assessed. Much of the current terrorist activity comes from small groups that are operating independently and without state support. Those involved are often uninhibited by the fear of punishment—many are willing to become human bombs to make their point. These circumstances make intelligence judgements about the current situation difficult and estimates about the future uncertain. In addition, our own culture and experiences cannot always penetrate the thinking of potential adversaries. Therefore, Steven Johnson, in his book about the discovery of how cholera was transmitted, provides a shrewd and insightful observation about the history of 'being wrong'. Johnson describes how even intellectual and knowledgeable people can unchallengingly accept canards and false leads. He also comments on the phenomena that it is not just that people can be wrong but that they hold to their beliefs in a 'tenacious and unquestioning way'.[7] Being creative and open to new ways of looking at problems is not an easy task. Critics of intelligence often are surprised to find that judgments derived by analysts are not supported or corroborated by irrefutable and persuasive evidence. Rather they are founded on fragments of information pieced together in a

[7] Johnson, S, *The Ghost Map* (London: Allen Lane, 2006) 126.

manner that may be clear to the analysts who have been following the problem but present an altogether indistinct representation when observed from the outside. The difference between intelligence judgements and evidence brought into a criminal case is markedly different. First, the criminal prosecutor probably will not bring forward a case for trial unless the evidence is sound and a conviction meets the Crown Prosecution Service threshold. Intelligence analysts have no such discretionary ability. They must draw conclusions whether the evidence is strong or weak. It is not possible to tell a policymaker during a crisis that a judgement cannot be ascertained. However, it is possible to caveat the judgements by stating that the evidence is not strong and there is uncertainty and caution about the conclusions.

There are some lessons here for policing intelligence, particularly in relation to the communication of intelligence. The CIA initiated a range of communication forms according to the needs of their customer. Traditional formal reports were produced alongside newspaper-style publications that allowed the readers to glean the headlines while a more detail account was contained elsewhere if they needed to read it. All too often, as Pease has insightfully noted in his response to systems and structures, the National Intelligence Model (NIM) prescribes how intelligence is conveyed. This method inhibits non-bureaucratic communication and non-systemized communication, which disempowers front-line staff and analysts. Nevertheless, NIM theorists would argue that there is still scope for urgent, real-time intelligence to be acted upon, and that the NIM ensures all relevant parties are informed as a result. Communicating intelligence is a major issue (as Lords Butler and Hutton as pointed out in the Weapons of Mass Destruction controversy), and that is as real in the police arena as it is in the security arena. In the CIA, analysts were encouraged to record their differing views, and footnotes in reports were utilized as a method for registering and recording such dissent. Dissenting voices can all too easily be overruled at Task and Coordinating meetings. There is no real mechanism for recording dissent in the current NIM process except in operation policy logs. Perhaps there are some lessons from how intelligence is communicated in the CIA that are relevant for policing intelligence.

In the build-up to the 2004 election in the US, political analysts often were unsure about who would win the election. Yet, we had extensive information about the candidates and polls assessing the voters' reactions, thousands of articles, endless talk shows, and experts assessing the information. The election in 2008 presents the same challenge but lack of information is not the problem, nor is good analysis. This begs the question of an intelligence organization's ability to assess the future when it involves closed societies or secretive groups with little or no information on the decision-makers or the decision-making process. For example, why would the policymakers or the public believe that intelligence could anticipate terrorist attacks planned by small groups in secret with greater confidence than political analysts could predict the outcome of an election in a country they live in and understood. Some of these issues can be explored by comparing the disciplines of foreign intelligence analysis and police criminal intelligence. It can be a useful way of using consilient thinking as our work in Northern Ireland for the IMC has shown. Unfortunately, there may be more mysteries than secrets to be uncovered in today's world. This is particularly true with an enemy that is 'imperfect'.

4

THE POLICE AND THE INTELLIGENCE SERVICES —WITH SPECIAL REFERENCE TO THE RELATIONSHIP WITH MI5

Professor Frank Gregory

INTRODUCTION

The organizational structures of national security and intelligence services are as varied as the organizational structures of police services. However, in most States there are organisations for the following functions: domestic security and intelligence, external intelligence, defence intelligence, and signals intelligence (sigint). There are two main linked approaches to understanding the relationship in a given State between the police and the intelligence services: historical and legal-institutional. The historical approach illustrates how a particular state has sought to provide for and govern a set of essential activities that may, in part, need to be both covert and deniable. The legal-institutional approach, by examining the statutory basis for such activities and the organizational structure, can help to clarify status, roles, inter-organizational relationships, and accountability mechanisms (Müller-Wille, 2006 and Venice Commission, 2007). Within Europe there is no common organizational model but rather a mixture of police and non-police types. A range of examples are illustrated in Table 4.1 below.

   In the UK there are three civilian security and intelligence agencies (National Intelligence Machinery, 2002): the Security Service (MI5) for domestic security and intelligence, the Secret Intelligence Service (MI6) for external intelligence '. . . in the fields of national security. . . in the interests of the economic well-being of the UK . . . (and). . . in support of the prevention or detection of serious crime,' (<http://www.sis.gov.uk/output/Page7.html>), and the Government Communications Head Quarters (GCHQ) for sigint and information assurance (<http://www.gchq.gov.uk/about/index.html>). In addition, under the Ministry of Defence there are the three service intelligence organisations and the Defence Intelligence Staff (DIS). The UK police

Table 4.1 Sample of European MI5 Equivalents

Country	Agency	Status	Recent Changes
Belgium	State Security Service (SE or SV)	Civilian agency	
Denmark	Security Intelligence Service (PET)	Part of Danish police	
France	Directorate of Territorial Surveillance (DST)	Part of Police Nationale	2007—a new internal security directorate will incorporate DST
Germany	Federal Department for Constitutional Protection (BfV)	Civilian agency	
Italy	SISDE (now known as ASI)	Civilian agency	Simplified structure under the Prime Minister as of 1/8/07
Netherlands	General Intelligence and Security Service (AIVD)	Civilian agency	
Sweden	National Security RPS/ SAK Service (Säpo)	Part of Swedish National Police	

also have their own specialist criminal intelligence bodies in the force intelligence bureaux, the specialist national units, for example, within the National Football Policing Unit (NPFU) as well as the Special Branch intelligence structure. Recent concerns about surveillance involving an MP (Rose, 2008) highlighted the specialist intelligence-gathering function of police prisons-intelligence units which operate under the guidance of ACPO's Prison Intelligence Working Group. New challenges can lead to the creation of additional police intelligence-gathering bodies as was recently the case in relation to gun crime with the establishment in April 2006, by the Home Office and ACPO, of the National Ballistics Intelligence Programme (NBIP). The work of the NBIP is supported by '. . . a multi-agency Joint Intelligence Cell' (Home Office Minister, Mr McNulty, Hansard, Written Answers, 18/10/06).

The police service's primary relationship is with MI5 and, historically, a major function of the police Special Branches (see Denning, 1963, HMIC, 2003 and Metropolitan Police, 2006), which focus on politically-related criminality, was to serve as the inter-agency link for that relationship. This relationship was codified in 1984 through Home Office guidelines to Chief Constables which stressed the Special Branches' 'interface' role between the Service and the police. The 1994 version of the guidelines highlighted the counterterrorism work by the Special Branches for MI5 but also referred to three other important areas of the working relationship: espionage, proliferation, and subversion, although, as former MI5 Director General Stella Rimington noted, '. . . this relationship has expanded significantly and now includes other parts of the Police Service. . .' (Rimington, 1994).

In essence, this relationship exemplified the prima facie separation of organisational roles in respect of suspect activities in the three main areas of political criminality: espionage, subversion, and terrorism. This relationship is governed by two important general principles. First, and with general applicability across the intelligence agencies, it was considered to be good practice as well as legally advisable to have '. . . a functional separation and sterile corridor between investigating (governed by the provisions of PACE) and intelligence . . .' (Harfield, 2006: 4). Secondly, the UK has always sought to maintain a distinction between the intelligence community and the law enforcement community, a principle expressed by Stella Rimington, when MI5 Director General: '. . . the Service has no executive powers. At the point where executive action is needed other agencies or departments (e.g. the police) take over' (Rimington, 1994).

Notwithstanding the role separation, there are degrees of similarity between the working environments of the police and MI5, as Rimington (1994) noted. Both the police and MI5 have investigation, collation, assessment, disruption, and prevention as '. . . core elements . . .' of their work and for both '. . . the protection of sensitive sources and techniques is central to the success of any operation.' However, the structural constraints in the relationship need to be clearly recognized. First, on the police side there is a considerable variation in the size and capability of the forces' Special Branches (HMIC, 2003). Secondly, and more importantly, from the perspective of MI5, there needs to be an awareness of the inherent limitations upon MI5 undertaking work outside core priority areas like counterterrorism by its small size in terms of personnel.

Currently MI5 is growing from a post-Cold War 'down-size' of around 1,800 in 2001 to around 3,200 in 2007 with a projected growth to 3,500 by 2008 and 4,000 by 2011 (Evans, 2007). By contrast, in England and Wales there were 141,892 police officers in post as of 31 March 2007 with a further 16,000 in Scotland and 7,500 in the PSNI, (see on England and Wales Home Office Statistics Bulletin 13/07, 26 July 2007). Thus on a rough calculation MI5 only has a personnel size equivalent to about 1.9 per cent of total UK police strength. However, it has been recognized, with regard to specialist functions that, as MI5's counterterrorism personnel element of its total strength increases, it is important '. . . to make sure that the police expand their counterterrorist capability in line with that of the security service . . .' (BBC News 24, 11 December 2007) in order to manage the intelligence flows from MI5.

Externally, MI5 participates in a range of networks of similar agencies covering, for example, G8, US, Commonwealth, and European links, especially the Counterterrorism Group (see further ISC, 2006; Rudner, 2004; Segell, 2004). Not surprisingly more attention has been paid to the potential significance of such networks post-9/11. This external activity is not, however, a feature of the working environment that distinguishes MI5 from the police. The UK police service participates widely in the growing arena of transnational police cooperation, (Sheptycki, ed, 2000). For example, there is the Police Working Group on Terrorism (PWGT) network of Counterterrorism and Extremism Liaison Officers (CTELOs) posted between European police headquarters in European capital cities and the network of police football intelligence units for countering football hooliganism. UK police officers are also seconded to Interpol and posted to the UK Bureau at Europol.

The other chapters in this collection cover the theoretical and methodological aspects of intelligence within a UK police organisational and operational context. Therefore this chapter will only touch on those areas in so far as it is necessary to the analysis of the inter-agency relationship which is the core part of this study. However, Nina Cope's analysis (2004) of 'Intelligence-led policing or policing-led intelligence' does provide some transferable findings that can be considered within this chapter. This is because Cope's study of an urban and a county force's intelligence unit focuses, in part, upon issues to do with the relationships between police officers and civilian staff. All the officers of Britain's three intelligence services are, in actual status, and more importantly in police 'culture' terms (see O'Neill, Marks and Singh, 2007), 'civilians'. Cope's study raises the following points of relevance which are set out below together with the linked issues that relate to the focus of this chapter:

- Analysts who were police officers felt that this status helped to 'legitimize' their work—did MI5 status confer equivalent 'legitimacy'?
- Police officers felt uncomfortable about accepting recommendations from non-police personnel—did this apply to recommendations from MI5?
- Do the providers of intelligence (in this case MI5) and the users of intelligence (the police) *understand* the needs and capabilities of each other?
- Were MI5's products targeted at police 'managers' or 'operational' officers?
- Did police officers see their roles 'as experts in matters of crime' (Cope, 2004: 197) challenged by MI5's entry into the SOC area?
- In general terms can it be postulated for police-MI5 relationships, as Cope does for police-civilian analysts relations, that it may mean the police 'recognizing individuals for their role, rather than their rank, which would require a cultural shift in how police and civilian roles are conceptualized' (Ibid 199)?

In order to explore these points further a short questionnaire, based on the above points, was sent to a small focus group of serving or recently retired police officers, ranging in rank from ACPO level to DC, with relevant career experience of working with MI5. The anonymized results of this survey are referred to in the concluding section in the context of the questions set out above, derived from Cope's study. Naturally some of the points need to be more fully addressed through further research. The chapter is structured in four sections: Understanding the Security Service; Counter-terrorism; Serious and Organized Crime, and Conclusion.

UNDERSTANDING THE SECURITY SERVICE

Tackling post-1968 Irish-related terrorism and especially MI5's assumption, in 1992, of lead agency responsibility (formerly held by the Metropolitan Police Special Branch) for countering Irish republican terrorism on the mainland, the end of the Cold War, and the Security Services Act 1989 are all key elements in the evolution of MI5 (or 'the UK's security intelligence agency' as it describes itself: <http://www.mi5. gov.uk>) away from its focus on counter-espionage and its major Cold War focus on counter-subversion. Nevertheless, it should be noted that counter-intelligence and counter-espionage still remain a serious commitment for MI5. Moreover, after 9/11 MI5 has moved overtly into the public consciousness through the widely-reported speeches of Director Generals (since Stella Rimmington), its website, and through the wider outreach of its protective security section, the Centre for the Protection of the National Infrastructure (CPNI, formerly NSAC—the National Security Advisory Centre and incorporating NISCC—the National Infrastructure Security Coordinating Centre).

The War Office and the Admiralty founded the forerunner to MI5 in 1909. In 1931 the service acquired its title of the Security Service and took responsibility for domestic intelligence-gathering on all threats to the UK except for those emanating from Irish groups and anarchists which then remained a police responsibility centred on the Metropolitan Police Special Branch (HM Government, National Intelligence Machinery, 2002; <http://www.mi5gov.uk/output/Page235.html>). In 1952 Prime Minister Churchill delegated the responsibility for internal security, a Crown prerogative function devolved to ministers, to the Home Secretary. The Home Secretary at this time, Sir David Maxwell-Fyfe, issued a directive setting out the functions of the service and the role of its Directors General.

This directive was renewed by succeeding Home Secretaries until it was replaced by the Security Service Act of 1989. This Act was amended in 1996 and it, like the Intelligence Services Act 1994 (covering SIS and GCHQ), is compliant with the Human Rights Act 1998. The most significant contemporary changes in the remit of MI5 came in 1992 when it assumed the intelligence-gathering responsibility from the Metropolitan Police for Irish-republican-related terrorism on the UK mainland and in 1996 when the 1989 Act was amended to allow MI5 to support police and other agencies in tackling serious organized crime. In 1992 MI5 also assumed the additional role of working with other agencies to counter WMD proliferation. The contemporary roles of MI5 cover intelligence work related to international terrorism, Irish-related terrorism, counter-proliferation, counter-espionage, and serious organized crime (this role was suspended with effect from 31 March 2006) and are shown in Table 4.2 below.

It is easier, by reference to the status and powers of MI5, to say what it is not than what it is. In the civil part of the public sector there are civil servants and local government officers with various kinds of powers over the citizens. A recent Centre for

Table 4.2 MI5's Core Work as Resource Allocation Percentage of Total MI5 Activities[1]

	International terrorism	Irish terrorism	Protective security
2001–2002	25%	32%	10%
2002–2003	32%	29%	11%
2003–2004	41%	25%	c.11.9%
2004–2005	44%	23%	13%
2005–2006	60.5%	16.5%	10%

[1] The Table is based upon figures in the Annual Intelligence and Security Committee Reports. It reflects changes in priorities but because the service was growing in this period it is not necessarily the case that a proportionate decrease means a decrease in resources in real terms.

Policy Studies Report (Snook, 2007) has identified 266 agencies with rights of entry into citizens' homes. Within the civil sector there are also the police holding the office and powers of a constable and the new SOCA officials with various powers. However, MI5 personnel are not, despite their origins, part of the military, nor are they civil servants or holders of the office of constable. They belong to the unique category of crown servants. They do not possess the powers of a constable but they do have investigative powers under the 1989 Security Service Act and are able to seek authorization for the interception of communications. They can of course seek assistance from the police especially from the Special Branches. MI5 has been succinctly described as '. . . primarily a security intelligence organization, not a policing department. Its job is the acquisition and assessment of intelligence and that is its fundamental skill' (Rimington, 2002: 215; Northcott, 2007: 467).

At the top of the service, the Director General is in a special position, as the head of a public-sector body. The Director General is accountable to the Home Secretary for the activities of the service, as specified through a Public Service Agreement (PSA) on an annual basis, in consultation with the Home Secretary, which includes agreed resource allocation priorities. For MI5 the PSA provides a very definitive remit whereas for the police service even the National Policing Plan (NPP) priorities and nationally-set performance indicators are subject to the mitigation in implementation of police discretion and the relative autonomy of chief constables with regard to local policing priorities. On occasion this may have implications for police decisions on resource allocations in relation to information flows from MI5, and the Intelligence and Security Committee was examining this issue, in late 2007, in respect of 7/7 bomber, Mohammed Siddique Khan (BBC News 24, 11 December 2007).

Because of MI5's extensive intrusive powers, it is important, as former Director General Stella Rimington wrote (2002: 191), that the service must not be 'the tool of government'. Therefore the Home Secretary has no powers to issue orders to the Director General as the Home Secretary can do in respect of civil servants. Moreover the Director General has the right of direct access to the prime minister, without going through the Home Secretary, because of the prime minister's ultimate responsibility for national security.

One method of assessing the extent to which MI5 has unique powers is to take a prime requirement for a security/intelligence agency, namely the possession of the requisite authority to conduct surveillance operations, and establish to what extent it has unique surveillance powers. In the UK this approach can be followed in respect of the Regulation of Investigatory Powers Act (RIPA; Harfield and Harfield, 2005). Under this Act, it can be seen from Table 4.3 below that MI5 exercises powers that are actually quite widely spread among a range of authorised agencies.

Whilst it is to be expected that MI5 and the police feature in all these authorized categories it may come as a surprise to the general public to learn that MI5's authorization under 'Deployment of Directed Surveillance' is shared with, inter alia, the Charity Commission and the Irish Lights Commissioners. Furthermore, 'Deployment of Intrusive Surveillance' is shared with the Office of Fair Trading and CHISs can also be deployed by the Financial Services Agency and the Gambling Commission. On

Table 4.3 RIPA Powers and Numbers of Authorized Agencies Including MI5

Powers	Number of authorized agencies
Deployment of Directed Surveillance	59
Deployment of Intrusive Surveillance	15
Interference with Property or Wireless telegraphy and Entry on Land	10
Covert Investigation of Computers	10—via interference with property 13—via Intrusive Surveillance 59—via Directed Surveillance
Examining Mobile phones	10
Investigation of Communications Data	7
Interception of Communications	11
Deployment of Covert Human Intelligence Sources (CHIS)	36

the basis of the above RIPA data, it can be argued that MI5, in terms of surveillance powers, is in no way unique but in fact operates as part of quite a wide group of public authorities whose work is deemed to require them to seek ministerial approval for the execution of such powers. Moreover, under RIPA, judicial oversight is provided by the Commissioner for Interception and the Investigatory Powers Tribunal.

Thus, in summary terms, MI5 is a small, statutory based and regulated, civilian public sector organization. Whilst it differs from the police in both the scale and status of personnel, both bodies have similar core features to their work. Moreover both MI5 and the police Special Branches, because they operate within the 'ring of secrecy', have sometimes been credited, in the wider police service, with possessing either extraordinary powers or unimaginably vast stores of information not available to ordinary 'coppers'. In other words there are elements of mythology surrounding the work of MI5 and the SBs (Phythian, 2005; West, 2005).

THE COUNTERTERRORISM (CT) RELATIONSHIP

When counter-espionage or counter-subversion was the main task of MI5, it had little need or requirement to engage with the wider Whitehall community or the general public. By contrast, tackling terrorism has become 'one of the most significant influences in changing the culture and working practices of MI5' (Rimington, 2002: 215). Under the current MI5 structure, CT is the responsibility of two branches (international terrorism and Irish and domestic terrorism) headed by the Deputy Director General. MI5 is very clearly the lead or tasking agency within this area of the relationship with the police. However, the amount of police resources allocated to these tasks is still subject to the discretionary decision of a chief officer.

For the police service, CT has its origins in the late nineteenth century with the need to tackle the mainland manifestations of the Irish problem of the period. The present system comprises, under the strategic oversight of the Association of Chief Police Officers-Terrorism and Allied Matters Committee (ACPO-TAM) and the more tactical oversight of the ACPO-TAM Advisory Group, a number of central police services and the specific Metropolitan Police Counterterrorism Command (SO15 or CTC—formed in 2006 by the merging of the Metropolitan Police Special Branch (SO12) and the Anti-Terrorist Branch (SO13)) plus the associated special units, the provincial police forces' Special Branches, and those other provincial police force assets that may be deployed, from time to time, in CT operations. Central coordination of non-operational Special Branch work is provided by the National Coordinator Special Branch (NCSB) and the National Coordinator Ports Policing (NCPP) who also oversees the dissemination of the police intelligence products from the National Ports Analysis Centre (NPAC) (Cabinet Office, 2007: 36).

On the basis of either a threat assessment or a risk assessment, only a few police forces other than the Metropolitan Police (eg North Yorkshire, West Midlands, City of London, and Greater Manchester Police) have brought all the relevant specialist sections together in a single CT unit or other form of centralized structure to date. The MPS continues to play its leading role in CT operations in London, nationwide, and internationally, especially through the role of the National Coordinator for Terrorist Investigations (NCTI).

In the early to mid-1990s, domestic intelligence reflected both an understandable preoccupation with Irish terrorism and an initial scaling down of counter-subversion operations post-1989. Irish-related CT operations were also generally regarded as having reached a success plateau after the IRA announced its ceasefire in 1996.

Counter-extremism intelligence, for example, on violent extremists within the animal rights movement, remained a police responsibility but MI5 did take on a small amount of work in support of police operations against serious and organized crime.

CT made MI5 more publicly visible via participation in inter-agency working and, post-9/11, in the very wide range of Whitehall 'Contest' CT strategy inter-agency committees (on 'Contest' see Cm 6888, 2006). This participation was also increased with the development of MI5's protective security outreach via the merger of the National Infrastructure Security Coordination Centre (NISCC) and MI5's National Security Advisory Centre (NSAC) to form the Centre for the Protection of National Infrastructure (CPNI) and the establishment, under the MI5 Director General, of the inter-agency Joint Terrorism Analysis Centre (JTAC). Moreover, CT requires that MI5 works very closely with the police through the Special Branch and CT units to develop intelligence, ideally into evidence that may be presented in court and where MI5 officers may have to give evidence themselves under cross-examination. MI5 also has to work very closely, at senior level, with the ACPO rank officer designated as the NCTI who chairs the Executive Liaison Group which agrees operational priorities, the ACPO rank officer who chairs the National Counterterrorism Tasking and Coordinating Group, and with Chief Constables in the development of anti-terrorist operations.

After having assumed lead-agency responsibility for intelligence-gathering related to mainland operations against Irish-related terrorism in 1992, in October 2007 MI5 also took over responsibility from the PSNI, for national security tasks in Northern Ireland, a responsibility that Dame Eliza Manningham-Buller noted as '. . . challenging to implement at a time of more general expansion and change for the Service' (ISC, Cm 6510: para 28, 14–15). However, the MPS CTC still receives copies of all intelligence on Irish republican terrorism in the UK as the CTC retains a national responsibility in this area under the lead responsibility of MI5.

New guidelines on the work of the police Special Branches were issued in March 2004 (Home Office, 2004: paras 20–21) and these make it clear that '. . . counterterrorism remains the key priority for Special Branch . . .' and that 'All intelligence about terrorism obtained by Special Branch is provided to the Security Service . . . (as the lead agency) . . . (and) . . . The Security Service sets the priorities for the gathering of counterterrorist and other national security intelligence by Special Branch.' The Special Branches' intelligence collection role is further defined by the '. . . requirements set out in the National Police Counterterrorism and Extremism Strategic Assessment and Control Strategy . . .' (Cabinet Office, 2007, 98).

MI5 took account of the variable size and resources of the Special Branches, before the introduction of the SB Regional Intelligence Cells, by negotiating annual Statements of Joint Working Objectives with individual force SBs (HMIC, 2003). It should be noted that the introduction of the SB RICs after 2003 did represent quite a low-level compromise when compared with the more significant reform options identified by HM Inspectorate of Constabulary (2003), because of the very variable capability of force SBs, such as a national SB structure. Following the introduction of the SB RICs, MI5 has developed eight 'regional offices' (about 25 per cent of MI5's staff total will eventually work outside London) to promote even closer cooperation between itself and the police. These stations now work with the three regional Counterterrorism Units (CTUs) or 'hubs', created following a decision by ACPO-TAM in 2006 in Birmingham, Leeds, and Manchester (the CTC in the MPS is the 'fourth' hub) following the abandonment of more ambitious government plans for police force amalgamations. The provincial CTUs have absorbed the relevant RICs and some of these are now referred to as Counterterrorism Intelligence Units (CTIUs).

The emphasis within 'Contest' upon the necessity to engage closely with communities in tackling terrorism has recently seen the development of more overt forms of engagement by the police Special Branches with communities in the process of information gathering, under MI5 tasking, which may produce more useable intelligence. This joint effort is known as the 'Rich Picture' approach (*The Independent*, 19 October 2006). In this area of intelligence gathering the Metropolitan Police has a very wide-ranging strategy related to 'Community Engagement to Counterterrorism' (MPA, 2006) including the Borough Operational Command Units (BOCU)-based 'Operation Delphinius' and the deployment of BOCU-based Counterterrorist Intelligence Officers (CTIOs). The locally-based CTIO approach is also developing within the provincial forces. The latest stage in this area of joint working is the announcement, by the prime minister in November 2007 of the formation of '. . . a new unit bringing together police and security and intelligence and research . . .[to] . . . identify, analyse and assess not just the inner circle of extremist groups but those at risk of falling under their influence—and share their advice and insights . . .' (BBC News, 14 November 2007). In order to arrive at a positive outcome from this initiative it will be essential that this process of unit formation builds upon existing good practice in joint working and is well integrated into the established key structures for joint working.

The most significant development in the analytical element of the UK's management of terrorism was the establishment in June 2003, on the initiative of Sir David Omand, the then Security and Intelligence Coordinator, of JTAC (Joint Terrorism Analysis Centre). In part, this was a response to criticisms of its more limited membership predecessor, the Counterterrorism Analysis Centre (CTAC—essentially MI5 staffed). JTAC operates under the authority of the Director General MI5, but has autonomy in its workings and its Director reports to an inter-agency management board. It represents a specific move to break down institutional barriers between intelligence agencies by the processes of co-locating the analysts and creating a new shared identity through JTAC membership. The personnel are primarily drawn from MI5, MI6, GCHQ, MoD (the three services and the DIS), and TRANSEC (the security directorate in the Transport Ministry). The FCO, Home Office, the police, the Office for Civil Nuclear Security, and the Health Protection Agency also participate in its work.

JTAC's remit is to provide long-term studies of international terrorism, for example, on the suicide bomber problem and immediate assessments of current threats. This remit actually breaks down into three components: the provision of country-based threat analyses and sector- or location-specific threat analyses for the UK which, from the available evidence, are used to set the security alert states for the UK; analyses of terrorist groupings and networks, including studies of key individuals; and terrorism trends analyses. The police service is an important contributor to and user of JTAC's products.

The intelligence-flow from MI5 to the police service regarding protective security has also been a rapidly expanding area of work. The police National Counterterrorism Security Office (NaCTSO), as this smaller police service with local force outreach was later named, was set up in 1998 as one of the responses to the 1996 PIRA bombing of Manchester City Centre. When the unit was set up, in January 1998, as the National Terrorist Crime Prevention Unit, it only had two officers, who were co-located with MI5's T4 branch. They acted as a channel for 'best practise' advice, mostly from MI5's T4 branch (later called the National Security Advice Centre—now subsumed into the Centre for the Protection of National Infrastructure (CPNI)) following the February 2007 merger with NISCC (National Infrastructure Security Coordination Centre), to police forces through their SBs. In October 2001, a further two officers were added to the unit and their remit was extended to include extremism and animal rights issues. Following 9/11, the unit's strength was further increased.

A national programme was put into place under which, by April 2003, all police forces had at least one Counterterrorism Security Adviser (CTSA) in post and the unit was retitled NaCTSO (National Counterterrorism Security Office). By 2004 there were 100 CTSAs in post in all police forces in the UK, Home Office and non-Home Office, with the largest concentration of CTSAs (13) in the areas covered by the MPS and City of London forces (NaCTSO, 2004). The CTSAs potential clients can range from local authorities, clearing bank branches, branches of chains/franchises, to very locally established commercial enterprises.

In the more operationally related aspects of the management of intelligence, the intelligence services are conscious of the need to prevent 'communication gaps' as happened on some previous occasions (ISC, 2006, on 5 July 2005 London bombings). The constraints on MI5 of the main forms of 'Need to Know' controls on information sharing—source protection, technical capacity protection, and external agency information sharing rules—are sensitively applied because of the 'Contest' strategy emphasis on public protection. A key issue is when, in the development of the chain of information through intelligence to evidence usable in court proceedings, might the decision be taken to intervene by carrying out arrests? The answer, from operational examples since 9/11, is as early as necessary to protect the public. In some instances, because of this protective emphasis, the useable weight of evidence for charging purposes was only finally uncovered just before the custody period ended (Gregory, 2006 (a) and (b)). Because of this increasingly operationally related flow of work for police forces, the forces themselves and their police authorities may also, in part, hold MI5 accountable for the consequences of operational decisions based upon MI5 intelligence. This might be especially so were those too often to lead to long-running, costly but inconclusive investigations and prosecutions or high-profile raids like Forest Gate that appear unproductive and produce negative results in terms of community relations. However, the ultimate responsibility for mounting a CT operation based upon intelligence from MI5 remains with the police. This point was forcibly made to the Commons' Home Affairs Committee in July 2004 (HC 886-I) in oral evidence by Chief Constable Todd of the Greater Manchester Police. Referring to an operation in the GMP area that caused controversy in a particular community, Mr. Todd said 'We had to carry out an operation to try to make sure we kept Greater Manchester and the UK as safe as possible from terrorism . . .' (Ibid Q 72).

SERIOUS AND ORGANIZED CRIME

This relationship, for MI5, was both bounded in terms of timeframe, 1996–March 2006, a temporary feature of the early post-Cold War era, and also structurally bounded in that it related to the upper levels of SOC. Moreover it reflects a reversal of relationships from that found in CT, as in the SOC area the police were the tasking body. It was principally conducted via two central police-run agencies, the National Criminal Intelligence Service (NCIS) and the National Crime Squad (NCS) both founded in 1998. The former drew its personnel from a multi-agency background that included Customs and Excise as well as the police and a small number of intelligence services personnel served at directorate level.

Therefore, as in the case of counter-espionage and counterterrorism, the relationship is not in the form of a general police-service-wide relationship with MI5. It was, rather, in the form of a 'need to know' link both at the top level within NCIS and to the NCS and at regional level OC units which existed until 1998. Moreover, the relationship reflected, certainly in terms of the Director General MI5's strategic allocation of resources, the most nationally- or Service-significant areas of SOC, namely drug-trafficking and organized immigration crime and, in terms of Organized Crime Groups (OCGs) operating in the UK, Irish terrorism and crime. In addition, in one other crime category, MI5 also provided assistance to the Serious Fraud Office (SFO) to help it secure its first four convictions for insider dealing (Times Online, 15 July 2007).

The general nature of the relationship between the police and the intelligence agencies on SOC can be discerned from the, albeit brief, mentions in the Annual Reports of the Intelligence and Security Committee (ISC). The SIS and GCHQ's functions have mostly been to '. . . generate intelligence on serious crime . . .' for use by NCIS and NCS (ISC, 2006: para 109), although the SIS retains an interest in counter-narcotics where there are either linkages to counter-insurgency work or where maintaining the counter-narcotics work link with a third country contributes to intelligence gathering. As the ISC reported (ISC, 2008, para 38) '. . . SIS is aiming to maintain the overall management and control of more sensitive operations, whilst transferring day-to-day practical management to SOCA, the police or HM Revenue and Customs . . .'. MI5's work in support of the police and other law enforcement agencies was mainly in the areas of '. . . operational, analytical, and assessment work on serious crime targets . . .' (Ibid para 108). Thus the intelligence agencies were helping with attempts to disrupt criminal organisations and they also provided some specialist training in deep-cover surveillance and associated technology (ISC, 2004: para 57). This type of help will be available, other agency priorities permitting, to SOCA.

One example of this relationship was '. . . the Reflex immigration taskforce set up in May 2000 [which] focussed on organized crime and involved the security services, immigration authorities and the police,' (Geddes, 2005, 334). Another example, of longer duration, is the role of MI5 in a ten-year National Crime Squad investigation (Operation Trinity) into a London crime boss, Terry Adams, who pleaded guilty at Blackfriars Crown Court to conspiracy to conceal criminal property. Adams was described as the 'managing director' of a family underworld empire, (*The Times*, 7 February 2007; *The Sunday Times*, 11 February 2007). The Adams case was illustrative of the targeted use of scarce MI5 resources against suspected leading OC figures otherwise known as ProNoms (Prominent Nominals) in NCIS terminology. MI5's current position on the SOC area was that it suspended work ongoing as at March 2006 but would consider working with SOCA again in the future '. . . where there is scope for collaboration and where resources allow' (ISC, 2006: para 108).

CONCLUSION

The relationship between the police service and MI5, in terms of intelligence gathering and the use of intelligence in relation to possible criminal activities of a political nature, is dynamic in character. From 1909 to 1931 there was a certain amount of overlap between the work of MI5 and the SB, then only existing in the MPS. From 1931 a more clearly delineated relationship was established with the MPSB having responsibility in relation to both Irish groups and anarchists. Between 1992 and 2005 MI5 was given the authority to be the lead body for all aspects of national security intelligence related to terrorism, espionage, subversion, and proliferation and was also clearly established as setting the priorities for the police in the gathering of counterterrorism and other national security intelligence through the medium of the SBs.

In the contemporary development of this relationship it is possible to discern comparable issues to those identified by Cope (2004) in terms of police officers working with 'civilians'. The responses to the questionnaire around Cope's findings, as adapted for this chapter, note problems of lack of clarity about what each side should expect from the other, issues with differences in organisational structures and rank equivalents (though these were also seen to apply, more generally, to police-civil service relations), and a concern, mostly from within the MPS, that MI5 might have been attempting 'empire-building' in the post-Cold War era. However, more generally it was seen that MI5's entry into the OC area was always going to be limited in terms of available resources. Indeed there was a consensus that initially the 'value added' of MI5's greater involvement was mostly in terms of technical capacity. There is a lingering concern that interpretations of the 'need to know' principle may still be a negative feature of the relationship; for example, service references to studies of a common problem may not always be followed up by the sharing of the findings of the particular study. However, the responses were unanimous in recording the view that relationships had greatly improved since the catalyst of 9/11.

Thus the response to terrorism, especially post-9/11, has seen the development of a rather broader form of relationship between MI5 and the police than was apparent in earlier periods. The MI5 regional working-levels, the volume of CT investigations, the 'Contest' inter-agency working groups, and the ACPO-TAM working groups are all having the combined effects of both multiplying and developing the working relationship at a number of levels between the police and MI5.

ACKNOWLEDGEMENT

As part of the research for this chapter a small number of semi-structured interviews were conducted, under Chatham House rules, with participants from both components of the core partnership. The author alone remains responsible for any errors of fact or interpretation.

REFERENCES

BBC News 24, 11 December 2007, 'MI5 expanding outside London', extracts from Part 2 of Gordon Coreara's BBC Radio 4 programme on MI5, <http://news.bbc.co.uk/1/hi/uk/713715.stm>, accessed 12 December 2007.

CABINET OFFICE, 'Security in a Global Hub—Establishing the UK's New Border Arrangements' (London: The Stationery Office, 2007).

CLUTTERBUCK, L, 'Countering Irish Republican terrorism in Britain: Its origins as a police function' *Terrorism and Political Violence* 18 (2006) 95–118.

Cope, N, 'Intelligence led policing or policing with intelligence?: Integrating volume crime analysis into Policing' *British Journal of Criminology* 44/2, (2004) 188–203.

COUNCIL OF EUROPE, European Commission for Democracy through Law (Venice Commission), *Report on the Democratic Oversight of the Security Services* (Study No 388/2006, CDL-AD (2007) 016, Strasbourg, 11 June 2007).

DENNING, LJ, *Lord Denning's Report (Profumo Affair)* (Cm 2152, London: HMSO, 1963).

EVANS, J, Director General MI5, 'Intelligence, counter-terrorism and trust', Address to the Society of Editors, 5 November 2007 <http://www.mi5.gov.uk/output/Page562.html>, accessed 7 November 2007.

GEDDES, A, 'Chronicle of a crisis foretold: The politics of irregular migration, human trafficking and people smuggling in the UK' *British Journal of Politics and International Relations* 7 (2005) 324–339.

GREGORY, F, 'The London Bomb incidents of 7 and 21 July 2005: "New Normality" or as predicted ?', (2006a), Working Paper 10/2006, Real Instituto Elcano de Estudios Internacionales y Estratégicos, Madrid, June 2006 <http://www.realinstitutoelcano.org/documentos/245.asp>.

——, 'Intelligence-Led Counterterrorism Operations in the UK Summer 2006: Issues and Consequences', (2006b), ARI Paper 106/2006, Real Instituto Elcano de Estudios Internacionales y Estratégicos, Madrid, October 2006, <http://www.r-i-elcano.org/analisis/1056.asp>.

HARFIELD, C and HARFIELD, K, *Covert Investigation* (Oxford: Oxford University Press, 2005).

——, 'SOCA: A Paradigm Shift in British Policing' *British Journal of Criminology* 46 (2006) 743–761.

HM GOVERNMENT, *National Intelligence Machinery* (London: The Stationery Office, 2002).

——, *Countering International Terrorism: The United Kingdom Government Strategy ('Contest')* (Cm 6888, London: The Stationery Office, 2006).

HM INSPECTORATE OF CONSTABULARY, *HMIC Thematic Inspection of Special Branch and Ports Policing—A Need to Know* (Home Office Communications Directorate, 2003).

HOME OFFICE, Scottish Executive, Northern Ireland Office, *Guidelines on Special Branch Work in the United Kingdom* (2004).

HOUSE OF COMMONS HOME AFFAIRS COMMITTEE, Oral Evidence, 'Anti-Terrorism Powers', (HC 886-i, Qs 48, 53, 62 and 72, 8 July 2004).

INTELLIGENCE AND SECURITY COMMITTEE (ISC), Annual Reports pursuant to the Intelligence Services Act 1994, all published as Command Papers by The Stationery Office, London.

——, *Report into the London Terrorist Attacks on 7 July 2005* (Cm 6785, London: The Stationery Office, 2006).

MANNINGHAM-BULLER, E, James Smart Memorial Lecture (2003).

METROPOLITAN POLICE, *Special Branch: Introduction and Responsibilities* (Freedom of Information Act Scheme Document, 2006).

METROPOLITAN POLICE AUTHORITY, *Community Engagement to Counter Terrorism* Report: 8b by the Commissioner, 27 July 2007 <http://www.mpa.gov.uk/committees/mpa/2006/060727/08b.htm>, accessed 19 October 2007.

MÜLLER-WILLE, B, 'Improving Democratic Accountability of EU Intelligence' *Intelligence and National Security* 21 (2006) 100–128.

NaCTSO, 'Survey of CTSAs in Police Forces', unpublished (2004).

NORTHCOTT, C, 'The Role, Organization and Methods of MI5' *International Journal of Intelligence and CounterIntelligence* 20 (2007) 453–479.

O'NEILL, M and MARKS, M, *Police Occupational Culture: New Debates and Directions* (UK: Emerald Group Publishers, 2007).

PHYTHIAN, M, 'Still a Matter of Trust: Post-9/11 British Intelligence and Political Culture' *International Journal of Intelligence and CounterIntelligence* 18 (2005) 653–681.

RIMINGTON, S, 'Intelligence, Security and the Law', James Smart Lecture, 3 November 1994, <http://www.mi5.gov.uk/output/Page380.html>, accessed 31 August 2007.

——, *Open Secret* (London: Arrow, 2002).

ROSE, C, 'Report on Two Visits by Sadiq Khan MP to Babar Ahmad at HM Prison Woodhall' by the Rt Hon Sir Christopher Rose, Chief Surveillance Commissioner (Cm 7336, The Stationary Office, 2008).

RUDNER, M, 'Hunters and Gatherers: The intelligence coalition against Islamic terrorism' *International Journal of Intelligence and CounterIntelligence* 17 (2004) 193–230.

SEGELL, GM, 'Intelligence Agency relations between the European Union and the U.S.' *International Journal of Intelligence and CounterIntelligence* 17 (2004) 81–96.

——, 'Reform and Transformation: The UK's SOCA' *International Journal of Intelligence and CounterIntelligence* 20 (2007) 217–239.

SNOOK, H, *Crossing the Threshold: 266 Ways the State Can Enter Your Home* (London: Centre for Policy Studies, 2007).

SHEPTYCKI, J, ed, *Issues in Transnational Policing* (London and New York: Routledge, 2000).

WEST, N, 'The UK's Not Quite So Secret Services' *International Journal of Intelligence and CounterIntelligence* 18 (2005) 23–30.

5

THE GOVERNANCE
OF INTELLIGENCE

Professor Allyson MacVean

Historically, literature relating to the governance of intelligence management has focused on the intelligence agencies (for example see Keegan, 2004; Herman, 1996a; Hinsley and Simkins, 1990). The wider governance of intelligence has seldom dominated mainstream policing as only specialist police departments, such as Special Branch, had until recently been concerned with intelligence systems and processes. Because of recent concerns that have arisen about the generation and use of intelligence by the intelligence agencies and politicians (see MacVean and Harfield, Chapter 7 below), the current advocacy of intelligence-led policing, articulated through implementation of the National Intelligence Model within mainstream policing, begs questions about governance and political motivation. Are there lessons for the police service in what has become known about the work of the intelligence services in recent years? Or is the use of intelligence in policing significantly different? These are key questions because, as Gregory identifies (see Chapter 4 above), the lines between police force and intelligence service are becoming increasingly blurred, not least with the appointment of a former MI5 Director General to head the new Serious Organised Crime Agency (Harfield, 2006).

FROM POLITICAL DENIAL TO POLITICAL
EXPOSURE: SPINNING INTELLIGENCE

It is of the essence of a Secret Service that it must be secret, and if you once begin disclosure it is perfectly obvious to me as to Honourable Members opposite that there is no longer any Secret Service and that you must do without it (cited in Andrew, 2004: 30).

This view of intelligence work, espoused by Neville Chamberlain when Foreign Secretary, has dictated attitudes, both practitioner and by default (because they know no different) public, for decades. The intelligence community was perceived as the guardian of national interest against transient and feckless politicians (Scott and Jackson, 2004). It was only towards the end of the twentieth century, with the Security

Service Act 1989 for instance, that government began to acknowledge openly the existence of intelligence agencies and the role they played in informing foreign and defence policy.

The premise of secrecy evaded the principle of governance. Even when the Security Service (MI5) was put on a statutory footing, the governance arrangements (Security Service Act 1989, ss 4 and 5, and associated schedules) were equipped with wide-ranging mechanisms for privileging secrecy over transparency, no distinction being made between material, method, and mechanism in intelligence gathering. The same rationale was applied to the Secret Intelligence Service (MI6) and Government Communication Headquarters (GCHQ) when they were re-established on a statutory basis (Intelligence Services Act 1994, ss 8 and 9). The 1994 Act additionally created the Intelligence and Security Committee 'to examine the expenditure, administration and policy of' MI5, MI6, and GCHQ (ISA 1994, s 10), a joint Parliamentary committee whose members are appointed from outside government by the prime minister, in consultation with the leader of the opposition. The Committee's annual report, redacted as the prime minister sees fit or is advised, is placed before Parliament. This is governance by the great and the good, rather than governance through Parliament.

Glees and Davies (2004) have argued that the processes and structures that govern official secret intelligence had been exposed to a lesser extent by the spate of public inquiries and spy scandals since the 1960s. For example, Lord Denning's Report in 1963 examined the operations of the Security Service and the adequacy of their cooperation with the police in matters of security in establishing if there was any evidence that national security may have been breached in the circumstances leading to Secretary of State for War John Profumo's resignation. In his report, Denning also published, as an appendix, the previously secret Maxwell-Fyffe Directive (1953), which was the Security Service enabling executive order that touched upon the workings of the Joint Intelligence Committee (Denning Report, 1963). But it took political controversy over the way in which intelligence appeared to have been manipulated and was suspected of having been misrepresented in the run-up to the 2003 invasion of Iraq to expose the workings of the intelligence community to public scrutiny as never before. Indeed, two unprecedented public inquires were held, and their reports published (Butler, 2004; Hutton, 2004).

As national security and military intelligence was exposed through the debate about whether Iraq had had Weapons of Mass Destruction at its disposal, sufficient to pose a credible threat and justify pre-emptive invasion, so, in subsequent terrorist attacks which may or may not have been in retaliation for the military action, counterterrorist intelligence came under the spotlight, particularly in relation to police counterterrorist operations.

This juxtaposed two markedly different attitudes to governance: the historically-based opaque governance of the intelligence community and the equally historically-based governance of policing founded upon local authority (Police Act 1964; Police Act 1996). But even within the more transparent governance of policing, the emerging specialism of intelligence (HMIC, 1997) was still seen to be largely the preserve of expert departments such as Special Branch (HMIC, 2003).

DEFINING INTELLIGENCE FOR ACTION

There has been a tendency for the police service to look to the military (the 1997 HMIC thematic report on intelligence is prefaced with a quote from Sun Tzu's *The Art of War*) and the intelligence community, as well-established experts in intelligence working, not least because of partnership working in counterterrorism (HMIC, 2003; Gregory, Chapter 4 above). But as such, these are experts in their own field, which is not policing. The community being policed provides most of the intelligence and information that contributes to police intelligence products: much of it is volunteered, very little has to be obtained covertly. Conversely, military and national security intelligence is acquired usually covertly from ally and foe alike.

Whether practice directly translates between these arenas is one debate much constrained by what material is available in the public domain, but this chapter focuses on the principle of effective governance and how this can be applied to intelligent policing given that public confidence in intelligence-working may have been seriously eroded as a consequence of the portrayal of the use of intelligence in the run-up to the Iraq war, in subsequent police operations such as the shooting of Jean Charles de Menezes at Stockwell tube station, and the execution of search warrants at a house in Forest Gate.

'The truth about the Stockwell shooting paints a picture of confusion, human error and faulty intelligence in the first definitive account of the day Mr de Menezes died' (*The Independent on Sunday*, 4 December 2005, Sophie Goodchild and Steve Bloomfield). A number of questions are raised about ownership of intelligence, from which will follow the construction of governance frameworks.

If intelligence is defined as information that has been processed for action, does this imply that the officer responsible for implementing the action has ownership, or is it the analyst who has provided the product, or is it senior management who are responsible for the implementing strategic policy and directives, or is it a collective responsibility? If ownership cannot be defined by those who generate or exploit the intelligence product, does then governance and political motivation define responsibility?

Does ownership or perceived ownership of intelligence play a crucial part in intelligence being accepted as credible? Or is it that endorsement of intelligence by the intelligence agencies bears more weight than intelligence submitted by government or other agencies, such as the police? If ownership is a key issue of intelligence, who then should be accorded ownership of the intelligence product and ought they to have ownership? Does settlement of ownership bring with it greater accountability?

There are numerous definitions of governance, but common to them all are systems and processes that oversee the overall direction, effectiveness, supervision, and accountability of an organization. For the purposes of this chapter, I define governance of intelligence as oversight of the role of intelligence institutions or departments and their structures of authority to define policy, allocate resources, and coordinate or control activity in society.

Academic theories regarding the governance of intelligence have sought to establish the relationship between truth, knowledge, and power—hence Herman (1996), whose literature sought to promote greater public understanding of intelligence. Herman contended that if the cloak of secrecy was, where appropriate, loosened and where possible the public had a stake in the governance processes, it would provide a safeguard against political manipulation and interference. Sir Percy Cradock, chairman of the Joint Intelligence Committee (JIC) from 1985 to 1992, persuasively sought to legitimize the view that the role of the secret agencies wase to provide objective, policy-free analysis assessments to policy and decision-makers. Cradock characterized the JIC as 'having an eye to the future and to British interests, and free from political pressures likely to afflict their ministerial masters' (cited in Scott and Jackson, 2004: 10).

Yet public confidence in the authorities and their use of intelligence is, in no small part, founded upon confidence that the authorities are doing the right thing in the right way. And if political institutions are not appropriate forms of governance on behalf of the people, then what might intelligence governance look like? And should it be the same for the intelligence community and the police, given the different arenas these two professions operate in, and given they engage in significant overlap in counterterrorism activity. While the police service has never denied using intelligence, it does so within a culture of secrecy. Has the culture of secrecy fostered by the official denial of the intelligence services influenced the way in which the intelligence has been constructed and developed in the police service? If so, what impact would this have for the governance of police intelligence given their unique relationship with the community, one that is being fostered and encouraged in the twenty-first century by both government and the police?

Do the different uses and applications of intelligence influence the processes and structures of governance? The intelligence services are concerned with national and international intelligence, as is SOCA. Both organizations are primarily concerned with information relating to terrorist and serious and organized criminal activities. However, whereas the police gather intelligence from a wider range of sources, it is generally only concerned with information pertaining to the geographical parameters of the force area. The intelligence service adopts different methods of intelligence storage, dissemination, and analytical systems to those adopted by the police service, and in general terms police intelligence is rapidly converted into evidence for use in court.

If the definition of governance is concerned with power of authority to define policy, allocate resources, and coordinate or control activity in society, then integrity and independence of intelligence must also be integral to the process.

INTEGRITY, INDEPENDENCE, AND DOING BUSINESS

In 1994, John Major commissioned a post-Cold War review into the purposes of the intelligence agencies. The review undertaken by the then Permanent Secretary of Defence, Sir Michael Quinlan, specifically made reference to the Joint Intelligence Committee[1] arrangement and cautioned about the importance of its integrity and independence:

[the JIC] . . . is internationally admired as a major British strength, but its integrity and prestige are at risk if it is not used just for guidance before policy decisions but for public presentation after them. We must not slide towards selectivity and advocacy which, in a different institutional environment, occasionally corrupts the use of intelligence in the United States (Quinlan, 2000)

This statement has significant implications for the police. The police have a history of traditionally separating intelligence analysis and those using the intelligence products for police policy or action. Part of that disconnection is to ensure that both functions remain independent and that the integrity of each is maintained. When these roles become blurred it can distort the line between content and presentation and assessment and advocacy (see MacVean and Harfield, Chapter 7 below) often leading to more weight being placed on the intelligence that it can bear.

While Major's open government initiative was embraced and further advanced by New Labour, with it came a more informal ministerial style and approach of transacting political business. This approach included by-passing traditional communication channels, not taking minutes at meetings and negating the democratic process by forming informal groups rather than formal committees. Consequently, key personnel who should have been informed of critical issues were not; no official records were available to document the decision-making processes and as a consequence, the traditional political power-base was distorted from the 'democratic collective' in favour of a few (Hennessy, 2004). Thus, it could be argued that the mechanisms set up to provide and facilitate government accountability slid into something more fluid and unstructured with little opportunity for dissenting voices to be heard.

During the same period of the open government initiative, a new global threat was emerging, al-Qaeda and terrorist activity, which also directly influenced the relationship between the police and intelligence services (Gregory, Chapter 4 above). The global al-Qaeda threat provided governments with the justification to reorder the nature of both local and global intelligence, and the way in which organizations responsible for collecting, analysing, and disseminating intelligence conduct their business (Butler, 2004; Hutton, 2004). Intelligence-led policing was espoused has the way forward in countering terrorist activity (Goodchild and Bloomfield, 2005). The police and intelligence agencies were required and directed to work together in an unprecedented approach. Yet, what does that mean for the police, who openly

---

[1] The JIC is part of the Cabinet Office and is responsible for providing ministers and senior officials with co-ordinated interdepartmental intelligence assessments that are important to national interests, primarily in the fields of security, defence, and foreign affairs.

communicate and request intelligence from the public, and M15 who traditionally operate clandestinely. How can secrecy be reconciled with the need to maintain integrity and independence in the management of intelligence? It is worth reviewing some the lessons that materialized from the Hutton and Butler reports and what specifically they mean for the police.

LESSONS FROM THE HUTTON AND BUTLER REPORTS

Political events in 2003 and 2004 prompted unprecedented public inquiries into the machinations of government use and representations of intelligence for the case of going to war with Iraq in 2003 (Butler, 2004; Hutton, 2004; Intelligence and Security Committee, 2003).

The Butler Inquiry focused on the structures, systems, and processes of intelligence by investigating, inter alia, the accuracy of acquired intelligence, what was known and when, and why there were such discrepancies between the intelligence as originally assessed and the facts when they became known (for a brief outline of the Hutton Inquiry see MacVean and Harfield, Chapter 7 below).

Jointly, the reports concurred that '. . . the Government, the intelligence services, and the BBC all fell short to some degree of what might have been hoped, or expected, of them at a time when the country was on the brink of being taken into a war' (Runciman, 2004: 3).

Read together, the two inquiries reveal the difference between intelligence assessment and political advocacy and who behaved professionally given that knowledge and information (Runciman, 2004). Lord Hutton assessed his evidence in terms of the charges made, leading to a series of 'acquittals', 'convictions', and 'non-proven' adjudications, while Butler functioned more as a contemporary historian 'reconstructing "reality" as best [he] could from documents, and oral evidence, recreating mood and context—if not motivation—as [he] went' (Hennessey, 2004: 64). Collectively, the publications created a new discourse for official secret intelligence as well as propelling it into the public consciousness in a way never witnessed before (Scott and Jackson, 2004). Consequently, there is greater public access and accountability of intelligence regarding national security in relation to terrorist threats. Whether this demand was fuelled by the public following the publication of the September and February Dossiers, or whether it was the result of the government and intelligence agencies trying to educate the communities in intelligence, remains obscure. But whatever the reason, it led to the unprecedented announcement in January 2007 by M15 that it was launching an email service to alert the public to terrorist threats.

The following themes from the Hutton and Butler reports are most pertinent to policing and the governance of intelligence:

• Who has input into the intelligence/analytical products?
• Who has 'official' ownership of intelligence that is used to inform strategy and direct operations?

- How do you ensure the intelligence is robust and valid?
- What cautions are required when intelligence is used for political advocacy (as it could be in intelligence that informs policy)?
- What caveats should or need to be put around the use of intelligence?
- How can consensus about public understanding of the presentation of intelligence (particularly with the emphasis on the participation of Independent Advisory groups) be achieved?
- How do the media portray police intelligence?

The police service has considerably more mechanisms for oversight than those of the intelligence agencies, but such mechanisms tend to be concerned with the service and behaviour to members of the public, and performance measurements rather then the systems that record and regulate the integrity of intelligence. The Crime and Disorder Act 1998 adds further nuance in directing police forces to work in partnership with other agencies and the local community to formulate and implement a strategy for the reduction of crime reduction and disorder at local levels, including publishing an audit of performance and providing a system for community dissent. Partnership raises further questions about governance. Does working in partnership provide an additional mechanism of accountability for the use of police intelligence? How might the different governance arrangements for the individual partners interact? Is there interoperability in governance? And in particular, how can the sharing of intelligence between partners be governed in the light of significant and fatal intelligence-sharing failures (Laming, 2003; Bichard, 2004; HMIP, 2006).

It can be argued that one means of achieving accountability in relation to integrity of intelligence is through the process of it being converted to evidence, which has to stand up to scrutiny through the trial process—evidence based on intelligence that is challenged and contested as part of the trial system.

SECRECY, TRUST, AND POWER

While the Hutton and Butler reports exposed tensions that naturally exist between the intelligence arena and the use of intelligence by policymakers, they illustrated that the traditional boundaries of discord had been exceeded by deliberate government interference. Political meddling blurs the distinction between intelligence as fact or information, and intelligence as political ideology. The same holds true for police intelligence. If the public, or specific communities within the wider public, come to view the police as primarily an intelligence agency (or as an extension of the intelligence community) rather than as a community safety and crime-fighting agency, it will irrevocably alter the nature of police/public relations and interaction. Such a development may make policing more confrontational as the last vestiges of policing by consent erode.

Christopher Andrew (2004) argues against the widely held notion that complete secrecy and nil parliamentary accountability foster an efficient and effective intelligence service. He builds the case for greater accountability, which he sees as necessary if the 'foul-ups of the past are not to be repeated in the future'. However, 'knowing the enemy' in the twenty-first century is more complex than the last century, particularly within the context of policing where not everyone is the enemy. Neighbourhood policing espouses policing by consent, where dialogue and interaction with members of the community is fostered and encouraged. The policing of antisocial behaviour for instance, arguably involves a social contract with the community. If members of the community are the 'ears and eyes' of the police, then intelligence by its nature must be explicit and overt. Social contract cuts both ways, and consideration is required when 'police intelligence' needs to be communicated to members of the community. How can governance, trust, and power be reconciled when the community is both the problem and the solution—indeed 'should we burden friends with secrets?'[2] What then are the implications for the transnational organized crime arena, where the enemies (eg drugs barons) may well be beyond the criminal jurisdiction of the agency concerned and, equally, include social enemies such as user demand for illicit goods and services (such as illicit migration services, drugs trafficking, and counterfeit goods)? In this scenario, the potential enemies are in fact elements within the community which the police and partner agencies are seeking to protect.

If the old difficulty was hunting out and collecting the secrets, neighbourhood policing has provided the challenge of working out what is secret in amongst the mass of information now available and who has got it when it is required (Hughes-Wilson, 2004). This difficultly has been succinctly identified by the intelligence agencies when the emergence of terrorism across Europe in the 1970s led to a dramatic shift from intelligence required for traditional warfare towards intelligence specifically on counterterrorism, and this has been further reinforced by the emergence of the new global terrorism of the twenty-first century: '. . . the nature of counterterrorism is to get ahead of the game to stop, frustrate or otherwise prevent terrorist activity. That is the primary goal but the reality is that we can never stop all such attacks and no security intelligence organization in the world could do so. An attack may get through our defences' (Report into the terrorist attacks on 7 July 2005, 2006: 14).

The counterterrorism experts also acknowledge the limitations of intelligence:

As attacks against the UK have been mounted and successfully disrupted in the period since 9/11, the intelligence community's understanding of the scale of the threat against the UK has advanced. I think the more we learned over this period of several years, the more we began to realise the limits of what we knew, and I think that remains the case (Report into the terrorist attacks on 7 July 2005, 2006: 14).

The current climate in which the secret services operate to gather intelligence, which is used to inform political decisions and direct action, is more complex and more uncertain. New and innovative methods of doing business by intelligence agencies have and are, taking place, as different forms of intelligence from non-traditional sources are required.

It is also true that policing in the twenty-first century is more intricate and complex. The extending police family have greater numbers of civilian staff including Community Support Officers who patrol streets but have limited powers. The

---

[2] Personal conversation with Professor John Grieve.

government's commitment in implementing neighbourhood policing ensured that the necessary funding and resources required to develop the scheme at the local level were available. Policing was to be more visible and more accountable, with every member of the public knowing who their local officer was and how to contact them. This suggests that if there is more contact between the police and members of the community then it is not unreasonable to expect a corresponding increase in the levels of intelligence. Such intelligence is incorporated into the National Intelligence Model, which directs the organic development of neighbourhood policing through targeting crime hotspots and by bringing more offenders to justice. The public also know who exactly is responsible for reducing crime in their area.

So while neighbourhood policing inspires greater involvement with the community it also provides greater intelligence from that interaction—intelligence which has to be distilled and refined through analysis into something that is purposeful and actionable. While the NIM provides a standard business system, the issues of governance and ownership of the intelligence products remain obscure.

CONCLUSION

This chapter demonstrates that intelligence as conceptualized by the intelligence agencies is very different to intelligence as defined by the police. The methods by which intelligence is collected by intelligence agencies and the police, the systems of classification and storage, methods of analysis, and the way it is implemented to inform policy or practice differ significantly. Yet, since the emergence of the threat by al-Qaeda, both the police and MI5 have increased the number of surveillance operations undertaken. These operations are underpinned by intelligence-led policing and yet intelligence-led policing still appears to be beset by problems in relation to governance. The intelligence services may have previously postulated their position as guardians of the national interest, and in that respect beyond governance, but the controversy relating to intelligence about Weapons of Mass Destruction gave rise to public concern about what was being done in their name. The same must hold true for police intelligence particularly if there is a greater emphasis through neighbourhood policing to secure more community intelligence. There has been an increasing tendency, post-7/7, to equate community intelligence with counterterrorism intelligence thus blurring the distinction between the intelligence and police services. But here is the rub. Community intelligence is not intelligence: it is information. Surveillance operations can only harvest information. Intelligence is information that has been processed so that it is available for action. Intelligence is information that requires judgement, context, and perspective. Information is as fragmented as the threats themselves, whether threats from terrorists or threats from criminal activity: a potent mix of professional and amateurs, legitimate and illegitimate, local and international. Fundamental decisions have to be made such as when to act upon information/intelligence. Context and circumstance can sometimes be as difficult and elusive as the intelligence itself. This was identified by the Metropolitan police's Deputy Assistant Commissioner, Peter

Clarke, about the anti-terrorist operation in Forest Gate: 'The purpose of the investigation, after ensuring public safety, is to prove or disprove the intelligence that we have received. This is always difficult, and sometimes the only way to do so is mount an operation such as that we carried out this morning' (Extract from full statement on the Forest Gate raid by Peter Clarke, Guardian Unlimited, Friday 2 June 2006).

On the other hand, not testing the intelligence can have disastrous consequences. Ignoring or failing to recognize the significance of intelligence is equally dangerous. Mohammad Siddique Khan, one of the suicide bombers responsible for the July bomb plot in London, was known to the police and MI5, but only through activities peripheral to the conspiracies they were tracking. Operating in such an uncertain environment necessitates that the process of governance and its attendant systems must be articulated if police intelligence is not to be hostage to political posturing. Even more pertinent is the use and concept of the term 'intelligence'. The lack of a robust definition of intelligence in policing is part of the problem. It could be argued that the police trade and deal with information and knowledge. If knowledge-based policing (Harfield and Kleiven, Chapter 18 below) more accurately characterizes police activity and action, perhaps it may the basis upon which to define a robust process of governance.

This chapter has posed a number of questions to which answers will only become apparent through wider debate and discourse. Recent controversy over intelligence that either is believed to be misrepresented or is believed to have been wrongly interpreted and erroneously acted upon has highlighted the absence of transparent governance and effective management of intelligence issues. There is a strong case for treating the governance of the intelligence community separately from the governance of the police service, but the increasing overlap between the intelligence working of these two professional communities, together with a greater role for partnership in the delivery of safer communities, has meant that intelligence governance, insufficiently sophisticated as it is, has become increasingly complicated just as the public are becoming less trustful of intelligence professionals.

REFERENCES

ANDREW, C, 'Intelligence, international relations and under-theorisation' in Scott, L and Jackson, P, eds, *Understanding Intelligence in the Twenty-First Century* (London: Routledge, 2004) 30.

BICHARD, M, *The Bichard Inquiry Report* (House of Commons, London: TSO, 2004).

BUTLER, Lord, *Review of Intelligence on Weapons of Mass Destruction. Report of a Committee of Privy Counsellors* (HC 898, London: TSO, 2004).

CRADOCK, P, in Scott, L and Jackson, P, eds, 'Journeys in Shadows' *Understanding Intelligence in the Twenty-First Century* (London: Routledge, 2004) 10.

DENNING, LJ, *Lord Denning's Report (Profumo Affair)* (Cm 2152, London: HMSO, 1963).

GLEES, A and DAVIES, P, *Spinning the Spies: Intelligence, Open Government and the Hutton Inquiry* (London: Social Affairs Unit, 2004).

GOODCHILD, S and BLOOMFIELD, S, (*The Independent*, 4 October 2005).

HANDEL, M, 'The politics of intelligence' *War, Strategy and Intelligence* 2/4 (October 1987) 5–46.

HARFIELD, C and HARFIELD, K, *Covert Investigation* (Oxford: Oxford University Press, 2005).

——, 'SOCA: A paradigm shift in British policing' *British Journal of Criminology* 46 (2006) 743–761.

HENNESSY, P, 'What we know now' in Runciman, WG, ed, *Hutton and Butler: Lifting the Lid on the Workings of Power* (Oxford: Oxford University Press, 2004) 61–81.

HERMAN, M, *Intelligence Power in Peace and War* (Cambridge: Cambridge University Press, 1996a).

HERMAN, R, *Iron Gate* (London: Pocket Star Books, 1996b).

HINSLEY, F and SIMKINS, C, *British Intelligence in the Second World War: Its Influence on Strategy and Operations: Security and Counter-Intelligence* Vol 4 (New York: Cambridge University Press, 1990).

HMIC, *Policing with Intelligence* (London: HM Inspector of Constabulary, 1997).

——, *A Need to Know: Thematic Inspection of Special Branch* (London: HM Inspector of Constabulary, 2003).

HMIP, *An Independent Review of a Serious Further Offence Case: Anthony Rice* (London: HM Inspectorate of Probation, 2006).

HMSO, *The Intelligence and Security Committee Report into the Terrorist Attacks on 7 July 2005* (May 2006).

HUGHES-WILSON, J, *Military Intelligence Blunders and Cover-Ups* (New York: Da Capo Press, 2004).

HUTTON, Lord, *Report of the Inquiry into the Circumstances Surrounding the Death of David Kelly CMG* (HC 247, Stationery Office, 28 January 2004).

INTELLIGENCE AND SECURITY COMMITTEE, *Iraqi Weapons of Mass Destruction—Intelligence and Assessments* (London: TSO, 2003).

KEEGAN, J, *Intelligence in War* (New York: Alfred A Knopf, 2004).

LAMING, L, *The Victoria Climbié Inquiry* (London: TSO, 2003).

NEWBURN, T, *Handbook of Policing* (Devon: Willan Publishing, 2003).

O'NEILL, O, 'Accuracy, independence and trust' in Runciman, WG, ed, *Hutton and Butler: Lifting the Lid on the Workings of Power* (Oxford: Oxford University Press, 2004) 89–109.

QUINLAN, M, 'The future of covert intelligence' in Shukman, H, ed, *Agents for Change* (St Ermin's Press, 2000).

RUNCIMAN, W, ed, *Hutton and Butler: Lifting the Lid on the Workings of Power* (Oxford: Oxford University Press, 2004).

SCOTT, L and JACKSON, P, *Understanding Intelligence in the Twenty-First Century: Journeys in Shadows* (London: Routledge, 2004).

SUN TZU, *The Art of War* (Oxford: Oxford University Press, 1963).

6

'INTELLIGENCE' AND THE DIVISION OF LINGUISTIC LABOUR[1]

Kalbir Sohi and Dr Clive Harfield

INTRODUCTION

Within law enforcement the phrase 'intelligence-led' enjoys much currency and there has been a great deal of practitioner and academic discourse about aspects of intelligence-led policing which has included recent publication of intelligence doctrine (see, for instance, Harfield and Harfield, 2008, Chapters 2, 3 and 5). But what has emerged from the discourse and doctrine is evidence to indicate that whilst 'intelligence' enjoys a common currency, it may not enjoy a common meaning. This has implications particularly at a strategic and policy level. At a time when intelligence product and its role in informing decision-making has come under particular scrutiny (Bichard, 2004; Butler, 2004; Hutton, 2004; HMI Probation, 2006) this chapter explores, from the perspective of the philosophy of language, the meaning and misunderstanding of 'intelligence' and considers the possible implications in the arena of policing organized crime.

PHILOSOPHICAL BACKGROUND

THE TRADITIONAL VIEW OF MEANING

For a significant period in the philosophy of language[2] a single view of what words mean was widespread. The view rested on drawing a distinction between two types of things that words can stand for. The first of these notions, 'the extension', was taken to be the set of object that it is correct to apply the word to. So, for the word 'horse', it is correct to apply this word only to horses and so the extension of the word 'horse' is the set of all, and only, horses. The second notion is best introduced through a somewhat hackneyed example in the philosophy of language. Consider the two compound

---

[1] Many thanks to Gabriel Segal for very useful comments on an earlier draft of this chapter.

[2] Putnam claims from medieval times (Putnam, 1979:215) but the philosopher that most forcefully presented this view of meaning was Gottlob Frege in 'On Sense and Reference' (Frege, 1892/1980).

terms 'creature with a heart' and 'creature with a kidney'. Since it is true that everything with a heart also has a kidney, these two terms have the same extension, all the things that it is correct to apply the first term to it is also correct to apply the second one too. However, it is clear that these two terms mean different things, so we cannot restrict our notion of meaning to the extension of a word or term. Instead, we must introduce the second of our notions of meaning, 'the intension'. Various different structures or entities have been considered to do the work of intensions. The key element that they have in common is that they distinguish things that the extension does not, as with the descriptions 'creature with a heart' and 'creature with a kidney'. The type of account that we will be using here is that which associates the intension of a term with the concept that it expresses.

Although there is considerable debate over what 'concepts' are, it is generally agreed that a concept is some sort of psychological state, perhaps similar to believing certain things,[3] being able to make certain inferences[4] or identifications, or just having had certain interactions with instances of the concept.[5] Since it is a psychological state, it can be considered as internal to the person who possesses that concept; so you having the concept 'horse' is dependent on certain things inside your head—beliefs about horses, for example.

The relationship between the intension and the extension is of interest. Typically, when we talk about what a word means we are talking about something like the intensions; that is, we are considering some information that we associate with the word which we use as a criterion to determine what is in the extension of that word. So, if someone were to ask us, 'What does "horse" mean?' we would reply with a list of characteristics of horses—'they are animals with four legs, hooves, etc'—such that the list would enable us to determine what it was appropriate to call a horse and what it is not. So, we can see that, on this traditional picture of meaning, the intension of a word determines the extension; it provides a criterion for working out what the word applies to.

The traditional picture can be summed up in the following ways:

1. The meaning of a word can be separated into two parts: the extension and the intension, where the extension is the set of things that is associated with the word and the intension is the concept that the word expresses.
2. The intension determines the extension; it provides a criterion by which things are judged to be in the extension.
3. The intension is a psychological notion and, as such, is internal to individuals; meanings are 'in the head'.

THE DIVISION OF LINGUISTIC LABOUR

In a seminal paper in the philosophy of language (Putnam, 1979), Hilary Putnam introduced a novel new way of thinking about words and their meanings.[6] He introduced

---

[3] So, to have the concept DOG, you may have to believe that dogs have four legs.

[4] It may be a condition of having the concept RED that one has to be able to identify red things say.

[5] So having the concept HORSE might be dependent on coming into contact with horses.

[6] Putnam was one of a group of influential philosophers including Saul Kripke (1980), David Kaplan (1989), and others who questioned the traditional picture of meaning.

a new argument against the traditional view. In particular, he aimed to argue that the points 2 and 3 above were not jointly true of a notion of meaning. In his arguments he introduced a particular type of scenario called 'Twin Earth'. Twin Earth is exactly the same as the real Earth but for one or two seemingly minor differences in the physical environment, differences that are external to any individuals. Putnam then uses this scenario to argue that when an individual on Earth and his molecule for molecule identical twin on Twin Earth say the same thing they mean different things—not because of anything that is different about them, their beliefs, or other psychological states but because of the differences in their external environments.

Putnam's thought experiments introduced a distinction between two ways of thinking about meanings. On the one hand we have the traditional picture of meaning as being intrinsic to individuals: it is what the individual associates with a word that determines what it refers to. On the other hand, we have the new picture of meanings being indelibly linked to the speaker's environment: a single change in the physical environment causes changes in what the speaker means by their terms, whether they are aware of it or not. The two positions have come to be known as 'internalism' and 'externalism' respectively. The type of externalism that Putnam's argument motivates is based around a particular picture of science and its relationship to language; it is science that determines the correct way to classify things in the world and our language respects this classification. We might call this type of externalism 'natural kind externalism', where a natural kind is the type of thing that science investigates. Typical natural kinds might be species of animals, scientifically individuated substances like water, or the basic entities of science like atoms and quarks. A superficial way of describing natural kind externalism might be as follows: the meanings of words are determined, at least in part, by the physical nature of the subject's external environment.

We can see that this flies in the face of the traditional view of meaning since the meanings of words are not wholly determined by the individuals that use them. In addition to natural kind externalism, Putnam and a second philosopher, Tyler Burge (Burge, 1979), also introduce a second way in which the meanings of words are determined by factors external to the subject. This second kind of externalism, called 'social externalism', is the main interest of this chapter. Putnam introduces this version by way of an example. Suppose that you are unable to tell the difference between elms and beeches; in fact, the information that you associate with the word 'elm' is the same as the information that you associate with the word 'beech'. Notwithstanding that fact, it is still the case that when you utter the word 'elm' you refer only to elms and when you utter the word 'beech' you refer only to beeches. Since the information that you associate with the two words (your internal state) is the same, it cannot be by virtue of your concepts, 'elm' and 'beech', that you refer to different things; it must be something external to you. In this case, Putnam correctly points out that if no one could tell what an elm was (or what a beech was) then there would be no use for the word 'elm' (or 'beech'). As a result, he holds that it is by virtue of there being experts that are able to tell the difference between the two trees that our words refer to different things.

In his example, Putnam is once again restricting his thesis to natural kind terms. Tyler Burge, in his arguments, extended the thesis so that it covers a wider range of terms. Burge's argument concerns an individual, Alf. Alf has certain beliefs about arthritis; he believes that he has arthritis in his knees, that it causes him pain, and that it gets worse in winter. One day, he wakes up and feels a pain in his thigh. He goes to the doctor and tells him that he thinks his arthritis has spread to his thigh. The doctor corrects him: arthritis is by definition an ailment of the joints and so his arthritis cannot have spread to his thigh. Now we consider Twin Earth, an exact duplicate of the real Earth with one minor change: on Twin Earth the term 'arthritis' is used to refer to a wider range of ailments than on Earth and, in particular, it also includes pains in the thigh. Twin Alf, Alf's molecule for molecule doppelganger on Twin Earth, has all the same beliefs about arthritis as Alf does and also wakes up one morning with a pain in his thigh. He goes to the doctor and informs him that his arthritis has spread to his leg. The doctor concurs and they get on with their business. Burge argues that Alf and Twin Alf express different concepts when they use the word 'arthritis'. Twin Alf expresses the wider, twin concept that includes the pain in his thigh. In contrast Alf expresses the concept 'arthritis', the same concept that the doctor (and any other relevant expert) does. Burge argues that Alf expresses the correct concept even when he has a false belief about one aspect of that concept. He does this by virtue of the fact that he has a partial understanding of the concept and is willing to defer to the expert.

Putnam and Burge identify these phenomena as engendering a division of linguistic labour. Just as in ordinary activities there is a division of labour between people with different skills in order to serve a common goal, Putnam proposes that in the case of some words there is a division of linguistic labour between producers, who determine what the words mean, and consumers, who use them.[7] In using the words, the consumers somehow defer to the expertise of the producers. Thus in the elm and beech case we are relying on the fact that there are experts who can tell the difference between elms and beeches (and that can use the words 'elm' and 'beech' correctly) when we use the words and it is by virtue of there being such experts that we latch on to the correct type of tree.

We can introduce the following principle then, which captures the division of linguistic labour (DLL): if a person (i) has a partial understanding of a word, w, and (ii) uses w with the intention of deferring to experts; then that person's use of w has the same reference as the experts' use.

So even when I have only a partial understanding of what the word 'elm' refers to, when I say 'elm' I manage to refer solely to elms because I intend to use the word in the same way the experts do. Both conditions (i) and (ii) are a little vague. The question of 'what sort of understanding constitutes "partial understanding"?' immediately arises. It is almost certainly the case that in order for DLL to be true, partial understanding has to be sufficient to determine what *type* of thing we are referring to; in the elm and beech case it is unlikely that the example would get off the ground if Putnam did not even know that these words refer to trees. There are many questions to be asked of DLL: what does 'deferring to the knowledge of experts' involve? How regularly does this type of deference occur in ordinary discourse? Is this the only version of DLL? The one that we want to look at in this chapter is this: what happens when there is more than one set of experts?

---

[7] This terminology (producers and consumers) is Kaplan's (1990) and is resurrected in Segal (2000).

DLL AND MULTIPLE EXPERTS[8]

ANOTHER TWIN EARTH EXAMPLE

Consider Police Sergeant Smith, an officer in the Someshire Police Force on Earth. PS Smith has a partial understanding of the word 'intelligence'. He uses the word from time to time, mainly to refer to information that has been collected on suspects of crimes in his Basic Command Unit, and has a general idea of some things that might count as intelligence in the policing context. Now consider a Twin Earth where everything about PS Smith is replicated by his doppelganger, Police Sergeant Twin-Smith. Twin-Smith is also an officer, in the Twin-Someshire Police Force and has an identical partial understanding of the word 'intelligence'.

So far, so identical. Let us introduce a difference between the two worlds then. On Earth the word 'intelligence', as used in a policing and security context[9] is used by the experts in line with the following definition:

Def1: Personal information of value to national security, the prevention or detection of crime or disorder, the maintenance of community safety, and the assessment or collection of any tax or duty of any imposition of a similar nature, other than that required to be held for legal or administrative purposes, which has been assessed for accuracy and relevance and in respect of which it is necessary to protect the identity of the source.

On Twin-Earth however, experts in the relevant field use a different definition of 'intelligence':

Def2: Information that has been subject to a defined evaluation and risk assessment process in order to assist with police decision-making.

So, the only difference between the two worlds is how the experts in the linguistic community use a particular word. This might seem to be quite a matter of little importance, especially in the case of Sergeant's Smith and Twin-Smith since they both have the same level of understanding of 'intelligence'. Our initial assessment of the situation might well be that when each of them use the word 'intelligence' they are talking about the same thing, since their understanding of the word is the same. However, when we introduce DLL into the picture, we see that, contrary to what our first thoughts on the matter may indicate, Smith and Twin-Smith are saying different things.

On the deference model of DLL when Smith utters the word 'intelligence' he means Def1 as the meaning of his word is determined by the set of experts on Earth. In contrast, but also as a result of DLL, when Twin-Smith makes the same noises in uttering 'intelligence' on Twin Earth he means Def2 since the meaning of his word is determined by the experts on Twin Earth who use 'intelligence' to mean that.

This Twin Earth example shows us that two individuals, identical in terms of their internal psychological structure, can express different meanings by using the same words, purely by virtue of what relevant experts take the word to mean. This is a result

---

[8] The key philosophical arguments in this section are due to Gabriel Segal and can be found in a similar form in Segal (2000).

[9] We use this disclaimer to exclude the concept of an individual's intelligence or 'braininess'. From here on we will drop the disclaimer but we still intend to refer to the policing and security context.

of DLL. If we hold that thesis to be true then we see that having communities with different expert meanings can result in people, with a similar partial understanding, expressing different meanings when they use the same term.[10]

A TWIN EARTH CLOSER TO HOME

Such science fiction examples are all well and good, but beyond their consequences for externalism in the philosophy of language, what effect can Twin Earth have on us? Well, in fact, this Twin Earth example is not so far away from home. The two definitions that we have used, Def1 and Def2 are not constructions from the authors' imaginations, nor are they used by organizations as far apart as the UK Police Force and the Twin-UK Police Force; they are actually definitions in current police literature as issued in guidance to police officers.[11] Now, let us shift our focus from Twin Earth to the real thing by considering the following, very plausible, scenario. ACC W of Police Force X and ACC Y of Police Force Z both attend a conference on the National Intelligence Model. In the afternoon there are various parallel sessions and they decide to attend different sessions, A and B. In session A, the session leader (an expert) talks about 'intelligence' using Def1, since he read the first document, and the session leader of B does the same, only this time using Def2 since he read the other document. The two ACCs arrived at the conference with a partial understanding of 'intelligence' and, since they were unable to pick up everything that their relative expert said about 'intelligence', they form an intention to defer to the respective experts in their use of the word 'intelligence'. As a result of this intention, DLL comes into play and their subsequent uses of the word 'intelligence' have the same meanings as those of their respective experts. In the coffee break after the sessions, ACCs W and Y get talking and W says, 'Intelligence-led policing is certainly the way forward', to which Y replies, 'It certainly is; intelligence will play a significant role in our future policing strategy'.

Now we have a conundrum. As a result of DLL, X and Y are expressing different things by their uses of the word 'intelligence'. Since their understanding of the term is largely the same it is unlikely that the difference in what they mean will turn up through further discussion. If they had listened carefully to the definitions that their respective experts proposed and picked up that information we could credit each of them with having a superior understanding of two different meanings and they would presumably eventually find out that this was the case, namely that they were talking about different things. However, if they did pick up that information, there would be no need for DLL as each would have a full understanding of the concept,

---

[10] It has been pointed out that the two definitions presented here need not be substantially different. In particular, if the 'defined evaluation and risk assessment process' of Def2 is the same as the processes laid out in Def1 then the two definitions would essentially be the same. However, since it is not specified what these processes are we will play on the possible ambiguities of the definition and hold that they are actually different.

[11] Def1 can be found in ACPO/HMCE (1999), Def2 in ACPO (2005: 13).

rather than a partial one, and would not need to defer to the experts but would in fact have an understanding similar to that of the experts. Since they have maintained their partial understanding and added an intention to defer to the experts, DLL entails that they end up talking at cross-purposes, with no way of finding out that they are.

The situation is worse when we consider a slightly different case. Consider what would happen if ACC W were now at a conference were there were two sessions on intelligence, both of which W attends. In the first session the speaker implicitly uses Def1 and in the second, the speaker implicitly uses Def2. ACC W digests the main parts of the talks and goes back to his Force to give a presentation on how to implement the strategies discussed by the speakers. When he gives this talk, he uses the word 'intelligence' copiously and in doing so, intends to refer to the same thing that the experts did. Which meaning does W use when he uses the word 'intelligence' in his talk? He intends to defer to the experts in using the word, so by DLL he expresses what the experts use when they use the term—but which of the two experts does he defer to? There is nothing to choose between the two experts: neither one has a greater relevance to W.[12]

What do we say about W now? None of the alternatives are especially appealing. Perhaps he expresses two meanings, one linked to each expert; perhaps he expresses a single meaning, which could either be one of the experts' meanings or his own understanding of the term. It is unlikely that he expresses two meanings even though he defers to two experts since it is not the case that he has decided that in some cases he will defer to one and in some to the other; he defers to both collectively and equally. If he did express two meanings we would be able to ask, 'How come "intelligence" sometimes stands for Def1 and sometimes for Def2?', a question that does not have any clear answer in our case. Similarly, if we try to force the issue and say that he expresses one of the experts' meanings and not the other, we are left with the same question: what decides which meaning he expresses? We could answer that he expresses both meanings and that what he expresses is Def3, which is essentially Def1 added to Def2. However, it could easily be the case that the definitions are mutually exclusive and that each one excludes the other one. Finally, we could say that W expresses just one meaning but that it is not the experts' meaning. This is essentially saying that DLL cannot cope with situations in which there is more than one set of experts and saying this would be a blow for the thesis since there are many cases where there are different sets of experts.[13] If we choose this option, we are also left with the problem of what meaning W does express when he uses the word 'intelligence': is it the partial understanding that he has or something else?

---

[12] We can assume that, for argument's sake, he uses their ideas equally and mixes what they say in his own discussion.

[13] Gabriel Segal gives some examples which exploit the differences between UK and US English (Segal, 2000) but it is easy to think of other examples along the lines of 'intelligence'.

CONCLUSION

DLL strikes many, both within and outside philosophy, as a plausible thesis. However, as we have seen in the previous sections, it can have some unpalatable consequences. If there are cases where more than one set of experts exist, and the experts have different understandings of how to use a term, then we get into problems, both when people are deferring to different experts and when a single person has two equally salient groups of experts to defer to. Whilst some of the examples that we have used here have a decidedly science-fictional nature, the consequences of these considerations is anything but. Firstly we have seen that in the case of 'intelligence' there are in fact at least two uses in play. If we take into account the myriad different ways in which 'intelligence' has been employed in the recent policing literature[14] there are almost certainly going to be further uses to take into account. If each person who defers to the experts in their usage is deferring to just one set of experts, with one particular usage, then we run into problems of the first type, where different groups of people with allegiances to different experts will talk at cross-purposes. If instead, each person is deferring to a mix of the different sets of the experts, then we run into problems of the second type. We have to ask, 'which of the experts' meanings are they expressing?', if that is, in fact, what they are doing.

We can also point out that deference occurs in chains. A police constable may defer to his chief constable who may defer to the ACPO lead who may defer to a particular set of academics. In this way, we can see that the same problems will filter down deference chains. However, the chains can terminate in different places. So far we have assumed that the relevant experts to whom people with partial understanding will defer are at the ACPO level. This means that the meanings are determined at a level higher than that of the Force and so people in different Forces can end up with the same meaning. An alternative model would be each chain terminating with the relevant individual at Force level, be that an ACC, DCC, CC, or someone different. In this case someone in Force A would defer to CC A for instance, whilst someone in Force B would defer to CC B. If CCs A and B have different conceptions of 'intelligence' then we have two Forces operating with different meanings; since there are 60 Forces and associated bodies in the country,[15] we could end up with 60 different meanings! This model is an unlikely one for the way that things actually work but it does raise questions about the interaction between the national bodies, such as ACPO, and those who are in charge in each Force. It is perfectly feasible that a CC somewhere could disagree with the ACPO guidance and thus introduce his own understanding of 'intelligence' but, arguably, that sort of situation is not useful for communication and understanding within the service as a whole.

We also have to be aware of the problems that occur when there is discourse between organizations. An example of the sort of problems that might arise can be

[14] The terms 'intelligence products', 'intelligence-led policing' and the 'National Intelligence Model' come to mind, but there are others. See Kleiven and Harfield (Chapter 18 below) for a discussion on the various interpretations of 'intelligence' discovered amongst staff from different national jurisdictions seconded to Europol.

[15] According to <http://www.police.uk/forces.htm>, accessed October 2007.

seen if we consider the case of the Serious Organised Crime Agency (SOCA). SOCA, which became operational on 1 April 2006, is the result of merging the National Crime Squad, the National Criminal Intelligence Service, the National Investigation Service of the former HM Customs and Excise, and the investigation arm of HM Immigration Service. SOCA has also recruited from the intelligence community and former MI5 and MI6 personnel occupy key posts (Harfield, 2006). These are all agencies with their own understanding of what intelligence is and how it should be used and, as a result, all agencies that potentially have different meanings for the word 'intelligence' (Innes and Sheptycki, 2004; Sheptycki, 2004: 326). Similarly academics conceptualize intelligence in different ways, for example the four modes model of 'criminal', 'crime', 'community', and 'contextual' intelligence (Innes et al, 2005: 44).

There is a particular distinction in understanding and usage between law enforcement and the intelligence community, and this influences approaches to organized crime. Whereas the law enforcement constituent elements of SOCA have a history of using intelligence to support evidence-gathering and prosecution, the intelligence elements have historically focused on disruption rather than detection and prosecution. When debating the statutory remit for SOCA, HM Government laid particular emphasis on disruption rather than detection as a key role for SOCA, thus demonstrating the influence of the intelligence community over the construction of SOCA.

SOCA will be a step change away from a classic investigation organization of investigation and prosecution toward employing the most effective and proportionate means dedicated to reducing the harm done by organized crime . . . SOCA will work in a fundamentally different way to its predecessors . . . SOCA will be a genuinely intelligence-led organization. Real knowledge and understanding of the problems must be its first responsibility. That in turn will drive decisions about which activities to target and the best means of attacking them (Caroline Flint MP, Hansard (Standing Committee D) 11 January 2005, cols 35 and 66).

This difference in emphasis in the way in which intelligence is used need not necessarily make a difference to what intelligence is for SOCA and the wider police community, or to what 'intelligence' means. However, if the types of things that count as intelligence in the disruption model are different to the types of things that count as intelligence in the detection and prosecution model then there could be a related shift of meaning.

The difference in emphasis from detection to disruption evidenced here has perhaps resulted in a difference in the things that are classed as intelligence and thus in a difference in how the word 'intelligence' is used. The implications of such a change of influence would be important and varied.

As a result of this kind of change those working within SOCA will defer to a different set of experts to those outside of it. Will this different usage of the term 'intelligence' distance SOCA from the rest of the law enforcement community?

Certainly discourse between SOCA and other branches of the law enforcement community will be affected. At the level of the BCU (level 1 of the National Intelligence Model) partial understanding of the term 'intelligence' is bound to be rife. If officers at this level defer to the experts of ACPO when using the term then a substantial difference will exist between what they say and what members of SOCA say.

Have the different perceptions of intelligence and the ensuing difference in word meaning between the intelligence community and law enforcement interrupted the continuum articulated in the NIM? Does 'intelligence-led' now mean something different according to which part of the law enforcement community one is working with? How does this influence partnership-working between the conventional police service and the new investigators of SOCA? These are questions that are raised by our foray into the theoretical areas of the philosophy of language that seem to be anything but theoretical.

REFERENCES

ACPO, *Guidance on the National Intelligence Model* (Wyboston: NCPE, 2005).

——/HMCE, *The Recording and Dissemination of Intelligence Material: Code of Practice* (London: NCIS, 1999).

BICHARD, M, *The Bichard Inquiry Report* (HC 653, London: The Stationery Office, 2004), available online at <http://www.homeoffice.gov.uk/pdf/bichard_report.pdf>, accessed October 2007.

BURGE, T, 'Individualism and the mental' *Midwest Studies in Philosophy* IV (1979) 73–121.

BUTLER, Lord, *Review of Intelligence on Weapons of Mass Destruction: Report of a Committee of Privy Counsellors* (HC898, London: The Stationery Office, 2004), available online at <http://www.butlerreview.org.uk/>, accessed October 2007.

FREGE, G, 'Über Sinn und Bedeutung' *Zeitschrift für Philosophie und Philosophische Kritik*, 100 (1892) 25–50. Translated as 'On sense and reference' by Black, M, in Geach, P and Black, M, eds and trans, *Translations from the Philosophical Writings of Gottlob Frege* (3rd edn, Blackwell, 1980).

HARFIELD, C, 'SOCA: A paradigm shift in British policing' *British Journal of Criminology* 46 (2006) 743–761.

—— and HARFIELD, K, *Intelligence: Investigation, Community, and Partnership* (Oxford: Oxford University Press, 2008).

HMIP, *An Independent Review of a Serious Further Offence Case: Anthony Rice* (London: HMIP, 2006), available online at <http://inspectorates.homeoffice.gov.uk/hmiprobation/inspect_reports/serious-further-offences/AnthonyRiceReport.pdf>, accessed October 2007.

HUTTON, Lord, *Report of the Inquiry into the Circumstances Surrounding the Death of Dr David Kelly CMG* (HC247, London: The Stationery Office, 2004), available online at <http://www.the-hutton-inquiry.org.uk/>, accessed October 2007.

INNES, M, FIELDING, N and COPE, N, 'The appliance of science? The theory and practice of crime intelligence analysis' *British Journal of Criminology* 45 (2005) 39–57.

—— and SHEPTYCKI, J, 'From Detection to Disruption: Intelligence and the changing logic of police crime control in the United Kingdom', *International Criminal Justice Review* 14 (2004) 1–24.

KAPLAN, D, 'Demonstratives' in Almog, J, Perry, J, and Wettstein, H, eds, *Themes from Kaplan* (Oxford: Oxford University Press, 1989) 481–563.

——, 'Words' *Proceedings of the Aristotelian Society* Supplementary Volume 64 (1990) 93–120.

KRIPKE, S, *Naming and Necessity* (London: Blackwell, 1980).

PUTNAM, H, 'The meaning of "Meaning"' in *Philosophical Papers, Volume 2: Mind, Language and Reality* (Cambridge: CUP, 1979) 215–271.

SEGAL, GAM, *A Slim Book About Narrow Content* (Boston: MIT Press, 2000).

SHEPTYCKI, J, 'Organizational pathologies in police intelligence systems: Some contributions to the lexicon of intelligence-led policing' *European Journal of Criminology* 1/3 (2004) 307–332.

PART II

THE ROLE
OF ANALYSIS

INTRODUCTION TO PART II:
ANALYSIS—PROVIDING
A CONTEXT
FOR INTELLIGENCE

Sir David Phillips

One way and another the writers in this section ask us what we think about 'intelligence' by reflecting upon the dilemmas of the 'analyst'. After all there is a reasonable consensus that 'intelligence' is about the reduction of information to a distillate of meaning; it is not simply the possession of 'information'—albeit that in common usage, particularly and ironically amongst professional customers, intelligence is a term naively used as a synonym for the 'golden nuggets' of raw data. Furthermore, if the task of distilling the 'product' from the 'data' were merely mechanical we would not need to call upon their Delphic skills. To this end we are indebted to Abram Shulsky for his insight that intelligence has the defining characteristic that it is to be adduced from information otherwise denied and likely to be wreathed in deceit—the rest is research. That said, the fashion amongst the more liberally minded commentators, following the noble tradition of the *éminence grise* of intelligence, Sherman Kent, is to downplay the capture of information by clandestine means and emphasize the 'open source' route. Evans in his contribution, for example, makes no mention of covert collection as being vital or even important to the new world analysts of the PSNI—rather their contribution is to be 'community focused' seemingly as a political requirement. But both the 'puzzles' (what is knowable) and 'mysteries' (what can only be speculated upon) of the intelligence game, to follow Gregory Treverton's useful distinction, however the clues are unearthed, presume some level of intellectual discovery (if not oracular interpretation). To this end the analyst stands out amongst the successive roles in the so-called 'intelligence cycle' as the creative spirit.

Despite claiming the intellectual high ground, the analyst remains a figure of ambiguity: at times bearing the taint of Cassandra, or, as observed in the contribution of McVean and Harfield, underrated, under-taxed, and lacking influence. It is true Evans sounds a more optimistic note but he admits real evidence of effectiveness has yet to be obtained and we might ask whether what he records has more than a touch of 'early-adopter' enthusiasm.

The story of Captain Joe Rochefort, the eccentric American code-breaker and analyst, sacked as head of the United States Navy's Pearl Harbour cryptanalysis centre for proving his superiors wrong, should perhaps be read by every analyst tyro before taking on the job. Rochefort's brilliant work fathomed the Japanese plan for an attack upon Midway Island and eventually revealed the entire battle plan from a painstaking examination of decrypts. His priceless contribution gave Admiral Nimitz the opportunity to destroy the Japanese carrier fleet thereby turning about the naval forces of Admiral Yamamoto and, as was to be seen, the fortunes of the Pacific War (Hughes-Wilson, 1999, Chapter 4).

Rochefort's demise is illustrative of the uncertain and intermediate position of the analyst. Exactly because he or she is employed to speculate on the most likely interpretation when everything is not or cannot be known, he or she can only speak in degrees of significance, which of course affords no certainty. The successful use of intelligence is about dialogue and the balance of probabilities not absolutes, but in uncertain and faltering hands such ambiguities and ambivalences as are inevitable when only part of the picture is clear, are more likely to be used unscrupulously either to justify excessive caution or foolhardy enthusiasm. Rochefort's eccentricity (a penchant for working in a silk dressing gown over his uniform) stands as a metaphor for the analyst in another way too. As McVean and Harfield observe, the centre ground of the dilemma is that analysts usually work for ordered and hierarchic employers yet their contribution at the highest level probably turns upon a freewheeling imagination and lateral thinking to challenge conventional wisdom. The modern appetite for doctrine is so easily subverted into doctrinaire prescription and even worse, when intelligence practice is within the call of those who do not understand it, instead of being tasked it is merely bureaucratized. It is not surprising therefore that most studies of 'intelligence failure' have condemned the presuppositions of the policymakers and decision-takers not the errors of intelligence analysts as such. Indeed, in the Butler and Hutton reports it is difficult not to see 'intelligence' as having been used after the fact as an alibi for policy. There is certainly no indication that 'intelligence alerts' were the mainspring of policy change. The simple truth was that there was insufficient information for the analysts to make strong predictions and a failure of collection is not a failure of analysis—although dossiers produced after the event to put the best gloss on a poor situation may well constitute its subornation.

Intelligence literature is rich in critiques, an understandable consequence of the fact that, almost by definition, we will hear more of intelligence failures than we ever will of intelligence successes. Hopefully, this compendium provides more than that. McVean and Harfield explore a number of ways in which the inherent unreliability of intelligence might be counterbalanced, most notably by suggesting ways in which the 'users' might be held in check by third party auditing. If the history of 'intelligence reform' in the United States is anything to go by, institutional reforms have a nasty habit of atrophying or simply being subverted in what Richard K Betts called 'the illusiveness of solutions' (Betts, 1978, Vol 3: 73)—and as we choose our political leaders and sometimes our commanders because they hold opinions rather than for their objectivity, the prospect of reforming the 'users' may also have its limitations.

Sissens takes us in at the ground floor and tells us what crime analysts think about their world. Their responses confirm the litany of organizational pathologies researchers in general have identified and she concludes that the 'NIM' expectations of analysts are a long way from being fulfilled. It is difficult not to get the impression from the comments she cites that 'intelligence' has been something foisted on the operational police officer in the absence of evidence to illustrate its bounty. Every homicide investigator has pressed their crime scene manager for the merest strand of DNA ever since its discovery—if 'intelligence' is a comparable boon why routinely are the wrong demands made of its producers? The focus of research has been very much on the qualities of the recipients rather than the quality of the intelligence as such—or for that matter the quality of the data available for analysis. Sissens sees James Sheptycki's critique of organizational maladjustments as pretty much substantiated by her own research. But Sheptycki's criticisms in the end could be levelled at any complex organization and do not explain why there is so little evidence of the organic growth of effective intelligence use. One is tempted to ask the question as to whether the analysts have yet to come up with the goods even if they have to swim against the tide to do so—after all, Joe Rochefort met with every objection but in the end his case was sufficiently compelling for Admiral Nimitz to bet the fortunes of the US Navy on his analysis. More to the point perhaps, the NIM, making intelligence synonymous with managerial deployment decisions in the hierarchy of command, is itself the liability. The language of the 'Information State' is about networks not platforms.

The intelligence analyst is looking for renditions of a problem that will be sufficiently revealing to provide opportunity for a telling response. The theory is that new insight will make the case for a redeployment of effort. Instead of merely being busy damping down the *symptoms*, forewarned we strike at the *causes*—both tactically, by neutralizing the immediate threat, and strategically, by changing the context. For this approach to work there are some preconditions: the host organization has to sustain a learning culture; analysts have to be part of a network not filters in a hierarchy; and intelligence has to be integrated with operations, not presented as an alternative. Sissens's research tells us the mission of the NIM is not being achieved, but do we judge the use of intelligence by its form or by its results? Organizational problems are capable of being managed. The larger question is why they are not addressed.

'Intelligence' is about thinking: making sense of the data to produce a synthetic model of the problem and using analysis to extract examples that can be acted upon. It is a collaborative effort because it relies on feedback and suitable collection. It is not simply a choice amongst competing police strategies; strategy is not possible without intelligence, and tactics without results analysis never develop beyond the mundane. To this end intelligence is an intellectual endeavour and relies on educated minds not training. Most of the writers sense policing has adopted the rhetoric of the 'enlightenment', today wrapped up in a valueless vocabulary of 'management speak', but not its essence. Problem solutions come from imagination, rationality, and empiricism—all three—entailing a constant struggle with preconception and cliché (the resort of the parvenu). Analysts may be speculators but they are also empiricists; they use intuition but they rely on evidence; perhaps they have a tough time because, as Jacqueline Sissens suggests, they are on the fault line of a culture clash—at once mildly threatening to the lore of the craftsman on the ground floor and the cliché of the 'change management' elite up in the command suite.

Lest all seem doom and gloom, we can take some comfort from the review of Ridley who sees steady if not abundant progress in the field of organized crime and terrorism. In his description of the 'Ghent methodology' he takes us much nearer to the heart of intelligence as 'description'—comprehensive understanding of how the *target problem* works as a system; eliciting the contingencies of context, not simply identifying the players and the places. And whilst he outlines the inevitable difficulties of data flow and inter-agency cooperation, they seem surmountable exactly because the delivery organizations know they are dependant on intelligence and have more realistic expectations of it.

Lack of success perhaps makes us a little obsessive about the irritations within a complex mission and alternatively nothing kindles enthusiasm and interest more than resounding achievement. Interpretation from information as a precursor to activity is the essence of intelligence: it is the difference between chance encounter and a plan. Great achievements are rarely the outcome of unplanned encounters and thereby the case for the analyst should be secure. Most of the irritations researchers have uncovered, once acknowledged and understood, are resolvable if the law enforcement world can grasp the essence of the thing and perhaps detach itself a little from the prevailing political obsession with measure and form.

REFERENCES

BETTS, R, *Analysis War and Decisions—Why Intelligence Failures Are Inevitable* (Princeton: Princeton University Press, 1978).
HUGHES-WILSON, J, *Military Intelligence Blunders* (London: Robinson, 1999).

SCIENCE OR SOPHISTRY: ISSUES IN MANAGING ANALYSTS AND THEIR PRODUCTS

Professor Allyson MacVean and Dr Clive Harfield

INTRODUCTION

The theme underpinning this edited volume is that of consilience, the imaginative and innovative recourse to and utilization of ideas and learning from different disciplines to achieve new insights. It is born out of effectively contemporaneous epidemiology investigation (Johnson, 2006), and philosophical consideration (Whewell, 1847). This chapter, founded upon the concept that consilient thinking is a key attribute in effective analysis, reflects upon aspects of analysis as currently practised within the overall intelligence profession in British policing. It draws upon the personal experience of one of the authors (CH) as police intelligence manager and on the wider considerations brought to bear by an academic specialist on intelligence issues (AM). It sits within a context defined by Cope (2004) and Dunninghan and Norris (1999) and considers first how analysts are perceived and utilized, and then issues concerning the use of analytical product. Not unintentionally, more questions are posed than answered.

WHAT SHOULD BE DONE WITH ANALYSTS?

It is well established that the National Intelligence Model (NIM) is a business process intended to achieve efficient and effective policing through informed targeting of resources (for a general discussion of the NIM and relevant literature see Harfield and Harfield (2008), particularly Chapter 5). On taking up the post of Basic Command Unit (BCU) intelligence, one of the present authors (CH) was advised by senior colleagues at police headquarters that extra funding had been made available to recruit two additional analysts for the BCU intelligence department. This largesse coincided with implementation of the National Intelligence Model in order to meet the target date of 1 April 2004. The appointment of two additional staff brought the analytical team up to four persons. Within a couple of months, however, one of the analysts was transferred elsewhere within the organization thus transforming the unit into a team of three with one vacancy.

The BCU commander had been equally delighted to receive additional funding for extra analysts but now he was confronted with conflicting priorities. Salaries were devolved to BCUs and by keeping the fourth analyst post vacant, the extra salary money could be off-set against the efficiency savings and cash recovery targets imposed on BCU commanders by HQ financial managers. The fourth analyst was never replaced. From this perspective, the most valuable contribution of the analysts' team to the BCU's overall performance came from the individual who was never employed! Not that the BCU commander is to blame for what some might regard as an absurd situation. The commander's role involves reconciling as best possible conflicting priorities and making difficult decisions. But how is it that the police service has got itself into a position whereby, in order to meet efficiency targets, a BCU commander is forced to under-resource a system of working that is intended to help make the police service more effective and efficient?

This vignette provides the backdrop for the following reflections on the purpose and profession of analysts based on the experience of one who used to have to manage, referee might be a more appropriate term, senior officers' expectations against analysts' aspiration.

The answer to the question, 'what should be done with analysts?', in part is defined by expectations characterized in organizational culture (for an international perspective on the relationship between analysts and decision-makers see Marrin, 2007). Failure to understand or appreciate the role of analysts will inhibit their contribution, no matter how much effort the analysts individually or collectively expend. Cope (2004) identified significant negative perceptions within the context of police service organizational culture including:

- Police officer analysts seem to enjoy more credibility amongst police colleagues than civilian analytical staff.
- Police officers feel uncomfortable accepting recommendations from analysts who are not police officers.
- Non-police analysts are excluded from and/or intimidated by the police organizational culture and consequently their expertise is unrecognized or ignored.
- Senior investigators and managers often side-line the role of analysis.
- Analysis is often used retrospectively to justify decisions already taken, rather than to inform strategic and operational decision-making.
- There is often confusion between analysis supporting management decision-making and analysis supporting operational decision-making to the extent that analysts employed to interpret information in order to provide intelligence are often diverted into supporting performance management.

None of the attitudes disclosed through research evidences positive affirmation of the value of analysts or their role. Sissens has revisited these issues (Chapter 9 below) and has arrived at conclusions that tend to corroborate rather than challenge Cope's findings.

Three distinct types (or generic expectations) of analytical work in the UK police service have emerged: business analysis, crime pattern analysis, and intelligence analysis (the latter vulnerable to being equated with servicing the NIM process). Contributing to the confusion surrounding the purpose of analysis, these different activity areas can constrain creativity or disguise the fact that analysis in support of intelligence-led policing is not actually happening. In the absence of developmental intelligence work and with the prevailing political emphasis on performance management, it is all too easy for analytical effort to focus on performance and patterns rather than intelligence development and interpretation.

What guidance does the NIM offer? Superficially it emphasizes the importance of analysis within the overall profession of intelligence work but didactically it provides a menu of products that analysts are expected to produce within a prescribed chronological framework. The concern is raised that this focus on scheduled analytical products defines and dictates the way analysts work and think to the detriment of lateral creativity.

NIM can be used as a reactive performance management tool rather than a proactive intervention tool, not least because the information feeding it is reactive and historic due to the lack of a meaningful intelligence development (analytical) capacity. This is a resource issue. The NIM product timetable and the number of analysts servicing it meant that there was little or no time for the analysts CH worked with to create new lines of enquiry through deep, thorough, and creative analysis. The weight of demands placed upon them, including servicing the tasking and coordinating schedule, significantly inhibited capability and capacity to undertake the sort of analysis that could truly and innovatively inform tasking and coordinating.

SKILLS RECOGNITION AND RETENTION

Given that intelligence analysts are vulnerable to efficiency savings, diversion into supporting performance management, and process demands rather than being driven by purpose, it is perhaps not surprising that retention of analytical skills within the police service is proving problematic. Individuals who embarked upon their analytical careers in the police service only to discover they are not being asked to do the sort of work they thought they were going to do, have not infrequently gone onto to analytical opportunities elsewhere that were often, for whatever reason, more attractive than the opportunities within the police service. How might such losses be stemmed?

One argument, not unpersuasive, is that there should be a career structure for analysts within the service, providing progressive stages of career and salary enhancement. But there is a counter-argument, equally cogent. Why, if retention of analytical skills within the organization is the issue, would analysts be given the opportunity to escape within the organization as well as outside it? That argument asserts that there should be no career structure for analysts. Either individuals want to be analysts or they want to be managers. In the latter case there are plenty of other career opportunities. Retention of analytical skills, following this train of thought, can be achieved by providing analysts with the flexibility to be laterally creative thinkers and by paying the sort of salary that would otherwise only be available through managerial promotion. It would also go some way towards enhancing the professional status of analysts (for international perspectives on this see Marrin and Clemente, 2006). But that is a significant challenge to an organizational culture in which professional perception, peer respect, status, and salary are all inextricably linked to a quasi-military rank and hierarchy.

Making the automatic equation between qualification and professional status, there have been moves to encourage analysts to achieve workplace-based National Vocational Qualifications (NVQs). But what message about organizational values does it send to analytical staff when those with degrees, as well as those without, are required to seek a vocational qualification at NVQ level 4? Is the organization saying that they have wasted their effort in putting themselves through tertiary education? Are the skills they have previously acquired and brought with them, presumably in response to recruitment criteria, being undervalued?

The value of analysts can be recognized by giving them the tools and time to the job; by recognizing the skills they bring to the role from outside; and by rewarding with a view to retaining the most skilled analysts in the front line of criminal investigation and intelligence development where their skills are of most value to the organization.

RESILIENCE AND RIGIDITY

Not unconnected with the issue of retention is that of resilience. If analysts are to be classified within a tripartite system of specialisms what, if any, resilience can be built into such a system? Preparation for this chapter identified a police service business analyst who wished to investigate performance data alongside crime pattern analysis in order to shed some further light on some performance issues. Perceiving a need for an introduction to crime pattern analysis methodology, the analyst requested appropriate training and was advised that the basic intelligence analyst training had to be completed first before the individual could be proposed for a crime pattern analyst training course. The analyst started thinking outside the box, and the system responded with an obstacle.

This raises a number of issues about the rigidity of the infrastructure within which police analysts are asked to operate. Why are there separate training courses for different types of analysis? What does that achieve? Why do the courses have to be attended in sequence? Are apparent but false specialisms being created within familiar and comfortable concepts, namely a hierarchy of skill and ability? Is the ability to engage in spontaneous creativity and lateral thinking, argued to be the qualities of a skilled analyst, really something that can be taught and trained?

An alternative perspective presents itself. Why have such specialist training at all? If the potential exists to recruit intellectually adept individuals from a variety of backgrounds with demonstrable skills or academic ability, why is the police service recruiting in order to train? Is the service in the business of recruiting skills and ability or recruiting novice individuals it can then train and educate within the paradigms of conventional wisdom? And if it is the latter, what is the business case for the police service as an education provider if there is the alternative model of recruiting the skills? One fact appears to be fully corroborated by the sheer weight of examples: the police service is training individuals who, having gained analytical work experience, then depart for more attractive opportunities in the private sector where the organization values their skills differently and rewards them differently. From that perspective the service has ended up in a situation in which it appears to be addressing and servicing the analytical needs of other organizations and not its own.

Perhaps there is a yet wider question. If the service is recruiting the right people for the right reasons, and the recruitment process identifies that individuals have previously acquired and demonstrated the requisite skills and abilities prior to appointment, then there should be no need to train analysts. Colleagues have suggested in informal debate that there is no training course that can do justice to the role of an analyst within law enforcement. Has the training need been misunderstood here? Should the service not be recruiting individuals with demonstrable analytical skills and then training not them but their managers on how to achieve the best with such individuals?

Regularly rotating staff between different types of analytical work is a means of promoting the flexible environment within which creative thinking may flourish. It can also be a means of breaking down the presumption of specialisms identified by analyst colleagues during the preparation of this chapter; specialisms that impede resilience, flexibility and creativity. Much depends upon how the police service and analysts within the service choose to define the analyst profession. Too much structure may not be a good thing. Is the police service imposing upon its analysts roles, functions, and status consistent with traditional police hierarchies and working models when in fact the added value of the analytical profession to policing is the very fact that it provides a means of transcending traditional thinking to offer new insights? Are analysts being provided with the room and flexibility within which to explore all available sources and data or are constraints imposed upon them that have more to do with processing data than with what could be argued to be the ultimate purpose of analysis within the police service: locking up criminals and enhancing community safety.

WHAT SHOULD BE DONE WITH ANALYTICAL PRODUCTS?

The challenge must be to provide a police environment that will foster in analysts the experience and competence to bring not only logic and critical thinking to their analytical considerations, but also the ability to link these skills with lateral thinking, creativity, and innovation. However, applying these two philosophies collectively in an analytical context can have implications for both the analysts and the analytical products.

Logical and critical thinking is underpinned by scientific rationale; it is a process derived from thinking about events and incidents sequentially, generally in terms of causes and consequences. Thus, logical thinking implies following a train of thought based upon the interpretation of previous or existing circumstances to predict what will happen if the same circumstances continue to prevail. Analytical products developed from logical application allows the tracking of past events to forecast the immediate future.

Creative and innovative thinking involves creating something new and valuable. It goes beyond thinking about events sequentially; it requires a range of cognitive skills including flexibility, originality, fluency, elaboration, imagery, and abstract and allegorical thinking. Innovative thinking is to stimulate inquisitiveness and foster divergence. In addition to requiring knowledge, comprehension, application, synthesis, and evaluation, it also includes skills such as comparison, use of analogies, inductive reasoning, judgement, instinctive and intuitive perception—skills, regarded as craft-like, or philosophical rather than scientific.

The distinction between the characteristics of scientific and philosophical models in the context of the analytical process and analytical products can be considered further. Take, for example, mathematics as a scientific discipline: arithmetical codes, such as differentiation and binary formulae, are integral to both traditional and modern mathematics and are fundamental to the analytical process. The routine application of such mathematical codes in the analysing procedure validates and substantiates the analytical products, ensuring robust and reliable products; they are codes and formulae which have been tried and tested over time, and are not usually contested when used in analytical applications. However, such codes and formulae are generally not accessible or available for more innovative philosophical thinking. Such thinking is often open to interpretation, opinion, judgement, experience, and wisdom; it goes beyond the constraints of traditional analytical practice. If conventional codes and formulae are not readily accessible for innovative analytical interpretation, what analytical methodologies exist that enable philosophical reasoning to be routinely applied to the data-analysis process? See Juett et al (Chapter 12 below) and Bhatti (Chapter 13 below) for excellent examples of some lateral thinking, creativity, and innovation in the analytical process.

The role of the analyst is to seek for truth and value in intelligence sources by the process of gathering, analysing, and making use of information in order to understand a particular environment and therefore create options for intervention. However, the analytical product is only one element in the decision-making process for intervention and the enlightening facets that analytical products may provide are not always absolute and unflawed. Despite routine checks and tests to establish the reliability and robustness, why is it that some products of analysis are more credible, while others more dubious? Why is it that some analytical products stand up under scrutiny and others do not?

LEARNING LESSONS

In seeking to provide an explanation, it is useful to consider what lessons can be transferred from the specialized intelligence agencies to the use of intelligence by policing agencies. In particular, are there lessons from the Hutton (2004) and Butler (2004) reports and the intelligence about Weapons of Mass Destruction, which are pertinent to the use of intelligence in the police environment?

Both Hutton and Butler provide a glimpse into the complex interrelationship of truth, value, trust, and power in intelligence. The reports also highlight that intelligence, once covert, is now more widely used by government in public debates and such disclosure into the public domain brings with it responsibilities. While police intelligence, by its very nature as evidence, is often presented in the public domain through the criminal justice process, nonetheless the reports convey aspects about the use and political power of intelligence, with the attendant risks which that might involve.

Hutton and Butler were not so concerned with who behaved well and who behaved badly, so much as who by their behaviour made a difference to the way the intelligence was represented, portrayed, justified, and authenticated. The reports also emphasized the potential consequences of presenting intelligence as truth and fact while failing to qualify margins of unreliability. Intelligence, which has been misrepresented by according it more credence than it deserves, crosses the fine line of assessment to advocacy. The shift from intelligence as assessment to intelligence as advocacy, as exposed in both the Hutton and Butler reports, changes both the substance and integrity of the intelligence product.

The Butler report severely criticized the way in which the intelligence on Iraq was analysed, assessed, and then incorporated into the Joint Intelligence Committee (JIC) assessment documents for government ministers and other influential policy advisors. The Hutton report revealed the pressure placed upon the JIC by Downing Street to produce a document for public presentation to justify the government's decision to go to war. The government's decision to use the JIC to produce a public document, although not unprecedented, was extraordinary. The shift from assessment to advocacy represented a shift from intelligence products as a tool (to assist the understanding and context of an incident or situation in order to develop a range of solutions) to intelligence as a form of political power in its own right.

Those who challenged the claims of Weapons of Mass Destruction and their deployment within 45 minutes asserted that the prime minister was either mad, bad, or had been had: mad if he had total and unjustifiable belief in the existence of Weapons of Mass Destruction of which there was no reliable intelligence; bad if he had wilfully orchestrated a public dossier for the purposes of taking the country to war and knowingly exploited unreliable intelligence; or had if he had been deceived by the intelligence agencies that the intelligence was accurate and robust (for a US perspective on the same issues see Herbert, 2006).

CONSIDERATIONS ARISING FROM THE BUTLER AND HUTTON REPORTS

Three considerations emerge from the Hutton and Butler reports that are applicable to this chapter. First, it was not the decision to take the country to war that was in question; it was the way the intelligence was presented—in a dossier endorsed by the JIC in order to make it appear more reliable than it really was. Second, the initial distribution of the intelligence for review and comment prior to its publication was limited, so it bypassed the agencies with the greatest analytical expertise and skills. Third, the presentation of the intelligence was in a format which was unsuitable for its audience. The public are not educated customers of intelligence; they are unfamiliar with the rhetoric and the caution that is associated with intelligence products. Crucially, the dossier failed to detail the normal caveats when intelligence is utilized for decision-making or informing policy.

These three issues are a potential risk for all managers dependent upon intelligence. The JIC, an intelligence agency staffed by skilled analysts and experienced experts, in the mist of what could be described in policing terms as a 'critical incident', failed to qualify the reservations about the quality of the information underlying the judgements that it passed on to government. As both the Hutton and Butler report emphasized, neither the intelligence services nor the government did enough to safeguard against the possibility that the information may not have been reliable. Nor did they highlight that the dossier emphasized the potential inaccurate and subjective character of intelligence. However, it is important to remember that two different and competing agendas were at play. The JIC and secret intelligence services failed to caveat reliability whereas the government presented as fact what it could not be certain was true. Thus, the intelligence failure was collective and cumulative.

Observing the failure of the JIC, what measures can be put in place to guard against police intelligence being perceived as absolute and reliable? How can unreliability be qualified if, as Hutton and Butler have pointed out, the assessment of intelligence is a complex and often tortuous exercise in which certainty is elusive, blind alleys commonplace, and even the most apparent reliable sources can turn out to be nothing of the kind?

HUNTLEY AND BRYANT: LESSONS IN ASSESSING PUBLIC PROTECTION NEEDS

The Bichard Inquiry into the murder of Holly Wells and Jessica Chapman illustrated unreliability inherent in the incompleteness of intelligence and the dangers of accepting information at face value without questioning the merit or context of the data. One of the key failings identified by Bichard was the inability of the police and social services to recognize Ian Huntley's pattern of behaviour soon enough as a result of ineffective information sharing. More specifically, Humberside police acknowledged that there were systematic and corporate failures in the way in which they managed their intelligence systems. The process of creating and maintaining records on their local intelligence system was fundamentally flawed and officers, at all levels, were alarmingly ignorant about the processes of the system. This ignorance was, in part, responsible for the ineffective management of intelligence, allowing vital information to be lost.

A report on the murder of Naomi Bryant by Anthony Rice voiced similar concerns about partial information, taking intelligence on face value, and the lack of recording the decision-making process. Her Majesty's Inspectorate of Probation, who undertook the inquiry noted with concern that vital intelligence relating to the previous convictions of Rice was missing during his assessments for parole and the Multi-Agency Public Protection Arrangements (MAPPA), despite the information being readily available on police data systems.

The report also asked why insufficient questions were asked and inadequate evidence sought about Rice's previous offending by the police and other agencies involved in managing him. While the desirable outcome of MAPPA is effective risk management, it also provides a forum to demonstrate critical and searching assessment of intelligence and defensible decision-making based upon that assessment.

Three further key issues arose in relation to intelligence processes from the inquiry into the death of Naomi Bryant. First, who ultimately is responsible and has ownership of the assessed intelligence? Second, mistakes, misjudgements, and miscommunication, both intra- and between agencies, can very quickly lead to cumulative failure both at the assessment stage and in the analytical product of intelligence. Third, the inquiry identified the need for independent assessments of the intelligence process.

Both the Bichard and Naomi Bryant inquiries, along with the Butler and Hutton reports, illustrate the dilemmas for intelligence particularly relating to unreliable data, missing information, and the unquestionable acceptance of intelligence and intelligence products. However, the issues from the inquiries and reports provide a test framework to assist in managing unreliability in intelligence.

TEST FRAMEWORK FOR MANAGING UNRELIABILITY

A test framework for managing unreliability is suggested here, comprising seven elements.

Accountability v Ownership

While analysts analyse the data, subject it to critical and creative thinking models, who actually has ownership of the products and who legitimately can represent intelligence on behalf of the organization? What are the cautions in disseminating intelligence more widely, particularly to uneducated customers? Establishing comprehensible instructions about the uses and limitations of intelligence and products should be ascertained as a matter of good practice.

Assessment v Sophistry

While intelligence assessment is utilized for advocacy in many instances, what are the consequences when it becomes manipulated for political sophistry? Who will be the moral advocates? What techniques/procedures are required to ensure that sophistry is minimized? Would it be useful to deploy independent advisory members, and who would undertake this role?

Reality v Perception

When the processes and systems designed to ensure robustness and validity of intelligence become blurred, so does the distinction between reality and perception. Operators and analysts who do not fully understand the intelligence systems that they operate are liable to misinterpretation and misjudgement.

Content v Presentation

How can content and fact be presented in order that they will be received and understood by the audience for which they are intended? Intelligence is often required for a variety of different audiences with distinct messages for each. What mechanisms are in place to ensure appropriate information is included and highlight what is missing? What instruments are available to demonstrate how the intelligence was utilized to inform the decision making process?

Badges of Credibility v Truth

Badges of credibility, while important in some cases have the capacity to weaken the case for truth. The badge of the JIC imprinted onto the September dossier misled the public into believing that the intelligence contained in the document must have been reliable and true. What are the specific implications for the organizations of embellishing a badge that represents credibility? How can truth be reliably presented, even when it is difficult or unpalatable and whose duty is it to deliver the truth?

Facts v Value

In the case of the Weapons of Mass Destruction, the Butler and Hutton reports illustrated that fact and value had become inextricably linked. Intelligence analysts often have a clear idea about what their political masters want to hear and this, in turn, may produce a desire to please. Different facts will have different values to different audiences. Consequently, there is an inherent danger that differing values will digress from the actuality of the fact, and myths and false assumptions may begin to emerge. There is also caution required about communication that aims at accuracy, communication that is casual about accuracy, and communication that deliberately aims to mislead.

Power v Caveats

Analysts are the experts in analysing information and intelligence and have a duty to speak truth unto power, however, difficult or inconvenient this may be. The use of caveats, documenting limitations and cautions about the use and application of intelligence products, may be a method of overcoming this.

As the test framework model above illustrates, there is a connection between proper processes and management accountability and political responsibility. The Butler report highlighted that informality and the circumscribed character of government procedure reduced the scope for informed collective rational judgement. Butler also asserted that under the prime minister's regime, traditional formal meetings and minute-taking procedures had started to become more informal and routine processes had begun to disintegrate. Different leaders have different ways of conducting business, and while it is possible to reconcile due process with informal style, there is a risk that informality can slide into something more fluid and unstructured, creating an environment where advice or dissent may not be offered nor heard. Leaders are only as powerful as their colleagues permit them to be. Good orderly inclusive procedures that also record the decision-making process instil rationality into the process. Procedures for ensuring truth and accuracy are typically embedded in professional and institutional structures (O'Neill, 2004:94). The routines of fact-checking and verifying sources, of checking records and calculations, of submitting work to peers, and of selecting and testing caveats are all part of good practice and essential in achieving a level of precision and truth when making claims that draw upon intelligence.

As can be evidenced by the reports referred to above, post-evaluation is very sterile in recreating moods and context, particularly where critical decisions are not contemporaneously recorded. Post-inquiries cannot capture the uncertainty or ambiguity surrounding the real-time decision-making which is informed by intelligence products during times of crisis. Also apparent from the reports was not just the failure of the agencies to check and probe for information and intelligence but their apparent inability to explain this state of affairs. The Butler, Hutton, and Bichard reports together with the inquiry into the murder of Naomi Bryant have provided an insight into some useful lessons for those who analyse and those who manage police intelligence. As Peter Hennessy as commented, intelligence just provides catseyes in the dark on a very difficult road through dangerous countryside. Intelligence is rarely a floodlight (Hennessy, 2004: 65). Braudel, in his book *History of Civilisations*, observed historians, like their fellow hunter-gatherers in the intelligence world, have to draw out from imperfect and incomplete strands of 'the thin wisp of tomorrow which can be guessed at and very nearly grasped' (1993: xxxviii).

CONCLUSION

This chapter has raised questions about attitudes towards analysts and analysis in the police service and has gone on to consider what good analysis looks like. It raises some debates about different approaches and methodologies for managing unreliability and uncertainty, successful management of which will directly influence perceptions of analysts. Good analysis goes beyond the application of mathematical formulae: it also requires an inquisitive and enquiring mind that blends scientific and creative methodologies, building bridges between different disciplines.

Analytical products have considerable power attached to them. They inform strategy and direct resources. They have the ability to close down other forms of enquiry. With power comes some appreciation of the influence, ownership, and trust of the products. Intellectual paradigms can make it more difficult to establish the truth even if the analysts are attentive and methodological in their research. Learning to listen to reason takes time particularly among those who do not want to hear. Dissenting voices often remain unheard or are lost in the process. Learning to see can be equally challenging when people are blinded by politics, personal ambition, or their own ideas. Independent reviews provide impartiality and another perspective on the analysis process.

How can expectation and aspiration be managed in the twenty-first century, where both media and politicians demand immediate answers and solutions? There needs to be a formalized mechanism for managing unreliability, in order that collective and accumulating intelligence failures, such as those identified in the Laming, Hutton, and

Butler reports and the HMIP report into the death of Naomi Bryant are to be avoided in the future. Inherent imprecision in intelligence work means that the profession may never qualify as a science, but through acknowledging the value of analysts and their contribution, and through sophisticated utilization of their product, the dangers of sophistry can at least be avoided.

REFERENCES

BRAUDEL, F, *A History of Civilisations* (London: Penguin, 1993).

COPE, N, 'Intelligence-led policing or policing-led intelligence?' *British Journal of Criminology* 44/2 (2004) 188–203.

DUNNINGHAN, C and NORRIS, C, 'The detective, the snout and the Audit Commission: The real costs in using informers' *The Howard Journal* 38/1 (1999) 67–86.

HARFIELD, C and HARFIELD, K, *Intelligence: Investigation, Community, and Partnership* (Oxford: Oxford University Press, 2008).

HENNESSY, P, 'The lightening flash on the road to Baghdad' in Runciman, W, ed, *Hutton and Butler: Lifting the Lid on the Workings of Power* (Oxford: Oxford University Press, 2004).

HERBERT, M, 'The intelligence analyst as epistemologist' *International Journal of Intelligence and CounterIntelligence* 19/4 (2006) 666–684.

JOHNSON, S, *The Ghost Map: A Street, an Epidemic and the Two Men who Battled to Save Victorian London* (London: Allen Lane, 2006).

MARRIN, S, 'At arm's length or at the elbow? Explaining the distance between analysts and decision-makers' *International Journal of Intelligence and CounterIntelligence* 20/3 (2007) 401–414.

—— and CLEMENTE, J, 'Modelling an intelligence analysis profession on medicine' *International Journal of Intelligence and CounterIntelligence* 19/4 (2006) 642–665.

O'NEILL, O, 'Accuracy, independence and trust' in Runciman, W, ed, *Hutton and Butler: Lifting the Lid on the Workings of Power* (Oxford: Oxford University Press, 2004).

WHEWELL, W, *The Philosophy of Inductive Sciences Founded upon the History* (New York: Johnson Reprint Corporation, 1847).

8

CULTURAL PARADIGMS AND CHANGE: A MODEL OF ANALYSIS

R Mark Evans OBE

Policing with the Community and its strategic component, Intelligence-led Policing (ILP), cannot function without a timely stream of high quality crime reporting information and a skilled analytical capability. The Crime Analysis Centre, created early in the change process, quickly developed into a centre for excellence, with a reputation recognised nationally and internationally. The central unit and district analysts are a critical component contributing to progress (Oversight Commissioner, 2007)

Policing in Northern Ireland has gone through radical change in the last 10 years. The Police Service of Northern Ireland (Crime) Analysis Centre deploys some 95 staff across more than 30 sites including Territorial, Headquarters and Specialist Units.[1] This case study explores the Analysis Centre as a model suitable for supporting an intelligence-led, community-focused style of policing. It will explain the importance of building critical mass, focusing on support for decision-makers, and emphasizing analyst learning and development as critical success factors in addressing cultural paradigms and supporting change to shape the future.

A FRAMEWORK FOR CHANGE

In September 1999, after a lengthy period of review and consultation, and under the title '*A New Beginning*', the Independent Commission on Policing for Northern Ireland published its findings (Independent Commission on Policing for Northern Ireland, 1999). Widely referred to as 'The Patten Report', it made 175 recommendations

---

[1] As at March 2007 The Police Service of Northern Ireland comprised 7,500 full-time regular sworn officers, 1,677 reserve officers and c3,250 non-sworn police staff. The ratio of police analysts to full-time officers is 1:90 (the Analysis Centre establishment includes a number of non-analyst positions).

and dealt with every significant area of policing—including Human Rights; Oversight and Accountability; Policing with the Community; the Structure and Composition of the Police Service; and Recruitment and Culture, Ethos and Symbols.

The Commission had much to say about the state of policing in Northern Ireland. As would be expected in any review of a major public service organization, the picture was mixed. While many saw no need for reform, other groups felt an 'entirely new' police service was required. In publishing its findings, the Commission drew heavily on the experience of key local, national and international opinion-formers and, in many respects, made proposals that could be seen as reflecting best practices from around the world. Arguably, the Commission set out a vision for policing services that might be seen as a model to which not only the police in Northern Ireland, but others internationally, might aspire.

The report outlined challenging targets for reform, represented a clear break with the past, and set out a very significant 'blueprint' for change. The government subsequently published an implementation plan which included the creation of a team of international observers to monitor progress and report regularly.[2]

Building on a process that had been underway since the mid-1990s, the Commission emphasized the importance of a policing style that promoted, valued, and understood the need for community engagement. It made seven specific recommendations that dealt with policing with the community including: 'The Northern Ireland Police should, both at a service-wide level and at patrol-team level, conduct crime pattern . . . analysis to provide an information-led, problem-solving approach to policing . . .'. Additionally, the Commission (under the heading of 'management and personnel') set out the requirement that: 'District Commanders should be required regularly to account to their senior officers for the patterns of crime and police activity in their district and to explain how they propose to address their districts' problems'.

By referring to 'information and problem-solving' and by linking this to patterns of crime, performance, and accountability within a framework of much wider (organizational) reform, the Commission created space for the 'new' discipline of crime and intelligence analysis to take root. But the notion that the Patten report was the *sole* driver for a better analytical capability for the policing service in Northern Ireland needs to be avoided. As early as 1995 the RUC had conducted its own fundamental review and many of Patten's recommendations reflected the findings of this report. In April 1999 an internal (RUC) review of the 'Crime Intelligence Model' had stated: 'The [review] team strongly supports the provision of civilian crime analysts in each of the Regional Intelligence Units and the Force Intelligence Bureau'. Following the Patten report there was an expectation that the analytical service would be benchmarked

---

[2] The international team of observers was established as the Office of the Oversight Commissioner under a Chief of Staff. It included experienced representatives from policing in the USA and Canada and called on expert consultancy resources and, in the early stages, on the support of the International Association of Chiefs of Police.

against the best in the world, would be central to a more modern policing approach and that it would support the cultural transition needed to move to a less reactive policing style—particularly in tackling crime and other quality of life issues. While Northern Ireland had (and in many respects may still have) a reputation for sectarian violence and terrorism, the core business of local policing reflects the sort of day-to-day priorities that might be found anywhere in the world.

While the Patten report created an urgency around police organizational reform that (in UK terms at least) may be unique, it afforded little guidance about how to create and implement an effective analytical service to support the new style of policing that was demanded. Against this backdrop the PSNI Analysis Centre Model was founded on four key strategic principles:

- support for the *cultural and organizational* changes needed to embed the use and application of an effective police analysis service (as a matter of deliberate choice it was decided to avoid use of traditional labels such as 'crime analysts' or 'performance analysts' to reflect the fact that staff in PSNI would be multi-skilled and work across functions);
- promoting *intelligence-led policing* (based on the principles of the UK National Intelligence Model) focused on tackling crime and priority policing problems;
- aggressively pursuing *continuous professional development* (and later reflected in the concept of *'creative intelligent analysis'*[3]);
- adopting a clear focus on *support for decision-makers* and *making an operational impact.*

These guiding principles have been central to the Centre's development. While the context may be unique to Northern Ireland the framework has application across global policing (and indeed the wider law enforcement community).

KEY STRATEGIC PRIORITY 1: CULTURAL AND ORGANIZATIONAL CHANGE

The Commission noted that the 'culture and ethos of an organization include both the way in which it sees itself and manages itself internally and the way in which it sees and interacts with its clients and others outside the organization' (Independent Commission on Policing for Northern Ireland 1999). In recommending that policing with the community should be the core function of the police service it recognized that this had ' . . . implications for the structure of the police, for management,

---

[3] The term 'Creative Intelligent Analysis' was devised during a series of meetings/workshops with John Grieve and was introduced to PSNI analysts at the 1st annual PSNI analyst conference in 2004. It has been further developed since and is manifest in the PSNI analyst competence framework under the headings of 'Encouraging innovation', 'Developing knowledge and practice', and 'Contributing to the development of the knowledge and practice of others'.

for culture and for training' (Independent Commission on Policing for Northern
Ireland 1999).

The 'cultural web' provides a useful way to reflect the reality of policing as described
by the Commission in the late 1990s[4] (see Figure 8.1). It points to an organization
strong on professionalism/service, responsive to demand but with limited experience
of policing in a transparent, fully accountable environment (power, controls); it was

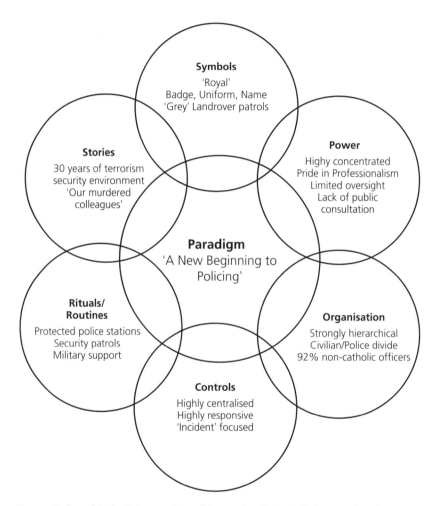

Fig 8.1 Cultural Web-Crime and Intelligence Analysis: Policing Services in
Northern Ireland 1999

[4] The cultural web is adapted by the author from Johnson and Scholes (1997). For the purposes of this
report Organizational Culture has been defined as 'the deeper level of basic assumptions and beliefs that are
shared by members of an organization, that operate unconsciously and define in a basic taken-for-granted
fashion an organization's view of itself and its environment'. Combined with the organizational paradigm
('A New Beginning to Policing') it comprises the cultural web (as seen from a crime and intelligence analysis
perspective) for the policing services in Northern Ireland in 1999.

still structured in the main to reflect the demands of fighting a 30-year terrorist campaign (symbols, stories, rituals) and (crucially in this context) it was strongly hierarchical with only limited involvement of non-sworn staff in contributing to decisions that really mattered (organizational).

Establishing the notion that crime and intelligence analysis had 'something useful' to offer in such circumstances was challenging and required a strategic and planned approach. 'Change', as noted by Senior (1997), 'is about nothing if it is not about persistence.'

KEY STRATEGIC PRIORITY 2: INTELLIGENCE-LED POLICING (NIM)

Ratcliffe refers to Intelligence-Led Policing (ILP) as a 'business model and managerial philosophy' and highlights the pivotal role of data analysis and crime intelligence in tackling crimes and wider policing problems' (Ratcliffe, 2008). ILP is about focused activity against 'criminally active' individuals, and initiatives against local (strategic) policing problems (Audit Commission, 1993). Its central aim is to allow (some) officers to escape the shackles of demand-led policing and to identify and tackle issues in a more selective, strategic fashion (Maguire and John, 1995).

ILP is manifest in PSNI through the practices and frameworks described in the UK National Intelligence Model (NIM). The Analysis Centre embraced its principles very early on. NIM provides a common language, processes, and the thread that runs through other aspects of core operational business. From 'concept' NIM has now become the way PSNI does the bulk of its volume, serious and organized crime business and this is locally joined-up with wider national security work. Structured meetings set direction within Districts, Regions, and key Headquarter Units. Part of the success of NIM for PSNI arises from the clear link that has been established with the planning process and to crime performance management. Analysis at all levels (local, regional, national) informs the setting of annual policing priorities. Delivery against plan targets is focused through regular risk-based assessments. At a Northern Ireland level progress is monitored through a monthly 'Top Team' meeting which ensures that key and emerging issues are subject to informed decision-making at the right (senior) organizational level. The link to performance is captured through regular forward-looking reports and conferences focused on crime and other policing problems. These support a robust, but flexible, management-driven review process. NIM provides the cultural and organizational framework that values more forward-looking, evidence-based approaches to decision-making and problem-solving at every level. NIM is a framework that aligns *actual* resources against *real* problems.

ILP in PSNI reached a tipping point five years after implementation when all local command units and key specialist units had regular and reliable access to a professional police analyst service utilizing broadly consistent organization-wide processes. Arguably, seven years after implementation, the full benefits are still to be felt. It is certainly clear that there remains room for further improvement. For example, individual decision-makers can still undermine its value by failing to properly understand and use the products of crime and intelligence analysis; and there is not (yet) compliance with the necessary systems and processes to make ILP 'work' everywhere. But from a standing start, progress has been rapid. Amongst the critical success factors are:

- a clear link between local (volume crime) problems and intelligence collection activity;[5]
- a determination to embed new management processes to *action* the products of crime and intelligence analysis;
- *consistent* leadership from the top—three successive Chief Constables and their Assistant Chief Constables responsible for crime—have all been advocates of the ILP approach;
- critical mass—while the technical aspects of NIM don't need to be fully understood by everyone, a few staff promoting it in isolated areas is a recipe for failure; over the longer term NIM is a way of thinking and working every day, not a concept that can be applied once and then forgotten about;
- PSNI experience indicates that, more than anything, ILP needs long-term commitment in order to become embedded.

The Oversight Commissioner recognized the importance of police analysts in supporting many of these critical success factors in his final report:

District and departmental analysts produce information essential for identification of priorities and the allocation of patrol and investigative services. Analysts deployed to DCUs provide support for commanders in developing their action plans and informing their DPPs [District Policing Partnerships] and other community forums about crime patterns and other issues. The Analysis Centre performed a major role in the introductory phase of the National Intelligence Model, and participated in the initial training of neighbourhood policing teams. More recently there has been an increase in the frequency of crime analyst presentations to public forums, including DPPs (Oversight Commissioner 2007).

KEY STRATEGIC PRIORITY 3: CONTINUOUS PROFESSIONAL DEVELOPMENT (CREATIVE INTELLIGENT ANALYSIS)

To some, 'learning' is synonymous with 'training'. In a fast-moving operational environment it is clear that they are not the same at all.[6] Aristotle said, 'We are what we repeatedly do. Excellence then is not an act but a habit'. The Analysis Centre model strongly values 'experience by doing'. The process of professional development for PSNI analysts begins during the recruitment phase. Applicants go through an exhaustive selection process—involving multiple testing, problem-solving, a group exercise,

---

[5] For example Dedicated Source Handling Units aligned to each District boundary increasingly work against a list of priority offenders. This dynamic list is updated regularly and provides a focus for intelligence collection.

[6] To 'learn' means 'to enhance capacity *through experience* gained by following a track or discipline'. Quoted in Peter Senge (2007).

the delivery of an effective presentation, and a final interview. An information evening is held to ensure new recruits know what is expected of them. For some it is a surprise to learn that they will be working on 'real' problems alongside police officers and that they are expected to contribute their own thoughts and ideas very early on.

The PSNI Analyst Development Programme (ADP) was launched in 2000. The ADP is designed to provide a solid foundation in the core skills required to perform effectively as a police analyst. It comprises two stages: stage 1—an initial seven-week training course and stage 2—a two year development programme which is monitored and managed by the Analysis Centre and delivered in partnership with line managers and host units. Most staff (over 95 per cent) are recruited as 'trainee police analysts' and are required, as part of the programme, to maintain a portfolio of evidence across five key work (competence) areas. They are assessed at regular intervals and (for those who are ready) required to sit a formative interview at the end of this period to assess suitability for promotion to police analyst.

Building on the success of the ADP initiative, in April 2005 the Centre launched its Continuous Professional Development (CPD) Programme—which challenges staff to continue learning throughout their career. I have previously stated that:

In establishing the Analysis Centre we set out to create a centre of excellence. Skills and knowledge improvement, through a structured learning programme, was a guiding beacon. This flexible framework—underpinned by portfolio building and rigorous work based assessment—provides Police Analysts with the opportunity to contribute original thinking in ways that will improve policing for all the people of Northern Ireland (Evans, 2005).

The process of review and reflection is critical to the Analyst Professional Development Programmes (Jeapes, 2007).

Experience indicates it takes at least two years for trainees to become competent in the role. Beyond this, analysts need a further period of time before they are capable of contributing in a significant way to the development of better products, new techniques or more effective ways of doing business. Because policing is constantly evolving, the role demands continuous improvement and learning. It is also clear that the link between professional development and analyst career paths and pay/reward systems is critical. Over the medium/longer term it is increasingly difficult to sustain one without the other. At more senior levels the key requirement for PSNI analysts is to demonstrate competence around the notion of 'creative intelligent analysis'.

CREATIVE INTELLIGENT ANALYSIS

All PSNI analysts at every level are monitored against a corporate competence framework which requires evidence in respect of information management, professional development/managing relationships, liaison, analysis, and presentation/performance. Creative Intelligent Analysis is an additional concept developed to *require* more experienced staff to stretch the boundaries of their work. It fits within the overall framework.

In promoting the notion of creativity the Centre seeks to encourage innovation, risk-taking, and change. It particularly values the ability to 'think differently'. There are three parts of *intelligence* described in Sternberg's Triarchic Theory : *analytical, creative and practical*. Analytical ('book-smart') intelligence refers to the ability to problem-solve; creative ('imaginative') intelligence refers to the ability to deal with new situations by drawing on existing knowledge—it requires going beyond learnt skills; practical ('street smart') intelligence requires the ability to solve real everyday problems—often by applying learnt skills to new or unusual situations. According to Sternberg, success requires a balance of these three types of intelligence. Analyst recruitment in PSNI seeks to uncover individuals with this balance—and then through structured professional development to improve and develop them. In reality, all individuals are stronger or weaker in different areas so shared ideas and mutually

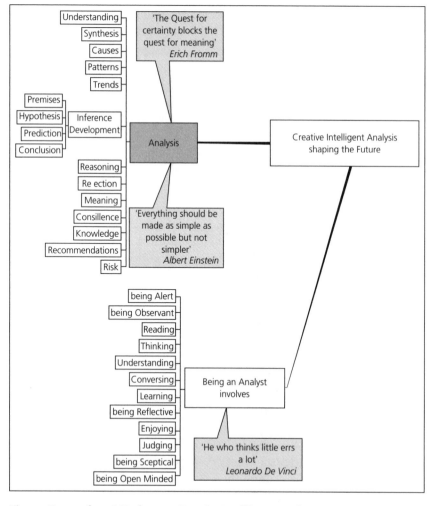

Fig 8.2 Extract from Mindmap—Creative Intelligent Analysis

Source: Analysis Centre: Intrepretation, Evaluation, Direction

supported learning are critically important. Successful analysis requires understanding, inference development, reasoning, reflection, consilience, and (particularly) the ability to make recommendations.

The Centre makes extensive use of mind-maps to convey ideas. Figure 8.2 illustrates the value of visualization to bring focus to decision-makers and to simplify often complex messages.

In the workplace, to be able to demonstrate creative intelligent analysis, analysts are required to provide evidence in three areas:

- Area 1: Innovation. The Centre has been guided by *practical* notions associated with 'innovation': 'The ability to see, think and formulate things in new ways is the basis of creativity. Yet the creative process contains many steps and it may take a winding path'(Nobel Museum, Stockholm). It is expected that staff will try to improve on existing systems, processes, products or other aspects of analytical work. *Small* steps rather than fundamental new ways of working are required. Evidence of innovation is shared in many ways—for example at the PSNI annual analyst award ceremony (which recognizes excellent work) inspirational music provides the backdrop to a photostory slide show: 'The Analysis Centre: A Year in Pictures'.
- Area 2: Developing own knowledge and practice. This requires monitoring advances, implementing good ideas obtained from others and synthesizing new knowledge in ways that are relevant and effective. Staff are expected to apply learning—for example the best analysts will reflect lessons learnt at a monthly training day in developing a 'new' analytical technique in their subsequent products.
- Area 3: Contributing to the knowledge and practice of others. 'If it's easy for people to connect, communicate and share knowledge, they will do it. If it isn't they won't' (Browne, 1997). This is achieved through learning and development days, delivering presentations, attending workshops or conferences, mentoring, undertaking short-term international placements, and (crucially) by publishing products to the Analysis Centre intranet—which enables them to be viewed by all other analysts.

While 'Higher' analysts operate within areas of responsibility, 'Senior' analysts (who will have more experience) are expected to influence the wider work of PSNI—see Figure 8.3.

Competence Area	Higher Police Analyst	Senior Police Analyst
Creative Intelligent Analysis	1. Encourage innovation in **your area** of responsibility	1. Encourage innovation in **your organization**

Fig 8.3 Roles of Higher and Senior Analysts

KEY STRATEGIC PRIORITY 4: SUPPORTING DECISION-MAKERS AND OPERATIONAL IMPACT

In a world without analysts (and indeed intelligence) decision-making still goes on. But, used and understood, the work of analysts can provide significant added value and reassurance. Good analysts provide the information necessary to proactively tackle problems. They help manage risk, provide justification for why things are done (and, often more importantly, why other things are not done) and can help generate audit trails that facilitate accountability and oversight. 'Once you've internalized the concept that you can't prove anything in absolute terms, life becomes all the more about odds, chances and trade-offs. In a world without provable truths, the only way to refine the probabilities that remain is through greater knowledge and understanding' (Rubin, 2003). Ratcliffe explains that:

... the analyst's role is to construct an image of the criminal environment and convey that picture to decision-makers ... The real target audience [is] the police chiefs who decide who does what ... by changing the thinking of a few key individuals, it is possible to positively influence the way that policing is conducted in large areas that cover millions of people (Ratcliffe, 2004).

The focus on decision-makers has been a fundamental principle in the evolution of the Analysis Centre model. It is manifest in many ways:

- Line management is through local (senior) operational commanders—who have (over time) become advocates for the analytical service and are able to 'translate' requirements in ways that facilitate corporate application.
- Analytical work is regulated through a series of robust but flexibly applied service-level agreements. This ensures that analysts are tasked in ways that are appropriate, valid, and focused on actual policing problems.
- While all analysts belong to 'the Centre', they are physically deployed at multiple locations—working directly alongside those operational staff who have the authority to deploy resources.
- There has been continual pressure on the organization by the leadership of the Analysis Centre to implement the management structures necessary to *action* the products of crime and intelligence analysis. Without such structures even the very best analytical work has little or no chance of making a difference.

Robert Chesshyre, in a study of police officers in South London, made the unsurprising, but generally neglected, observation that 'Most police officers have one very specific goal in mind, to produce guilty people before the court and to see them justly convicted. Everything else—specialization, community policing, public order—pales beside that aspiration' (Chesshyre, 1989). This reality has been critical in driving notions of 'impact', and the Analysis Centre model in the early years was unapologetic in relying heavily on achieving results around crime detection and reduction. This 'created space' to allow success measures in other (perhaps more difficult) areas (such as crime prevention) to emerge over time. As Schaffer succinctly puts it 'The essential idea is to focus immediately on tangible results ... instead of trying to overcome resistance to what people are *not* ready to do, find out what they *are* ready to do...' (Schaffer, 1995). While all analytical measures of 'impact' require the collation of statistical data (for example on the type and range of products generated) the most useful and reliable feedback is obtained from those operational commanders, senior police officers, government officials, and other decision-makers who use the analytical service on a daily basis:

During my performance meetings with both Response and Sector Inspectors I have heard nothing but the highest praise for the quality and timeliness of the information being made available to their officers [by the analysts, researchers, and CIOs]... The identification of hotspots, crime patterns and suspects has added great value to their patrolling... I am also greatly encouraged that random patrolling has now been replaced by focused intelligence led patrolling. Our recent successes bear this out (District Commander, PSNI Urban Region).

CHANGE AND THE NEW CULTURAL PARADIGM: A MODEL OF CONSILIENCE?

Implementing a crime and intelligence analysis change strategy cannot be done simply by putting in place new IT systems, carrying out training initiatives or devising plans. These, and many other practical factors, may be important, but promoting the Analysis Centre Model also required a clear focus on what Buchanan and Boddy (1992) refer to as 'backstaging'. This is '...concerned with the exercise of power skills; with intervening in political and cultural systems; with influencing, negotiating and selling, and with managing meaning'. According to Kanter (1983) '...change masters [are] skilful in obtaining backing for what they felt need[s] doing, gaining approval and legitimacy and being able to make a good case. Much of this [comes] from their ability to develop quality relationships through networking within [the] organization'. Leadership is clearly important '... [the Director] has a very unique personality. I think he is driven. He is a real zealot when it comes to driving issues through' (Kennedy, 2007).

The 'new' (2007) cultural web—as seen from a crime and intelligence analysis perspective—is shown at Figure 8.4 below.

The crime and intelligence analysis service has been both *part of* the programme of change and *responsive* to it:

• The emphasis on 'service' and 'communities' is now part of the day-to-day (symbolic) language. Acceptable standards of analysis in the early days have now been replaced by a more expectant and demanding culture.
• Power: The 'battle to win acceptance' is now being fought in pockets (and mainly in support areas, which in many ways are much less responsive than front-line operational areas). Effective analysis is widely seen as supporting a more professional, progressive police service. As one senior officer commented: 'District Commanders [now] fight over the loss of an analyst before they fight over the loss of a Chief Inspector' (Kennedy, 2007).

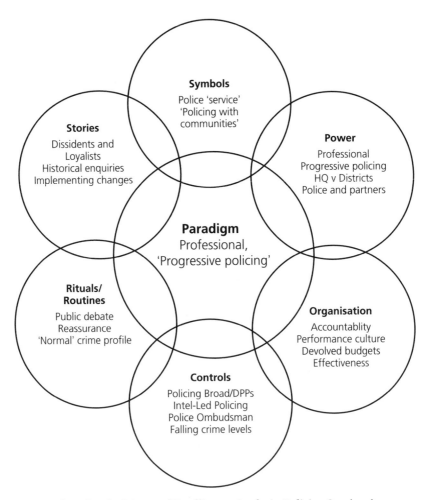

Fig 8.4 Cultural Web-Crime and Intelligence Analysis: Policing Services in Northern Ireland 2007

- Key strategic and tactical *organizational* crime decisions are now much more likely to benefit from evidence-based products—with consequent benefits for efficiency. While rigorous analysis of 'effectiveness' has not (yet) been carried out, there is unambiguous anecdotal evidence that commanders *feel* local performance is better because of the analytical work being carried out.[7]
- Controls: Police analysts support the oversight work of the NI Policing Board, local District Policing Partnerships, and the Office of the Police Ombudsman. NIM is

---

[7] While the Centre collects a good deal of both qualitative and quantitative data reliable measures of impact have not yet been developed. This is a complex matter and no reliable approach that adequately addresses this complexity has yet been identified.

associated with better accountability and has coincided with broadly falling crime levels over several years.

- Rituals and routines: The public and local media debate around crime still lacks genuine insight. But it is slowly improving, informed in part by much better police advice and information. 10 years after the Patten inquiry the crime profile in Northern Ireland—once dominated by public order and terrorism—is now more normal.
- The legacy of the past and the *stories* associated with it remain a very significant influence on policing in 2007. Dealing with history remains important, and significant analytical resources are committed to it. Reputation and trust is crucial in providing public reassurance. Once established they need to be renewed on a frequent basis.

The new Paradigm, 'Supporting Professional, Progressive Policing',[8] requires the out workings of the Analysis Centre Model to be quite deliberately 'hard-edged'. Products, briefings, advice, and (particularly) *recommendations* to support day-to-day policing priorities are the key requirements. Whilst not necessarily apparent to front-line (non-analytical) staff, these products are inspired by education, science, business, literature, music/photography, and philosophy. *Education* and *science* (and particularly the ideas associated with crime science[9]) have shaped learning and development and a more evidence-based approach to tackling crime (though in the world of operational policing true converts remain in a minority). The world of *business* has shaped much of the Centre's work—around leadership, planning, competition, and management. *Literature* is studied for the latest thinking. *Inspirational music* and *photography* are used to celebrate success and achievement. But it is perhaps a single strand from the world of *philosophy* that best captures the essence of the Analysis Centre model:

Knowledge is a great treasure, but there is one thing higher than knowledge, and that is understanding. Mere information by itself is worth little, unless it is arranged in ways that make sense to its possessors and enable them to act effectively . . . To make sense of information—to understand it—one has to put it into fruitful relationship with other information, and grasp the meaning of that relationship, which implies finding patterns, learning lessons, drawing inferences, and as a result seeing the whole. The task—achieving understanding—is . . . the task of [law enforcement analysis]. . .[10]

It is necessary to *apply* thinking from other disciplines in ways that are *practical and valuable*—to avoid the inevitable criticism that staff are spending time on things which it may be hard to justify as core business.

---

[8] In February 2007 a major international policing conference was held in Belfast. It was attended by eminent policing experts from North America, UK, Europe, and further afield. The theme of the conference was 'Policing the Future' which builds upon the current notion of 'Professional, Progressive Policing'.

[9] The Jill Dando Institute of Crime Science has played a key role in shaping these perspectives. JDI, through Director Gloria Laycock, has engaged in running workshops, conferences and providing peer review and support for the work of the Centre.

[10] Adapted from Grayling (2004): in the original text the words 'law enforcement analysis' are replaced with the word 'philosophy'.

CONCLUSION

The PSNI model has promoted the notion that a group of analysts, committed to providing a professional world class service, can help improve policing. Creating a truly corporate analytical service to support an intelligence-led, community-focused style of policing requires three key things. First it is necessary to *build critical mass* (enough analysts to affect behaviour across the organization) including a willingness to invest in the (sophisticated) information technology, data collection, management, leadership, and other systems and processes needed to underpin this approach. Second, *support decision-makers* by focusing squarely on impact through the delivery of products, ideas, advice, and assistance which add real value. Encourage analysts to ask questions, take (acceptable) risks and challenge (safely) 'the way things have always been done'. Finally, supporting change to shape the future requires reflection, review and an emphasis on creative intelligent analysis. For every police analyst *learning and development* must be a mantra. Borrow good ideas from other disciplines and integrate these with the best that law enforcement has to offer.

REFERENCES

AUDIT COMMISSION, *Helping with Enquiries* (London: HMSO, 1993).

BROWNE, J, 'Unleashing the power of learning' *Harvard Business Review* (Sept–Oct 1997).

BUCHANAN, D and BODDY, D, *The Expertise of the Change Agent* (London: Prentice Hall, 1992).

CHESSHYRE, R, *The Force Inside the Police* (London: Sedgewick and Jackson, 1989).

EVANS, M, *The Analysis Centre: Professional Development Programmes* (Belfast: PSNI, 2005).

GRAYLING, A, *The Mystery of Things* (London: Weidenfeld and Nicolson, 2004).

HASTINGS, C, *The New Organization: Growing the Culture of Organizational Networking* (London: McGraw-Hill, 1993).

INDEPENDENT COMMISSION ON POLICING FOR NORTHERN IRELAND, *A New Beginning: Policing in Northern Ireland* (9 September 1999—The Patten Report).

JEAPES, L, PSNI Analyst Professional Development Programmes (2007, unpublished).

JOHNSON, G and SCHOLES, K, *Exploring Corporate Strategy* (4th edn, London: Prentice Hall Europe, 1997).

KANTER, R, *The Change Masters* (London: George Allen & Unwin, 1983).

KENNEDY, J, 'Critical success factors to entrepreneurial activity in the public sector: A case study of the police service of Northern Ireland' Unpublished MBA thesis, Queen's University, Belfast, 2007.

MAGUIRE, M and JOHN, T, *Intelligence, Surveillance and Informants: Integrated Approaches* Police Research Group Crime Detection and Prevention Series (Paper 64, London: Home Office, 1995).

OVERSIGHT COMMISSIONER, *Overseeing the Proposed Revisions for the Policing Services of Northern Ireland* May 2007.

RUBIN, RE and WEISBERG, J, *In an Uncertain World: Tough Choices from Wall Street to Washington* (London: Random House, 2003).

SCHAFFER, R, quoted in Peters, T and Waterman Jr, RH, *In Search of Excellence* (reprint, London: Harper Colins, 1995).

SENGE, P, ed, *The Dance of Change* (London: Nicholas Brealey, 2007).

SENIOR, B, *Organizational Change* (London: Pitman, 1997).

STERNBERG, R, 'The theory of successful intelligence' *Interamerican Journal of Psychology* 39/2 (2005).

RATCLIFFE, J, ed, *Strategic Thinking in Criminal Intelligence Analysis* (Sydney: The Federation Press, 2004).

——, *Intelligence-Led Policing* (Devon: Willan Publishing, 2008).

9

AN EVALUATION OF THE ROLE OF THE INTELLIGENCE ANALYST WITHIN THE NATIONAL INTELLIGENCE MODEL

Jacqueline Sissens

INTRODUCTION

This chapter presents new research undertaken to establish whether the function of the intelligence analyst in relation to the requirements of the National Intelligence Model (NIM) has been achieved (on the NIM see ACPO, 2005). The overall aim of the research was to evaluate the role of analysts to establish if their function is rhetoric or reality and whether professionalism have been achieved through dedicated and specialized training. The objectives of the research were four-fold: to establish theory with regard to the role of analysis; to evaluate the role of intelligence analysts within UK police forces and other agencies; to determine any differences in theory and reality; and analyse why any disparity between theory and reality occurs.

The chapter will assert that the role of the analyst has, to date, not been sufficiently or adequately developed. Three particular factors are explored to determine their impact upon the role and function of the analyst: the analyst as an individual, analysts as a group, and organizational issues. Significantly, in relation to organizational issues, police culture and organizational pathologies were identified as being the most challenging issues in ensuring the utilization of analysts as the NIM dictates.

THE FUNCTION AND CHARACTER OF THE ANALYST

Previous research on the role of the analyst within a NIM context has included a study by John and Maguire, based on fieldwork carried out in 2002, and drawing upon information from the NIM implementation teams about police force progress towards NIM compliance prior to the target implementation date of 1 April 2004

(John and Maguire, 2004a). In relation to analysts, the report specifically identified concerns around recruitment and retention, training, education and experience, role, and impact. John and Maguire concluded that there were large knowledge gaps amongst all ranks of police officers, and this needed to be remedied to secure the effectiveness of the NIM. At the outset of the research, a lack of commitment to the NIM from all ranks highlighted that leadership and ownership were imperative if the model were to succeed.

RECRUITMENT AND RETENTION

The report also drew attention to the fact that analysts were difficult to recruit and retain. John and Maguire argued that this was due to the lack of police service experience in the field of analysis. Additionally, flat career structures and lack of promotion prospects within the police service resulted in higher than expected staff turnover as other agencies, private sector companies, and forces competed for the most experienced and highly trained intelligence analysts. This finding was corroborated by the Council of Europe (2001), which found that where police officers and civilians were employed as analysts and were fulfilling the same role, the pay disparity between officers and civilians were found to be significant, thus affecting the motivation of the civilian analysts. The promotion hierarchy was limited: analysts could only become a senior analyst, a strategic analyst, or a manager. Consequently, many of them would leave the discipline after a few years. Dixon (2003) compared different European approaches to intelligence management and identified good practice. His study acknowledged the need for comprehensive selection processes and subsequent training as key to quality analysis within any intelligence processing model.

THE ROLE

Two studies (Cope, 2004; Ratcliffe, 2003) also provide excellent insight into the role of the analyst within intelligence-led policing. Cope found a 'poor understanding of analysis amongst police officers and a lack of understanding of policing amongst analysts' (Cope, 2004: 188). The study concluded that training and development of both police officers and analysts is crucial to develop a productive working relationship. Moreover, the report found that when police officers undertook the role of analysts their analytical products were held in higher regard than the work of civilian analysts. The issue was not one of work quality but the lack of acceptance of the 'civvie' employee by sworn colleagues. Police officers felt uncomfortable accepting recommendations from analysts where the analysts were 'civilians' rather than 'police' and were thus therefore perceived as lacking experience in an operational role. Cope (2004: 189) suggests that because analysis aims to provide an unbiased overview of intelligence it is in conflict with a police officer's personal analytical process. Police officers' traditional reliance on experiential knowledge implies that the analytical process may be biased by such familiarity. Thus, for example, such prior knowledge could influence how crime problems were perceived by officers, without them necessarily having widely experienced the crime problem. Gill (2000: 94–96) discusses that an officers' tendency to rely upon experience results in them continually rounding up the 'usual suspects'. Therefore, the role of the analyst has been introduced to challenge this established way of working and offer new options for consideration: to provide and recommend an variety of tactics for intervention that can and do challenge normal police tactics.

LIMITATIONS AND OPPORTUNITIES OF INTELLIGENCE-LED POLICING

Ratcliffe (2003: 4) discusses some of the limitations and opportunities of intelligence-led policing. He looks at the unrealistic expectations placed upon the analyst when, for example, 'an intelligence analyst is unable to precisely predict the next, date, time, and place of a burglary'. Unrealistic expectations are, in part, founded upon failings in the systems infrastructure underpinning intelligence processing and analysis. Michael Mansfield succinctly highlighted the need; James Sheptycki, the problems. Mansfield stated:

There plainly has to be a compendious and effective local intelligence gathering operation in existence that can be accessed quickly by officers at any time, day or night, especially when those officers may not be familiar with the locality. The information itself should be categorised in such a way that it can be called up by reference to name, or description, or address, or offence, or modus operandi, or vehicle or associates. Computerisation must clearly have made this possible for the future (Stephen Lawrence Inquiry transcript Michael Mansfield QC closing speech, p 11055 2–12).

Sheptycki (2004: 308) provides an excellent introduction of the inception of criminal intelligence systems and the complexity in which they are developed and integrated into the policing organization. He describes how law enforcement agencies are able to take advantage of interoperable information technology systems. Sheptycki identifies and categorizes these dilemmas as eleven organizational pathologies, illustrating how these can affect the role and production of intelligence analysis. Considering the impact of organizational pathologies also emphasizes the disconnected approach to intelligence gathering and sharing to which Michael Mansfield's statement above alludes.

Sheptycki's eleven organizational pathologies in police intelligence systems (Sheptycki 2004) are as follows:

1. Digital divide—plethora of non-interoperable IT systems.
2. Linkage blindness—incomplete data denies opportunities to identify crucial links.
3. Noise—glut of low-grade intelligence clouding interpretation.
4. Intelligence overload, including compulsive data demand—forcing analysts to sort data rather than analyse it.
5. Non-reporting or non-recording—labour-intensive recording procedures create a disincentive to report/record data.
6. Intelligence gaps—failure to link intelligence between the NIM's three levels of criminality.
7. Duplication—multiple agencies undertaking parallel investigations on the same subject due to lack of intelligence coordination.

8. Institutional friction—disparate working systems inhibit collaboration.
9. Information hoarding and information silos—lack of horizontal communication linkages between databases, individuals, or units.
10. Defensive data concentration—duplication of data collection because of system interoperability problems.
11. Occupational subcultures, including intra-agency and inter-agency occupational subcultures—beliefs and perceptions held amongst workers inhibit adoption or sharing of good practices and new ideas.

Sheptycki's key point is that the very nature of the intelligence systems utilized by the analyst may prevent them from producing a product that can be taken at face value. 'The organizational pathologies outlined [above] show that the processing of criminal intelligence is not as rationally ordered as may appear in the pages of the strategic analyses that are its product. . . . Given the catalogue of organizational pathologies that affect the policing intelligence system, it will be necessary to use the analytical products of that system with circumspection' (Sheptycki, 2004: 328).

PSYCHOLOGICAL ISSUES AROUND ANALYSIS

The literature discussed so far has focused on the practical issues around analysis, but the psychological issues surrounding analysis are also relevant when considering the role and impact of the analyst. The psychological perspective is concerned with how analysts make judgements and assessments, and how this can affect the quality and therefore the application of products they generate.

Herbert Simon (1997) first advanced the concept of 'bounded' or limited rationality fifty years ago. He argued that because of limits in human mental capacity, the mind is not capable of coping with the complexity of the world, so it constructs a simplified mental model of reality. Rational behaviour within the mental model would occur but it may not reflect the reality of the outside world. The concept of bounded rationality is recognized as a portrayal of judgement and choice, and as an adjustment to the limitations of the mind. Bounded rationality is influenced by factors that include past experience, education, cultural values, role requirements, and organizational norms, as well as by the specifics of the information received. Simon's theory provided a significant insight on how analysis occurs within the mind. Therefore, Simon's model of bounded rationality explains why individual analysts would interpret the same information differently.

Ekblom advances the issue of critical and creative thinking in the analytical process: 'Crime analysis is an exploratory process; it is more akin to composing a picture than to the slavish following of the fixed steps of a cookery book. It follows that people who carry out crime analysis need, above all, to appreciate the essence of the approach, its context, objectives and limitations' (Ekblom, 1988: 1).

Allen (2001: 78–79) also investigates this issue in analysis and discusses the 'dichotomy of aims and interests' within analysis and more specifically the issue of hypotheses that are designed to turn assumptions into facts. He suggests that analytical hypotheses are 'tenuous if not invalid if not based on careful calculation of all the strengths and weaknesses of all the factors in the equation'.

THE RESEARCH

The present research was conducted via a self-completion postal questionnaire sent to intelligence analysts accredited under the UK National Intelligence Analyst Training (NIAT) programme. There were 57 respondents: a sample size not dissimilar from the national data set utilized in John and Maguire (2004a), and the response rate was 76 per cent, therefore eliminating sample bias. The respondents included a variety of ranks and roles within analysis. The chosen method overcame the three main issues of geographical constraint, risk of interviewer bias, and confidentiality.

A combination of dichotomous and multiple-choice closed questions was utilized to prevent any bias towards one type of data collection and to maintain the interest of the respondent. The responses were analysed for trends and patterns in the responses and then this was referenced with secondary information from previous research to ensure that a valid hypothesis had been reached. None of the questions posed required participants to breach their responsibilities to the Official Secrets Act or expose sensitive police tactics.

As with all research, there are limitations. The sample of 57 analysts come from fifteen organizations and therefore the responses may not be representative of how the NIM is working throughout law enforcement in the UK. The consistency of the data presented speaks for itself. Taking into account the literature reviewed above, the present research illustrated that analysts working within the NIM framework utilize nine analytical techniques to produce four intelligence products.

RESEARCH FINDINGS

The research indicated a high percentage of respondents do not produce NIM products. Over 80 per cent of analysts are not involved in the production of strategic assessments. This may be because the role of producing strategic assessments lies with a senior or strategic analyst. It should be noted that in the research, only three respondents were senior analysts and therefore it is important not to read a particular significance into this.

According to John and Maguire, the core products that NIM requires analysts to produce in their role are Strategic Assessments, Tactical Assessments, Problem Profiles, and Target Profiles (John and Maguire, 2004a: Table 4.3). However, the respondents in this present survey illustrated that this is not core business for them. Target Profiles were the most produced, with 58 per cent of respondents producing them (compared with 70 per cent in John and Maguire's national survey). Only 30 per cent of respondents produced Problem Profiles (compared with 80 per cent) whereas 42 per cent produced Tactical Assessments (compared with 75 per cent).

One respondent noted, 'We could be doing more NIM related products, this would help standardise the work of analysts'.

This statement was supported by three other respondents who alluded to the lack of production of NIM products. Another respondent commented, 'Some analysts just produce a technique in isolation, techniques should form part of a product, otherwise the analysis and the context is lost'.

Part of the research was concerned with the analytical techniques that were utilized and the results demonstrated significant differences between techniques. Of particular interest were the techniques not routinely employed in the day to day work of the analysts. Over 72 per cent of respondents stated that they did not utilize Risk Analysis, whereas 90 per cent did not use Results Analysis. Moreover 78 per cent of respondents claimed that they did not employ Operational Intelligence Assessments.

The most utilized analytical techniques were Network Analysis, with 88 per cent of analysts stating that they used this technique and 66 per cent stating they exploited Crime Pattern Analysis. These findings support Maguire (2003: 30) who had established that analysts were inadequately or poorly trained in the use of Results Analysis and Risk Analysis. The above results lead to the conclusion that only a small percentage of the Tactical Tasking and Coordination Groups (TT and CG) fully understand the NIM (12 per cent) and the role of the analyst (22 per cent). This statement was substantiated by the 42 per cent of respondents who felt that only the minority of the TT and CG understood the NIM and only 32 per cent of respondents felt that the minority of the TT and CG understood the role of the analyst. These findings support research undertaken by Cope (2004) and Ratcliffe (2003). Cope found that there was a lack of understanding about intelligence analysis amongst police officers, but conversely there was a lack of understanding of policing amongst analysts.

In addition, four respondents made reference to Standard Operating Procedures (SOPs). One respondent stated: 'In the absence of ongoing training on the NIM, SOPs come in useful when a NIM product is tasked as it helps define the format that the document should take'. This illustrates a lack of understanding around the contents of NIM products, not only for police officers and the TT and CG as product customers but also amongst analysts. This finding is supported by the research of John and Maguire (2004a) who also found a lack of consistency and ongoing training on the NIM.

The final section of the research explored analysts' perceptions of their role, and what changes they would recommend to ensure that both the NIM and analysts are fully utilized and integrated into policing. Here, 65 per cent of respondents felt that their skills were not fully utilized. The research also identified five key areas to improve the utilization of analysis.

1. Analysts to spend less time on administration or support and more time spent conducting 'analysis' (22 per cent)

One respondent suggested 'because we are civilians we are associated more with administrative functions than operational support. This needs to change if analysis is to be taken seriously.' Forty-eight per cent of respondents stated that up to a quarter of their day was taken up with administrative functions; whereas 36 per cent of respondents stated that between a quarter to a half of their day was taken up with administrative functions. Twelve per cent of respondents stated that between a half to three-quarters of their day was taken up with administrative functions, but 4 per cent of respondents stated that all of their day was taken up with administrative functions.

2. Improve understanding of analysis amongst product customers (21 per cent)

As a respondent noted, 'my D[etective] C[hief] I[nspector] is a really good cop but he still does not understand what I can offer as an analyst. It is not that he can't understand, I sometimes think that it is because analysis is such a foreign concept to old school coppers because they haven't gone through their career with it.' This is illustrated by the findings of John and Maguire who, in their research, found that 'only 36 per cent [were]... familiar with the operation of NIM, and 45 per cent with the operation of the TCG' (2003: 52).

3. Improve organizational data collection and storage methods (14 per cent)

One respondent commented, 'I spend more time writing reports on how I can't write the reports because the data I can access is incomplete or it has been collected with a different purpose in mind.' This statement echoes the debates outlined in Sheptycki's discussion around organizational pathologies.

4. Act upon intelligence gaps and recommendations provided by analysts to prove worth of analysis and motivate analysts (11 per cent)

As one respondent noted, 'Very few of my products seem to get acted upon, I identify gaps that need filling but it is rare that these get acted on.' This was in contrast to another respondent who asserted. 'One thing that works very well in our unit is the tasking process. I can make recommendations and they will be discussed and allocated. I get the feedback and can update my work. I think that is the benefit of working in a multi agency unit [CDRP], everyone has their organization to represent and no one wants to let their side down.'

5. Improve ongoing training and train the behavioural side of analysis (11 per cent)

As one respondent shrewdly observed, 'when everyone talks about improving intelligence analysis, they refer to the quality of writing, types of analytical products, relations between intelligence analysts and product customers, no one in the intelligence analysis world seems to talk about how analysts minds should work or try to improve this. I think it is a huge concern, we are all from differing backgrounds.'

The research also addressed some issues around training, education, background, and experience. Respondents demonstrated that the police service generally recruits graduates for analytical roles. Thirty-two of the 57 respondents had an educational achievement of tertiary degree level or higher. Previous experience varied widely: some analysts had been recruited directly from university, while others had private sector experience. Only six of the respondents had transferred into being an analyst from other civilian roles within law enforcement. Two of the respondents were police constables.

The research also provided other valuable insights into the use of analysts and issues that they face. In particular one respondent referred to the issue of unrealistic expectations, and this is supported by Ratcliffe (2003: 4). Other respondents alluded to this same issue without categorizing it as 'unrealistic expectations'. Other respondents viewed it as a training issue. One analyst scrutinized 'occupational culture' in relation to Police versus Civilians debate as affecting their ability to be effective in their role. One respondent noted that, 'Analysts are mainly young, civilian and female and if they are in the police then they are mostly of a low rank. This causes problems with the communication process with managers within the police culture.' Another alluded to this by noting that the benefit of being a police constable conducting analysis was that it 'helped to legitimise the product'. On the different perceptions of analysis undertaken by police and civilian staff see Cope (2004).

Despite the acceptance of a product, seven of the respondents noted that they were not confident in the judgements and recommendations there were making due to a lack of knowledge of the context of the problem they were working with. This supports the statement by Cope (2004) who found a 'lack of understanding of policing amongst analysts'.

On a positive note, 82 per cent of respondents did feel that they provided 'added value' to the role of their organization yet only 66 per cent felt that their role was perceived in a positive light by their non-analytical colleagues.

Thus, the main findings of the research can be summed as follows:

- There is a lack of use of NIM products and of certain analytical techniques amongst analysts.
- There is a lack of understanding amongst the TT and CG and customers of analytical products.
- Civilian analysts suffer from issues with police organizational culture and lack of knowledge around policing policies and practices.
- Training for analysts and customers is not sufficient to ensure that the NIM is reinforced and updated.
- Organizational data collection and retention causes analysts difficulties.
- Analysts are incorrectly utilized by managers.
- Analysts do feel that they add value to their organization.

As stated above, analysts are not producing NIM products—Strategic Assessments, Tactical Assessments, Problem Profiles and Target Profiles. The research has indicated that there are several possible reasons or combinations of reasons for this. These can be broadly defined as: lack of understanding of analysis, lack of training on NIM, poor management, and organizational pathologies of intelligence systems.

Most analysts are managed by police officers and while this is not problematic in itself, it does pose some unique concerns. Respondents noted that despite available training, there remains generally a lack of understanding of what analysis is amongst managers. The paucity of training on analysis affects not only the analysts and managers but also impacts upon the ability of the customers to ask the right question when requesting analysis. It was noted that many managers do not understand what type of training an analyst needs (for example, court appearances, law on disclosure, criminological theory, or thinking processes). One respondent even noted a manager's lack of understanding of what resources an analyst requires to be able to produce an analytical product.

A lack of communication and understanding was evident amongst the responses. Respondents were concerned about middle and senior management who do not always use analysis correctly and they felt this was due to a failure to appreciate its contribution. There remains a lack of training and education for the customers of analytical products to develop their knowledge of what they might expect if they requested an analytical product. John and Maguire (2004b: 3) noted that this was also an issue with ownership and understanding of the NIM. He observed 'large knowledge gaps about the NIM among all ranks of officers'.

Several respondents noted the issue of thinking processes as a concern. Although their perception of the problem differed, they all alluded to being concerned about their lack of understanding of their own thought processes and how this impacts upon the judgements they make. This problem has the potential to impede accurate intelligence analysis. Mental processes are amongst the most important but most difficult to deal with and to educate about. Intelligence analysis is fundamentally a mental process and understanding this process is hindered by a lack of conscious awareness of the workings of our own minds. Respondents also noted a lack of 'mind training' to understand how the human mind works and to therefore understand how they analyse problems. Training on thinking skills will develop a conscious reflection on analytical processes.

These findings and the associated recommendations that the respondents have made may go someway to addressing the individual and group issues of why intelligence analysts are not functioning in compliance with NIM theory. There are also broader issues around the functionality of intelligence systems that would affect the role of the analyst even if the issues were rectified, these include the issues of organizational pathologies of intelligence systems.

As discussed earlier, the intelligence system structured in the NIM has been configured not as a web but rather as a hierarchically organized information environment in which there is not one centralized information system but a number of sometimes competing intelligence systems. These are structural issues, of which intelligence analysts have a good understanding as they deal with them on a daily basis.

CONCLUSION

This chapter has demonstrated that analysts do not yet fulfil the role that the NIM intended. There is a requirement for recognition within law enforcement organizations of the organizational pathologies and cultures that hamper the effectiveness of analysts, as observed by Sheptcki (2004). In addition, there exists a requirement for more specialized training around thinking processes if analysts are to understand the impact of their mental model on the product that they are working on. It needs to be acknowledged that, in an organizational culture that has not historically relied on evidence-based analysis to inform decision-making, analysis as a specialism has many barriers to overcome before it can be considered as a tool imperative to the policing function. Analysis, especially strategic and volume crime analysis, offers an important and valuable function that cannot be undertaken 'in the heads or mindsets' of police officers. A change in culture will have to take place before analysis can really take effect and, while there is evidence that this is happening, the integration of these two widely different cultures will have to take place over a long time period as analysis is contrary to established and traditional policing practices.

REFERENCES

ACPO, *Guidance on the National Intelligence Mode* (Wyboston: NCPE, 2005).

ALLEN, GW, *None So Blind: A Personal Account of the Intelligence Failure in Vietnam* (Chicago: Ivan R Dee, 2001).

COPE, N, 'Intelligence-led policing or policing-led intelligence? Integrating volume crime analysis into policing' *British Journal of Criminology* 44/ 2 (2004) 188–203.

COUNCIL OF EUROPE, *Crime Analysis: Best Practice Survey No 4* (Strasbourg: Pc-s-Co, 2001).

DIXON, T, *Intelligence Management Model for Europe* (London: Home Office, 2003).

EKBLOM, P, *Getting the Best Out of Crime Analysis* (Crime Prevention Unit Paper 10, London: Home Office Crime Prevention Unit, 1988).

GILL, P, *Rounding Up the Usual Suspects* (Ashgate: Aldershot, 2000).

JOHN, T and MAGUIRE, M, 'Rolling out the NIM: Key challenges' in Bullock, K and Tilley, N, eds, *Crime Reduction and Problem Orientated Policing* (Devon: Willian Publishing, 2003).

—— and ——, (2004a) *The NIM: Early Implementation Experience in Three Police Force Areas* (Cardiff: Cardiff University, 2004).

—— and ——, (2004b) *The NIM: Key Lessons From Early Research* (Cardiff: Cardiff University, 2004).

MAGUIRE, M, 'Criminal investigation and crime control' in Newburn, T, ed, *Handbook of Policing* (Devon: Willan Publishing, 2003).

RATCLIFFE, JH, (2002a) 'Intelligence-led policing and the problems of turning rhetoric into practice' *Policing and Society* 12/1 (2002) 53–66.

——, (2002b) 'Damned if you don't, damned if you do: Crime mapping and its implications in the real world' [Electronic version] *Policing and Society* 12 (2002) 211–225.

——, 'Intelligence-led policing' *Trends and Issues in Crime and Criminal Justice No 248* (Canberra: Australian Institute of Criminology, 2003).

——, ed, *Strategic Thinking in Criminal Intelligence* (Sydney: The Federation Press, 2004).

SHEPTYCKI, J, 'Organizational pathologies in police intelligence systems' *European Journal of Criminology* 1/3 (2004) 308–332.

SIMON, H, *Administrative Behaviour* (London: The Free Press, 1997).

10

PAN-EUROPEAN LAW ENFORCEMENT STRATEGIC ANALYSIS: TRENDS AND CONCERNS

Dr Nick Ridley

The events of 1989–2001—the break up of the former Soviet Union, the Balkan civil wars, the emergence of and the reaction to new manifestations of fundamentalist religious terrorism—resulted in new and more complex problems of organized crime afflicting Europe. These cataclysmic international events influenced criminality and defined developments in law enforcement strategic analysis in the EU.

THE ADVENT OF 'NEW' ORGANIZED CRIME

The 'new' (post-1989) organized crime in Europe comprised emerging criminal groups and organized crime structures from the former Soviet Union and Eastern Europe, apparently conforming to traditional conceptions: monolithic, large scale, hierarchically organized entities. These post-Soviet groups quickly established their presence, firstly in the transition democracies of Central and Eastern Europe, and then within the EU itself.

Responding to this proliferation, law enforcement analysts in several EU Member States collaborated in the mid-1990s to produce common criteria defining 'organized crime', such definition being intended to facilitate law enforcement prioritization and resource deployment. The 12 criteria (at one stage it was 14) were individual characteristics which, when applied to an identified grouping of criminals, would place the group within or outside the definition of organized crime. Four of the criteria were 'mandatory'; others were variables. Despite the level of theoretical investment, in practice they were found to be too numerous and the whole analytical structure cumbersome. Consequently analysts within EU Member States formulated a more trenchant definition of organized crime. By the late 1990s, the concept of 'organised crime group' was also being reassessed. Traditional monolithic hierarchical structures were no longer viewed as the sole model. Organized crime groups, smaller in terms of membership, based upon ethnic affinity, and operating in narrow geographical areas became apparent. These groups engaged with each other in common criminal enterprises.

Accordingly a 're-evaluated model' of organized crime groups was evolved by analysis posing questions as to the exact the extent and breadth of organized crime.[1] Strategic intelligence discerned criminal groups, particularly those originating from Eastern Europe, not as omni-competent and omni-powerful with strict pyramid hierarchies, but rather as individual groups of criminals operating, either continuously or periodically, in some form of loose association of vertical criminal structures. At one stage the change was emphasized as moving 'from criminal collectives, initially organizations, later on to criminal networks, then to the individual organized criminal' (Europol, 2006).

By 2005 within the Russian Federation, authorities estimated that there were between 300–400 important organized crime groups, of which only 15 criminal organizations possessed network structures (Council of Europe, 2005). Information from Russian law enforcement, when analysed within Europol, revealed that there were just over 130 criminal groupings, comprising 1,200 individual organized crime groups operating in cooperation and cohesion, engaging in common criminal enterprises.

Criminal groups, each contributing specialist activities, sustained long-term criminal enterprises through networking. Criminal services were franchised between groups, for instance storage of imported drugs, or laundering criminal proceeds. Strategic analysis identified high levels of violence and intimidation as core modus operandi of organized crime groups. These activities were carried out at two levels of criminality; one level consisted of extortion and robbery whilst the other level was more economic-crime based. This second level involved commodity fraud, money-laundering, and discreet infiltration of economic sectors.

Analysis identified numerous other organized crime group attributes for use as long-term strategic indicators. The degree of international cooperation between the groups grew significantly and the geographic extent of those links widened. There were numerous links between organized crime groups within the EU and the Accession States, as well as with groups throughout the rest of the world, including North America, China, Colombia, Iran, Morocco, Nigeria, Pakistan, Surinam, Turkey, and Vietnam.

The 're-evaluated model' of organized crime was corroborated by the work of van Duyne (1996), Savona (1999), and Levi (2003). Van Duyne emphasized the fragmented nature of the groupings, frequently utilizing the term 'disorganized crime', and concluding that organized crime groups' disposable criminal assets were much smaller than the massive profits formerly ascribed to them.

---

[1] In fact within various EU criminal intelligence units over a period of several years there have formulated no less than seven differing 'models' of organized crime, some with overlapping characteristics, but nonetheless distinguished by other methods of operating and long-term criminal objectives. For simplicity, only the salient points and the outline of the process of re-evaluating organized crime have been covered.

EUROPOL—ANALYTICAL DIFFICULTIES, DATA PROTECTION, AND 'REMIT'

In response to both this new threat and the removal of internal EU borders, a new EU organization, Europol, was established, initially outside the EU framework but subsequently incorporated in the Treaty of Amsterdam 1999. Based in The Hague, its official remit is to support criminal investigations involving two or more Member States through EU-wide intelligence exchange and analysis of criminal intelligence. Each Member State seconds law enforcement staff to Europol, which also hosts liaison officers from Third Party States.

One issue that pervaded pan-EU intelligence exchange was that of data protection. At the outset Europol needed to gain the confidence of the intelligence contributors. Member States were the main contributors of intelligence. The electronic architecture of information exchange was so constructed that analysts and individual Member States had access only to the data given by that Member State. Whilst these arrangements conformed to data-protection provisions, assuring the contributing Member State that its body of data remained under its control, they nonetheless severely hampered real-time intelligence exchange between the various Member States.

Initially, low staffing levels necessitated that Europol's remit was confined to certain crime categories, thereby further limiting intelligence exchange and constraining potential analysis data.[2] One extensive case of money-laundering taken by Europol involved six Member States over a period of 12 months. Information was exchanged and strategic indicators were identified. The criminal proceeds originated from suspected drug-trafficking, illegal immigration and arms trafficking. However, because arms trafficking was not then within the remit of Europol, the information concerning activities relating to arms trafficking could not officially be stored or even accepted, despite the fact that the financial data concerning arms trafficking was intermingled with the financial data from the other two criminal activities, and the fact that the same group of international criminals were perpetrating all three criminal activities. For over five years such intelligence dilemmas occurred hinging upon the issue of whether potential cases and the accompanying intelligence were within the legal remit of Europol.

The related issues of whether intelligence data could be accepted and how it should be stored thus impeded full strategic and operational analytical work of the EU's criminal intelligence agency. These issues overshadowed the fundamental objective of using, analysing, and disseminating the intelligence. Such difficulties have been overcome, and there has been undoubted progress in strategic analysis on an EU-wide

---

[2] A significant indicator of the various political and legal difficulties was in the name itself; for the first twelve months the official name of the organization was *Europol Drugs Unit* with the sole remit of drug-trafficking and money-laundering from drugs proceeds. This was at the insistence of Customs organizations of various Member States—including the UK—who wished to preserve equality with police forces and primacy over drug-trafficking. After one year the name Europol was official, with it being designated the official EU police and law enforcement organization, and new crime categories fell within its operational and strategic remit.

basis. However such progress has taken time. As recently as August 2007, a management strategy document outlining the role and future of Europol highlighted,

the ensuing debate demonstrated limited awareness of ,or trust in, Europol by the national competent authorities. . .the vicious circle . . .a number of Member States express criticism towards the support and services provided by Europol, while, in turn Europol calls attention to the shortcomings in the co-operation afforded by Member States (Europol Management Board, 2007: 1).

These shortcomings included the area of strategic analysis.

ORGANIZED CRIME AND ECONOMIC SECTORS— THE GHENT ANALYTICAL METHODOLOGY

The analytical work of formulating criteria and elements for defining organized crime was pursued by academia and law enforcement agencies within the Member States in Europol throughout the 1990s. Building upon this work, a ground-breaking analytical methodology was formulated in the early 2000s by Belgian Federal Police in cooperation with several EU law enforcement bodies and the University of Ghent. Labelled 'the Ghent methodology', it gave valuable insight to assessing the nature of organized crime, financial crime and the vulnerabilities of financial sectors to infiltration, subversion, and criminal exploitation.

With two key elements, an information-gathering target involving an integrated spectrum of business enterprise and the element of risk assessment, the Ghent methodology strategically analysed organized crime, treating it as an enterprise or business. Using this approach, organized crime was perceived to follow free-market dynamics, responding to economic opportunities. The Ghent methodology was adopted and deployed as part of strategic analysis by law enforcement organizations across the EU. It shifted the traditional methodology focus from solely concentrating on major organized crime groups to concentrating on the activities of organized crime within the legal economy. In doing so it afforded law enforcement a more open-minded approach in order to identify criminality proactively. Legal and illicit markets are analysed together with the environmental factors and wider international political factors affecting these markets. In the analysis of the market itself the Ghent methodology reconciled and combined predictive indicators of market vulnerability and synthesized all of them in a standardized risk assessment. Europol Situation Reports on Organized Crime (2002, 2003) include specific sections on political factors and economic factors that can be partly attributed of the Ghent methodology.

However, from the point of view of strategic analysis undertaken for law enforcement purposes, three factors must be borne in mind when using the Ghent methodology. Although the development of the Ghent methodology was a synthesis of academic and law enforcement expertise, the initial and formative stages of the methodology were conceived entirely in an academic background. The various stages of the

Ghent methodology are designed to combine a quasi-mathematical series of equations, leading to a definitive figure in terms of vulnerability of an economic sector to organized crime exploitation. In practical terms criminal activity is more adaptable and pragmatic, although no less harmful in terms of human casualties and long-term economic damage.

Secondly, there is the time factor. It is three years since the Ghent methodology was completed and although it has been used on a number of occasions it has never been adapted or updated. Organized crime and criminal groups do not remain static, but adapt modus operandi, and change tactics and engage in other types of crime, often on a short-term basis. For example, Islamic extremist cells within the EU since 2004 have engaged in several differing and changing forms of local, low-level crime for fund-raising purposes, such changes occurring with bewildering rapidity to strategic analysts attempting to monitor trends.

Thirdly—and fundamentally—the Ghent methodology departs from the basic law enforcement principal of concentrating upon the criminal or criminal groups. The starting point of the Ghent methodology is industry, the economic sector, and business enterprise given their potential vulnerability to criminal exploitation by organized crime. This is of value, albeit in a peripheral or indirect manner, to intelligence regarding particular criminals or organized crime but only on the broadest level. The Ghent Methodology takes no account of essential and up-to-date operational intelligence on criminals. Nonetheless, in the evolution of strategic evaluation and analysis of organized crime, the Ghent methodology stands as an important milestone.

TRIAL AND ADAPTATION OF ANALYTICAL METHODOLOGIES

Within the EU during the late 1990s and early 2000s strategic analysis in both academic and law enforcement institutions sought to define organized crime by means of matrices and linear depiction of criteria elements, all giving differing 'scores' according to certain activities or characteristics.

The laudable strategic objective was to identify to law enforcement planners particularly active organized crime groups thus facilitating intervention prioritization. Unfortunately, this type of strategic analysis proved inefficient in identifying and successfully analysing the phenomena outlined in the emergence of various criminal groups impacting upon the EU. The rigid basis on which pan-EU analysis was undertaken overemphasized certain criteria leading to a focus on the existing known organized crime groups and overlooking indicators which may have revealed the emergence of new groups or crime trends. Strategic analysis during this period, on an EU basis, concentrated on the vulnerability of sectors of society and economies to organized crime activity, and did not take sufficient account of the differing crime categories being engaged upon by criminal groups either simultaneously, or in close succession. Such omissions were eventually rectified by changes in strategic analysis products.

First, there was a shift from strategic situation reports to threat assessments. Situation reports produced by Europol and individual EU Member States' analytical units provided a broad situation overview, with predictions. The new-style threat assessments produced by Europol took into account threat levels of various criminal groups impacting upon the EU and future changes.

Second, more attention was given to a crime category approach with strategic overviews focusing on individual crime categories such as drug-trafficking and illegal immigration which were being undertaken on an EU-wide basis. These overviews outlined the various criminal groups involved, but also took into account the interrelated nature of different crime categories: for example, common criminal enterprises and shared international routes, illicit trafficking of all commodities, and the accompanying criminal growth of service crime industries such as stolen or forged passports which facilitate the primary offending.

CASE STUDY—STRATEGIC INTELLIGENCE OVERSIGHT AND ALBANIAN CRIMINAL GROUPS WITHIN THE EU

During the 1990s, the strategic intelligence constant held by international law enforcement was the dominance over the international heroin trafficking by Turkish organized crime groups. Other Balkan groups were held to be of comparative insignificance. Such was the 'received wisdom' within which intelligence was analysed. Strategic analysts came to revise radically their interpretation on realizing that their preconceptions had impeded recognition of emerging trends.

By 1993, Albanian/Kosovar organized crime groups across Europe were gaining an estimated 1 to 2 million US dollars annually as a result of heroin trafficking. By 1996 in Denmark 90 per cent of all heroin trafficked into the country was under the control of Albanian/Kosovar criminal groups. In the same year in Sweden organized prostitution in Stockholm was under Albanian criminal group control, and the heroin trafficking groups based in Norway were coordinating activities with a group in southern Sweden. The UK Metropolitan Police increasingly had to deal with trafficked prostitutes, forcibly engaged in sexual slavery, organized and controlled by Albanian/Kosovar criminal groups.

By 2002, Albanian Yugoslav/Kosovar criminal groups were dominating heroin trafficking across Europe and were expanding their activities in other areas of organized crime. These groups were present in several urban centres in Germany, including Hamburg and Munich, and in Hesse and Bavaria they had ousted and broken the monopoly of Turkish heroin dealers. They had established their activities in two areas of eastern France and a *quartier* in Paris. They had penetrated throughout Switzerland, causing authorities to openly speak of a heroin epidemic. Based in the northern Czech Republic areas of Liberec and Jablonec-Nisu and in Prague, where they wrested control from one Ukrainian organized crime group, they were the dominant organized crime group controlling the transit flow and domestic supply of heroin (Czech Republic Police, pers comm, 1994). They also commenced importing prostitutes to service Prague nightclubs.

Whilst these groups had wrested control of heroin trafficking from Turkish groups in Germany, and had established monopoly control in Switzerland, in other locations they arrived at pragmatic rapprochement with Turkish and other criminal groups over supply and distribution of heroin.

The whole process of Albanian/Kosovar organized crime groups establishing themselves within Europe and dominating the heroin market occurred over a period of a decade. During this period EU law enforcement analysis units, whilst occasionally alluding to certain regional occurrences, and acknowledging that there were organized crime groups of Albanian origin, did not adequately explore the possibility that such groups may be extensively active on a pan-EU basis.

Four points are worthy of note regarding the overall strategic analysis and final—delayed—recognition of the full significance of Albanian criminal groups.

Firstly, the insidious penetration and gradual establishment of Albanian organized crime was either not recognized at all, or else recognized only within individual EU Member States. The EU-wide pattern was not spotted by analysts.

Secondly, when the massive collapse of neo-classical pyramid investment frauds disrupted the Albanian economy and society in 1996, analysis of the possible criminal impact on the rest of Europe suggested that the only adverse consequence was likely to be increased illegal migration from Albania to the rest of Europe. The possibility of the frauds being associated with other forms of criminality was not considered. International heroin trafficking, for instance, was still perceived as being firmly under the domination of Turkish organized crime.

Thirdly, essential characteristics of Albanian organized crime groups were overlooked. One of these was the intensely pragmatic and versatile nature of their criminal activities. Once established in heroin trafficking, the crime groups diversified and devoted resources to engaging in organized illegal immigration, trafficking in human beings, and organized theft of high-value vehicles. Another characteristic was that the groups' avoidance of rigid hierarchical structures. They operated as a confederation of criminal groups, in contact with each other, but nonetheless self-contained.

Finally there were the common ethnic origins shared by the Albanian/Kosovar groups, all of whom originated from just four small geographical areas. This close-knit ethnic, regional, and linguistic affinity of the groups ensured internal discipline, loyalty, and highly secure inter-group contact.

THE LAW ENFORCEMENT RESPONSE TO EMERGING GLOBAL TERRORISM

The terrorist attacks in New York and Washington in September 2001 were a catalyst for the redefinition of policing in terms of national security rather than regional or community safety. One former British senior police officer observed that the response required 'a complete re-prioritization of law enforcement tasks as all of us who work in law enforcement formerly knew them' (David Veness, Chief Security Advisor, United Nations, addressing a Europol meeting, January 2002).

Prior to 2001 intelligence analysis of terrorism within the EU was carried out principally on a bilateral Member State basis, where two mutually impacted Member States would exchange information. Post-9/11, a more pan-European approach was adopted.

The lack of a comprehensive and coherent definition of terrorism (Carlile, 2007) hampered strategic analysis which, as has already been seen in relation to organized crime, is conceptualized in terms of a standardized definition in order to facilitate resources allocation and intervention prioritization. One promising opportunity to obtain such an agreed and multinational consensus on such a definition occurred in the hastily convened international US-EU and Asian regional law enforcement meetings in New York and Washington in September 2001. Yet, paradoxically, the crisis necessitating such meetings were the very reason no consensus was even attempted on this occasion:

With the still-smouldering twin Towers visible from our respective emergency meetings, we would have been ridiculed and damned for ever if it became known that we spent even one minute of valuable time trying to obtain an academic and legal definition of terrorism (Europol Director, briefing to Europol staff, October 2001).

Thus at a time when law enforcement was being expected to deal with a new scale of threat in a new way, the creative thinking and consensus that arguably are crucial to the success of international cooperation and collaboration were assumed on the basis of acquiescence and non-dissent rather than negotiated and debated: hardly knowledge-based policing, even less consilience.

This lack of preparation merely prepared the way for strategic impedimenta later on. At an intelligence experts meeting in Moscow in 2004, a delegate from one EU Member State stated that the principal barrier to strategic assessment of terrorism was a lack of definition, asserting in this context that his nation was the leading State in Europe in considering the impact of terrorism and in attempting to combat it. Provoked, the UK and Spanish delegates justifiably pointed to their own expertise, their countries having been subjected to the worst terrorist attacks in Europe for over a generation. The offending remarks were withdrawn. The incident is noteworthy, not for the misunderstanding causing an intense exchange, but for as an example of how the failure to achieve an agreed definition complicates international strategic approaches and cooperation because of the absence of a clear framework.

The preferred Spanish and English model for counterterrorist action, formulated through long years of experience, was that of a five-strand counterterrorist strategy— preparatory action, preventative measures, proactive operations, post-event investigations, and consequence management/community involvement—to be deployed on an EU basis. In this strategic context the elements of particular importance were people, equipment including weapons and explosives, finance, accommodation, storage, transport/travel, and communications.

Simple strategic analysis of al-Qaeda attacks fully revealed the advantages retained by the terrorist, namely the element of surprise and choice of weaponry, the ability to change targeting at will, the option of returning to a target if a previous attack was unsuccessful, and, above all, access to individuals who are prepared to die in order to achieve their operational objectives. Consequently, within the area of counterterrorism and financing, since 2001, EU law enforcement analysis has stipulated that it is essential not just to concentrate upon the suspects, means, and motives, but also to consider the changing nature of the target, and the choice of target being changed at will by the terrorist (Weston, 2004: 78).

Refocusing effort on EU-based multilateral analysis, rather than the bilateral collaboration that had predominated prior to 2001, enhanced this approach. Instead of examining the financing of individual groups within individual countries, effort was redirected towards trying to understand the financing of terrorism generally throughout Europe.

Banking institutions were viewed as potentially important vehicles for fund transfer and therefore were vulnerable to exploitation for terrorist financing purposes. Financial intelligence was exchanged between banks and law enforcement agencies, evolving to produce fewer, but more timely, suspicious transaction reports. This intelligence was integrated in support of a wider strategic intelligence picture being compiled on the trends relating to suspected terrorist cells and their individual members.

TERRORISM AND THE NEXUS WITH ORGANIZED CRIME

The possible nexus between organized crime and terrorism has been, and continues to be, the subject of long-standing academic debate (see for example, Bratton, 2007; Holmes, 2007). The extremes of the debate are epitomized, on the one hand, by the somewhat abrasive assertion of experienced Dutch criminologist Petrus van Duyne who suggested to an international financial crime seminar held in Sofia, Bulgaria in March 2007 (under the aegis of the US EWMI and the Bulgarian Financial Services Authority) that, 'the connection between organized crime and terrorists only exists in the narrow minds of Police officers'; and, on the other hand, the prediction of Schweitzer half a decade ago, who asserted that distinctions between terrorism and organized crime were 'fading fast' and that both groups take advantage of 'breakdowns in State authority to facilitate and continue illicit profitable enterprises' (Schweitzer, 2002; see also Levi, 2003; van Duyne and von Lampe, 2004).

Shelley postulated links between drug-trafficking and terrorism, identifying potential narco-terrorist groups whose activities had political as well as criminal objectives. Later, Shelley identified other organized crime groups making common cause with domestic terrorist organizations, not for political change but for 'destabilising' objectives, nullifying effective government, and enabling criminal groups to continue their widespread activities unimpeded (1999). Shelley's assertions coincided with the works of Makarenko scrutinizing the nexus between organized crime and terrorism.

In simple operational terms, Makarenko identified a key point in her 'common convergence of causes' (2003) where, either in developing, transition, or failing States, domestic terrorist groups make common cause with organized crime elements. In this situation organized crime and terrorism combine to maintain the status quo of the partial breakdown of government and law enforcement, and stultify democratization and economic development in order to perpetuate their activities for either political separatism or criminal profits.

This academic identification of an organized crime-terrorism connection was paralleled by law enforcement strategic analysis. In the aftermath of 9/11 a pan-EU Counterterrorism Task Force was formed, comprising Member States' law enforcement representatives, Europol officials and analysts, and the representatives of the Member States' security services. The Task Force—the first on a pan-EU basis—was inevitably beset by the difficulties regarding information exchange already alluded to above. An additional barrier to effective strategic analysis was the continuing doctrine amongst representatives from the security services of the Member States' within the Task Force that terrorism and serious crime were separate issues, with the perpetrators in each category having no significant intermingling. These difficulties were resolved partially by the reform, realignment and de facto creation of a second EU Counterterrorism Task Force in 2004 based at Europol. Through its work, associations between individuals linked to suspected terrorist organizations and individuals linked to criminal groups became apparent.

A UK practitioner expert offered an unofficial estimate that two-thirds of the organized crime groups in the UK are involved with some form of terrorism (Commander, Metropolitan Police Service, pers comm, March and April 2005). This epithet does not only cover individuals active and wittingly engaging in full-time collusion in terrorism, but also embraces a variety of other associations such as criminality with distant terrorist-group connections and 'one-off opportunist' criminals carrying out services for single payments from representatives of terrorist groups who conceal the identity of their organization. Europol has noted the continued association: '. . .the links are indirect but indisputable. Terrorism is using the ways and paths that are already paced by organized crime' (Europol Senior Strategic Analyst, interview with author, June 2007).

The essentially pragmatic methods of differing terrorist cells within the EU in raising revenue for terrorist purposes have confirmed the trend, particularly evident since late 2004. Professional financial crime and money-laundering has always demonstrated a continuity of modus operandi in the gaining of criminal proceeds and, in the laundering process, the financial structures of interlocked companies and investment vehicles were long established; transaction flows through these institutions were continuous. However, in the area of terrorism, different terrorist cells across the EU countries engage in various forms of low-level criminality to raise funds for their activities and daily expenses. The criminal activities change—in strategic intelligence analysis terms—in a relatively short space of time and there is no consistently preferred method. The funds themselves are transferred quickly, on a short-term basis, by various transfer methods. Fund movements sometimes involve contact with representatives from organized crime groups for mutual short-term enterprises in the area of storing and disposing of funds. This whole trend of pragmatic, short-term criminal fund-raising further corroborates the growing indicators of the nexus between terrorism and criminality.

A GENERATION OF EU STRATEGIC ANALYSIS— POSSIBLE CONCERNS

Over the last two decades law enforcement strategic intelligence has unquestionably made progress. The profession enjoys more resources and personnel, the innovation and implementation of technological and digital aids to handle and deploy massive amounts of data, and an overall acceptance of the value of skillful analysis. However, there have arisen four areas of possible concern.

Criminal to Crime—A Change in Focus

Initially, in keeping with basic law enforcement through prosecution, analysis was termed 'Criminal Intelligence Analysis' and focused on the criminal. Gradually analytical focus expanded then significantly shifted to include analysis of crime, crime areas, even definitions of crime categories, and, as has been outlined, definitions of organized crime groups. Whilst such a shift in concentration is inevitable and enhances the strategic and long-term preventative planning benefits, the original focus of intelligence analysis in law enforcement, that of intelligence being deployed against the criminal(s), should not diminish.

The Possible Diminution of One Essential Analysis Component

The original intelligence cycle, designed to be simple and operationally effective, consists of the five elements: gathering, collation, evaluation, analysis, and dissemination. Arguably, one key element, evaluation of the information prior to analysis, has been relocated within the cycle and its role changed. Evaluations now review the final analytical product and assess possible course(s) of action. The original elements of evaluation was far more fundamental and vital: evaluating the data and ascertaining what reliability could be placed on certain pieces of information after collation but before analysis, in order that to ensure that analytical hypothesis were constructed from reliable information. Even within differing law enforcement agencies where evaluation of incoming information occurs, evaluation systems are not totally standardized. The cardinal maxim holds true that 'analytical technique, no matter how elaborate or eloquent, will not replace good data, or make up for poor or inadequate information' (Inane and Reuses, 1990: 67).

Timescale for Strategic Analysis

Strategic intelligence analysis always has a time-lag deficiency. It is dependent upon raw operational data, which is rarely imparted during the course of the operation. Therefore trend recognition and review is frequently founded upon data up to six months old. On an EU dimension this time lag is inevitably compounded by the transmission of such data from national Member States to Europol, which involves necessary further pre-dissemination sanitization.

In stark terms, operational analysis is based upon piecemeal intelligence. Full real-time operational information is rarely available to the analyst, who must nevertheless formulate real-time hypothesese and intelligence products with data to hand. Whilst this is an intrinsic part of successful operational analysis such data, when appropriately disseminated for strategic purposes, may be incomplete in that significant indicators are missing and strategic trends cannot be fully extrapolated.

Deadlines for Strategic Analysis

The rigidity of political and institutional deadlines for information sits uneasily with full, comprehensive, dynamic strategic analysis. Strategic analysis is a long-term evolving task, taking into account developing trends, necessary reassessments, and re-evaluations. The tasking of compiling reports on a periodic basis, either annually or quarterly for international organizations and national governments, involves strict deadlines which may cut across evolving criminal trends. Therefore the periodic 'snapshot' strategic report may give a distorted or incomplete picture, with the full significance of some trends or developments omitted.

EU-WIDE STRATEGIC INTELLIGENCE ANALYSIS IN RETROSPECT

The areas of concern outlined above, and the failure to identify the emerging Albanian/Kosovar threat, should not detract from the indisputable progress in strategic intelligence analysis that has occurred over the past 20 years within EU law enforcement. This progress has involved:

- handling a sudden influx of large amounts of data regarding the criminality of the hitherto unknown area of Eastern Europe;
- identifying the post-1989 organized crime groups originating from Eastern Europe and their impact upon the EU;
- reassessing the nature, scope and extent of these groups within the overall context of assessing the whole criminal phenomena of organized crime;
- developing and adapting evolving analytical methodologies, so synthesizing with academic development of research methodologies;
- overcoming difficulties of data-gathering, collation, and strategic analysis on an EU-wide scale;
- resolving the weaknesses of static strategic EU situation reports by complementing and supplementing these with the development of EU strategic EU threat assessments;
- responding to the challenges of strategically analysing post-2001 terrorism and its potential impact upon the EU.

Such challenges have been successfully resolved. The ongoing progress in strategic analysis continues to produce added value to law enforcement efforts on a national and EU scale against global organized crime and terrorism. Learning the lessons of the last two decades will sustain future progress.

REFERENCES

ALBANESE, J, *Organized Crime in America* (Cincinnati: Anderson, 1997).

BLACK, B, VAN DER BEKEN, T and DE REUVER, D, *Measuring Organized Crime in Belgium: A Risk-Based Methodology* (Antwerp-Apeldoorn: Maklu, 2000).

BRATTON, W, 'The unintended consequences of September 11th' *Policing: A Journal of Policy and Practice* 1/1 (2007) 21–24.

BUNDERAMT FUR POLIZEI, *Swiss Police Reports* (Bern: Strategic data from Working Group Onkel, Operation Benjamin, Working Group Bakony, 1995).

BUNDESKRIMINALANT, *Organized Crime Situation Report* (Wiedesbaden, Germany, 2004).

CARLILE, Lord, *The Definition of Terrorism* (Cm 7052, London: TSO, 2007).

COUNCIL OF EUROPE, *Organized Crime Situation Report: Focus on the Threat of Economic Crime* (European Commission Octopus Programme, Brussels, 2005).

EUROPOL, *Analytical Guidelines* (The Hague: Europol, 1999).

——, *Annual Report* (The Hague: Europol, 2004).

——, *Organized Crime Threat Assessment* (The Hague: Europol, 2006).

—— MANAGEMENT BOARD, *The Strategy for Europol* (MBS 1342007, 2007).

GRANT, RM, *Contemporary Strategic Analysis* (Oxford: Blackwell Publishing, 2005).

GUNARATNA, R, ed, *The Changing Face of Terrorism* (London: Marshall Cavendish, 2004).

HOLMES, L, ed, *Terrorism, Organized Crime and Corruption* (Cheltenham: Edward Elgar, 2007).

INANE, FAJ and REUSES, E, 'Network analysis' in Andrews, A and Peterson, M, eds, *Criminal Intelligence Analysis* (California: Loomis, 1990) 67–74.

LEVI, M, 'Organizing financial crimes: Breaking the economic power of organized crime groups?' in Siegel, D, van den Bunt, H and Zaitch, D, eds, *Global Organized Crime Trends and Developments* (Studies of Organized Crime Series, Kluwer Academic Publications, 2003).

MAKARENKO, T, *The Crime-Terror Nexus* (London: Hurst, 2003).

SAVONA, E, *European Money Trails* (New Jersey: Harwood Academic Publishers, 1999).

SCHWEITZER, GE, *A Faceless Enemy—The Origins of Modern Terrorism* (Cambridge, Mass: Perseus, 2002).

SHELLEY, L, 'Identifying, counting and categorising transnational organized crime' *Transnational Organized Crime* 5/1 (1999).

SMITH, DC, 'Paragons, pariahs and pirates—a spectrum-based theory of criminal enterprise' *Crime and Delinquency* 26/3 (1999).

VAN DER BEKEN, T and SAVONA, E, *Measuring Organized Crime in Europe: A Feasibility Study of a Risk-based Methodology across the European Union* (Antwerp-Apeldoorn: Maklu, 2004).

VAN DUYNE, P, *The Phantom and Threat of Organized Crime* (London: Kluwer Academic Publications, 1996).

—— and VON LAMPE, K, eds, *Threats and Phantoms of Organized Crime, Corruption and Terrorism* (Nijmegan: Wolf Legal Publications, 2004).

WESTON, K, 'The terrorist threat: the British Police response' in Gunaratna, R, ed, *The Changing Face of Terrorism* (London: Marshall Cavendish 2004) 74–83.

PART III

CASE STUDIES— INTELLIGENCE AND PARTNERSHIP

INTRODUCTION TO PART III: CASE STUDIES—INTELLIGENCE AND PARTNERSHIP

Dr Clive Harfield

In Chapter 4 above, Frank Gregory's exposition of the evolving relationship between British national security structures and the domestic police service coincidentally offered a study of inter-agency partnership. Within the context of failed intelligence-sharing between partners, as highlighted in the murders of Victoria Climbié, Jessica Chapman and Holly Wells, and Naomi Bryant (Laming, 2003; Bichard, 2004; HMIP, 2006), the themes of partnership and intelligence run throughout the government's current vision for community safety (Home Office, 2004): there are 81 references to partnership and 80 to intelligence. To ensure increased effectiveness in neighbourhood policing and community safety, the government proposed the following seven measures, the outcome of which is annotated in italics at the end of each proposal. Much of the work was, of course, already underway before the 2004 White Paper was published:

- A more tightly focused National Policing Plan: *enacted through the Police and Justice Act 2006, section 2 and Schedule 2.*
- A new Code of Practice to help embed the systematic application of the National Intelligence Model: *published (ACPO, 2005).*
- A new grading mechanism for police performance—with new arrangements for rewarding success and addressing under-performance: *undertaken through inspection and engagement with the Home Office Police Standards Unit.*
- A new National Policing Improvement Agency and the rationalization of existing national policing bodies: *enacted through the Police and Justice Act 2006, section 1 and Schedule 1.*
- A review of police force structures: *undertaken, radical proposals for infrastructure rationalization postponed indefinitely* (HMIC, 2005).
- A review of the partnership provisions of the Crime and Disorder Act 1998, undertaken during 2007: *completed but not publicly available at time of writing.*
- Changes to strengthen the membership and role of police authorities: *enacted through the Police and Justice Act 2006, section 2 and Schedule 2.*

(Home Office, 2004:102)

In particular, 'the Government regards the National Intelligence Model as providing a cornerstone on which policing in the 21st century should be built. . . . The

National Intelligence Model can also be used in the context of partnership work to reduce crime and disorder within communities' (Home Office, 2004: 106). The message could not be clearer. But to what extent is partnership working becoming more effective, more intelligent?

The White Paper went on to mention in passing the Greater Manchester Against Crime (GMAC) partnership business model as an approach government 'would like to see taken up more widely' (Home Office, 2004:106). The first contribution in Part III comes from Sarah Lewis of Salford District Council who coordinates the work of the Greater Manchester Community Safety Partnership Team. She examines the working of the GMAC business partnership model to date which is trying to implement an effective intelligence-led partnership based on the NIM and CDRP intelligence analysis.

The sharing of information and intelligence between partners to understand the impact of drug and alcohol abuse in London, the better to inform interventions and intelligent policing, is the subject of the next contribution from the Greater London Alcohol and Drug Alliance (GLADA). The practitioner authors of this study, Laura Juett, Rebecca Smith, and John Grieve, are two senior policy officers from the Greater London Authority as well one of the present editors who served as a former independent Chairperson of GLADA having previously been a Deputy Assistant Commissioner in the Metropolitan Police.

Partnership-working need not necessarily be solely based on inter-agency collaboration. Successful community-safety policing involves partnerships between agencies and the communities they serve, and this means understanding the communities. Adrian Bhatti, a Community and Diversity Officer (CaDO) with Thames Valley Police, takes an innovative look at the relationship between policing and communities through the development of sophisticated community impact assessment methodology. His experiences are informed not only by the diverse demography of the Thames Valley Police area but by the organizational and community learning following the arrest of terrorist suspects in High Wycombe in August 2006 (Thornton and Mason, 2007).

Radicalization as manifested in terrorism reminds us that threats once thought of as largely external and extraordinary have, with increased globalization, become increasingly internal and more commonplace. Together with the threats to economic and social stability posed by transnational organized crime, this highlights the need for effective partnership and intelligence-working across national borders. The next two contributions to this section explore perspectives on transnational and international partnership and intelligence.

In relation to bilateral relationships Ludo Block, a former Dutch police liaison officer in Moscow, uses his own experiences of the practicalities involved in intelligence and partnership-working to illustrate both what works and what does not work. It is a case study that exposes the rhetoric of international law enforcement cooperation to the spotlight of reality through its discussion of how intelligence is understood, how liaison is understood, and how a liaison officer posted overseas deals with the context and culture into which he or she is temporarily immersed.

The final contribution is the presentation of a small-scale study undertaken at Europol exploring within the international arena some of the issues raised by a previous study of intelligence-working within English police forces (Kleiven, 2007). Both authors, Kleiven and Harfield, have practitioner experience in transnational policing and international law enforcement cooperation. If international intelligence cooperation is to be effective, there has to be some common understanding and some accessible collaborative mechanisms. This, in part, was the vision of Europol. The extent to which the vision has been or can be realized is raised by this exploratory reconnaissance into the understanding of intelligence at Europol which, quite independently, corroborates some of the practical experiences recounted elsewhere in this volume by Ridley.

In combination, these contributions offer the reader an anthology of partnership and intelligence-working case studies in a variety of contexts and structures. This diversity inhibits the extent to which significant like-for-like comparative analysis can be undertaken but it serves to reinforce the point that intelligence and partnership are terms which are invested with a multiplicity of meanings. The progress apparent within the domestic arena is episodic and individual, but progress there has been and although the 2004 White Paper offered little more than exhortation, individual projects have demonstrated what can be achieved. The extent to which the GMAC business partnership model could be replicated elsewhere rather depends on the relationship between police areas and CDRPs. The debate about police force mergers is dormant but, given the 250-year history of policing in England and Wales, will undoubtedly reawaken. Had mergers gone ahead in 2006, there may have been greater scope immediately to translate the GMAC model elsewhere. Could approaching policing provision from a functional community-safety partnership perspective rather than from an organizational-form perspective be the catalyst that eventually re-engages politicians, practitioners, and public about whether a still largely Victorian infrastructure is the best way of delivering twenty-first-century policing? The GLADA experience reveals what can be achieved in the open-source arena, providing the always valuable reminder that intelligence is not confined to material and data that has to be sought and gathered surreptitiously; and at a time when the value of community intelligence, largely ignored in the original implementation of the NIM (Kleiven, 2007), is being reassessed now that the al-Qaeda threat may be more likely to come from resident converts than from external agents, the learning offered by the CaDO model about approaches to understanding the community is all important.

The Dutch/Russian and Europol studies illustrate how intelligence and partnership working in the international arena inevitably involve the collision of practical policing (and, it should not be forgotten, due process) with diplomacy, international relations, and foreign policy (Bigo, 2000). Here the actors and practitioners still have much to learn about their own professional community and how it can work more effectively. That having been achieved, the professional community will then have to engage with the wider public community to ensure that international law enforcement and intelligence cooperation does not fall into governance gaps, a consequence which would deny the opportunity to secure public support and confidence in such international and transnational working.

REFERENCES

ACPO, *The Recording and Dissemination of Intelligence Material: Code of Practice. Police* (London: ACPO, 2005).

BICHARD, M, *The Bichard Inquiry Report* (House of Commons, London: TSO, 2004).

BIGO, D, 'Liaison officers in Europe: New officers in the European security field' in Sheptycki, J, ed, *Issues in Transnational Policing* (London: Routledge, 2000) 67–99.

HMIC, *Closing the Gap: A Review of the 'Fitness for Purpose' of the Current Structure of Policing in England and Wales* (London: HMIC, 2005).

HMIP, *An Independent Review of a Serious Further Offence Case: Anthony Rice* (London: HM Inspectorate of Probation, 2006).

HOME OFFICE, *Building Communities, Beating Crime: a Better Police Service for the 21st Century* (Cm 6360, London: TSO, 2004).

KLEIVEN, M, 'Where's the intelligence in the national intelligence model?' *International Journal of Police Science and Management* 9/3 (2007) 257–273.

LAMING, L, *The Victoria Climbié Inquiry* (London: TSO, 2003).

THORNTON, S and MASON, L, 'Community cohesion in High Wycombe: A case study of Operation Overt' *Policing: A Journal of Policy and Practice* 1/1 (2007) 57–60.

11

INTELLIGENT PARTNERSHIP

Sarah Lewis

INTRODUCTION

This chapter describes a model for partnership-working that has been developed by the Greater Manchester Community Safety Partnership Team (GMCSPT). Application of the model to partnership-working has led to collaborative successes and has identified ways in which partnership-working can be improved. With recent government emphasis on locally delivered neighbourhood policing in partnership with other community-safety actors (Home Office, 2004; 2008), the innovation and initiative being developed in Manchester may offer food for thought for agencies in other geographical areas planning knowledge-based collaboration and intelligent partnership.

The GMCSPT works closely in partnership with the ten local authorities within the Greater Manchester urban area (each of which hosts a corresponding Crime and Disorder Reduction Partnership (CDRP)), Greater Manchester Police, the Greater Manchester Fire and Rescue Service, Greater Manchester Probation (local office of the national Probation Service), the Greater Manchester PCTS, together with the Greater Manchester Police Authority and the Greater Manchester Passenger Transport Executive. Although with no statutory obligations or responsibilities, the GMCSPT is, in essence, a meta-CDRP. The partnership model is called Greater Manchester Against Crime (GMAC, available at <http://www.gmac.org.uk>) and has been formally evaluated by a team led by Tim John at the request of the GMCSPT (John et al, 2006). The Home Office has recently expressed interest in the project and has commissioned its own review of the partnership initiative, which is being undertaken by the Jill Dando Institute for Crime Science at the time of writing. The partnership was established in 2003 with the strategic purpose of building 'a structure whereby a multi-agency approach across ten local authorities can contribute to a pooled resource for the conurbation' (John et al, 2006: 1). The discussion that follows considers the background, structure, and method for delivering the GMAC approach in relation to the collection, analysis, and use of information in order to achieve the goals of reduced crime and increased safety of the public. Underpinning the work of GMAC is the Partnership Business Model (PBM), which will be described in detail together with the key decision-making documents in relation to crime and disorder: the Greater Manchester Strategic Assessment, the Opportunity Strategy, and Delivery Plan. The chapter concludes with a description for the future planned developments for GMAC and the GMCSPT.

The GMAC PBM is an initiative that seeks to extend the potential of the National Intelligence Model in the partnership arena. The National Intelligence Model was launched in 2000 and it aims to be:

a means of organizing knowledge and information in such a way that the best possible decisions can be made about the use of resources. It ensures that actions are coordinated between the various levels of delivery and that lessons are continually learnt and fed back into the system (John and Maguire, 2003:38).

Under the National Policing Plan (originally enacted under the Police Reform Act 2002, s 1, now replaced by the National Community Safety Plan), the Home Secretary required of all police forces in England and Wales that the National Intelligence Model be adopted and implemented by April 2004. It was therefore timely in Greater Manchester to seek to involve partners in order to strengthen the delivery of the model in a partnership context. The Association of Greater Manchester Authorities (AGMA) had produced a paper 'Sharing the Vision' which detailed a partnership approach to tackling crime and disorder, setting out a clear direction for partnership working; it was these two developments that set the scene (2003).

Prior to the creation of the GMCSPT, partnership-working was taking place across Greater Manchester but was working to 10 different community-safety structures and processes, each of the ten local authorities hosting its own statutory CDRP. There was a collective sense from partners that this could be done better and that there was scope for coordination. The initiative was intended to build upon successful local working arrangements and to bring real benefits for the public by supporting organizations' key business objectives in relation to community safety and helping in the reduction of crime and the fear of crime.

THE PARTNERSHIP BUSINESS MODEL

The GMAC PBM complements provisions within and provides a delivery mechanism for key government legislation and policy including the Police and Justice Act 2006, the Crime and Disorder Act Review (Home Office, 2007), Local Area Agreements, and localized delivery of public service. The model offers a common method for Crime and Disorder Reduction Partnerships (CDRPs) to manage their core business towards achieving their desired outcomes. In particular the model provides for:

- the collection, analysis and interpretation of information relevant to the business of a partnership;
- a method for presenting the information to Partnership Business Groups (PBGs) in order that decisions can be made, priorities for action set, and resources appropriately targeted;
- a logical annual sequence of meetings with a clear relationship between strategic and tactical groups responsible for delivering action;
- a common business model that operates at a local and Greater Manchester level with a clear and beneficial relationship between the two levels.

The common annual cycle of meetings is structured to fit with business planning cycles and budget-forecast meetings for all the partners. The model provides a clear and beneficial relationship between local priorities and action and complementary activity at the Greater Manchester level. This in turn fits into local authority and Greater Manchester arrangements and also national planning frameworks such as those in the CDRP review (Home Office, 2007). This complementary activity at local and Greater Manchester level relies on information and analytical products transferring easily and logically between the levels. As crime and disorder manifest themselves at a local level, GMAC, via a consistency of process across all ten CDRPs, provides an effective method of working across borders, to share information, disseminate effective practice, and take common action where necessary or desirable.

The Greater Manchester groups need to assimilate and consider the common priorities and issues of ten local-partnership arrangements in order to add value and support local delivery in the most effective way. There is enough commonality for this to be achievable. Where there are individual priorities unique to a given authority, GMAC provides the mechanism through which these can be accommodated or through which conflicting interests can be mediated. To fulfil this, the annual cycle of meetings at the Greater Manchester level is offset by at least one month to create the time to understand and present information to the Greater Manchester Partnership Business Group.

The GMAC model is built upon, and its continued development depends upon, the cooperation and enthusiasm of a range of key stakeholders. The ten CDRPs across Greater Manchester are all at differing stages in relation to alignment to the PBM. Where CDRPs are better aligned there is the beginning of some evidence of a link to improved performance, in particular around delivery to Public Service Agreement 1 (at the time of writing this focuses on a reduction in the volume of key crimes but the PSAs are subject to review and will be reconfigured from April 2008). Implementation of the model in two of the most aligned CDRPs has in particular resulted in ever-improving partnership relationships and continuously improved data-share leading to improved tasking and coordination of the relevant resources within the partnership. Cross-agency development of innovative solutions has been achieved using improved analytical products. There is enhanced intra-partnership accountability and tangible outcomes have been achieved in terms of crime reduction and public perceptions.

The Home Office commissioned-review being conducted by the Jill Dando Institute will assess PBM compliance across the ten CDRPS, and the outcome of this will be individual action plans for each partnership to implement in order to improve this area of their work. Additionally, a Greater Manchester-wide action plan will be compiled that the GMCSPT will take forward and develop across Greater Manchester.

CRITICAL SUCCESS FACTORS

The PBM is underpinned by five critical success factors:

1. Quality data
2. Effective IT solutions

3. Skilled and equipped strategic analysts
4. Core decision-making documents
5. Effective use of resources-tasking and coordinating

Quality Data

The availability and quality of data upon which CDRP Strategic Assessments and other key documents are based is of clear importance in accurately driving the business of each Partnership Business Group.[1] The data hub is hosted by Greater Manchester Police and networked to the ten CDRPS. It acts as a central repository for information which is integrated into a commercially available analytical solution (i2) that permits mapping analysis, network analysis, and data mining. The data hub represents a significant investment in drawing together anonymous data-sets from a range of agencies, including Greater Manchester Fire and Rescue, Greater Manchester Passenger Transport Executive, Greater Manchester Police, the probation arm of the national Offender Management Service, and Greater Manchester Ambulance Service. The data-sets also include neighbourhood profiles, lifestyle, census data, and crime pattern analysis.

The data hub has been described as a 'complex database-solution using geo-coding and postcodes as a common reference with common information entities to search preloaded data' (Rigby, 2005). Maintenance of the partnership data, including collection, cleaning, and loading is currently contracted to AGMA, which provides the independence required to reassure partners that they have access to the shared data and are not merely providing data to the police as host agency for the hub.

Effective IT Solutions

As stated above, the purpose-built data hub is hosted by GMP and networked out to the ten Community Safety Teams. A range of commercial software tools are utilized in analysis and problem-solving, including: *SPSS*, a statistical analysis package; *i2*, a software package that holds partnership data in one location; *Mapinfo*, a GIS mapping tool; *Crisis*, used for data manipulation; *Hotspot Detective*, for analysing hotspots; *Crimestat*, a spatial statistical tool free from the internet; and *Georeveal* studio, a tool that allows analysts to author and publish data on maps. But ultimately IT solutions are just tools and therefore only as effective as the use to which they are put either by individual agencies or partnerships.

Skilled and Equipped Strategic Analysts

Five strategic analysts are located in the GMCSPT offices at Greater Manchester Police HQ and 12 located across the 10 CDRPs (employed by GMP and local authorities respectively). A buddying system has aligned each of the five GMP HQ-based analysts with two local authority counterparts based within the local authorities. There

---

[1] Currently separate from the Strategic Assessments required under NIM implementation, CDRPs are required to undertake annual Strategic assessments from April 2008, under Home Office guidance contained in *Delivering safer communities: a guide to effective partnership working* (2008). GM partnerships have been doing their own Strategic Assessments for the past four years and a GMAC conurbation-wide document has also been completed for the last four years.

are 13 additional users located within partnerships (for example, operational tactical analysts working within GMP and additional local authority analysts with a role-specific need to access the data hub). The analysts are line-managed by Community Safety Managers and GMP Local Authority Liaison Offices, thereby ensuring the link between the two areas of work. All analysts are fully trained, attending a high-level intensive two-week training programme delivered by the GMP training section plus training delivered by the Jill Dando Institute, University College London. The analysts have access to CADRAD (the Crime and Disorder Research and Development group co-chaired by GMCSPT and AGMA), a monthly meeting framework which provides support and supervision in addition to access to a virtual intranet workgroup that provides the opportunity to share good practice and discuss common problematic areas of work. Lastly, thinking and reading time is encouraged to aid their development.

The central partnership teams experience has illustrated that a project-management approach to producing documents such as the Strategic Assessment provides the support and guidance that analysts benefit from. It is also recognized that the work involved in managing the business process is significant. Some CDRPs have appointed a 'Partnership Business Coordinator' to effectively manage the activity and business process. The analytical teams benefit directly as the posts fill a gap that existed between post-holders. It also addresses in part the sometimes isolated role of the analyst and offers them support, guidance, and supervision from someone who understands their role.

Core Decision-making Documents

The CDRP Strategic Assessments are the key documents within the GMAC process, providing analysed data, and are the documents that form the basis for the opportunity strategy and delivery plan. Via the use of strategic analysis the 'bigger picture' can be captured accurately. It provides the ability to critically review how the business of crime and disorder is undertaken, and enables the identification of high, medium, and low priority neighbourhoods and themes. This can be undertaken particularly by the use of the Vulnerable Localities Index (VLI), a method for measuring indicators of community cohesiveness whereby information from a number of data-sets is linked to a geographic information system which is then used to identify localities where cohesiveness is at risk. Priorities for partners can be accurately identified and prioritized and crime can therefore be identified in the context of communities, linking quantitative and qualitative data geographically.

Whilst initially a model for 'strategic alignment and business planning', GMAC has provided the environment in many CDRPs for operationally relevant, timely intelligence sharing that enables the coordination of a wide range of partners' resources. This has led to the production of a monthly Partnership 'Tactical Assessment'.

Effective Use of Resources—Tasking and Coordinating

A recognized difficulty with the National Intelligence Model on which the PBM is based is that language and terminology had become seen as a barrier to implementation at force, local, and individual levels. Even when the model started to be embedded, the technical jargon used throughout the model was often viewed as obstructive rather than conducive to gaining an understanding (John and Maguire, 2004).

Considerable efforts were therefore made to adjust the language used within GMAC to avoid similar difficulties, while retaining the overall structure and process. In particular the NIM 'Tasking and Coordinating Groups' are renamed 'Partnership Business Groups'. These groups are responsible for setting priorities, developing delivery plans, tasking, coordinating resources, performance management delivery, and identification of effective practice. Currently across Greater Manchester, partnerships are at differing stages in terms of integrating the structures for delivering partnership-working, with some still running dual police and community-safety structures and others delivering to one single structure. In the CDRPs that are better aligned to the PBM, they are operating to the single structure and meeting-cycle, which involves all partners in the delivery to the partnership agenda.

THE STRATEGIC ASSESSMENT

Although the importance of the data hub cannot be underestimated, the content of the Strategic Assessment should not be limited to the hub; a process of local commissioning enables the documents to provide local and/or specific information to fully inform the prioritization process. The Greater Manchester Strategic Assessment (produced by GMCSPT) covers issues that have been identified by the majority of local partnerships across Greater Manchester and/or have been, or could potentially be, coordinated, developed, and delivered at a Greater Manchester level. Additionally, this years' Strategic Assessment has utilized a range of colleagues—experts in their field—not only as critical readers but expert advisers, to advise during the compilation of the document. Throughout the document an extensive range of data and sources are used to provide detailed analysis of key issues. Clear links are made to the local strategic assessments. On a national level, and particularly within the context of the Crime and Disorder Review (completed in September 2007) and the requirement upon CDRPs to undertake Strategic Assessments (Police and Justice Act 2006, ss 19–22 and Schedule 9), the Strategic Assessment at both a local and Greater Manchester level can be viewed as making a significant contribution to developing the knowledge-base upon which CDRP decisions are informed and taken.

The GMAC PBM has therefore placed Greater Manchester ahead of the game in terms of the infrastructure to support such developments.

THE OPPORTUNITY STRATEGY

The local Strategic Assessments are produced in June of each of each year with a six-month review in December. The Greater Manchester document is produced in September; the recommendations from the assessment help to form the 'Opportunity Strategy'. The intervention opportunities fall into three broad categories which capture all aspects of partnership activity. These are prevention, information gathering, and enforcement. These priorities are detailed in the Opportunity Strategy. This document is used to communicate priorities throughout an organization and may also be useful as a means of communicating with local communities. The Opportunity Strategy will describe the priority action but will not detail the steps to be taken to implement or deliver the activity.

THE DELIVERY PLAN

The Delivery Plan falls out of the Greater Manchester Strategic Assessment and the Opportunity Strategy, and at both a Greater Manchester and local level is used tactically to aid local delivery. The Delivery Plan gives a more detailed explanation of how the priorities for the partnership will be delivered, formatted in a clear and concise manner. The delivery plan is owned by the Partnership Steering Group and is reviewed on a regular basis to ensure that actions are completed in a timely manner and any difficulties or blocks to delivery are addressed rapidly. Clear timescales and leads for each recommendation are highlighted in the plan. Each year the team endeavours to ensure that the plan is 'owned' by partnership colleagues as there can be a tendency for the delivery to fall to the GMAC central team.

FUTURE DEVELOPMENT

The GMAC model provides a clear framework based on a proven business model. By following the key steps in the model outlined above a standard method of working is achieved which allows for flexibility but respects the integrity of existing structures. The future of GMAC needs to focus upon an increase in public accountability and confidence, addressing the issues that are raised in the Crime and Disorder Reform Programme. This question of public accountability and confidence will in part be covered via the implementation of the Single Point Project, a web-based mapping system which is a complement to existing analytical resources and processes. The system has been developed with an external software company and designed to be of maximum use to decision-makers in the GMAC Partnership. It is easy to use, comprising powerful and flexible maps which display a range of partner data-sets for use by practitioners through a web browser. The project was officially launched for practitioners to use on 15 October 2007 with a planned roll out for public use by mid-2008.

PARTNERSHIP AND THE MANCHESTER EXPERIENCE

Inter-agency partnership has long been a cornerstone of successive administrations' approach to community safety and policing. The Morgan Report (Standing Committee on Crime Prevention, 1991) reasoned that crime prevention and community safety were not the sole responsibility of the police service. Current policy regarding community safety was outlined in *Building Communities, Beating Crime*, which calls for 'more effective partnership working' (Home Office, 2004: 5). Byrne and Pease remind us that partnership is not an end in itself, accepting as they do so that they risk allegations of political heresy by suggesting 'partnership working is not always appropriate' (2003: 295). Within the wider context of political emphasis on partnership, their paper helpfully summarizes three partnership pitfalls that the GMAC project has sought to avoid (Byrne and Pease, 2003: 296):

• a high ratio of talk to action;
• lengthy delays between decisions to act and action;
• varying enthusiasm for partnership-working among local authority departments with people-processing departments generally more keen than those who make physical changes.

Manchester has hosted significant and successful innovation in local authority partnership in a variety of arenas (see for instance Evans, 2007). This is no different in the field of community safety and policing, as the GMAC initiative has demonstrated. There are still areas for improvement, including the need to achieve universal compliance with the GMAC model in terms of coordinating meeting and planning schedules and of properly distinguishing between strategic and tactical contexts and content. The central partnership team is clear that business-planning for the coming twelve months must include working closely with our CDRP partners to ensure that there is a clear understanding of the model and that appropriate guidance and support is provided for CDRPs to ensure consistent implementation and application. The outcome of the Jill Dando Institute of Crime Science Review of Partnerships, commissioned by the Home Office, will assist greatly in this process.

In terms of community safety, the outcome to date has been encouraging. Comparison with BCUs across the north-west region (see Lancashire Constabulary BCS Tracker Tool available at <http://www.lancashire.police.uk/index.php?id=680>), reveal that four of the 10 CDRPs in the Greater Manchester urban area have particularly enhanced their performance since adoption of the partnership business model, and none have demonstrated poor performance overall. In terms specifically of recorded crime, three of the ten CDRPs have witnessed notable reductions whilst the others are demonstrating an acceptable level of performance.

There is a considerable amount of effective and promising multi-agency practice taking place across Greater Manchester; Bolton CDRP, located in the north-west of Manchester, have made significant inroads into addressing crime rates. Bolton's neighborhood policing teams do not just comprise police staff but widen as 'virtual teams' to include housing officers, environmental services staff, and community-safety development officers, and many others who, thanks to the shared intelligence and information they jointly hold, are in the right places, at the right time, in the right numbers, responding to the needs of local people and local communities. Not only have crime levels decreased by over a third, but some types of crime, such as burglary, have fallen by 65 per cent. More pleasing are the reductions in perceptions of antisocial behaviour and local drug dealing which have also halved. Bolton's multi-agency evidence-based and intelligence-led approach, and subsequent achievements in tackling the issues that matter most to local people, have undoubtedly contributed to its Beacon Status award for 'Preventing and Tackling Anti-Social Behaviour' (Beacon Awards 2007–8), one of only four in the country and the only one on the North.

Additionally, Bolton have been awarded Beacon Status for their approach to 'Reducing Reoffending' in the Beacon Awards 2008–9, and are one of four national 'Beacons' in this category. The application of GMAC PBM is a core factor in the partnership success and recognition for 'Excellence in Public Service'.

The successes achieved and the lessons being learned through the work of the Greater Manchester Community Safety Partnership Team are an example of consilient thinking in practice, articulated through the CDRP model for enhancing community safety. A work in progress, it illustrates what can be achieved through strategic partnership-working.

REFERENCES

AGMA, *Sharing the Vision* (Manchester: Association of Greater Manchester Authorities, 2003).

BYRNE, S and PEASE, K, 'Crime reduction and community safety' in Newburn, T, ed, *Handbook of Policing* (Devon: Willan Publishing, 2003) 286–310.

EVANS, B, 'The politics of partnership: urban regeneration in New East Manchester' *Public Policy and Administration* 22/2 (2007) 201–215.

HOME OFFICE, *Building Communities, Beating Crime* (Cm 6360, London: TSO, 2004).

——, *Delivering Safer Communities: A Guide to Effective Partnership Working* (London: Home Office, September 2007).

——, *Neighbourhood Policing Pledge* (London: Home Office, March 2008).

JOHN, T and MAGUIRE, M, 'Rolling-out the national intelligence model: key challenges' in Bullock, K and Tilley, N, eds, *Crime Reduction and Problem-Oriented Policing* (Devon: Willan Publishing, 2003).

—— and ——, *The National Intelligence Model: Early Implementation Experience In Three Police Force Areas* (Working Paper Series No 50, Cardiff: University of Wales, 2004).

——, Morgan, C and Rogers, C, *The GMAC Partnership Business Model: An Independent Evaluation* (Treforest: University of Glamorgan, 2006).

RIGBY, BV, *A Review of the GMAC Partnership Business Model Structures, Processes and Personnel Used in the Production of the Local Strategic Assessments Across the Greater Manchester Crime and Disorder Partnerships* (Manchester, 2005).

STANDING CONFERENCE ON CRIME PREVENTION, *Safer Communities: The Local Delivery of Crime Prevention through the Partnership Approach (The Morgan Report)* (London: Home Office, 1991).

12

OPEN-SOURCE INTELLIGENCE —A CASE STUDY

GLADA: 'LONDON: THE HIGHS AND LOWS' 2003 AND 2007

Laura Juett, Rebecca Smith, and Professor John GD Grieve CBE QPM

INTRODUCTION

This chapter considers intelligent policing in its widest sense. It describes the approach and methodology used by the Greater London Alcohol and Drug Alliance (GLADA) to develop robust evidence-based reports in relation to the impact of drug and alcohol use in London. It provides detailed discussion on the challenges and benefits of partnership-working as a route to intelligent policing. The factors that contribute to crime and disorder are complex and therefore the police must have tools at their disposal that do justice to that complexity, bringing together a wide range of perspectives on the same set of issues, and melding them to create a complete picture. These tools support intelligent policing which is empathetic and proactive, rather than reactionary.

OPEN-SOURCE INTELLIGENCE AND CONSILIENT THINKING

Open-source intelligence is any source of information that is readily available. Such sources of intelligence are often overlooked yet provide vital evidence when attempting to paint the real picture and tell the real story. It is in bringing together open-source intelligence from a variety of sources that a depth of understanding and ideas for action can be achieved. The police have recognized the value of open-source intelligence for some time. Yet there was and continues to be some caution about this approach. The juxtaposition of these three words has produced shudders from officers working in this area because of the implications for opening up and making less threatening other aspects of intelligence (Grieve, 1998 and 2004).

Effective use of intelligence from a wide range of sources can, and should, lead to 'consilient thinking'. Consilient thinking refers to a process in which a theory from one discipline is used to inform the ideas of another. It is derived from the word 'consilience' meaning unity of knowledge.

The value of consilient thinking was most recently illustrated in *The Ghost Map* (Johnson, 2006), where the central characters analyse patterns and connections (including human experience) from various sources to identify the cause of cholera outbreaks in nineteenth-century London. In his book, Johnson reminds us not just about the value of combining knowledge and experience, but the value of local community intelligence and local experts. Johnson referred to 'social intelligence' and its value in challenging what we believe—in this instance that cholera was not caused by contaminated air but by contaminated water.

Consilient thinking suggests that knowledge is best generated by bringing people from different disciplines and experiences to work together thereby creating connections not previously conceived. Ultimately, consilient thinking can provide clarity—an ability to see the patterns and causes and connections across disciplines and knowledge bases.

Open-source intelligence and consilient thinking are both central to GLADA's approach to reviewing and updating the evidence-base on the level and impact of drug and alcohol use in London. London is often dubbed the 'drugs capital' of the UK. The city plays an important part in the global drugs trade and is a significant market and centre of consumption. Alcohol too is consumed widely in the city and plays a significant role in London's night-time economy. Relying on open-source intelligence and aiming towards consilient thinking are obvious choices when attempting to understand the complexities of a city like London and issues like alcohol and drugs.

THE LONDON CONTEXT

London is the most populous city in Western Europe, home to over 7.5 million people and is densely populated with nearly 4,800 people per square kilometre. It is one of the most ethnically diverse cities in the world. Alongside New York and Tokyo, London is often described as a 'global city': a place that has strong cultural, political, and economic links to communities across the globe and that has a tangible and direct effect on global affairs. London is a place where humanity's diversity comes together and is celebrated as the 'world in one city' (Sassen, 1991).

Currently over 30 per cent of Londoners are from non-white ethnic groups. Londoners practice 14 faiths and speak over 300 different languages. The ethnic and cultural make-up of London is constantly changing and evolving. Figures suggest that over the next 15 years the proportion of Londoners from non-white ethnic groups will continue to grow.[1]

London is the economic centre of the United Kingdom and a significant contributor to the national and global economies. It is hardly surprising then that it has the

---

[1] Greater London Alcohol and Drug Alliance, *London: the Highs and the Lows 2* (London: GLA, 2007).

greatest proportion of high disposable-income households in England. Yet despite this great concentration of wealth, three of the five most deprived boroughs in England are in London and 41 per cent of London's children are living in poverty (London Child Poverty Commission, 2007).

This mix of people with wide-ranging ethnic and cultural backgrounds, and the extremes of wealth and deprivation means that London is vibrant and cosmopolitan but also a city that faces many challenges, of which the harm caused by alcohol and drugs is one.

THE MAYOR AND THE GREATER LONDON ALCOHOL AND DRUG ALLIANCE (GLADA)

The Greater London Authority (GLA) provides a unique form of regional government for London—made up of a publicly elected Mayor and Assembly. The Mayor has a duty to promote economic and social development in London. Improving health, promoting equality, and creating sustainable communities are all key priorities, as is community safety, including policing in its widest sense.

Following his election in 2000, Mayor Ken Livingstone, sought to improve real and perceived safety and to show leadership in reducing the harmful effects of alcohol and drugs in the capital. He aimed to reduce the number of drug and alcohol related crimes, the number of injuries and deaths arising from drug and alcohol misuse, and to improve the availability of support and treatment services for all of London's diverse communities.

The Mayor acknowledged that London's complexity means that thoughtful and innovative approaches are often required to achieve change. He identified partnership action as the best way to meet the enduring challenges that drugs and alcohol present. To this end, in 2002 he established a new strategic partnership, the Greater London Alcohol and Drug Alliance, GLADA.[2] GLADA is a network of networks, a grouping of organizations and agencies with responsibilities in addressing the various challenges associated with drug and alcohol use. Members come from the health, criminal justice, treatment, and voluntary and community sectors. The Mayor appoints an independent chair to the partnership, a symbol of its autonomous status.

GLADA aims to address strategic pan-London issues through partnership working. It seeks to provide added value by addressing priorities that are not fully dealt with through local structures or through a single agency. Its strength is its independence and the rich breadth of disciplines, knowledge, experience, and diversity of its members. They work together to identify strategic priorities and areas where they can affect change, or at the least develop a shared understanding of the issues.

The diversity of its knowledge, opinion, and experience makes GLADA an ideal vehicle for consilient thinking. One of GLADA's guiding principles has always been to

---

[2] The members of GLADA are: Adfam, London Councils, Government Office for London, Greater London Authority, London Alliance of Service Users, London Area Prisons Drug Strategy Directorate, London Drug and Alcohol Network, London Drug Policy Forum, London Probation Service, Metropolitan Police Service, National Treatment Agency (London Region), London Regional Public Health Group, NHS London, the National Addiction Centre, and The Federation.

base all decisions on evidence and continuously review the nature and impact of alcohol and drug use. In this way, the partnership aims to dispel myths and stereotypes and bring clarity to debate in this area of policy-making.

A CASE STUDY—LONDON: THE HIGHS
AND LOWS 2003 AND 2007

OVERVIEW

Following its formation in 2002, one of GLADA's first priorities was to establish an accurate picture of the nature and impact of drug use in the capital. The partnership recognized that policy and practice in this area can be informed not by evidence but by anecdote, prejudice, and a sensationalist media. The two editions of *London: the Highs and the Lows* (2003, 2007) (hereafter 'Highs and Lows') pull together information from different sources to provide a reliable evidence base.

The first Highs and Lows report was published in 2003 and concentrated on issues associated with drug misuse. The second edition, published in 2007, covered both drugs and alcohol, and future editions will continue to cover this broader range of substances. The four-year gap between the publications of the two reports allowed for long-term mapping of patterns and trends in the level and impact of substance misuse. It is envisaged that this frequency of reporting will continue to ensure that each report captures any significant changes in drug and alcohol use and impact rather than year-on-year fluctuations.

PRODUCING THE REPORTS—BARRIERS AND SUCCESSES

The Highs and Lows project teams brought together representatives from nine different organizations which work on aspects of drug and alcohol use in London. They included representatives from strategic governance and policy organizations such as the Government Office for London, the Greater London Authority (GLA), London Councils, and the London Drug Policy Forum; operational organizations such as the National Treatment Agency, London Probation Service, and the Metropolitan Police Service (MPS); and from health information specialists, the London Health Observatory.

At the beginning of each process, the project team started out by drawing up a basic framework, outlining the sections to be included in the report, and which organizations would be able to provide the information required in each section. Although the structure outlined in this initial framework changed over the course of the project, it was essential to set out the intended shape of the report at its inception in order to facilitate discussion between project team members, and to reach a shared understanding about the aims of the project.

The various organizations involved provided information in quite different ways. The strategic policy organizations mostly provided material that was already in the public domain. This included publicly available reports such as the General House-hold Survey for England and the British Crime Survey as well as regional and national strategies such as the Mayor's Best Practice Guidance to Managing the Night Time Economy and the Home Office's National Drug Strategy. These organizations also provided commentary on the implementation of strategies, noting any particular challenges and opportunities that these strategies presented.

In contrast, the organizations that have a more operational role, such as the MPS were able to offer raw data that had not previously appeared in the public domain. This data was sourced primarily from routine monitoring and performance management processes. The inclusion of this depth of data was essential to the rich-ness and currency of the report. Much of the data included in the final version of the Highs and the Lows 2 (published in January 2007) described activity up until late 2006.

Sharing this current data posed some problems for the organizations involved. Standard organizational sign-off procedures had to be followed in all cases before the data was released for publication. This meant that there was often a time lag between when the data was originally put forward for inclusion and when it was officially released. At times this time lag affected the analysis that could be conducted. Given that the different sets of data worked together to paint a fuller picture, uncertainties about the inclusion of particular pieces of evidence affected the analysis of evidence from other sources. The project team mitigated against this by keeping close track of how certain pieces of data related to others and highlighting those areas of the report that had to be kept consistent with one another.

There were also sensitivities about one organization's data being analysed, or re-analysed, and then published by other organizations—in this case GLADA and the Mayor of London. It is usual practice for organizations to aim to present data in a format that shows their work in a favourable and positive light. However, for the GLADA reports, the primary aim was to present robust and reliable information with analysis that was to be completely impartial. The project team discussed these neces-sities at the outset and reached a joint understanding about the nature of the analysis and commentary that would accompany the data, and agreed that the Mayor would publish the reports, on behalf of GLADA. Team members also communicated this to all contributors. It was important to establish that the GLA had final editorial control of the published document, but also to regularly circulate drafts of the document to all contributors well in advance of the final publication date. This allowed any con-cerns about data inclusions and exclusions and analysis to be discussed throughout the process.

The organizations involved in the preparation of both Highs and Lows reports contributed their data in a spirit of goodwill and mutual trust. Early in each proc-ess the project teams agreed that bringing their data-sets and experiences together and presenting them in a GLADA/Mayoral document would allow them to say more than they could individually. This allowed the Mayor to use his unique voice to high-light and raise awareness about issues, challenges, opportunities, myths, or data gaps in a way that no one organization could do. This agreement was perhaps the most important aspect of consilient thinking for the projects as it allowed the reports to become holistic overviews of the level and impact of drug and alcohol use in London, rather than collections of discrete data-sets. This is the key advantage of the partnership approach that GLADA exemplifies.

The highly collaborative approach described above could have led to fairly weak recommendations for future work if the authors had been reticent about highlighting the shortcomings of their partners. However, this was not the case with the Highs and Lows reports. The 2007 Highs and Lows report included a full set of recommendations to those working in the alcohol and drug fields about how responses and service provision could be improved. Again, it was the way the information was openly and positively shared that made this possible. The project team adopted a 'no surprises' policy so that all partners had early notification of recommendations that were relevant to them. This did not mean that partners had the opportunity to change the recommendations, but rather that they were involved in the thinking, and made aware of all decisions well before publication.

WHAT DO THE TWO 'HIGHS AND LOWS' REPORTS TELL US?

Both Highs and Lows reports presented an array of data that had been collated by different organizations to serve different purposes. The data was collected at varying levels ie national, London-wide, sub-regional (eg Inner or Outer London), and at local authority level. Thus, it was imperative to be clear about the population covered by any particular set of data. It also meant that a great deal of care was required when making comparisons across data-sets, as often they referred to quite different populations.

It was essential that the analysis in each report was rich enough to convey the complexity of drug and alcohol issues. Equally important was the need for clarity and accessibility. Achieving this balance required careful decision-making about which levels of analysis were most appropriate for each topic—for example, whether it would be most useful to provide a comparison between London boroughs, or between men and women, or ethnic groups. Similar decisions had to be taken about when to provide comparisons between London and the national picture and when to look at the differences within London. In some cases it was worthwhile to explore all these elements of one issue, but in others, for simplicity and clarity of message, it was better to slice the data one way.

In many cases national reports have London-specific data embedded within them. Particularly useful are those that provide annual updates of standard data-sets—such as the British Crime Survey. Lifting data out of these reports and plotting it over time enabled the project team to analyse some London-specific trends that were not presented in any of the source reports. Again, this posed challenges as data-collection methods and parameters often change over time, even within one set of reports.

As stated in the introduction to this chapter, the 2003 Highs and Lows report considered only the level and impact of drug use in London. The report presented British Crime Survey data showing that Londoners were more likely than people in other parts of the country to report using illicit drugs, and Class A drugs in particular. The data showed that 14 per cent of Londoners reported using Class A drugs in the previous year, and six per cent in the previous month. Cocaine was found to be the most widely used Class A drug. The most recent data at the time of publication showed that levels of cocaine use had increased sharply in recent years, and that the level of use in the capital was more than double than those in other parts of the country.

The report indicated that these high levels of drug use were reflected in high levels of recorded drug offences. The most recent data at the time of publication showed that 55 per cent of all recorded crack cocaine offences, 39 per cent of cocaine offences, 13 per cent of heroin offences, 15 per cent of ecstasy offences, and 25 per cent of cannabis offences were in London. In all, 23 per cent of recorded drug offences in England took place in London.

The report also described some of the health and social impacts of drug use. The authors noted that many Londoners use illicit drugs recreationally and without negative health or social consequences, but that despite this there were at least 70,000 problem drug-users in London. The report also cited London Health Observatory analysis of Hospital Episodes data, which showed that between 1998 and 2000 there were 854 drug-related deaths due to drug misuse in London, meaning that every 30 hours a Londoner died as a result of drug misuse.

The 2007 Highs and Lows report updated much of the data presented in the first report and provided new data describing the level and impacts of alcohol use. It provided a more complete picture of substance use in the capital, noting both the differences between alcohol and drugs as well as the similarities and instances in which their use and impacts overlap. The report showed that Londoners were still more likely than people in other parts of the country to report using illicit drugs and that reported cocaine use had continued to rise. However, it was reassuring to see that according to British Crime Survey data, the proportion of Londoners reporting illicit drug use had dropped steadily from 14.7 per cent in 2003/04 to 11.2 per cent in 2005/06. Also reassuring was the finding that young Londoners are less likely to use illicit drugs than young people in other parts of the country.

The patterns for alcohol consumption were slightly different. General Household Survey figures showed that, on average, Londoners drink less often and at lower levels than people across the rest of England. Plotting this data over time showed that, contrary to public opinion and media reporting, the proportion of Londoners reporting that they have drunk alcohol in the past week had dropped significantly from 62 per cent in 2001 to 54 per cent in 2005.

The 2007 report included figures provided by researchers at Glasgow University including the most recent estimate of the number of problematic drug users in London—74,000 people. It also provided Department of Health estimates of the number of dependent drinkers in London—approximately 370,000 or 5 per cent of London's population.

The relationship between problem drug-use and crime was given even more detailed consideration in the second report, due to the ongoing expansion of drug testing in the criminal justice system. National Treatment Agency data showed that the number of positive drug tests completed in London has increased significantly since the introduction of testing on arrest on March 31 2006.

Due to continually improving data-collection systems, the 2007 report also provided considerably more London-specific evidence than was contained in the first report. This included more detailed analysis of the differential impacts of drug and alcohol use in inner London and outer London boroughs, illustrating that drug and alcohol-related crimes and death rates were significantly higher in inner London. Much of the data was also aggregated according to gender, ethnicity, and age. This allowed some consideration of the particular impact of drug and alcohol use on black and minority ethnic communities, young people, and women.

Drug and alcohol issues are constantly changing as new drugs become available, methods of drug and alcohol use change, and criminal networks become more complex. The two Highs and Lows reports demonstrated that policy-makers should look to locally specific evidence is essential to understanding London's situation rather than being guided by national and international findings, which may or may not match the experiences and needs of people living in London. For this reason, the authors of both reports emphasized the need for local authorities and a range of other organizations operating in London to continue to collect evidence and monitor changes within their communities, and to share this evidence with colleagues across London.

WHAT DO THE HIGHS AND LOWS REPORTS SHOW US? INFORMATION DESIGNED FOR ACTION

The authors of the Highs and Lows reports set a challenging objective of presenting information designed for action: that is, information that could inform, and potentially lead to changes in the activities of those working on drug and alcohol-related issues. Knowledge-management experts make clear distinctions between data, information, and knowledge (Fig.12.1). 'Data' is described as lacking context or meaning,

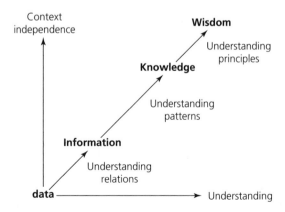

Fig 12.1 The Data/Information/Knowledge Axis

Source: Contribution to an account of police intelligence as 'fragmentary; the pieces have yet to be put together, and the full jigsaw puzzle revealed'.

while 'information' entails an understanding of the relationships between pieces of data. In contrast, 'knowledge' is derived from an understanding of the patterns and implications of information. In other words, information becomes knowledge when it enables action (Bellinger, 2002).

In preparing the reports, the authors focused on the audience they hoped to reach and considered how this audience would receive and use the information provided. The target audience consisted of people working not just in policing but also in the drug and alcohol sector, as well as the health and criminal justice sectors, across London. This was a broad audience with wide-ranging perspectives and remits, but with a common need for reliable London-specific data that could guide decision-making and deployment of resources to respond to drug- and alcohol-related needs in the capital.

The report was designed to support a 'needs assessment' approach by providing detailed data on the experiences of communities across London, and of different groups within these wider communities. This meant looking more closely at the data to reveal the trends within the trends and also the gaps in evidence that could have a significant impact on the picture as a whole. For example, the evidence shows that cannabis is the most widely used drug in London while cocaine use is increasing steadily and the level of use of other drugs is actually decreasing. Yet drug services, and particularly clinical treatment services, continue to focus primarily on opiate users.

Another example of a disjuncture between the evidence and current practice relates to London's age demographic. London's population is younger than other parts of the United Kingdom with nearly one-third of the population falling within the 15–34 age group. National data shows that young people are more likely to have used drugs and consumed high levels of alcohol in the past year. There is an array of policies focusing on the need for drug and alcohol education and prevention initiatives aimed at young people. However, there is very little data describing the consumption of alcohol among young Londoners.

There was a similar lack of data on drug use among older people, both in London and at national level. For example, people over 60 years of age are currently not asked to complete the drugs component of the British Crime Survey because of the assumed low level of drug use among this age group. Yet due to the success of treatment programmes many long-term drug users are now surviving into older age, meaning that better evidence is needed about the experiences and needs of older people who use drugs.

Due to the identification of these data gaps, both Highs and Lows reports included recommendations about improving data collection and monitoring practices. GLADA used the reports to make the case for organizations operating across London to measure what they really need to know, rather than operating on the basis of what is measured most easily. However, even with the most comprehensive and detailed data-sets, the pieces of data do not simply fall together to make the full picture. The various data-sets presented in the Highs and Lows reports do not tell the complete story of drug and alcohol use in London. Instead, they often reveal more about government priorities and which aspects of drug and alcohol use and impacts are easily quantifiable. The Highs and Lows authors decided to accept an element of incompleteness, rather than fall into the trap of waiting for an elusive last piece of the puzzle.

The project team also sought to make use of community intelligence, such as that provided by voluntary and community organizations. Evidence derived from the experiences of local communities is often not given the credence accorded to data from more 'official' sources. Nonetheless, it often complements other data sources, providing information that is difficult to capture from outside the communities in question. The Highs and Lows reports included data from a number of voluntary and community organizations, particularly in the sections of the report that focused on the wider impacts of drug and alcohol use, beyond police and hospital data. For example, data collected by Childline (a national free helpline for children and young people), provided insight into the impacts that parental/carer alcohol and drug misuse have on children. Similarly, data provided by charities Crisis and St Mungos revealed the strength of relationship between drug and alcohol use and homelessness. The Highs and Lows reports demonstrated the value of this type of evidence, and how it can be utilized to support data from other sources.

CONCLUSION

Consilient thinking was essential to the process of drawing the various disparate pieces of evidence together so that the final Highs and Lows reports were more than merely a collation of data. It was clear that the data could have been drawn together in many different ways to produce quite different pictures of the level and impacts of drug and alcohol use. The project teams working on the two reports had to come to early agreements about the 'totality' they were aiming for. As described above, the various contributors were naturally protective of their data and the story it might tell, particularly when combined with data from other sources. In several cases bringing the different data-sets together served to challenge various organizations' claims of success and good performance. Again, this is not to say that organizations were attempting to cover up poor performance, but rather that the rigidity of performance monitoring mechanisms and the focus on particular targets can blinker organizations to the wider implications of their work.

Placing data-sets within a wider and often more challenging context might be expected to lead to finger-pointing and tension between the various agencies and organizations within the drug and alcohol sector, and related sectors. This was not GLADA's experience in preparing the two Highs and Lows reports. In fact, bringing the data together led to increased understanding of the agendas and priorities that the various organizations were focusing on and a greater sense of shared responsibility. The Highs and Lows reports show that data should not just be collected and valued within the context of performance management but should be used to illustrate, inform, and educate, and ultimately to lead to action and improvement.

REFERENCES

BELLINGER, G, 'Emerging perspectives' *Systems Thinking*, available at <http://www.systems-thinking.org/kmgmt/kmgmt.htm>.

GREATER LONDON ALCOHOL AND DRUG ALLIANCE, *London: the Highs and the Lows* (London: GLA, 2003).

——, *London: the Highs and the Lows 2* (London: GLA, 2007).

GRIEVE, J, 'Sitting on the lid' *Policing Today* 1(October 1994) 11–14.

——, 'Intelligence as education for all' in O'Connor, L, O'Connor, D and Best, R, eds, *Drugs: Partnerships for Policy, Prevention and Education* (London: Cassell, 1998) 3–10.

——, 'Developments in UK criminal intelligence' in Ratcliffe, J, ed, *Strategic Thinking in Criminal Intelligence* (Sydney: Federation Press, 2004).

JOHNSON, S, *The Ghost Map* (London: Allen Lane, 2006).

SASSEN, S, *The Global City: New York, London, Tokyo* (Princeton NY: Princeton University Press, 1991).

SIMS, J, 'What is intelligence?' in Shulsky, A and Sims, J, *What is Intelligence?* (Working Group on Intelligence Reform, Washington: Georgetown University, Consortium for the Study of Intelligence, 1993).

13

'THE MOBILES ARE OUT AND THE HOODS ARE UP'

Adrian Bhatti

INTRODUCTION

This chapter explores the relationship between policing and the communities around us. It is based on 'gnosis', a form of experience as learning rather than taught knowledge and seeks to demonstrate what is meant by consilience and its practical application to the 'seven C's' which Thames Valley Police have identified as being at the very core of assessing the significance of events on communities and their structures. The title of this paper encourages the reader to acknowledge the different component parts of an event and how an integrated map of thinking will inform our opinion that 'something' is about to happen. The component parts of the assessment can be defined as the 'seven C's'. Each component forms part of the larger mechanism; in order to appreciate the depth and complexity of the mechanism we can use different lenses to review core issues between communities and policing. Quite often the *catalyst* (which is one aspect of the 'seven C's') requires 'something'—in this case, a reaction resulting in an event. The catalyst indicates that a situation has changed and an individual or group may be in *confrontation* with another. The reaction of the police and the community begins with *causality*, an examination of cause and affect. Analysis will be undertaken by the police to examine these three themes, resulting in a *Community Impact Assessment* (CIA), enabling the police to understand the process of different groups uniting and then coming into conflict with others. This process can be seen as a form of *crystallization*, a course of action whereby groups of individuals have formed, defining themselves as having a common purpose. They share the same resonance and can be easily recognized as a group or a community.

Within the police there is one principal individual charged with the responsibility of identifying the consequences of the catalyst. Within Thames Valley Police, that function is performed by the Community and Diversity Officer (CaDO).[1] It is their responsibility to *communicate* the potential or actual impact of a *critical incident*.

[1] The development of the role of the CaDO can be benchmarked through a series of courses run in partnership with the John Grieve Centre for Policing. The expanded definition of a critical incident was the result of several discussions with Professor Allyson MacVean and this formed the basis of the section on critical incidents. My practical experience of critical incident management has been gained through my employment with Thames Valley Police as a Community and Diversity Officer and my involvement in a number of policing operations.

This chapter is divided into two sections, the first dealing with the role of the CaDO. The second section applies the 'Seven C's' to the concept of critical incidents.

COMMUNITY AND DIVERSITY OFFICERS

The Community and Diversity Officer or CaDO, embodies a number of core responsibilities that enable Thames Valley Police to develop a better understanding of communities across six strands of diversity. This foundation naturally generates improved intelligence within the management process that underpins critical incidents and further enables the Basic Command Units (BCU) to understand the variance of tensions within a community, incorporating action into strategy.

Many of the strategies used by the CaDO are or can been seen in *The Book of Five Rings* written in 1645 (Musashi, 2005) and can be applied to the operational policing. Musashi encourages us to 'think of what is right and true'. In application, moving from the insubstantial to the substantial, we are given a direction to differentiate reality from the actual picture that is being presented. A well-informed proactive CaDO will form an intimate knowledge of a community group. Intimacy and an appreciation of the variety of factors that enables the structures of a community to grow will reveal the social history of a community and, more importantly, identify key incidents that have shaped their interaction with the police. Moreover, this knowledge enables the police to be better placed in order to learn about the context of the situation and how behaviours and attitudes influence conflict. When learning from key incidents and unpacking the context, the police can demonstrate to the community the ability to be sensitive and emphasize the recognition that is needed to grow and change. Applying learning also prevents the same mistakes from being repeated.

The key to learning from incidents is to substantiate formal and informal contact with a key independent network of individuals from within the communities prior to and during the incidents, followed by post-incident assessment. Evidenced information allows those involved in the management CIA's to avoid the predictability of assumption. Through the elimination of assumption, the CaDO is to provide accurate assessments of communities on a regular basis in order to empower critical-incident management.

Thames Valley Police use the CIA to plan and manage community issues within the critical incident. The CaDO seeks to understand the issues and identify a number of risks and impact factors. The initial assessment attempts to identify the methods that need to be utilized within specific cultural frameworks to enable the police to adapt to a constantly fluid situation. Put simply, the CIA is the optimum tool that can be used to assist in the management of communities within critical incidents—underpinned and supported by a CaDO that can demonstrate an intimate knowledge of the community.

If you have an individual or group of CaDOs that are confident in the 'practice and cultivation of the science', ie the preparation of WTAs and CIAs, you already have a cell that can be divided and given specific responsibilities. The processes involved and associated with CIA are not fixed and they themselves are organic and constantly refine themselves. This is an emerging methodology, a method that is not based on routine, assumption, or speculation. Over the past few years CaDOs have put theoretical frameworks into action by becoming an integral element in critical-incident management.

A CaDO provides regular analysis of emerging critical incidents. Contact is maintained with the community through several strata. Initially the CaDO will speak with members of Independent Advisory Groups (IAGs). The CaDO will also interact with members of a Key Individual Network (KIN). A KIN represents a variety of people who can provide advice or opinions on the potential impact of an incident on the community. This contact with the community and those affected enables the CaDO to provide meaningful WTA assessments and incorporate members of the public to act as critical friends during the CIA process.

KIN contact and preparation of reports on a weekly basis inform opinion and measure the degree of tension in an area. The reports are not restricted to monitoring significant incidents and hate-crimes. The Weekly Tactical Assessment (WTA) is extensive as it incorporates open-source intelligence and raw information from the community, demonstrating knowledge of the community in the broadest sense of the word, and providing a framework to appreciate the subtle fluctuations in community power-structures and record the impact of an incident on the well-being of community. This empowers the CaDO, through training and guidance, to incorporate the WTA into the preparation of CIAs. It could also be argued that this incorporates another aspect of the *The Book of Five Rings*, 'acquaintance with the arts'. Arts in the classical sense of the East would refer to poetry or even performance associated with the Japanese tea ceremony. Arts for our purpose would refer to negotiation skills, intelligence retrieval, and rapport-building. These are core principles. The development of negotiation and rapport-building is not restricted to working with the community. In actuality, CaDOs often use these skills to negotiate within the critical-incident process to identify and resolve flashpoints or prevent confrontation with the police. More often than not, this happens when two distinct cultures collide. Ultimately, the CaDO is seeking the optimum route to return to normality, even though the benchmark given to a situation may have shifted. The return to normality must be sensitively managed, recognizing that the community itself must decide the level of the normality.

What has been identified is that within isolated communities the impact of an incident can have ripple affects on a local and national basis, shifting the concept of what is normal, and perhaps imposing a false normality on a community. Intimate knowledge of communities, values associated with kinship, and cultural understanding need to be included when considering CIAs, as it ultimately guides and empowers the BCU in truly understanding the complexity of critical-incident management. Applied learning can consciously shift the understanding of communities and reduce the opportunity of those that seek to exploit resentment within communities.

If we recognize the harm in situations, it becomes easier to identify the potential benefits. Therefore critical-incident management identifies the need for the police to accept their role in the situation. The police also need to be sensitive in understanding how their role is perceived by the community. This can have positive consequences and fulfils a responsibility which creates a positive consequence and directly affects the status of the incident from the perspective of the community. It may be that the police have to identify their own potential culpability in a situation by acknowledging and understanding any harm they may unwittingly have caused.

There are many examples to highlight perceived insensitivities to a particular religious custom or the treatment of young people, such as the stereotyping of people who wear hoodies. Examining insensitivities will lead to enhanced communication on all sides and the revealing of truth. Often the truth of a situation lies underneath different levels of misunderstanding and controversy. Consilience requires individuals and organizations to acknowledge how different strands of information, when drawn together, can have a dramatic affect on procedures and results. By understanding the harm that can be caused, the police are in a better position to act in an informed and compassionate manner. It is often the reflective contemplation of the CaDO combined with the focused direction of intelligence-gathering that can better inform and encourage others to consider carefully what is being presented.

DEFINING COMMUNITY IMPACT ASSESSMENTS

Managing the operational response to critical incidents has been a part of mainstream policing since its inception. However, community impact assessments (CIA) and risk management plans have only recently been acknowledged. Moreover, it has been the development of the CIA model that has generated a detailed understanding of the affects of critical incidents on the awareness of the community. The 'Seven C's' manifest themselves at various levels within the methodology of community impact assessments and offer a framework to contemplate the impact of an incident on a specific community group.

A CIA is a document that aims to define the causal relationships between events, facilitate understanding of the impact of an event on a group of people, produce measures known as risks, and develop a methodology to understand and prevent the risk from increasing, known as control measures. The end result is a document that seeks to manage a fluid situation by deploying a variety of policing resources based on intelligent and informed decisions.

Over the past five years, Thames Valley Police have sought to refine the methodology of the CIA, to produce an impactive and flexible document that can be used in a variety of contexts. Thames Valley Police do not claim sole rights to the use of the document; however we have developed its methodology and, based on its practical application, we can celebrate its success. The application and its usage are extensive, varying from reactive policing through to planning or proactively policing the 'potentialities' of a particular incident.

The CIA and its supporting document, the Weekly Tactical Assessment (WTA), are intrinsically linked to the policing of critical incidents. The WTA is a document used to measure the degree of community tension within a specific policing area. It uses the Woodland[2] method of analysing information across three areas. The WTA examines the 'experience' of communities and in this section the CaDO is encourage to summarize 'what the community is telling us'. This is raw information gathered by the CaDO through community engagement techniques. Where possible this information is fed into the National Intelligence Model. The second section of the WTA refers to 'evidence' or the data that the police have such as intelligence reports, analytical information, and calls from the public resulting in incidents that have been recorded on police databases. Finally, the information from the first two sections is compared to inform the reader and suggest the 'potential' or what may happen. When combined with local knowledge and future events the potential of an incident can be mapped out at a very early stage in the conflict cycle.

TAT TVAM ASI (THOU ART THAT) OR UNDERSTANDING CRITICAL INCIDENTS

TVP use the following definition to understand a critical incident as:

The unique circumstances of the incident or the effectiveness of the response to it could have a significant impact on the confidence of the victim; their family and/or the community

When applying the model of the critical incidents, CaDOs or those tasked with completing the CIA will often include the following addition to the definition:

An incident or event which has, or is perceived to have, an effect upon a specific or non-specific community resulting in significant impact on the confidence or consciousness of victims, their families and/or the community *and which has a quantifiable variance on tensions that may exist within communities.*

Whilst it is accepted that any significant or critical incident will have an impact on a community, this chapter will detail the complex methodologies through which the impact is comprehended by different groups.

The impact of an incident is dynamic and incorporates a diverse range of factors including the interrelationships which may exist between the different strata that make up a community. In particular, hybrid impact factors may emerge at specific nexus points—for example, territorial ownership, different ethnic and cultural identities, and perceived imbalance of power within that community—thereby creating a

---

[2] DC Ron Woodland worked for the Metropolitan Police Service and assisted the John Grieve Centre in developing the training courses for the Community and Diversity officers in Thames Valley Police.

range of potential 'hubs' in which community impacts and tensions can develop and emerge.

CIAs cannot be viewed as a linear process nor defined as a set procedure; rather, they are a convoluted organic process which develop in relation to the environment in which they exist.

'YOU CAN'T SEE THE WOOD FOR THE TREES' OR EMPATHETIC APPROACHES TO UNDERSTANDING COMMUNITIES

In order to understand the application of the CIA it is necessary to be aware of the different approaches to understanding the communities which the police serve. Neighbourhood policing seeks to acknowledge a variety of cognitive groups, identified by the label 'communities'. The term community is sometimes misleading. The term relies on assumed knowledge of working definitions and the difference between the uses of the term by a number of different agencies. The Neighbourhood Policing Model in particular has influenced and informed my thinking.

When considering communities within the context of CIA and policing, we are cognizant of the interdependency and natural tension which exists between groups as defined by a number of factors including geographic location or ethnicity. With this in mind, communities can appear to be paradoxical. They can be vulnerable and resistant, unified and divided, depending on the environmental forces that are acting upon them.

It is clear that there is an organic nature to community groups and therefore communities can be viewed as ecosystems. Each of the definitions of ecosystems incorporates a common theme. They suggest complexity, acknowledgement of external and internal factors (which affect growth), and identify the sum parts of disparate factors into a single functioning unit. In order to develop and crystallize this perspective it is possible to explore a gentle analogy that allows for a less confrontational understanding of the nature of communities that are inherent in modern society.

For this brief moment imagine or visualize a wood. Begin to notice the diversity of the ecosystem. Continue to notice the variety of different trees at different stages of growth; consider how each tree could represent a different community. Although the wood is diverse, the root system of any tree is both subtle and complex, growing underneath us, absorbing nutrients from the soil with no external signs. Communities take root in particular environments and develop in relation to their environment, which occasionally conflict with their values and morals. Just as trees have complex root systems used to sustain and provide stability, communities have similar societal roots. For example, it could be possible to identify a shared sense of history that encompasses communities that have taken root in England. The explanation for the presence of a community could be colonialism, or post-war immigration/economic migration. Irrespective of its origins, a community needs to develop strong roots in order to survive; it will naturally consume resources, and this very act of natural growth can foster contempt and dislike amongst others competing for scarce resources.

How do we recognize communities? Is there only a need to identify a community when the differences become self-evident? In a wood, each tree performs a role and to a degree can fulfil a specific purpose in an ecosystem. For example, the trunk of a tree provides support to the branches as it enables different chemical and biological processes to occur, such as photosynthesis or osmosis. Within a community framework, the trunk provides a link from the roots to the branches, from generation to generation. This sense of stability will often reinforce both local and global identities. The branches of the tree represent different strands of growth, with one common feature of kinship to the trunk, strands united in fulfilling a common purpose. These can be likened to families, friends, and associates who form aspects of communities. The leaves of the tree serve to demonstrate the complexity of identity in modern society. Whilst superficially similar they demonstrate individual characteristics. Passing through stages of growth they provide photosynthesis and shelter and, having fallen from the tree, eventually replenish a tree by feeding the root system through decay. Trees are, by their very nature, intrinsic to the tapestry of the land, as much as communities are to the fabric of society.

With this knowledge in hand, a question arises: how does one catalogue and learn to understand the diversity of trees that populate the landscape? On whom do we place the responsibility of identifying and recording the information? Who is best placed to understand and explain the ecology of a tree? How can this individual seek to understand the competing resources that an organic life form needs, what risks are apparent, and what are the affects of external activity? These aspects of change can be affected by both internal and external factors.

Police forces should seek to understand communities through their structures, attitudes, and behaviours as this will often allow for a closer inspection of their culture; if we choose to apply the model of an ecosystem to communities, we can develop an understanding whereby we have the ability to interpret causality and its consequential effects on communities. We could liken this to a forest worker who can identify plants and trees without interfering with their mode of being. Within TVP we have developed the role of the CaDO to support Base Command Units (BCU). Within the last two years, the CaDO's role has been refined to concentrate on establishing how complex communities are, and apply CIAs and WTAs to monitor and respond to critical incidents.

UNDERSTANDING AND APPLYING THE COMMUNITY IMPACT ASSESSMENT

Having identified with the seven C's, are we better placed to analyse the effectiveness of the CIA? Have we reduced tension? Have we been able to understand the significance of the impact of the critical incident on the confidence or consciousness of victims, their families and/or the community? This is addressed within the CIA through the examination and refinement of 'control measures'. A control measure exists to manage a risk. Revisiting the title of the chapter through the prism of public disorder, it is possible to view youths gathering, in the context of sustained public-order activity and using mobile phones, as a risk. In order for the situation to be brought back to normality we may choose to take a number of actions such as a directed policing patrol. Alternatively, a CaDO may identify another control measure such as calling a youth worker to see if this is a normal occurrence and develop intelligence from the youth worker to assist with bringing normality to the situation. The second control measure enables scarce resources to be appropriately utilized. The contact between the youth worker and the young people is less inflammatory than police officers asking them to move on, and as a final incentive we develop information linked to the behavioural patterns of a group of people. CaDOs link control measures to the management of risk and impact factors. Through using a Community Impact Assessment, risk and control measures can be accurately recorded. This is significant, as this may influence a change in operational planning; when dealing with communities there is a very fine line between 'reassurance policing' and reassuring the police (ourselves) that nothing is happening. Where possible the independent views of community members and key stakeholders should be sought. This allows further consideration as many perspectives increase awareness and enable us to acknowledge the discreet and the obvious. Vital links between pieces of intelligence are casually hidden in obvious, day-to-day occurrences.

There is a requirement for the CaDO to be able to communicate knowledge through several different avenues. A Community Profile is one such avenue. A Community Profile can assist in building accurate and timely Community Impact Assessments.

Community Profiles are documents that identify the most vulnerable communities in our local area. The very nature of the document seeks to examine the core issues that matter to the community. It seeks to understand the historical context of a particular group within a specialized framework. By understanding social structures (the roots, trunk, and leaves), we can learn how to influence the community. Moreover, Thames Valley Police are constantly learning and being influenced by the community. This requires a level of critical reasoning and the willingness to listen. Whilst Thames Valley Police may not be responsible for the entire result of an incident, as members of the same community forming part of the richer tapestry of the land, we are required to signpost and where necessary support communities to empower themselves.

A Community Profile should seek to develop a holistic picture of communities within a community, providing valuable information to an agency and demonstrating understanding of the new, the vulnerable, and the disengaged.

CONCLUSION

Over the past five years, the methodology of CIA has developed to a degree where expertise can identify the most impactive incident on the consciousness of a community. In order to support the CIA and provide a monitoring system for emerging critical incidents, Thames Valley Police use the WTA to understand the contemporary reality of communities. Huntingdon (2002) provides the perfect summary to contextualize and understand the CIA in relation to critical incidents. The CIA and WTA enable the police to:

- order and generalize about reality;
- understand causal relationships among phenomena;
- anticipate and, if we are lucky, predict future developments;

- distinguish what is important from what is unimportant;
- show us what paths we should take in order to reach our goals.

It would be difficult to present every aspect of the above on a regular basis for the diversity of communities which we serve. Therefore, we seek to prioritize the information on behalf of the agency. We use a rationale developed from or by an understanding of an impact on a community. We utilize a form of corporate knowledge to develop strategies to minimize or reduce harm. By doing so we learn that communities themselves have a number of traditional routes that are open to resolving conflict. The critical incident provides a catalyst, a momentary space in a reaction, a channel whereby affective intervention strategies can be employed to reduce risk.

If we review our amended definition, we can clearly identify that it is operating on three levels. First, the significant impact on the community, followed by the further impact on the confidence or consciousness of the victim/family and by default the community, and lastly the quantifiable variance on the tension that may exist within communities.

It is critical to identify the component parts of the catalyst through the WTA and develop intervention strategies through the CIA. With effective prior engagement there will be, or ought to be, lines of communication which remain open to influential members of the community. Key to communication is integrity. Thames Valley Police also recognize that communication is a flowing process. It relies on confidence in the individual both from communities and from within the police. We would also suggest that communication should not be restricted to tried and tested formats. During the Lozell's disturbance of 2006, one of the key media, through which a 'message' was communicated, was a pirate radio station. This allowed myth and rumour to perpetuate itself. Moreover, young people in hoodies have a wide range of media available through which to communicate, such as email, photography, video phones, voice messaging, and SMS/internet. As communication can also act as a barrier during critical incidents, it is imperative to acknowledge the most effective form or style of engagement. Therefore, it would make operational sense to talk to the public through the very same radio station. Thames Valley Police suggest that by profiling the community and identifying individuals with influence we can quickly learn about the affects of an incident on a particular group. Thus, analysing and identifying those who are best placed to impart a message is one role of the CaDO during a critical incident. This would enable the police to improve its style of communication. More often than not the message given out by the police is contrary to the understanding of individuals and communities that are either directly or indirectly involved in the incident.

Understanding the scope of the context will provide a greater impetus to get to the heart of matters. The police are then in a better position to evaluate information and intelligence. Crucially, the police will also have generated a healthier appreciation for the effects of our actions. This in turn identifies a need to continually review the process, method, and style of communication. The police need to constantly review to ensure that they are listening and talking to the most appropriate people; this would enable the police to consider if the style and purpose of engagement is appropriate. It is crucial to consider if there are new lines of communication with individuals and groups that exist outside normal structures. Establishing informal engagement relies on identifying individuals with influence, and whose core values and beliefs lend themselves to the successful resolution of the situation. This enables the police to move forward positively and tackle myth and rumour. During a critical incident we may also have to take note of stereotyping and challenge this at a later stage. More often than not, this role is provided by a 'critical friend'—an individual recognized for their judgement and understanding. It is up to the critical friend to provide the capacity to deliver reasoned understanding during sensitive events.

It is widely acknowledged in policing circles that specialized officers are often required that have an in-depth knowledge of a group of people. These individuals can communicate clearly within the confines of a tasking and demonstrate the ability to innovate. Innovation is the key to maintaining focus in long-term critical incidents. Innovation in the technological sense allows the police to think outside the box, developing the ability to use different tools to engage with different sections of the community.

There is also the need to carefully balance the capacity that the police have to receive new forms of knowledge and react in an appropriate manner. Are we able to perform and manage expectations whilst dealing with day-to-day business? Capacity can sometimes be overlooked in the management of critical incidents. There is also the question of the community's capacity; how much can a community tolerate before the tension rises to an irreconcilable level?

The CIA is the tool that is utilized to unify disparate threads within the context of a critical incident. The CIA enables the police to keep a record of the development of the incident, monitors what information and decisions have been taken or discarded, and provides a rationale for policing activity. The document enables the CaDO or author to consolidate the information in a format that is informative yet easy to digest.

REFERENCES

HUNTINGDON, S, *The Clash of Civilizations: And the Remaking of World Order* (London: Free Press, 2002).

MUSASHI, M, *The Book Of Five Rings* (Cleary, T, trans) (Boston: Shambala Publications, 2005).

NATIONAL POLICE IMPROVEMENT AGENCY (Neighbourhood policing section) available at <http://www.neighbourhoodpolicing.co.uk/publication.asp>.

SUN TZU, *The Art of War* (Griffith, S, trans) (Oxford: Oxford University Press, 1971).

Primary source material

Community and Race Relation Officers Training, Latimer House, February 2003: a two week course which established the scope to develop the role of the Community and Diversity Officer.

CIA workshop chaired by ACC Anton Setchell, 2005 (TVP).

Community Impact Assessment training (TVP) with the John Grieve Centre for Policing: a series of training courses over the period 2003–5.

14

CROSS-BORDER LIAISON AND INTELLIGENCE: PRACTICALITIES AND ISSUES

Ludo Block

INTRODUCTION

Most European law enforcement agencies are currently aware that the coordination of criminal intelligence at local, regional, and national levels is at the heart of combating serious and organized crime. Nonetheless, putting this to practice effectively and efficiently remains difficult to accomplish, particularly as activities undertaken within the boundaries of the territorial jurisdiction increasingly do not suffice to successfully investigate serious and organized crime. A few decades ago neither the places where offences were carried out, nor the places where damage or harm from crime occurred varied considerably. The competent authority to investigate and prosecute, the citizenship of offender, investigator, and victim—and last but not least the actual whereabouts of offender, victim, and proceeds of the crime—were largely territorially based and relatively more clearly defined and fixed than they are today (Marx, 1997). Nowadays serious and organized crime almost by definition involves activities in more than one jurisdiction. Successfully combating this new dimension of crime requires law enforcement to seek partnerships across borders in order to obtain adequate intelligence on the criminal activities they are facing and investigating.

This chapter describes and analyses the practicalities and issues of cross-border liaison and intelligence alongside a case study of European law enforcement liaison officers stationed in the Russian Federation.[1] First, the development over the past decades of the use of law enforcement liaison officers in European cross-border intelligence exchange in general and their deployment in the Russian Federation in particular will be considered. Thereafter a brief description of the complex Russian law enforcement structures that form the working environment for the liaison officers in the Federation will be presented. Third, an in-depth examination of the daily practices of European law enforcement liaison officers in the Russian Federation will be

---

[1] The focus of this chapter on liaison officers is simply a matter of choice and makes no judgement as regards the crucial relevance of other operational arrangements (eg the Police Working Group On Terrorism, Cross Channel Intelligence Conference, Europol) for cross-border liaison and intelligence in Europe.

undertaken with a focus on the actual activities and process of criminal intelligence exchange. Fourth, based on these practices as well as some other available research findings in this field, a number of obstacles to cross-border intelligence exchange will be discussed. The chapter concludes with the highlighting of some significant points that emerge from the practicalities of cross-border liaison and intelligence. Before starting the analyses, however, some clarifying words on the concept of intelligence as used in this chapter are necessary.

THE CONCEPT OF INTELLIGENCE IN DAILY PRACTICE

Throughout the literature on (criminal) intelligence there is an ongoing discussion on the concept of intelligence and the difference between information and intelligence (Müller-Wille, 2004; Ratcliff, 2004; Robertson 1994). Some contributors identify intelligence as a process, others as a product of a process with secrecy and analysis as core ingredients through which intelligence can be distinguished from information. This chapter, however, with a view to its central subject, avoids a lengthy discussion on the concept of intelligence and offers a practitioners' point of view. Intelligence is simply understood to be information that enables law enforcement agencies to make decisions in order to successfully investigate crime. What turns information into intelligence is therefore in the eye of the beholder; it is what is needed at some moment in time for a particular decision to be made. For decisions concerning strategies in combating crime police might need intelligence derived from multiple-source analysed information. However, in practice for most criminal investigators at the tactical level, the intelligence needed are those pieces of information that help them to understand the particular crime and criminal activities they are investigating. Hence, what some designate as single-source raw data—for example the billing list of a particular phone or some 'pocket litter' containing the serial number of a particular 40ft shipping container—could be the piece of intelligence that provides a breakthrough in an investigation. Acquiring actionable intelligence in a timely fashion from across borders, however, poses a major challenge in the daily practice of many investigators. The role and use of liaison officers stationed abroad in engaging this challenge has considerably increased in the past decades.

THE USE OF LIAISON OFFICERS

LIAISON OFFICERS IN EUROPEAN POLICING

The use of liaison officers in cross-border law enforcement cooperation emerged in Europe in the second half of the 1970s. It started most prominently in the domain of the combat against drug-trafficking and quickly spilled over to combating organized crime and counterterrorism (Bigo, 1996).[2] Liaison officers are in fact law enforcement officers stationed in another territorial jurisdiction without any formal powers. They are tasked with maintaining contacts and acting as intermediary between their agency and the law enforcement agencies in the host country. Their role, according to Nadelmann (1994), can be quite ambiguous as they are both official representatives on behalf of their agency as well as a fixer, ie a facilitator of requests from and to their home country for information, evidence, interrogations, searches, arrests, and extraditions. Bigo sees liaison officers as the human interface between the various national police forces and from that perspective argues that their role is 'crucial for policing in Europe, because it is they who manage the flow of information between their respective agencies' (Bigo, 2000: 67).

Some developments within the EU, like, for example, the growing role of Europol and the Police Chiefs Task Force (PCTF) in the cross-border exchange of intelligence, could have a decreasing effect on the need for liaison officers. At present EU law enforcement agencies still make extensive use of liaison officers with around one hundred deployed inside the EU. This estimation only includes the bilateral liaison officers and not the so-called Europol liaison officers (ELO) who are stationed by the Member States to Europol. In 2006 there were 105 ELOs stationed at Europol (Europol Annual Report, 2006). The approximate number of EU law enforcement liaison officers stationed outside the Union in third countries is considerably larger and can be estimated at 250.[3]

EUROPEAN LIAISON OFFICERS IN RUSSIA

One country where multiple law enforcement liaison officers from EU countries are stationed is the Russian Federation. Table 14.1 shows the development [4] from 1992 to 2004 when the total number of EU law enforcement liaison officers in the Russian Federation had risen to 31 representing 17 EU Member States. Together they formed the majority of foreign law enforcement representation in the country; the number of foreign law enforcement representatives of non-EU Member States stationed in the Russian Federation in 2004 was 23.

The steady growth since 2000 can in part be attributed to EU Member States deciding to establish a first liaison, which includes liaison officers from the 'new' Member States in 2004. The other part of the growth can be ascribed to the increase of liaison officers per Member State, now varying from one to seven liaison officers for an individual country. Most liaison officers are stationed in their respective embassies in the

[2] To compare with US practices in this field, the FBI sent its first special agent abroad in 1939 (Nadelmann, 1994: 151) and its' legal attaché (LEGAT) program started after the Second World War with LEGATs stationed in Latin America, London, and Ottawa (Ibid, 152).

[3] Both estimations are based on open sources and field research by the author. The exact number strongly depends on which definition of 'law enforcement liaison officer' is used, for example whether one includes immigration liaison officers and liaison officers from security and intelligence services in this definition. Here these are *not* included.

[4] This table is based on the information provided by liaison officers of 13 Member States who took part in a survey conducted at the end of 2004, supplemented with information following from personal observations by the author between 1999 and 2004.

Table 14.1 Total Number of EU Member States' Law Enforcement
Liaison Officers Stationed in the RF

1992	1	1999	15
1993	4	2000	15
1994	5	2001	16
1995	9	2002	22
1996	10	2003	25
1997	12	2004	31
1998	13		

capital Moscow while Estonia, Finland, and Sweden chose to have (additional) liaison officers in St. Petersburg due to their geographic proximity to the north-west part of the Russian Federation. For similar reasons a Norwegian liaison officer was stationed in Murmansk. In comparison, the Russian Federation Interior Ministry had only four liaison officers posted in Europe in 2004, respectively in Germany, Spain, Poland, and Finland[5] and the Federal Security Service had two liaison officers posted in Europe, respectively in Germany and Sweden.

The European liaison officers stationed in the Russian Federation differ considerably in background, functional and geographical competence, and assigned tasks. Most liaison officers are police officers with a background in criminal investigations, some liaison officers have a background in customs investigations, and a few have a border guard or immigration background. Generally speaking police liaison officers deal with 'police' matters, and customs liaison officers deal with 'customs' matters—although their actual practices hardly vary. Also, for example, the Nordic liaisons[6] and the liaisons of the UK Serious and Organized Crime Agency (SOCA) have a competence in both customs and police matters.

A small number of the liaison officers in Moscow only cover the Russian Federation territory while most cover various countries of the former Soviet Union. Before looking into the daily practices of the liaison officers, the next section first offers a brief description of the context in which they operate.

THE CONTEXT: RUSSIAN LAW ENFORCEMENT AGENCIES

The organization of law enforcement in the Russian Federation is complex with various functional and geographical overlaps. Four agencies in the Russian Federation can be pointed out that engage on a regular basis in intelligence exchange with the

---

[5] 'Politsiya bez granits' in *Rossiskoy Gazete* 22 January 2004.

[6] The five Nordic countries, ie Denmark, Finland, Iceland, Norway, and Sweden, have been developing close police cooperation since 1972. In 1984 they established the Police and Customs Cooperation in the Nordic Countries (PTN), which includes a joint liaison network. In 2005, 38 'Nordic' liaisons representing all Nordic police and customs authorities were stationed around the world (Swedish Customs Annual Report, 2005).

European liaison officers. These are the Interior Ministry (MVD) in which the police is organized, the Federal Security Service (FSB), the State Customs Committee (GTK), and the Federal Drug Control Service commonly known by its Russian abbreviation 'Gosnarkokontrol'.[7] There are other law enforcement agencies with which some of the liaison officers cooperate like the General Prosecutor's Office and the Financial Monitoring Committee. The four agencies discussed in this section are however the most frequently contacted by almost all liaison officers.

The MVD consists of geographically and functionally organized departments. In each of the eighty-five territorial subjects of the Russian Federation exists a so-called Main Department of the Interior (GUVD) which can be described as a relatively autonomous regional police force with all basic police functions organized in its structure. In addition, the MVD has a number of functionally organized police departments at the federal level like, for example, the Department for Combating Organized Crime and Terrorism (DBOPiT, formerly known as GUBOP).

Various departments of the MVD, both at federal and regional level, have an international cooperation unit within their structure. Furthermore some officers from operational units, like the operational investigative bureau for combating drugs of the DBOPiT and the Moscow Police Criminal Investigations Department (MUR), have frequent direct contacts with the liaison officers. In this respect the National Central Bureau of Interpol in Moscow (NCB Moscow) is worth mentioning as it functions as an important and frequently contacted counterpart to the liaison officers. Requests made by the liaison officers by default get a higher priority within the bureau than those received through Interpol channels. In addition to intelligence exchange, the NCB Moscow supports the liaison officers by connecting them to direct contacts within various departments and units in the Interior Ministry or other law enforcement agencies.

The Federal Security Service, one heir of the notorious KGB,[8] has, besides its main responsibilities in the field of national security, counterintelligence, and counterterrorism, also broad law enforcement functions including the fight against serious and organized crime and drug-trafficking. The FSB has full powers of criminal investigation and a decentralized presence across the Russian territory which mirrors that of the MVD. Therefore, it is an equally important partner for the liaison officers in relation to the exchange of criminal intelligence.

For the liaison officers who are mainly occupied with customs cases, the State Customs Committee is the most frequently contacted cooperation partner. However, as the Customs Committee has full investigative powers for crimes resulting from cross-border movements of goods or valuables, most police liaison officers also frequently exchange intelligence with the Committee, particularly in cases of drug-trafficking and cigarette smuggling.

'Gosnarkokontrol' (with its 40,000 employees) was established in 2003 formally to more effectively combat drug-trafficking in the Russian Federation. The organization was staffed largely with employees of the simultaneously disbanded Tax Police and did not receive exclusive competence for combating drug-trafficking—the MVD, FSB

---

[7] Gosnarkokontrol is the abbreviation of the former official name of the Federal Drug Control Drug Service, though is still widely used in both media and official speech.

[8] The other 'heir' of the KGB is the Foreign Intelligence Service (SVR), which used to be the KGB First Directorate.

and Customs retained their competences and capacities in this field. Therefore, the role and effectiveness of this new agency is still somewhat unclear.

All Russian law enforcement agencies are characterized by excessive bureaucracy and strong hierarchical organization and culture. Between the agencies exist overlapping mandates, which trigger fierce competition and limited inter-agency cooperation. There is virtually no inter-agency intelligence coordination. None of the agencies could be pointed out as the central point for intelligence exchange on which the liaison officers can focus and there is no equivalent of what in the UK used to be the National Criminal Intelligence Service. The consequential impact thereof on the work of the liaison officers will be elaborated in the next section which focuses on their actual practices.

DAILY PRACTICES OF LIAISON OFFICERS IN RUSSIA

Tasks and Activities

It is important to note that no (European) standard for the work of liaison officers exists.[9] Instructions are based on national practices and regulations, although a number of common elements can be distinguished. Some of the European liaison officers stationed in Moscow emphasize the maintenance of good high-level relations as their main priority and spend little time on operational matters. For most liaison officers, however, the main element in their daily task is the actual exchange of intelligence with Russian law enforcement. Many liaison officers also facilitate judicial cooperation through preparation and support of the execution of international letters of request (ILOR and otherwise known as *Commissions Rogatoire*). They furthermore assist with extraditions, and organize non-operational technical cooperation like training and exchange of knowledge. Some, though not all, liaison officers also contribute to immigration tasks, visa procedures, and security matters in their respective embassies. This usually entails assisting the consular department of the embassy in reviewing visa applications as well as an advisory role with regard to the security of embassy staff and property. An example of diverging practices and regulations is whether a liaison officer is tasked and allowed by his agency (the regulations of the host country on this subject left aside) to run covert human intelligence sources.

The first priority of most liaison officers is to handle requests coming from their national law enforcement agencies and to see that these are properly and swiftly dealt with by one of the Russian agencies. Two reasons, however, encourage liaison officers also to accept requests from the Russian law enforcement agencies. First and foremost, there is a need to cultivate and maintain reciprocity even though in general the exchange of criminal intelligence is not governed by a strict quid pro quo principle. In practice it is not acceptable for a liaison officer to only bring 'questions' to his counterparts and

---

[9] The use and task of liaison officers has been discussed in Europe (in the cooperation under TREVI) since 1986 and is to some extent laid down in a 2003 EU Council Decision (*Official Journal of the European Union (OJ L 67 12.03.2003)*) recently amended by Council Decision 2006/560/JHA of 24 July 2006 (*OJ L 219 10.08.2006*). This Decision defines, in article 2, the 'task' of liaison officers which, however, leaves ample room for variance. There is little indication that this Council Decision has had much impact on the actual practices of the liaison officers (see for example the evaluation of this Decision in EU Council Document 8357/05 of 21.04.05).

never 'answers'. To some extent reciprocity can be offered by providing technical assistance and sending Russian colleagues to training courses and on other trips abroad. In the end, however, both parties need their investigative successes so to maintain a reciprocal 'intelligence relation' is a crucial aspect in the daily work of a liaison officer.

Second, every request inherently contains information on criminal activities, structures and involved actors, and could shed a light on security threats in the liaison officers' home country that otherwise might have escaped the focus of the law enforcement agencies. In practice therefore all liaison officers handle cases originating from their own country as well as cases from Russia.

Looking closer at the actual practices, liaison officers tend to handle mainly cases that, because of their complexity, sensitivity, or urgency need more active support than the average simple information-exchange that could pass through Interpol channels. Through their personal contacts and knowledge of the system, liaison officers are in a position to circumvent the sometimes mindless Russian bureaucracy. For example, in most agencies incoming and outgoing intelligence disseminations have to be approved on various subsequent hierarchical levels. They are sent up and down the hierarchical ladder meanwhile collecting stamps and signatures without any obvious added value as there is usually no case-management system in place. Liaison officers are, particularly when they present a request in person, often able to directly obtain approval at the highest level necessary and then to ensure the direct transfer of the request to a competent case officer. This prevents information leaks and can speed up the handling of the request considerably, which are crucial advantages compared to sending a 'paper' request that has to find its own way in the organization.

Significance of the Liaison Officers' Work

The EU Member States' liaison officers in the Russian Federation handled in 2004 approximately 4,000 cases with the actual number varying between 60 and 500 cases per Member State.[10] In comparison, the NCB Moscow also handles approximately 4,000 cases yearly of which the great majority—that is 70 to 80 per cent—relate to European countries.[11] Some caution is needed in interpreting these figures, however.

There is, as with many other concepts regarding operational law enforcement cooperation, no widely shared definition of a 'case'. Most liaison officers are, for governance and accountability purposes, obliged by their agency to file every new inquiry or intelligence dissemination as a separate 'case'. For example, the Netherlands liaison officer has to open a file for each new investigation regardless whether it originates from his home country or from Russia. This file will contain all incoming and outgoing communications regarding that investigation. This serves two basic functions. First is to keep a register of the exchanged information in order to comply with the relevant data-protection laws in the Netherlands. Second, the registration contributes to what Scharpf (1999) distinguished as 'output legitimacy' (ie the

---

[10]   These figures are based on results of the survey at the end of 2004.

[11]   The total number of cases as well as the percentage of 'European cases' are based both on several conversations with officials from the NCB Moscow and on extrapolation of data mentioned in a press release (*Sotrudniki Interpola v Rossii v etom godu podgotovili i osushestvili 15 ekstraditsiy iz-za rubezha b Rossiyu. RIA Novostu* 14–09–04).

effectiveness and efficiency) of the work of the liaison officer. However, a simple case, especially if the work can be done by e-mail and fax, could entail nothing more than a one-time information-exchange taking less then one hours' work. In contrast, a complex case could entail the exchange of various pieces of intelligence followed by the facilitation of multiple (formal) requests for (or the coordination of) investigative actions. Such cases could involve hundreds of messages, various meetings, and extensive travel, which together would take numerous hours of work during several months. This would still count as one 'case' and as a result placing too much emphasis on the exact number of cases is tricky. Nonetheless the workload of the liaison officers represents a fairly large, if not largest, part of the criminal intelligence exchange between European law enforcement agencies and the Russian Federation, particularly if one considers that no significant cooperation channels exist other than Interpol and the liaison officers (Block, 2007).

Process of Intelligence Exchange

Taking a request for intelligence from the liaison officer's home country as an example, the first step a liaison officer usually takes in each case is to properly channel the request. This means finding the appropriate legal context and the (most) competent agency (and sometimes person) to deal with the actual substance of the request. As was pointed out before, there is no single central point for intelligence exchange and the agencies have overlapping mandates. The FSB has a single point of contact for the liaison officers but within the MVD even various different department could be competent to handle the same request. Therefore liaison officers de facto can choose the agency they see best fit to handle their request. As there is little inter-agency coordination and intelligence sharing, the flipside of this situation is that relevant intelligence could remain untapped. Of course a request could be sent to multiple receivers though unwritten rules prescribe the liaison officers then to inform the requested agencies accordingly. In practice they then run the risk that none of the receivers would give much priority to the request. So usually the liaison officers choose, depending on the substance of the case, past experience, and personal preference, a single agency to deal with a particular case.

Significant effort then goes into the translation of the request although the actual linguistic translation into the Russian language forms only a minor part of it. More effort is often needed to adapt inquiries to meet the Russian Federation legal and operational requirements for the case to be dealt with quickly. This entails providing sufficient information in the preferred format of the requested agency, rephrasing the actual questions so they fit into their world of comprehension and, if possible, match the way information is stored there. Then the case is presented to the agency, if necessary in person. In the discussions on the follow-up of the request considerable attention is given to the process of the intelligence exchange (eg the classification and handling of the intelligence) as standards and protocols on this often differ.

Answers from the Russian partners are in their turn translated, where necessary annotated with additional explanations and advice, and then sent back to the requesting agency. Some liaison officers actively use local open sources to supplement received intelligence or to provide the law enforcement agencies in their home country with background knowledge on criminal developments in the area. All these efforts are aimed at a timely support for investigations and the intelligence process in the home country. That task, however, is not always simple. The next section will discuss some of the main difficulties in this practice.

OBSTACLES TO CROSS-BORDER INTELLIGENCE EXCHANGE

LEGAL OBSTACLES

The impediments to intelligence exchange, which are met in practice by the liaison officers, can roughly be divided in those of a legal and those of an organizational nature. On the legal side the Russian Federation has signed and ratified a number of Conventions regarding mutual cooperation in criminal matters with the Council of Europe. Examples include the European Convention on Mutual Assistance in Criminal Matters (1959) and the European Convention on Laundering, Search, Seizure and Confiscation of the Proceeds from Crime (1990). Also, all European countries with a liaison officer posted in the Russian Federation have concluded one or more bilateral agreement(s) on law enforcement cooperation with the Russian Federation authorities. These agreements, however, differ in level—inter-agency versus intergovernmental—and vary widely in content, from regulating technical assistance, to the exchange of information and intelligence, placement of liaison officers, and combinations of these issues. Still, having these multilateral and bilateral legal instruments in place does not necessarily provide for an unhampered intelligence exchange between the different legal systems. Diverse coercive powers and roles for investigators and a different place and value for intelligence in the investigative process are usually not given much attention in formal legal agreements. Therefore liaison officers (and investigators) regularly have to fall back on the national legislation of the involved jurisdictions to determine the exact possibilities for intelligence exchange.

Although differences in legal systems can obstruct the exchange of intelligence, in practice inadequate knowledge of the differences in legal systems often proves to be much more obstructive than the differences themselves. Other research (Tak, 2000) shows similar findings. Moreover, the fragmentation of legal infrastructure is not necessarily obstructing cross-border cooperation; it also can be used to find the most suitable jurisdiction for certain operations. Examples include choosing an optimal jurisdiction for the debriefing of Covert Human Intelligence Sources (CHIS), determining the best jurisdiction for particular interventions and obtaining evidence where it is more easily accessible. Liaison officers frequently have an advisory role in such decisions. This means that having adequate knowledge of the relevant legal differences and expertise in translating operational needs and possible options across legal traditions and systems is a core competence for them.

One generic issue, the difference in disclosure rules, remains problematic. In the UK Public Interest Immunity exemption provides a strong and effective tool to avoid exposing sensitive techniques or a CHIS in court (Harfield and Harfield, 2005: 21). However, this possibility to protect certain sensitive techniques or sources is in many other jurisdictions not available to the same extent. For example, under Netherlands disclosure rules all intelligence known to the investigator during the investigation becomes accessible for the defence at the trial. No exception exists for 'unused intelligence' relating to the investigation and known to the investigator, nor is Public Interest Immunity exemption available to protect sensitive techniques. Only the identity of a CHIS debriefed by Netherlands police intelligence officers is formally protected, all other sources of intelligence will in the end be disclosed in court. The following is an example showing that liaison officers should maintain a high awareness of the sensitivities and vulnerabilities concerning the handling of intelligence provided by their international counterparts. In a particular case Russian law enforcement held intelligence on a dangerous contraband transport arriving in the Netherlands. The intelligence was obtained through a Russian CHIS located inside a foreign, largely ethnically homogenous, criminal organization. The Russian authorities made the intelligence available to the Netherlands liaison officer but were unaware of disclosure requisites in the Netherlands. If the intelligence had been used any subsequent court file in this case would have had to disclose Russian law enforcement as the source of the intelligence. This fact, even while the actual use of a CHIS obviously was not mentioned in the received intelligence, would have been sufficient for the particular criminal organization to identify the 'leak'. In order to avoid jeopardizing the safety and position of the CHIS there was a limited choice: (a) do nothing or (b) seize the shipment but not to prosecute or (c) ask the Russians to channel their intelligence through a trusted third party.

Another example where differences in disclosure rules caused problems in the exchange of intelligence can be found in the 2005 Joint Investigation Team between the United Kingdom and the Netherlands (cf Rijken and Vermeulen, 2006).

ORGANIZATIONAL OBSTACLES

On the organizational level, impediments to intelligence exchange and cross-border liaison are often the result of the complexity of the different law enforcement systems as well as diverging interests and cultural differences. As is particularly visible in the Russian Federation with its rivalling law enforcement agencies, overlapping mandates result in ambiguity for the liaison officers about the intelligence positions of their cooperation partners. But differences given to the value of intelligence in the investigative process, and the lack of agreed standards for collecting and transmitting intelligence, also contribute to this ambiguity. Of course there are different standards for the evaluation of source and intelligence in use in the European countries but these are more or less comparable. For example in the UK the so-called 5x5x5 model is in use to indicate source, information, and handling code while in the Netherlands police use a 4x4x5 model. The Russian system however, differs considerably and every law enforcement officer could be in charge of his own intelligence collection, evaluation, and dissemination. For a liaison officer it is often impossible to obtain a proper evaluation of the disseminated intelligence by his Russian counterparts.

Additional obstacles for intelligence exchange with the Russian Federation can be found in the excessive bureaucracy and strong hierarchical organization and culture of the agencies some examples of which have already been discussed. These obstacles become particularly cumbersome if swift intelligence exchange is needed in ongoing operations, although law enforcement officers can be resourceful in finding solutions as the following example shows. Most Russian law enforcement agencies have strict regulations in place for (foreign) visitors on their premises. These regulations include obtaining a so-called 'propusk' (permission), a process that easily could take several days. In one operation real-time coordination of investigative measures required the unplanned though urgent on-site presence of the Netherlands liaison officer. As there was no possibility of obtaining a timely propusk, the liaison officer was smuggled into the premises of the agency in question sitting in the back of an official service car. The case officer picked him up some blocks away from the premises and provided him with the service identity document of a Russian officer. Taking advantage of lax security practices and an overstretched respect for hierarchy in his own organization he instructed the liaison officer to look 'grim' and 'flash' the ID when the vehicle entered the premises. It worked perfectly and the coordination contributed to the investigative results in the operation.

Endemic corruption forms a particular organizational impairment for cross-border liaison with Russian Federation law enforcement. Corruption in Russian society has been ubiquitous in the last century (Brovkin, 2003) and structural corruption inside Russian law enforcement has been widely documented. The risk of corruption limits the level of trust liaison officers can place in the law enforcement agencies and even if liaison officers choose their direct contacts carefully further mitigating measures inevitably obstruct the intelligence exchange to some extent. Finally cross-border cooperation is influenced by the relative direct political steering and dependence of the Russian law enforcement agencies as well as by its political functions. These are, although apparently less than under the communist party of the Soviet Union, still present (Shelley, 1996). Manifestations thereof include, on the one hand, the use of law enforcement agencies to target persons who are out of political grace with the case against Mikhail Khodorkovsky as most prominent recent example. On the other hand, persons who are part of the ruling class or have their support enjoy relative impunity.[12] As a consequence, liaison officers could be confronted with requests for intelligence as well as refusals to provide intelligence which only can be understood if regarded within a wider political context.

CONCLUSION

This chapter offers a brief overview of some practices in cross-border liaison and intelligence, largely based on a case study of European liaison officers stationed in the Russian Federation. It is recognized that an intelligent organization of the cross-border liaison function is a crucial requisite for the investigative process at a tactical

---

[12] See for instance 'When Children of Privilege Get Into Trouble', *Moscow Times*, 3 June 2005.

level but it can also greatly contribute to the strategic (national) criminal intelligence position. However, building effective and efficient cross-border partnerships requires adequate knowledge and understanding of legal and organizational particulars of the jurisdictions in which partnerships are sought.

For law enforcement cooperation within Europe multiple arrangements, like, for example, Europol and the Police Working Group on Terrorism, provide an accumulated body of knowledge and experience for this challenge. In environments where such established arrangements are absent, the deployment of competent liaison officers has proved to be an effective and efficient alternative strategy. Learning from liaison officers' practices might in turn contribute to designing robust intelligence systems particularly where there is a need to exchange intelligence and amalgamate partnerships across jurisdictional or institutional boundaries.

REFERENCES

BIGO, D, *Polices en réseaux: l'expérience européenne* (Paris: Presses des sciences politiques, 1996).

——, 'Liaison officers in Europe: New officers in the European security field' in Sheptycki, J, ed, *Issues in Transnational Policing* (London: Routledge, 2000) 67–99.

BLOCK, L, 'International policing in Russia: Police cooperation between the European Union Member States and the Russian Federation' *Policing and Society* 17/4 (December 2007) 367–387.

BROVKIN, VN, 'Corruption in 20th Century Russia', *Crime, Law and Social Change* 40/2–3 (2003) 195–230.

EUROPOL, *Annual Report*, 2006.

HARFIELD, C and HARFIELD, K, *Covert Investigation* (Oxford: Oxford University Press, 2005).

MARX, GT, 'Social control across borders' in McDonald, WF, ed, *Crime and Law Enforcement in the Global Village* (Cincinatti: Anderson, 1997) 23–39.

MÜLLER-WILLE, B, *For Our Eyes Only? Shaping an Intelligence Community Within the EU* (European Union Institute for Security Studies Occasional Paper 50, 2004).

NADELMANN, EA, *Cops Across Borders: The Internationalization of U.S. Criminal Law Enforcement* (PA: Pennsylvania State University Press, 1994).

RATCLIFFE, J, ed, *Strategic Thinking in Criminal Intelligence* (Annandale NSW: Federation Press, 2004).

ROBERTSON, KG, 'Practical police cooperation in Europe: The intelligence dimension' in Anderson, M and den Boer, M, eds, *Policing Across National Boundaries* (London: Pinter, 1994) 106–118.

RIJKEN, C and VERMEULEN, G, *Joint Investigation Teams in the European Union: From Theory to Practice* (The Hague: TMC Asser Press, 2006).

SCHARPF, F, *Governing in Europe: Effective and Democratic?* (Oxford: Oxford University Press, 1999).

SHELLEY, L, 'Post-Soviet Policing: A Historical Perspective' in Marenin, O, ed, *Policing Change, Changing Police* (London: Routledge, 1996) 205–221.

SWEDISH CUSTOMS, *Annual Report*, 2005.

TAK, P, 'Bottlenecks in international police and judicial cooperation in the EU', *European Journal of Crime, Criminal Law and Criminal Justice* (2000) 343–360.

15

EUROPOL AND THE UNDERSTANDING OF INTELLIGENCE

Maren Eline Kleiven and Dr Clive Harfield

INTRODUCTION

Historically, intelligence has often played a peripheral role in approaches to policing, being something that *added* to the investigative picture (Ratcliffe, 2004b; Kleiven, 2007) or *supported* the operations (Nicholl, 2004: 55) rather than informing policing strategy and style. Expert advocates have long argued that intelligence is the key to success in policing (Grieve, 2004), but only recently has intelligence enjoyed strategic pre-eminence. The 1990s saw the emergence of intelligence-led policing, with resources reassigned from investigation to intelligence gathering and processing. The implementation of intelligence-led policing has not been without problems. Many police organizations have lacked an inherent intelligence-focused culture. Definitions of intelligence have been problematic, with consequential confusion about function and purpose, about the necessary knowledge required of the intelligence generators and users, about different sources of intelligence and the operational implications thereof, and the purposes for gathering and using intelligence (Kleiven, 2007).

Internationally, the importance of information and intelligence exchange was recognized with the establishment of Interpol (created in 1923 and reconstituted in 1956: Deflem, 2002, Chapter 5). Within the European Union (EU), the removal of internal border controls provided the rationale for enhanced criminal intelligence exchange amongst Member States made manifest in the establishment of the European Drug Intelligence Unit which in turn became the European Police Office (Europol), the legal foundation of which is the Europol Convention 1995 (Official Journal of the European Communities C 316, 27 November 1995). Europol now sits at the heart of the European vision for an area of freedom, security, and justice. This paper, based on research interviews with Europol staff, will explore some of the challenges around the conception of intelligence amongst staff at Europol and considers if Europol, as a modern institution, is able to look beyond traditional approaches to intelligence towards a more knowledge-based approach.

EUROPOL

The Europol Convention came into force in October 1998. Based in The Hague, the Netherlands, Europol is now the centre for the exchange of police, customs and security information and intelligence analysis between Member States in the EU and cooperating Third Party partners. It is a unique international institution because it has been established to have access to and use personal data for the purpose of analysis, although like Interpol it has now direct operational powers. Europol can participate and provide intelligence and analytical support in joint operations where two or more EU Member States are involved. The organization is staffed by senior police, customs, or security officers delegated and seconded from their domestic organizations either as Europol Liaison Officers (ELOs), Serious Crime Experts, or as analysts (Monar, 2001: 206; see also Harfield, 2006: 746). It also directly employs its own staff. An ELO is placed in the Europol building to coordinate information exchange and the resulting measures between Member States and with Europol. The analysts provide assistance from within the Europol Analysis Unit, both within strategic and operational analysis (Europol, 2000: 5). Europol was established to carry out specific tasks on behalf of the member States (Ibid), and tasking will derive from three main sources (Europol, 2000: 8):

- Europol National Units located within Member States;
- the political framework of the EU (see Mitsilegas et al, 2003);
- Europol self-tasking (internally identified issues).

The tasks vary in nature: from providing expertise from ELOs or Europol personnel to operational teams, to providing training for national police officers and supporting investigations, though it has no operational powers of its own. Another important task is to provide strategic intelligence, and this is mainly done through the annual Organized Crime Threat Assessment (OCTA) reports (Europol, 2007). Intelligence Analysis is a core function at Europol, and the Europol Convention 1995 (Article 10) gives direction to how the analyst will work within the organization (Europol, 2000: 6). The intelligence analyst must consider all available sources and Europol has categorized three main sources of information and intelligence (Europol, 2000: 17):

- open sources—information publicly available including, for instance, media sources, scientific journals, data bases, academic reports, and libraries;
- closed information—information collected for a specific purpose with limited access or distribution;
- classified information—information collected by tasked covert means, including human and technical sources.

Europol's Analytical Guidelines state that it is vital that the analyst must 'avoid becoming a victim to the concept that only closed or classified data sources have authority' (Europol, 2000: 17), and that open source information can offer important contextual knowledge (Ibid, 18). Though the Director of Europol, Max-Peter Ratzel, states in the introduction that 'Europol is the European Union Law Enforcement Organization that handles *criminal* intelligence' (Europol, 2007, emphasis added), the Analytical Guidelines remind readers that the term 'Intelligence Analysis' is deliberately preferred instead of 'Criminal Intelligence Analysis' to underline the need for the incorporation of a wide spectrum of disciplines (Europol, 2000: 4).

INTELLIGENCE AND KNOWLEDGE

Europol defines Intelligence as 'Knowledge (processed information) designed for action' (Europol, 2000, insert 1). Within this construction, knowledge is information that has been interpreted by analysts based on the quality and quantity of information and on the analysts' knowledge and expertise. Dean and Gottschalk identify a 'hierarchy of police knowledge': data—information—intelligence—knowledge. Intelligence is viewed as facts and other data organized 'to characterize or profile a particular situation'; whilst knowledge comprises judgements and assessments informed by belief, (perceived) truths, and expectations (Dean and Gottschalk, 2007: 5). Butler states that 'intelligence merely provides techniques for improving the basis for knowledge... The most important limitation on intelligence is its incompleteness' (2004: paras 47 and 49). For these commentators, knowledge has conceptual primacy over intelligence. Knowledge, which logic dictates must include community knowledge as well as practitioner, policymaker, and expert knowledge, provides the context within which judgements about the proportionality of proposed intelligence-led responses should be considered (Harfield and Kleiven, Chapter 18 below).

RESEARCH

The present research investigated perceptions and understandings of intelligence amongst Europol staff, and whether this modern institution is developing philosophies and methods beyond the traditional use of intelligence towards a more knowledge-based approach. Therefore, the aims of this research investigation have been:

- to identify what officers and analysts at Europol understand by 'intelligence', 'knowledge' and 'information';
- to identify how well functioning the sharing of intelligence and knowledge is within Europol;
- to identify factors that could contribute to a more successful brokering of intelligence and knowledge.

METHODOLOGY

Semi-structured interviews were conducted in English (a working language of the EU and its institutions) with five serious-crime experts, four analysts, and two European

Liaison Officer (ELOs). One analyst and one expert from this data-set subsequently also answered follow-up questions of clarification. The data were gathered during fieldwork conducted by Kleiven during the spring of 2006.

Due to the nature of this research, which involved police intelligence and therefore sensitive data and personnel, some key ethical principles were followed (Hayden and Shawyer, 2004: 65). Official access was sought through senior police officers. All participation was voluntary and the candidates were asked in advance to participate. Some of the interviews were arranged through the interviewee's leaders and it is therefore important to recognize that this may have influenced their willingness to volunteer. Due to the nature of the topic the candidates were not questioned about personal information and all the data obtained has been kept anonymous and confidential. For this reason alone, there is no categorization of gender or age. Finally, the interviews did not contain questions likely to disclose sensitive intelligence material.

FINDINGS

Europol aspires to modern, sophisticated, state-of-the-art intelligence analysis. The aim of this research has been to examine if Europol, as a centre of excellence in intelligence analysis, has been able to function as a pioneer within this field, moving intelligence-led policing a step further towards knowledge-based policing, which some view theoretically as an enhancement of intelligence-led policing (see discussion in Harfield and Kleiven, Chapter 18 below). The quality and experience within this field of expertise varies to a vast degree in the different European countries. Europol recognized this early on and produced its 'Analytical Guidelines' to ensure that the analysts, regardless of nationality, 'speak with the same voice' (Europol, 2000: 3). 'Without such an approach it will be difficult for intelligence agencies of the Member States to fully understand each other's methods' (Ibid, 12). Despite the Guidelines, many of the interviews illustrated a lack of mutual understanding around many aspects of intelligence-led policing, including definitions of common terms.

Definitions of Intelligence Amongst Europol Staff

Europol defines intelligence as 'Knowledge (processed information) designed for action' (Europol, 2000, insert 1) thus, coincidentally, applying the reverse logic to that of Dean and Gottschalk (2007: 5). Given the defining characteristic of intelligence within the raison d'être of Europol, interviewees were asked to outline their personal definition of intelligence, and the responses showed different interpretations of the term. A majority of the interviewees merely equated intelligence with information, whereas a minority looked upon intelligence as information that has gone through a process, as data in need of more assessment. For example: 'Intelligence is information that has been processed. Raw data that has been evaluated, analysed and filtered.' (interview B3).

Another interviewee defined intelligence as being information exclusively from a covert source: 'I like to see a protection level. It has to be some sort of secrecy. I like the word covert connected to intelligence. Police data is not intelligence' (A1).

Since Europol's definition of intelligence is structured around the terms 'knowledge' and 'information' it was important to identify what the interviewees themselves understood by those terms. As stated above, a majority felt that intelligence and information are the same thing. For the rest, there were several suggestions as to what information might be although most interviewees thought it was everything and anything that gives added value. One thought surprisingly enough that information is: '. . .much more crime related than intelligence. It is provided in a more structured way than intelligence, more directed' (C1).

Definitions of Knowledge Amongst Europol Staff

When it came to the definition of knowledge, approximately half defined it as science, where the rest elaborated on that, saying it is something you gain through studying, training, and experience. Given Europol's definition of intelligence, it is interesting to note that almost all of the interviewees saw a distinction between intelligence products and knowledge products, terms which have very specific definitions within the UK National Intelligence Model for instance (ACPO, 2005). When it came to intelligence products, several interviewees expressed frustrations:

It is a problem that a lot of countries don't have a grading system. Translate that into 25 countries—how can you understand as an analyst from Finland what or how a Greek has graded the intelligence? (A2)

When one establishes an institution like Europol it is important to make sure one has a common understanding of what intelligence is. Internally here in the building there is a difference in the comprehension of what Europol should do and of what intelligence means (C2).

Europol wishes to share knowledge in this area with all authorities of the EU (Europol, 2000: 3), being a 'knowledge-broker' (Cambell, 2004: 696). Though this is a stated aim for Europol, concerns were raised:

Knowledge-based policing? We're still struggling with intelligence and the sharing of information (A1).

Language is a constraint. Then you have to have compatible police structures. Before you can have knowledge-based policing, you need all the countries to do intelligence led policing, but many countries don't. It is still a long way to go (B2).

Largest problem is that we are so much depending on the MS. We can create knowledge on our own, but that might not be what the MS wants. Though we might want to go one way, the MS might say, no we want to prioritise differently (B1).

Europol recommends in its Guidelines that all sources of intelligence must be used, specifically underlining the need for addressing the unilateral use of closed information. The all-source analyst must use open source to give credibility to the final product and give it a detailed contextual knowledge (Europol, 2000: 17–18). Despite these auspicious words, one analyst stated: 'In my personal perception it needs to be from a *covert* source, like informants, surveillance, and wire taps. Open sources, for example from phone books, is just information, it's not intelligence' (A1).

A majority of the interviewees defined open-source information as knowledge and not intelligence:

I gather knowledge from the intelligence we get from open sources. Operational criminal intelligence would be from the Member States (B1).

I think we neglect open sources and other sources like University environment—methodology especially. We stick to the old way here in Europol instead of applying new, modern knowledge (B4).

Europol as an organization is not the node where knowledge comes to, it is completely dependent on the people within the organization (C1).

Data Sharing

Information and intelligence are stored in the Europol Information System (Europol's internal information system) and for a specific operational project within an Analysis Work File. Data in a work file is strictly controlled and Europol is based on a 'need to know and a right to use' principle (Europol, 2000: 5). Almost half of the interviewees expressed a clear concern around this philosophy and the lack of horizontal sharing:

The legislation is a constraint. 'The more you share the more you get'. There has to be a level of trust (B5).

There is a lack of horizontal sharing of information. Everybody is sitting in their own room. If the guys in terrorism find a link to my type of crime, they won't tell me. This is something that should have been done by a knowledge-broker, but we don't have one. I have my own contacts within the 25 Member States. Much faster than within this house (C1).

A rigid framework is absolutely a hindrance. The Europol convention makes it difficult to share information internally. A work file has information—a telephone number can pop up in three or four work files. We should have someone that sees the whole picture—a horizontal approach, a cross check (C2).

If you read the convention there are too many limitations. The mandate is too rigid. (C3).

These views, perhaps unsurprisingly, are diametrically opposite to those held by civil liberties organizations. In particular Statewatch (<http://www.statewatch.org>), a UK-based organization, monitors EU developments and has frequently expressed concerns about the extent to which Europol and other institutions are empowered to share sensitive and personal data (Statewatch, 2005a, 2005b, 2006). Essentially the Europol staff are highlighting restrictions on the use of data submitted to Europol but still 'owned' by Member States, an issue also examined by Ridley (Chapter 10 above).

Member States

Europol states that it has been has been 'created to carry out specific tasks on behalf of the Member States of the EU' (Europol, 2000) and that each Member State should use Europol for all it has to offer, whether it is in the form of information exchange, analysis, or support of on-going investigations (Europol 2000: 5). A majority of the interviewees expressed clear frustration around the lack of involvement, awareness, and commitment from the different Member States:

The member states tend not to use us, and we cannot go further than the Member States want us to (B1).

We are struggling to get information from Member States and also from the people behind (B2).

The Member States have the knowledge about the crime—they lack the knowledge about what is Europol and what Europol can do (B5).

The problem is that the Member States only see their own country (the little picture)—they don't see the bigger picture. That's where the constraints lie. Europol should have more powers to tell the MS to *prioritize important cases!* (That is not investigatory powers, but the powers to steer the countries) (B1).

Some of the interviewees had a different approach, pointing out that it is easy to forget what the different nations have to struggle with. They underlined that Europol is a very young organization:

I have confidence in the Member States when it comes to sharing of knowledge, but they have to be reminded from time to time. If police officers would be more aware of Europol and what we can do, then I am sure much more information would come in (C1).

Member States would be more active if Europol could give a clear sign on what Europol wants (C3).

The Analytical Guidelines recognize that geographical distance and differences can influence the work of the analyst (Europol, 2000: 8). One of the interviewees states:

You still have many countries, which have many law enforcement agencies. Different legislations, different hierarchies, management, different heads of investigation, different styles, language, and cultural differences (C2).

Europol acknowledges in the Analytical Guidelines that other international and national organizations also produce important analytical work within a law enforcement environment and seeks to avoid a duplication of effort (Europol, 2000: 7). On the Europol homepage there is listed a number of EU bodies and other international organizations: European Commission, OLAF, UNODC, World Customs Organization, European Central Bank, and Interpol. The nature of this cooperation was elaborated upon by one of the interviewees:

With some non-EU countries or international bodies Europol has operational agreements (exchange of personal data allowed) or strategic agreements (no exchange of personal data allowed). The agreements with the Commission and OLAF are (so far still) 'administrative' agreements (allegedly, because they do not handle operational data)—which is basically the same as strategic (B2).

The interview design was such that future longitudinal studies could be undertaken to assess and measure the extent to which such apparent variable understanding amongst Europol staff changes over time as the organization matures during its second decade.

DISCUSSION AND CONCLUSION

Why, in an era when 'intelligence-led policing' features regularly in law enforcement and political rhetoric, are Member States apparently perceived as not making the most of an intelligence agency? The responses suggest a confused understanding (amongst all parties) of the relationship between Europol and relevant authorities within the EU Member States. Both the EU institutions and the individual Member States are clients of Europol. Yet Europol is also, to a significant degree, dependent as a client upon Member States for the information it analyses and disseminates. Not only may Member State governments have different individual expectations of Europol but the different policing, intelligence, border security, and customs authorities within each Member State may have different individual needs and expectations.

From this relatively small data-set emerge several characteristics of intelligence conceptualization and the processing of intelligence within Europol:

- There is no common understanding amongst Europol staff of how intelligence is defined, nor agreement on how it should be defined.
- There consequently appears to be no strong theoretical or conceptual basis under-pinning capacity and capability within Europol.
- There are strongly-held perceptions of data silos and a general lack of horizontal intelligence sharing, even to the extent that some staff consider it faster and more effective to contact a Member State directly than to contact the relevant ELO stationed at Europol.
- A rigid Convention framework is perceived as making it difficult to share information internally.
- There are different opinions held internally about the nature and function of Europol.
- There are perceived to be significant differences in philosophy towards and effort invested in Europol amongst different Member States.
- There is perceived to be a lack of knowledge externally amongst Member States domestic agencies about the support that can be given by Europol.

Taken together, this set of characteristics identified within this study illustrates generally-held perceptions of seemingly significant cultural and organizational barriers and impediments to the efficient and effective functioning of Europol. Whilst not necessarily equating with actuality, perceptions (even if misconceived) nevertheless define 'reality' for those working in any given environment. In a rather different study Ridley (Chapter 10 above), himself a former strategic analyst with Europol, provides corroboration for some of the findings above when discussing the failure of Europol to identify the emergent Albanian organized crime threat in the 1990s, just the sort of emerging strategic threat that the organization was set up to identify. Nevertheless, this present study could usefully be supplemented through repetition and through a study of perceptions held amongst practitioners in Member State domestic agencies. Instead of being used as an opportunity to highlight success stories (a response that could reasonably have been anticipated), this study has tapped into a rich vein of frustration that Europol could achieve more than it is achieving.

Indirectly the study has raised a number of governance issues. Practitioner complaints about overly-restrictive data-sharing regulation must be tempered with alternative views about the need for transparent governance. Abuse of institutional power or data access does not serve the community interest. Yet neither, too, does a dysfunctional institution. Europol makes bold claims: 'Information and communication may be considered, as law enforcement enters the new millennium, as the most important strategic means of dealing with the major social problems which will impact upon the EU' (Europol, 2000: 12). Law enforcement now operates within an information age that is making new demands of and is generating new expectations amongst the public and public servants alike. A number of cases in the UK over the last decade or more (the murders of Stephen Lawrence, Victoria Climbié, Jessica Chapman and Holly Wells, Naomi Bryant: summarized in Harfield and Harfield 2008, Chapter 2 and Kleiven, 2007) have identified lessons to be learnt and areas for improvement for law enforcement agencies as the profession of criminal intelligence continues to develop.

In the case of Europol it is important to maintain its development into an institution that is able to filter, manage, and interpret the levels of data generated by the information age in a professional manner. Europol, and society in general, are standing at a crossroads where decisions about secrecy or sharing, purpose, and proportionality have to be made. Practitioners advocate a new way of thinking where the focus is towards 'the more we share the more we get' rather than a 'need to know'. But this cannot be an end in and of itself. There is a need for a knowledge-based approach where effectiveness is rated higher than efficiency in order to tackle the challenges of the future.

REFERENCES

ACPO, *Practice Guidance on the National Intelligence Model* (Wyboston: Centrex, 2005).

BICHARD, M, *The Bichard Inquiry Report* (HC653, London: The Stationery Office, 2004) available at <http://www.bichardinquiry.org.uk/>, accessed on 20 October 2004.

BUTLER, Lord, *Review of Intelligence on Mass Destruction* (HC 898, London: TSO, 2004) available at <http://www.thebutlerreview.org.uk>, accessed on 18 October 2004.

CENTREX, *Guidance on the National Intelligence Model* (Hampshire: Centrex, 2005).

CAMPBELL, E, 'Police narrativity in the risk society' *The British Journal of Criminology* 44/5 (2004) 695–714.

DEAN, G and GOTTSCHALK, P, *Knowledge Management in Policing and Law Enforcement: Foundations, Structures, Applications* (Oxford: Oxford University Press, 2007).

DEFLEM, M, *Policing World Society: Historical Foundations of International Police Cooperation* (Oxford: Oxford University Press, 2002).

EUROPOL, *Analytical Guidelines* (The Hague: Europol, 2000).

——, *OCTA—The Organized Crime Threat Assessment 2007* (The Hague: Europol, 2007).

GRIEVE, J, 'Developments in UK criminal intelligence' in Ratcliffe, J, ed, *Strategic Thinking in Criminal Intelligence* (Sydney: The Federation Press, 2004) 25–36.

HARFIELD, C, 'SOCA: A paradigm shift in British policing' *British Journal of Criminology* 46 (2006) 743–761.

—— and HARFIELD, K, *Covert Investigation* (Oxford: Oxford University Press, 2005).

HARFIELD, C and HARFIELD K, *Intelligence: Investigation, Community, and Partnership* (Oxford: Oxford University Press, 2008).

HAYDEN, C and SHAWYER, A, *Research Methods and Research Management* (Open Learning Materials, Institute of Criminal Justice Studies, Portsmouth: University of Portsmouth, 2004).

HOBBS, Z, 'Police informants—opportunities and temptations: How can it lead to unethical police practices?' (MSc Dissertation, Criminal Justice Studies, University of Portsmouth, 2001).

KLEIVEN, ME, 'Where's the intelligence in the national intelligence model?' *International Journal of Police Science and Management* 9/3 (2007) 257–273.

LAMING, Lord, *The Victoria Climbié Inquiry* (2003) available at <http://www.victoria-climbié-inquiry.org.uk/index.htm>, accessed on 1 May 2005.

MACPHERSON, W, *The Stephen Lawrence Inquiry* (London: The Stationary Office Limited, 1999).

MITSILEGAS, V, MONAR, J and REES, W, *The European Union and Internal Security: Guardian of the People?* (Basingstoke: Palgrave MacMillan, 2003).

MONAR, J, 'Institutionalizing freedom, security, and justice' in Peterson, J and Shackleton, M, eds, *The Institutions of the European Union* (Oxford: Oxford University Press, 2001) 187–209.

NCIS, *The NIM* (London: NCIS, 2000) available at <http://www.homeoffice.gov.uk>, accessed on 10 August 2004.

NICHOLL, J, 'Task definition' in Ratcliffe, JH, ed, *Strategic Thinking in Criminal Intelligence* (Sydney: The Federation Press, 2004) 53–69.

RATCLIFFE, JH, (2002a) 'Intelligence-led policing and the problems of turning rhetoric into practice' *Policing and Society* 1 (2002) 53–66.

——, (2002b) 'Damned if you don't, damned if you do: Crime mapping and its implications in the real world' *Policing and Society* 12 (2002) 211–225.

——, 'Intelligence-led policing' *Trends and Issues in Crime and Criminal Justice No 248* (Australian Institute of Criminology, 2003).

——, ed, (2004a) *Strategic Thinking in Criminal Intelligence* (Sydney: The Federation Press, 2004).

——, (2004b) 'The structure of strategic thinking' in Ratcliffe, JH, ed, *Strategic Thinking in Criminal Intelligence* (Sydney: The Federation Press, 2004) 1–9.

—— and SHEPTYCKI, J, 'Setting the strategic agenda' in Ratcliffe, JH, ed, *Strategic Thinking in Criminal Intelligence* (Sydney: The Federation Press, 2004) 194–209.

STATEWATCH, (2005a) 'EU Policy Putsch: Data protection handed to the DG for law, order and security' *Statewatch Bulletin* 15/2 (2005) 1.

——, (2005b) 'Interoperability—the end of checks and balances on EU databases' *Statewatch Bulletin* 15/6 (2005) 1.

——, 'EU—Eight years on the data protection fiasco continues' *Statewatch Bulletin* 15/2 (2006) 1.

TILLEY, N, (2003a) *Problem-Oriented Policing, Intelligence-Led Policing and the NIM* (London: Jill Dando Institute of Criminal Science, 2003) available at <http://www.jdi.ucl.ac.uk/publications>, accessed on 10 August 2004.

——, (2003b) 'Community policing, problem-oriented policing and intelligence-led policing' in Newburn, T, ed, *Handbook of Policing* (Devon: Willan Publishing, 2003) 311–339.

WILLIAMSON, T, 'Policing's community challenge' in *Jane's Police Review* (1 July 2005) available at <http://www.policereview.com>, accessed on 8 August 2005.

YIN, RK, *Case Study Research—Design and Methods* (Applied Social Research Methods, Volume 5, 3rd edn, London: SAGE Publications, 2003).

PART IV

BENCHMARKING THE WAY FORWARD

INTRODUCTION TO PART IV:
THE FUTURE OF INTELLIGENCE

Professor Allyson MacVean

Policing in the twenty-first century is characterized by complexity, globalization, and new forms of threat. The need for wider strategic vision and unifying traditional cultural divides are imperative in securing confidence and trust in policing.

Throughout this volume, there is a concurrence that the terrorist attacks of 11 September 2001 in America provided a watershed for change. The previous localized structures and territories delineated by specific organisation roles and functions were proving counterproductive. Hawley, in opening his chapter portrays the cultural gaps between intelligence and operations that was encapsulated in The Commission on Terrorist Attacks upon the United States (9/11 Commission Report). Hawley argues that the cultural gap is the greatest challenge to intelligent policing today. Drawing upon the lessons learnt from the cultural divide between the intelligence and investigational areas of the Federal Bureau of Investigation (FBI), the Australian Federal Police (AFP) is reforming intelligence doctrine and processes. The key objective is to foster and enhance relationships between intelligence units and their operational and executive partners.

Hawley provides a historical narrative to the intelligence failures of the past and how such failure impacts upon organisational efficiency. Tribal rivalry and turf wars both within and between intelligence and operations inhibit the capacity for the development of a consilient approach to the intelligence process. The Australian Federal Police are redressing this issue through a partnership programme of change including education and the development of doctrine and process. But, as Hawley points out, the success of intelligence ultimately depends upon a discourse involving consilient relationships to develop intelligent policing rather than intelligence per se.

Stanko brings the global back to the local. Exploiting strategic intelligence using a consilient range of methodologies and partners can assist police organisations to understand better the concept of harm. This chapter provides an insightful reflection on how neighbourhood policing provides a mechanism to structure knowledge gleamed from local districts and translate it into strategic intelligence about crime problems that have yet to be fully developed. Using a unique and creative approach, Stanko challenges the traditional paradigm in which theories are translated into practice and, instead, attempts to map theoretical wisdom onto organisational ways of working. By applying innovative methodologies that are grounded in local information and local needs Stanko has been able to develop research, map-making, and analysis in the same vein as Dr John Snow and Reverend Henry Whitehead in their search into the cause of the cholera outbreak in Victorian London.

Stanko advocates the benefits of multi-partnership, multigenerational dialogue, including members of the community, as 'smart use' of information in shoring-up and developing community confidence. Intelligent policing for Stanko, is not about harvesting new and additional information, but about promoting a culture in which the existing recorded-crime information is fully understood and exploited as part of policing strategy for the detecting and prevention of crime.

Just as Stanko challenged the limitations of collecting and accumulating more intelligence without embracing any strategic purpose, Harfield and Kleiven explore the limitations of intelligence-led policing. They argue that the term 'intelligence-led' is a nebulous concept which has become embedded in professional rhetoric but which has not enjoyed practitioner common understanding. In part, this is because the original thinking of intelligence-led policing has been taken out of its original conceptual context; intelligence is only one element in a continuum of police knowledge: data—information—intelligence—knowledge. The emphasis on intelligence was greater than the other elements, skewing its terms of reference. This skewing was driven further forward by the introduction of the National Intelligence Model, which failed to consider the strategies chosen to manage criminality and disorder. Thus, intelligence-led policing was limited in what it could realistically achieve. Rather, for Harfield and Kleiven, they purport that knowledge-based policing provides a framework in which intelligence, as a concept, is only one part. The changing context of policing is at present challenging the inherent constraints of the NIM, but the authors invite readers to consider and reflect whether adopting a knowledge-based approach provides an alternative solution. They pose a series of searching questions for the reader to deliberate and, in so doing, reflect on what were the lessons learnt in the conceptualization and implementation of intelligence-led policing and the NIM. And how can these lessons be incorporated into a knowledge-based policing paradigm?

In relation to knowledge-led policing, Kelly looks at the ways in which effective knowledge management practice can contribute to enhance collaborative working relationships through Crime and Disorder Reduction Partnership (CDRP) fora. Kelly explores the distinction between explicit and tacit knowledge and the management framework which is required for both sets of knowledge to coexist in partnership working. Traditionally the culture of the police, with its hierarchical structure and strong sense of mission sits uncomfortably with the more open and trusting culture required for effective knowledge management partnership working. Kelly offers a model, in which police and CDRPs might operate collectively in knowledge management in order to further partnership.

Bowers, as one of the original architects of the National Intelligence Model, explores the interaction between knowledge management and the NIM, and how this might contribute to policing in the twenty-first century. If Stanko advocated the use of smart intelligence, Bowers promotes that the successful policing agencies in the future will move away from the compliance on policy towards a culture of learning and wisdom. Arguing that NIM is a business framework in search of a theory while knowledge management is a theory in search of a framework, he explores how tacit and explicit knowledge can postulate knowledge conversation as part of the knowledge process. Additionally, he identifies the development of sophisticated technology as a means of providing the potential for exponential knowledge-creation and exploitation. However, the key to success is focusing on effective interaction and communication between people rather than replacing the interaction with technology. Drawing on empirical research Bowers identified the need for knowledge workers with specific skill sets.

Sir Paul Scott-Lee et al takes us back to the natural tensions that exist between intelligence analysis and performance management. While there is a requirement for forces to have a robust performance management process, currently it has, as Sir Ronnie Flanagan's independent review of policing report has identified, generated perverse outcomes by creating tensions between neighbourhood policing and serious crime, including terrorism. Sir Paul articulated this effect as 'hitting the target but missing the point' syndrome. Sir Paul contends that while performance and intelligence are discrete disciplines, conflict between the two can be negated through better integration into the strategic planning and tactical implementation process. West Midlands Police have pioneered an innovative approach in bringing together intelligence and performance analysis techniques to reduce tensions and enhance the reduction of crime. In moving towards a more integrated intelligence/performance management process, managing the conflict between performance and intelligence professionals must be recognized and managed. This approach has created a framework that allows better alignment between the competing governmental priorities and issues that confront local communities. The creation of a joined-up approach between intelligence analysis and performance management provides a mechanism that allows police to respond swiftly to changes in the complex environment of policing.

Professor Pease, one of the most eminent consilience thinkers within academia, draws together a series of vignettes to illustrate the unsystematic formulaic process of the Police Funding Formula (PFF). He challenges the assumption that the policing needs of an area can be inferred by its demographics and other characteristics. The formula for measuring such characteristics and their interrelated associations detracts attention from the spirit of the PFF function. Drawing from a raft of intelligent research, Professor Pease challenges conventional Home Office wisdom on the way PPF is circumscribed and allocated. While it currently may provide political capital, it does so at the expense of a good integrated method of assessing and rewarding police performance.

This collection of essays provides some reflections for the future developments of intelligent policing. It has highlighted that while the relationship between intelligence and knowledge management is complex and exclusive, there are common elements within the disciplines that, as the authors above have demonstrated, can harness them together to provide a way forward. Knowledge-led partnership and communication provide a framework in which conventional assumptions and wisdoms of intelligence can be challenged, thus developing new forms of intelligent-policing strategy and process. As Professor Pease has demonstrated, this framework is not limited to just policing agencies.

This book concludes as Sir Ronnie Flanagan's thoughtful and articulate long-awaited independent review of policing report is published. The Flanagan report provides a pragmatic vision for law enforcement in the twenty-first century. The report acknowledges that traditional methods of policing are no longer applicable or effective; what are required are better forms of intelligent policing. The level of bureaucratic process and paperwork, and the insatiale requirements of target-related indicators can no longer be sustained. Formulaic policy, without fully understanding existing information and seeking out new knowledge to inform the process, will no longer be adequate to meet the demands of policing in the twenty-first century. This part provides some innovative, reflective, and pioneering examples of intelligent policing for the future.

16

CONSILIENCE, CRIME CONTROL, AND COMMUNITY SAFETY

Federal Agent Michael Hawley

INTRODUCTION

This chapter provides an Australian perspective on effective intelligence through the development of consilient relationships. It examines the relationship between criminal-intelligence units and their most significant clients: policing, executive, and operational units. It also examines the reasons behind what can often be a fractured relationship, the harm that this can cause to effective crime control and community safety, and how the Australian Federal Police (AFP) is attempting to build a consilient[1] relationship with its most significant clients through an initiative known as the Leadership in Criminal Intelligence Program (LCIP).

There is a perception by some that managers of law enforcement agencies fund intelligence sections for one reason only—to give them someone to blame when things go wrong. This cynical view is not a serious consideration of the relationship between intelligence and operational units, but it certainly indicates that these units do not always have a consilient relationship.

A long history as an operational detective has led to managing an intelligence area that identifies and develops intelligence best practice and, consequently, an enduring interest in the convergence of operations and intelligence. Of particular interest is the relationship between these two disciplines and the policing executive, many of whom have primary responsibility for operational areas.

Certain questions arise. Do intelligence units exist largely to be blamed when things go wrong? How many chief executives of law enforcement agencies really believe that their agencies are 'intelligence led'? How many want to be intelligence led? How many law enforcement executives understand the intelligence process or its limitations?

Law enforcement officials are used to hearing two dominant but opposing mantras: the opprobrious quips made in reference to intelligence units as a safe haven

---

[1] According to the *Macquarie Dictionary*, consilient derives from the noun consilience: a linking of knowledge and theory from one or more separate disciplines to create common groundwork of explanation (from Latin *con*- together + *salire* to leap), (Yallop, 2005: 314).

for 'broken biscuits', members who are incompetent or are physically incapable of operational duties; and the more positive 'intelligence-led policing', which suggests that intelligence holds a place of such respect and significance that it leads operational decisions.

With law enforcement resources critically stretched and societies faced by the ever increasing challenges presented by organized crime and terrorism, it is important that intelligence resources be used in the most efficient and effective manner. A key element in the effective use of resources is a consilient relationship between all sections of the organization, particularly the 'sharp-end' or 'front-line' units of intelligence and operational policing.

NEED FOR CONSILIENCE

The division between intelligence and operational areas varies in intensity across agencies and time, but it is real and harmful to the effectiveness of both areas. It also corrodes the relations of the agency with government and its other external clients.

This chapter contends that there is a reluctance to confront this issue and that, until this is done, communities are exposed to an unnecessary level of risk. It is simply not enough for government or senior executives to pronounce that agencies are intelligence led. An additional responsibility lies with them and with law enforcement staff at all levels to put aside tribal loyalties to their particular discipline, to learn more about the capabilities and expectations of the other's discipline and to begin to work more cooperatively together.

Overcoming the intelligence–operations divide is probably the single most important issue facing the degree of effectiveness of contemporary law enforcement. It is an issue that needs to be faced and understood, and positive measures need to be identified and taken to close this divide if more effective strategies to improve crime control and community safety are to be implemented.

THE WATERSHED FOR CHANGE

The National Commission on Terrorist Attacks Upon the United States (also known as The 9/11 Commission Report) inquired into the tragic circumstances of the terrorist attacks on New York and Washington in 2001. The Commission examined the causes of the failure to detect the events in advance and was critical of the cultural 'wall' that had developed between intelligence and investigational areas of the Federal Bureau of Investigation (FBI).

Prior to September 2001 cultural gaps that significantly affected performance were identified between intelligence and operations in the FBI. The report (2004: 79) states: 'The 1995 procedures dealt only with sharing between agents and criminal prosecutors, not between two kinds of FBI agents, those working on intelligence matters and those working on criminal matters. But pressure from the Office of Intelligence Policy Review, FBI leadership, and the FISA Court built barriers between agents—even agents serving on the same squads.'

This finding has provoked other law enforcement agencies to examine their own organizations and see if they have benefited from the revelations of the 9/11 Commission Report.

Until intelligence units are able to gain and maintain the respect and trust of both the executive and operational areas within their own agencies, the ability to develop consilience between the agency and their external partners is significantly impeded.

AN AUSTRALIAN PERSPECTIVE

This chapter discusses the journey that the Australian Federal Police (AFP) Intelligence is taking in reforming its intelligence doctrine and processes. The driving objective is to improve the effectiveness of the relationship that the intelligence unit has with its most significant internal client areas, particularly executive and operational partners. It is believed that by developing consilient relationships the AFP can build a strong and coherent organization, one that is able to win the respect of government and other external partners, both national and international.

The journey is being led by the National Manager Dr Grant Wardlaw and his executive team. Key to their deliberations is the work of the Leadership in Criminal Intelligence Program (LCIP). The LCIP was formed to identify, develop and implement best practice in criminal intelligence for the AFP and to advance the quality of internal relationships between the function and its client areas.

Although the journey has begun, it is not complete; nor is it without risk. Similarly, it is not easy, and the organizational commitment required is significant. But without a concerted investment and effort the results believed possible will not be gained. Without such commitment the risk to the business unit is high; but this risk is insignificant when compared to the risk to the organization and, more importantly, to the community. The task, therefore, is to identify barriers to building a consilient relationship with internal and external clients, developing and implementing effective cooperative mechanisms, and monitoring progress.

Like so many philosophical explorations this journey is ongoing and may never be completed, but progress has been significant.

NEED FOR A CHANGE IN FOCUS

As for most law enforcement agencies in advanced democracies, the tragic events of 9 September 2001 were a watershed in the AFP's policing arrangements. The intelligence community, released from its Cold War focus on state-sponsored espionage, had yet to come to terms with onshore terrorism and the demands that this would place upon it to engage in the full spectrum of the criminal justice process. Policing, similarly, needed a change in focus—to move into the national-security arena and learn to engage the intelligence community more cooperatively. Equally as critical, law enforcement agencies needed to be more proactive and accept that the key mission was not only the successful investigation of crime but also, preferably, the prevention of crime before it impacts on community safety. Intelligence fulfils this role.

The AFP Ministerial Direction (2006: 5), which guides AFP activity, expects the AFP to give special attention to 'preventing, countering and investigating terrorism under Commonwealth legislation' and to 'preventing, countering and investigating transnational and multi-jurisdictional crime'.

The Ministerial Direction clearly gives the same weight to 'preventing and countering' criminal activity as it does to 'investigating' crime.

It seems reasonable to argue that if, in the minds of government, preventing and countering crime prior to the overt act have equal standing to investigation then intelligence units within law enforcement have an equal and critical role to play in meeting this expectation. In addition, as intelligence units exist to provide well-thought-out advice to their internal and external clients, then it is essential that the relationships with these clients is such that they seek intelligence advice and have trust in its value once received.

DEFINITION OF INTELLIGENCE

Intelligence has been variously regarded as 'secret information' or a 'process'. The AFP, however, defines intelligence as a product derived from adding value to information to provide insight and influence decision-making.

This definition relates to the contemporary law enforcement environment in which a single intelligence assessment may contain relevant information that can range from 'nationally classified' to 'open source'. The key elements of this definition are:

- *Product*: Intelligence has no value if it cannot be communicated to those it seeks to influence. An intelligence product need not be a hard-copy report; it can be in any form suitable to convey the judgements made by the analysts.
- *Derived from adding value*: In modern law enforcement, analysts are often confronted by very large amounts of information. The task of the intelligence practitioner is to distil this information, thus providing meaningful analysis and comment.
- *Provide insight and influence decision making*: Intelligence practitioners do not become the decision-makers: this is the role of the executive. Intelligence supports the executive decision-making process by providing an appreciation of the issue under consideration and offering options and assessments of the viability of those options. The executive needs to consider this guidance in concert with advice from other stakeholders such as policy and finance before deciding on the course of action.

For the intelligence product to be accepted and valued by internal clients, intelligence departments need to have the respect of those clients. This is not always the case. Tribal rivalry between departments is not restricted to law enforcement. It can be just as corrosive to the commercial success of businesses as it can to the value of intelligence in law enforcement agencies. It is interesting to note that literature abounds on this dynamic in business. However, research on this subject in the law enforcement environment is meagre. This raises the question of whether this scarcity of research reflects a reluctance of law enforcement agencies to confront the dangers inherent in the divisiveness caused by tribal rivalries.

Law enforcement practitioners are well aware of tribal rivalries within their ranks. Writing on a joint agency investigation into a series of sexual assaults in Ontario, Alan Harman (1997: 106) refers to a subsequent report by Justice Archie Campbell which states: 'Ego clashes, turf competition and inherent rivalry between police services [were] a "natural everyday fact of . . . police life which got in the way of effective law enforcement".'

Similarly, such rivalries impact upon intelligence services, vital partners and clients of law enforcement in the fight against terrorism. Hitz and Weiss (2004: 10) quote a senior Central Intelligence Agency (CIA) operative as saying that geographic divisions of responsibility 'create jurisdictional and coordination squabbles that play right into terrorists' hands.' Furthermore, this operative admitted that internal politics 'were crippling our efforts to deal with one of the most important issues facing the administration . . . it all came down to turf . . . Obstructionism was rampant.'

Hitz and Weiss's comments raise several questions: why does the relationship between intelligence and operational areas sometimes fail, how does this failure in relationship impact upon the efficiency of the overall law enforcement process, and what has the AFP, through LCIP, done to develop and maintain consilience in the relationship between intelligence and operational areas?

WHY THE INTELLIGENCE/OPERATIONAL RELATIONSHIP CAN FAIL

Given the scarcity of information on tribal rivalry in the law enforcement context, an examination of this characteristic in business may provide some answers to the questions posed.

Business is driven by a profit motive, and results are generally more easily quantifiable than the successes of law enforcement endeavours. Furthermore, in many companies, departments exist as separate profit centres trading with each other in a manner not dissimilar to how they engage with external suppliers or clients. The internal environment in such companies is sometimes more competitive than that existing between the company and its external competitors. Paradoxically, however, the success of the organization depends largely on successful internal cooperation.

In law enforcement, however, intelligence and investigations form integral parts of a continuum, with a common mission to protect and serve the community. With a common mission and without an evident reason for enforced internal competition, it is reasonable to assume that cooperation would be the norm. This is not always the case, however.

So why does the relationship between intelligence and operational areas fail? Corrosive tribal rivalries in law enforcement are cultural. They develop through a process involving misunderstanding, competition for resources, and fear. Competition is sometimes introduced in the mistaken belief that it will stimulate efficiency. However, focusing on efficiency at the departmental level can sometimes be detrimental to the effectiveness of the organization as a whole. In other words, individual departmental successes do not necessarily contribute to the effectiveness of the organization as a whole.

Rivalry can sometimes be subtle and unnoticed, as Lewis et al (1997: 277) point out. Many conflicts in organizations become institutionalized through commonly-held attitudes, values and rituals, so conflict can become part of the organization's culture without members becoming aware of its presence. This rivalry not only impacts on the internal efficiency of the agency but also on how it is able to relate with external clients and government. Campbell (1998: 214) highlights this difficulty when she says that if internal competition, conflict, and aggressive behaviour typify an organization then it has a problem with 'relationship marketing'.

Despite the fact that some would believe tribal rivalry to be a natural phenomenon, additional factors influence the potential for disharmony in the relationship that intelligence has with its clients.

First, intelligence involves dealing with material that is often not available to other areas of an agency. Although secrecy is required, it can often become a wall—encapsulating intelligence, breeding egos, and separating the function from the very source of the information it needs to adequately perform its duties. Referring to a culture of secrecy Hitz and Weiss (2004: 13) state that the problem comes 'when secrecy is no longer considered a necessary evil, but the standard way of conducting business . . . Those on the "inside" can lose touch with those who are not . . . This can lead to unreasonable expectations from outsiders, and the dangerous insider belief that only those with secret access can provide useful analysis and relevant wisdom.'

Second, there exists a false expectation of the role of intelligence and its potential to know all the answers all the time.

Third, quality intelligence is not always acted upon. Stories of 'intelligence failure' abound—and many are well deserved. However, while some of these incidents reflect the inefficient application of the intelligence process, others actually represent situations where decision-makers and policy-makers have ignored intelligence advice. In addition to the expectation that intelligence should know the unknowable, decision-makers do not always trust the intelligence provided; intelligence is often under-resourced and there is pressure to deliver a product supporting a preconceived position.

Two well-known examples illustrate the so-called 'failure of intelligence'. Montgomery was provided with intelligence regarding considerable numbers of German forces in the Arnhem region of the Netherlands prior to the launch of Operation Market Garden in the Second World War. He chose to go ahead with the operation regardless of this advice—and the results were disastrous. Similarly, the invasion of South Korea was predicted although the exact date was not known. Ameliorating actions were not commenced because of cognitive dissonance—a refusal to believe a pattern of predicted activity that did not match an existing framework of belief. Marrin (2004: 655) claims that in March 1950, the CIA predicted that an attack could happen in June. Subsequently, military leaders were provided with about 1,200 reports indicating a massive North Korean military build-up. He goes on to say that in spite of these warnings and indicators of North Korean capability to attack, 'United States military commanders believed that geostrategic considerations would prevent North Korea from actually attacking. They were wrong, and for very similar reasons were wrong about the later Chinese intervention as well.'

A further factor influencing the quality of the relationship between intelligence and operations is a mistaken understanding of the nature of intelligence and, hence, an undervaluing of the specialization involved in the production of high quality analysis. Moreover, intelligence areas generally include a high proportion of non-sworn members. While they bring a richness to the analysis process through the addition of broad intelligence experience, this exacerbates the cultural divide between intelligence and operational areas, which are predominantly staffed by police.

The cultural divide also has a historical aspect. Many police have seen intelligence members assigned to perform data-input tasks and expect this to continue. Intelligence resources are scarce, highly valued, and seldom available for routine data-processing. However, this role is still mistakenly requested of intelligence areas, and refusal to assist is sometimes seen as failing to meet client requirements.

HOW RELATIONSHIP FAILURE IMPACTS ON ORGANIZATIONAL EFFICIENCY

The second question asks how the failure in relationship impacts upon the efficiency of the overall law enforcement process. As mentioned above, The 9/11 Commission Report clearly pointed to the impact of relationship failure between operational and intelligence areas of the FBI and the CIA. While these failures were brought sharply into focus by the investigation of the terrorist events of 11 September 2001, similar disharmony exists in most law enforcement agencies.

An examination of similar disharmonious relations between operational units in business can be a useful guide to the impact that they can have in a law enforcement context. A lack of shared understanding and respect between intelligence, decision-makers, and other key operational clients can have a number of negative impacts. These can include a lack of acceptance of the advice provided, a reduction in the funds applied to the intelligence process, and poor internal communication. Clearly these factors can combine to produce a self-perpetuating negative spiral. A perceived lack of a quality product can generate negative feedback. This can lead to poor morale within the intelligence environment and, in turn, can reduce the volume or quality of product produced and, consequently, funding. This negative spiral makes it increasingly difficult to generate the quality advice required by the most significant clients.

None of this excuses poor application of the intelligence process or substandard intelligence product. However, the responsibility for ensuring that this spiral is ameliorated lies not only with intelligence units but also with the executive and other significant clients. Schutz and Bloch (2006: 35) refer to the destructive turf wars in industry as a 'silo-virus'. They state: 'Ulcers, frustration, energy loss, hyperactivity and aggression are only a few of the long list of mental and physical reactions to the trench warfare on various fronts.' Significantly, they add that managers and employees are not only victims, but also the perpetrators of these problems. 'The carriers of the silo-virus are not only the functional areas themselves but the people working in them.'

So for whatever reason managers choose to criticize the quality of intelligence product and processes, they themselves become partly responsible for the quality of the product they receive. Intelligence staff are generally highly skilled and inquisitive. They seek to produce a quality product. However, negative comments about their work unit infuses their work life and can impact upon quality outputs—another self-perpetuating negative cycle. In 'Institutionalized competition and its effects on teamwork' Crow (1995: 54) comments: 'If a person can devalue himself and his work, this gives him permission to do substandard work. It affects [his] ability to provide a quality service'.

In order to produce more efficient and effective intelligence departments, the aim should be to limit the factors that produce internal competition and foster those that enable a capacity for working consiliently with internal and external clients. Both intelligence and operational areas need to recognize that intelligence is not a boutique area. Rather it is part of a team that seeks to achieve a common goal of protecting and serving the community. The team does this by contributing to a continuum of activity that commences with the assessment of threats and concludes with either the prevention of that threat or the arrest and prosecution of offenders.

Accepting that internal rivalry between intelligence and operations affects not only the ability of those units to work consiliently, but also impacts directly on the success of the relationship between the agency and other partner agencies, the third question of what can be done to develop and maintain a consilient relationship between intelligence and operational areas becomes critical.

ROLE OF THE AFP

In establishing and resourcing the LCIP, the AFP has taken positive steps in exploring the issue of organizational effectiveness and developing strategies to increase effectiveness. To understand the role of the LCIP within the AFP it is first necessary to understand the role that the AFP holds within the Australian law enforcement environment. The AFP is a national policing agency with responsibility for combating major organized crime and terrorism. The AFP also conducts community policing in the Australian Capital Territory and external territories, and it has a significant overseas presence with liaison officers in more than 25 countries and major peacekeeping and capacity building operations.

Operationally, the AFP is now divided into functions based upon crime type or role. These include Border; International; Counterterrorism; Intelligence; Economic and Special Operations; International Deployment Group; Protection; and Aviation.

Intelligence capability within the AFP formerly suffered from regional fragmentation, but the creation of an independent function allowed for central control of roles, product, and process. While this was a major advance in producing efficient intelligence services delivery, it also risked the reinforcement of a silo mentality. Recognizing this possibility and understanding the need to have a well-defined product to market to the executive and other functions, the Intelligence executive formed the LCIP area. It was accepted that there were no instant solutions; rather, it would be a journey towards the development of best practice and the communication and acceptance of best practice by most significant clients.

ROLE OF THE LCIP

The challenges given to the LCIP at the outset were to develop consistent and clearly articulated doctrine and process for the Intelligence function; to improve the understanding of the role and capabilities of the intelligence process throughout the broader AFP; and to identify, develop and implement world's best practice in criminal intelligence. Essentially the LCIP was tasked to create an international centre of excellence in criminal intelligence—and this became the mission statement for the programme.

The LCIP strategy to answer these challenges consists of four integrated processes. The first stage of the process is to identify critical issues. This task is undertaken by the LCIP team. The process includes the conduct of Functional Needs Analysis—face-to-face interviews with intelligence staff from all offices, and participation in various cross-function working groups and management forums.

The second stage of this process is research and development. LCIP intelligence officers and analysts research the selected topic with a view to identifying best practice and where it exists, developing new strategies, and identifying the most knowledgeable information sources on that issue. A colloquium programme is then developed in which law enforcement personnel from both Australian and international agencies are brought together with representatives from other relevant areas such as the academic community or appropriate non-government organizations. Colloquiums are facilitated and outcomes focused, with task groups usually working over three days. Depending on the security classification of the topic, discussions may be closed or open source. Colloquiums conducted by the LCIP to date have included 'Radicalisation—the journey towards terror', 'Illicit drug-trafficking', 'Transnational exploitation of women and children', 'Performance measurement in intelligence', 'Chinese organized crime—combating the criminal diaspora', 'Intelligence in the aviation environment', and 'The role of intelligence in peacekeeping and stability operations'.

The third phase of the LCIP is the intelligence-management training conducted in conjunction with the Australian Institute of Police Management. The LCIP recognized the need to create postgraduate-level training for intelligence managers and other law enforcement managers who have a close working relationship with intelligence. The Intelligence Management Development Program (IMDP) brings together intelligence and operations managers in a postgraduate environment to learn new skills and to develop and share a common understanding on issues of mutual interest. Successful participants receive a Graduate Certificate in Applied Management.

In addition to the normal range of public sector management skills required by all law enforcement managers, there are elements of management that are specific to intelligence portfolios. These include developing a strong understanding of the relationship between intelligence and policy, and being able to develop strategies that maintain the integrity of intelligence product while also meeting what may be competing client expectations.

The importance of the IMDP to furthering the goal of developing consilient relationships, both internally and with key partners, should not be overlooked. It is asserted that it is important for all areas of management to be able to develop an appreciation of the problems faced by the areas with which they interact: 'This ability to shift perspective must be applied and seen to be lived by general management. If this capability or the willingness to implement is lacking, the silo-virus will spread down the enterprise like a landslide' (Schutz and Bloch, 2006: 41). The IMDP allows managers of operational areas to gain a sound understanding of the role of intelligence and the services it can provide.

The fourth part of the LCIP is the Doctrine and Process Working Group (DPWG). This consists of a community of expert intelligence practitioners who provide the intelligence function with advice on the development of intelligence doctrine and policy. The DPWG provides the Intelligence executive with a powerful tool for effecting management change by encouraging intelligence staff to bring to management's attention inefficiencies in the process for management to consider effective amelioration strategies and then to assist in implementing those strategies.

THE AFP'S INTELLIGENCE SERVICES MODEL

Strategies developed by the LCIP include an innovative intelligence model that allows for the application of a consistent intelligence process across the AFP's very diverse functions and geographical regions, while still allowing for flexibility in application to meet functional or geographical requirements. Known as the Intelligence Services Model it involved first making an assessment of all the work performed by the Intelligence function and rationalizing this into eight services. These are Information Collection and Evaluation (ICE), Investigative Intelligence (IE), Target Development (TD), Operational Intelligence (OI), Strategic Intelligence (SI), Human Source Management (HSM), Undercover Services (US), and Counter and Security Intelligence (CSI). The appendix at the end of this chapter has further details of these services.

Business rules were then developed to support the negotiation of service agreements between AFP Intelligence and partner areas including regional offices and other functions. The purpose of these negotiations is to ensure that there is a clear understanding of the services that Intelligence will provide and the support expected by the client area. In addition, through this model (see Figure 16.1), the Intelligence function is able to implement common effective standards while still allowing partner units the flexibility required to achieve their particular goals. An important part of this negotiation is reaching an agreement on the balance of intelligence services required by the partner unit.

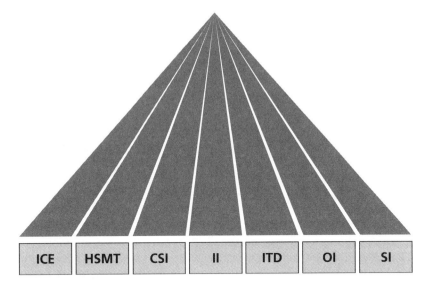

Fig 16.1 AFP Intelligence Services Model

While it is understood that intelligence staff may be required to deliver all of the abovementioned services at some time, the business rules determine where Intelligence will concentrate its resources to meet the demands of that partner unit. For example, the first application of business rules is the negotiation between Local Office Managers and the Local Office Intelligence Coordinators. Each office may have different requirements due to the nature of criminal activity in its area of interest. One Local Office Manager may request a focus on Target Development and Human Source Management while another manager may seek a concentration of effort on Intelligence Collection and Evaluation and Investigative Intelligence. The Intelligence Services Model allows for both a consistent application of intelligence principles and the flexible delivery of intelligence services.

In this model, Intelligence becomes both a service provider and a leader. This may seem contrary to the popularly espoused mantra of intelligence-led policing. However, it is a more realistic application of intelligence resources and generates a more harmonious and consilient relationship with operational areas who are often less than supportive of the notion of being 'led' by Intelligence.

The teams delivering the services described above produce the following products:

- *Intelligence Brief* (IB): This product is used to convey time-sensitive information to internal and external clients, usually about a single issue. Information may be strategic, operational or tactical in nature. Although detailed analysis is not required, the relevance of the information to the AFP should be explained. IBs are generally one to two pages long.

- *Intelligence Assessment* (IA): This product is used to report the results of more comprehensive intelligence taskings, other than those covered by the Intelligence Brief. They present detailed multiple-source, topic-specific analysis of a strategic, operational, or tactical nature.
- *Intelligence Watch Report* (IWR): This product is designed to provide the AFP Executive with current analytical assessments that are short, concise, and relevant to AFP business.
- *Strategic Intelligence Forecast* (SIF): The SIF is the major strategic product of AFP Intelligence. This biannual report provides an update on the criminal environment as it relates to AFP functional streams from information supplied in the form of Intelligence Advisory Reports. Analytical Services sends requests for information to local offices and liaison to provide input for this annual report.

The SIF is a document critical to the development of AFP policy. It represents a clear example of how the AFP is intelligence led. The SIF is presented at meetings of the AFP Strategic Leaders Group, the most significant executive forum. At these meetings issues are discussed and action items agreed upon as tasks for National Managers to pursue and report upon to the group at future meetings.

Other LCIP strategies are focused on the need to improve internal communication and knowledge development, including collection statements that clearly articulate what information each intelligence area seeks and how this information will be processed, and a set of internal communication tools designed to allow for corporate knowledge to be captured, developed, and shared.

The efforts being undertaken by AFP Intelligence through the auspices of the LCIP are ongoing but they have already produced mechanisms to improve consilience in the relationship between intelligence and its most significant clients. Nevertheless, culture is a strong determinant of all police activity and the cultural divide between intelligence and operations will not be easily bridged. In fact, it could be argued that achieving internal consilience will be a harder task than working cooperatively with external partners.

The first step in building a more cooperative partnership is to acknowledge that problems exist in the relationship in the first place. This starting point has not yet been fully recognized by all the parties involved. The difficulty of doing so is emphasized by McGuire and Hutchings (2006: 196) who provide a Machiavellian perspective on the internal and external forces driving change. In their discussion of the determinants of organizational change they refer to Ivancevich and Matteson (2002) who argue that 'internal factors are generally within the control of management, but can sometimes be more difficult to recognise and diagnose than external factors'. McGuire and Hutchings also refer to Machiavelli's acknowledgement that change is inevitable, and to his caution to agents of change: 'It should be borne in mind that there is nothing more difficult to handle, more doubtful of success and more dangerous to carry through than initiating changes.'

It is little wonder that creative and well-thought-out policies do not always achieve the results required. Schutz and Bloch (2006: 41) remind us of the impact of the behaviour of members in the organization, and that the 'tools of bridge-building management are only as good as the people who use them.' As stated earlier, building effective and consilient relationships between intelligence and internal and external partners is not the sole purview of intelligence, but the responsibility of all organizational members.

SUMMARY

The LCIP has researched intelligence best practice and developed measures to improve cooperativeness in the relationship between intelligence and most significant clients. Through engagement in the IMDP clients have been exposed to the challenges faced by intelligence in meeting their expectations. Intelligence doctrine and process have been developed that seek to both lead and serve clients through the thorough verification of their requirements and the production of products they can trust.

The change strategies undertaken by AFP Intelligence consist of the creation of a dedicated national function, the development of consistent doctrine and process, and the exploration and training of best practice through LCIP strategies. These strategies have substantially improved the degree of consilience between the intelligence function and operational partners and, consequently, organizational effectiveness.

As the consilience journey progresses, the LCIP continues to develop efficient intelligence practices and communicates these to clients. In doing so, the LCIP is making progress towards more efficient crime control and community safety by working in a cooperative manner with internal and external partners.

APPENDIX: AFP INTELLIGENCE SERVICES

Information Collection and Evaluation (ICE)

This is an important process in that it provides accountability for all information owned by Intelligence. ICE provides the initial processing of large quantities of this information. An example of this function is the correct management of Information Advisory Reports.

Investigative Intelligence

Intelligence officers and analysts work closely with Investigations by adding value to tactical information so as to provide guidance to team decision-making. This may be in the form of association charts, chronologies, target assessments, or post-operational assessments.

Target Development

This Intelligence process develops targets to a point where, on balance of probabilities, the likelihood of a serious crime is understood and targets identified. While the primary task of evidence collection, resolution, and brief preparation will be conducted by Investigations, target development teams will nevertheless collect evidence coincidental to their targeting activities.

Operational Intelligence

This is the identification of convergences between disparate pieces of information, criminal activity, and police operations across time, place, and crime type. It provides targeting opportunities and also supports strategic intelligence by identifying criminal trends.

Strategic Intelligence

Strategic Intelligence analysts form the knowledge-centre for the AFP on crime threats. Analysts produce intelligence which is designed to influence high-level decision-making and which provides a contextual framework for operational activities. Strategic Intelligence primary clients include the AFP executive, management of partner agencies, and government. Strategic Intelligence is a National Headquarters function only.

Human Source Management

Intelligence manages the recruitment, tasking, and deployment of human sources.

Undercover Services

Intelligence manages the selection, training, and deployment of the undercover programme. This service can support any of the eight core services mentioned on pages 220 and 221. It can also directly support investigations.

Counter and Security Intelligence

This involves intelligence related to the security of AFP operations.

REFERENCES

AFP Strategic Plan for 2004–2006 (Updated 2006).

CAMPBELL, AJ, 'Do internal department relationships influence buyers' expectations about external supply partnerships?' *Journal of Business and Industrial Marketing* 13/3 (1998) 199–214.

CROW, R, 'Institutionalized competition and its effects on teamwork' *Journal for Quality and Participation* 18/2 (1995) 46–54.

HARMAN, A, 'Inter-jurisdictional cooperation in Ontario' *Law and Order* 45/9 (1997) 106–108.

HITZ, FP and WEISS, BJ, 'Helping the CIA and FBI connect the dots in the War on Terror' *International Journal of Intelligence and CounterIntelligence* 17/1 (2004) 1–41.

IVANCEVICH, J and MATTESON, M, cited in McGuire, D and Hutchings, K, 'A Machiavellian analysis of organizational change' *Journal of Organizational Change Management* 19/2 (2006) 192–209.

LEWIS, DS, FRENCH, E and STEANE, P, 'A culture of conflict' *Leadership and Organization Development Journal* 18/6 (1997) 275–282.

MARRIN, S, 'Preventing intelligence failure by learning from the past' *International Journal of Intelligence and CounterIntelligence* 17/4 (2004) 655–672.

McGuire, D and Hutchings, K, 'A Machiavellian analysis of organizational change' *Journal of Organizational Change Management* 19/2 (2006) 192–209.

National Commission on Terrorist Attacks upon the United States, *The 9/11 Commission Report Including Executive Summary: Final Report of the National Commission on Terrorist Attacks upon the United States* (2004).

Schutz, P and Bloch, B, 'The "Silo-Virus": Diagnosing and curing departmental groupthink' *Team Performance Management* 12/1–2 (2006) 31–43.

Yallop, C, et al, *Macquarie Dictionary* (4th edn, Macquarie University, 2005).

17

STRATEGIC INTELLIGENCE: METHODOLOGIES FOR UNDERSTANDING WHAT POLICE SERVICES ALREADY 'KNOW' TO REDUCE HARM

Professor Betsy Stanko

Criminological research has argued for some time that there are some evidence-based ways of working to better prevent crime and minimize harm. Focusing on the places, most vulnerable victims, and the people who cause the most harm to communities should—by all reviews of the literature—mould an intelligence-led strategy leading to the reduction of harm. I use a definition of 'intelligence' here that is eclectic, drawing from Legg and Hutter's (2007) musings on the definitions of intelligence. They suggest that intelligence :

- is a property that an individual agent has as it interacts with its environment or environments;
- is related to the agent's ability to succeed or profit with respect to some goal or objective;
- depends on how able the agent is to adapt to different objectives and environments.

These aspects of intelligence are relevant to policing because intelligence is a combination of the way information is used by an agent within an ever-changing and complex environment. In this chapter, when I use the word intelligence I mean the following: *Intelligence is smart information which enables police and police organizations to minimize intentional (criminal) harm to individuals and communities.*

In the past seven years in the Metropolitan Police in London, I have tested a number of grounded methodologies to harness the ethos of the above and draw on everyday information held by the police and the public. Such methodologies help guide a better policing outcome for public need, because it uses the information supplied by the public themselves about what has harmed them. Listening to people and how they use the police to intervene to help them frames a more systematic approach connecting people's own resources to aid (or hinder) their resilience to crime. Of course, police must always be scanning for information which informs them about crimes not reported by the public or that the public 'don't see'. But this chapter will not be focusing on this kind of 'intelligence'. This chapter describes some of the methodologies for using routinely recorded police crime information—which largely comes from the public—as a form of intelligence in the reduction of harm to communities.

GROUNDING STRATEGIC INTELLIGENCE: A CRIMINOLOGIST ON THE INSIDE

After 25 years as a university professor, I joined the Metropolitan Police in London as its senior advisor for strategic analysis nearly five years ago (Stanko, 2007). Based at the heart of the largest police service in Europe, I brought scepticism of official crime data and extensive research experience into the silence of violence to the heart of UK policing (Stanko, 1985). My understanding of how victims' silence *outside officialdom* mutes an understanding of victimization is now being applied *inside officialdom*. Do victims who contact the police tell them about incidents which are so different from those victims who do not contact the police? Typically the criticism of police recorded data is so strong that the 'voices' of those who do contact the police are overlooked in an effort to highlight the plight of those who do not contact the police. What I find in exploring police recorded-crime information is a rich vein of knowledge about what was and is known about crime through the experiences of victims who talk to the police.[1] From my years of studying silence I now study voice—victim/police contact—and this voice is a critical ingredient of intelligence.

DATA-QUALITY ISSUES

Such an approach to police recorded-crime information may be considered misguided or naive to an outside observer. It might be considered to be folly according to many academic criminologists. After all, there are volumes of texts devoted to critiquing in great detail what is missed by and through the use (and misuse) of police-generated recorded information as a picture of crime. This might be pure folly in terms of preventing harm as well. Such critiques are not without their merit. Official crime records do not capture the 'universe' of illegal activity or the true picture of how people experience 'crime'. Incomplete police information is the result of many factors: victims themselves choose not to tell anyone about an experience, officials record some criminal events and not others, official crime categories distort the understanding of criminal incidents; these are some of the ways a 'truer' picture of crime is often distorted. All of the above occur with great regularity. The British Crime Survey, for instance, tells us that only 44 per cent of the crime the BCS measures is ever reported to the police.[2] So

---

[1] There is also good information about criminal incidents generated through police activity (such as cannabis possession arrests).

[2] There is a recurring debate about the 'incompleteness' of the British Crime Survey, as it too fails to capture 'all the crime'.

from outside the police services looking in, criminologists and statisticians have spent a great deal of time looking for and critiquing what the police do not know about crime from their own records or debunking what police and government publish as an 'official record' of crime. Of course, given the heightened concern about security from organized crime or terrorism, we could be missing what might ultimately cause the greatest harm in our communities. Clearly such forms of intentional criminality put many of us at risk, and certainly have a detrimental effect on health and well-being. But there are many chapters in this book focusing on how to ferret out what we need to know in order for security services and law enforcement to keep ahead of those who might wish to do harm to communities.[3]

PROBLEM-SOLVING

Criminologists have been advocating a 'problem-solving' approach to policing for many years now. But there have been sighs of frustration from many academics about why what they believe to be such a transparent 'good idea' just cannot be translated into systematic good practice as a matter of routine. This remains a challenge to the transformation of policing from a reactive service to a proactive service. In London, boroughs each have 'problem-solving advisors' working to assist better long-term approaches to dealing with local issues. Intelligence-led and citizen responsive—this is the aspiration for the kinds of information that drives strategy for crime prevention in London. Yet we still struggle to exploit our information efficiently and effectively.

So in response to the challenge I have begun to devise simple ways to harness what people tell us about the issues they have faced 'as crime' (crime reports) and using this information to help drive police proactivity. Data quality of course is critical to such analysis, and our crime data are never perfect, as I have stated above. However, this should not prevent us from learning about what it is that people are telling us as a police service—and how if we learn better how to deal with what they are telling us now, we can adapt to what they might tell us in the future. And with the arrival of local policing in the form of Safer Neighbourhoods teams in London, the opportunity to structure the knowledge gleaned from the local areas and translate it into strategic 'intelligence' about crime problems has yet to be fully developed.

This chapter uses three examples of these methodological approaches to capturing *grounded* knowledge as 'intelligence'. The first two examples draw on high-level analysis of public-generated crime reports and the third example taps the local knowledge of local police officers to build a strategic picture of a local drugs market. All three examples raise strategic questions about how we can find systematic ways of focusing on the harm of crime and, I suggest, enable a better dialogue with communities, senior police officers, and government officials about ways to minimize such harm. As an academic criminologist working in the heart of a police organization, I ask different questions from many 'police trained' crime analysts because I am raising strategic questions about what we are focusing on, how are we doing it, and

---

[3] I refer to this as information that is 'off piste' to crime records.

why we are really focusing on this problem rather than that one. While many of our analysts map, count, and show results about how units are 'performing' crime reduction, there is little understanding about the reasons why crime might fall, whether victims might have changed demographically, or whether or not the places and circumstances of crime have shifted. Such questions are necessary in order to build more innovative approaches to the analysis of crime and harm in London—one that is strategic in nature and applicable to tactical decision-making in time. At the heart of these examples highlighted here is a continuous spotlight on knowing—as much as one can from the available information—about victims, offenders, and locations. Nothing new here, you (the reader) might say. This 'holy trinity' of understanding crime—victims, offenders, locations—is an 'axiom' in criminological thinking. However, few criminologists have tried to apply systematically this approach and embed it in the strategic, tactical, and organizational learning of such a large organization. As I am constantly reminded, the internal culture of an 'in time' service must be transformed too.

The first example reflects the learning from what domestic violence and hate-crime *victims* tell us about violent crime and offenders. I draw on lessons from a project I led in the Metropolitan Police in 2001, 'Understanding and Responding to Hate Crime', a Home Office funded project under the Crime Prevention Initiative (see also Stanko et al, 2003). The second example highlights what *place* tells us about violent crime and offending. In London for example 1 per cent of the streets play host to 30 per cent of the serious violence. The prevention of violent harm to communities can be focused on where harm clusters. Problem-solving and identifying violent *offenders* can be targeted more efficiently because many offenders are indeed locally based. In the third example, I discuss the usefulness of a simple methodology for capturing local knowledge from the local police about a form of offending—open illegal drug markets—named by the local public as a serious matter of concern. This methodology enables us to see how an understanding about place, offending, and the community's concerns converge to generate more robust 'ground-level up' intelligence about the rising violence linked to the illegal drug economy.

As criminological theory, what I offer in this chapter is not new. However, I have learnt in the past seven years that theory is not readily or easily translated into police practice. The magic lies in mapping theoretical wisdom on ways of working which, for the police, achieve results in terms of crime reduction and the production of actionable information (thus giving front-line officers 'intelligence'), and, for the public, achieve noticeable differences on the ground.

EXAMPLE ONE: WHAT DO HATE-CRIME AND DOMESTIC VIOLENCE VICTIMS TELL US ABOUT THE DANGEROUSNESS OF OFFENDERS?

The first step in monitoring and creating strategic intelligence is to understand the nature of the kind of incidents people are reporting to the police. The aim of the Home Office funded project[4] (URHC) was simple: use routinely collected crime reports to carve out a victim-focused evidence base for corporate policy on the harm of domestic violence and hate-crimes (see Stanko, 2001a; Stanko, 2001b; Stanko et al, 2003). The project set out a systematic picture of the kinds of incident reported to the police, taking what people report as a proxy of the kinds of issues facing the policing of hate-crimes.[5] The project spawned an approach to using police data as a repository of the public's need for protection against hate and domestic violence. By no means was it complete—there were, for example, few reports of so-called 'honour-based' violence. However, the project interrogated crime data to tell us the circumstances of identified 'hate and domestic related' violence—the when's, the where's, and the who's, especially the relationships between victims and offenders.

The MPS crime records hold robust (but not always complete) data on:

- profiles of victims who contact the police (age, race/ethnicity/country of origin);
- profiles of offenders (single offenders, multiple offenders, ages, race/ethnicity/country of origin);
- profiles of places where offences occur;
- profiles of what happened and the range of crime classifications used to record such incidents (flagged as 'hate'; homophobic; domestic and other categories of violence);
- whether and what type of weapons are involved;
- repeat victimization and seriousness of incidents;
- whether an offender was identified and whether an arrest resulted;
- post-arrest decisions (sometimes!).

URHC set out to understand the nature of hate-crime and domestic violence through knowledge about its victims, the nature of victimization, the dimensions of offending behaviours, and its variation across local areas (borough and ward analysis

---

[4] The policing of domestic violence and hate-crime evolved in London as a response to a number of events. The first Domestic Violence Unit was established in 1988 in the MPS. Following the publication of the Macpherson Inquiry into the death of Stephen Lawrence in 1999, the Racial and Violent Crime Task Force was established expanding the remit of support to victims of targeting 'racial' and domestic violence to include homophobic violence following the three bombings in London during April 1999. The then Directorate's remit was to monitor all hate-crimes across London, develop strategy and policy in relation to investigation, victim care and the use of intelligence to prevent such crime. The first director of the Directorate was DAC John Grieve. The Directorate has transformed over the years in the MPS. Currently the Violent Crime Directorate has the remit for serious forms of hate, domestic, and other violence in London.

[5] See <http://www.met.police.uk/dcf/files/domestic_violence.pdf>; <http://www.met.police.uk/dcf/files/racial_fact.pdf>; <http://www.met.police.uk/dcf/files/homophobic_violence.pdf>; <http://www.met.police.uk/dcf/files/sa_fact.pdf>.

now available). The project developed a number of methodologies to examine common themes and patterns in the crime data which enabled the central policy unit to compare demands for police assistance across local areas as well as across teams. These methodologies included:

- a quantitative analysis of the MPS flagged offences for domestic violence and hate-crime over a set time (one month, three months, and so forth);
- an in-depth qualitative analysis of events occurring over a random 24-hour period to provide context and richness to the overall/patterns identified in the quantitative analysis (see Stanko, 2001 b);
- qualitative analysis of the most serious incidents to inform assessments of the dangerousness of offenders and the dangerousness of the incidents reported by repeat-users of the police service (what some call 'repeat victimization').

As has been widely documented, hate-crime and domestic violence involve a variety of criminal and antisocial behaviour—ranging from serious life-threatening attacks, criminal damage, harassment, and other abusive acts. There is an assumption that racist violence, faith violence, and homophobic violence have their roots in 'hatred'. Many also presume that distance, dissimilarity, and unfamiliarity motivate such 'hatred'. Our information demonstrated—and continues to demonstrate—that people call the MPS most often about the behaviour of their neighbours, business associates, and other acquaintances than the behaviour of strangers. The kind of incidents that come to police attention—be they threats, attacks, or other forms of abuse—are the kind of local encounters that are often difficult to avoid. People live and work, day in and day out, within the contexts of threat and danger. In some respects, homophobic and racist violence have similarities with domestic violence because commonly there is some kind of familiarity between victim and offender. Such familiarity mixed with features of vulnerability derived from intimacy and personal authority, sometimes mixed with problems associated with mental health, substance abuse, financial difficulties, and cultural factors, combined to propel people to reach out for assistance when 'private matters' move beyond people's own resources to stop the violence.

URHC demonstrated that crime-solving and intelligence-gathering can be enhanced using the lessons of what we know about victims' use of the police in times of crisis.[6] However it was clear from the growing analysis that the seriousness of some of the offending deserved more systematic proactive responses from the police. The project's analysis showed the links between sexual assault and domestic violence, and these links serve as clues to understanding the potential lethality of some domestic violence situations. Looking more carefully at repeat domestic violence victims who turned to the police for help told us a great deal about the offenders. These offenders were not only more persistent, but we could see the way in which violence escalated

---

[6] Racial and homophobic violence, for instance, is largely committed by local people—neighbours and school children in particular—and that this information can be harnessed as intelligence about offending and drive-focused crime prevention which can be directed at the times and the places where offending is most prevalent. The analysis of the racist and homophobic violence in London demonstrated that preventative intervention strategies should address the behaviour of neighbours and school children. Multi-agency cooperation, local dialogues supporting a more cohesive civil society, underpins police enforcement activity.

with seriousness and with frequency. Recognition of this link is now clearly embedded in the risk-assessment tool the MPS developed to focus intervention in the prevention of domestic homicide.

The policing of 'known' violence from a victim perspective means that the police reliance on 'incident based' crime analysis shifts to an acknowledgement of 'context based' criminal incidents. The low level and volume of many hate-crime and domestic violence incidents coming to the attention of the police are most likely to be resolved through consultation and problem-solving in its most local context. As we learnt from this project, the most serious violence—homicide, threats to kill, sexual assault—can be prevented by identifying and targeting the most dangerous of offenders. It is at this high-end of harm that we begin to see distinctions between the kinds of danger offenders pose, and the kinds of offending leading to such high levels of harm.

Victims tell us useful information that is actionable for police tactics and strategies in the prevention of violence; and when victims report crime in some places more than others, we can glean information about the kind of problems associated with the place. An analysis of *place* then also lends itself to strategic analyses of what kinds of harm befall some local communities more than others. It is to a discussion of place as a contributor to intelligence-led policing that I now turn.

EXAMPLE TWO: WHAT DO RISKY PLACES TELL US ABOUT OFFENDING AND OFFENDERS?

Braga (2006) has noted in a systematic review of 'hot spots' policing that a focus on place—'where crime' clusters—is a fruitful approach to reducing crime. I devised a simple methodology for the identification of key 'high reported-violent-crime' wards in London. In 2006/7 for instance, 10 per cent of total police-recorded violent crime occurred in only 23 electoral wards (3.7 per cent of the total of 624). Ten per cent of murders and grievous bodily harm (GBH) occurred in only 13 wards (2.1 per cent of wards) (Stanko and Hales, forthcoming).

Building on the lessons of the URHC project to develop an evidence-base to explain the rise of violent offending, my approach again was simple:

- Use people's reports of crime, especially forms of violent crime, to rank local wards—tapping people's use of the police in more local areas.
- Take a particular look at serious violence to see whether the places where drivers of violence (alcohol-related, domestic-related, weapon-related) differed.
- Compare the kinds of crime (including acquisitive crime) that occur in the top wards with the rest of the MPS.
- Recommend that the MPS take action and focus on these 'higher crime' areas, monitor progress, and share the lessons of successful reduction in violence.

In 2004 MPS strategic corporate analysis highlighted the contribution of alcohol-related violence to the overall increase of violence in London. Analysis in 2005 also demonstrated that not only does violent crime cluster, but the level of the volume of other crimes is higher and the nature of the violence in these small geographical is more serious. The result of the above analysis showed that 34 (5 per cent) of 624 wards had levels of reported crime twice that reported by other wards across London. What kind of offending was driving this difference?

Substance misuse—alcohol-related violence—dominated the kinds of violent offending reported in high-street town centres.[7] Adopted by the Violent Crime Directorate, the methodology identified 'challenged wards' using a basic ranking of a list of serious violent and volume crime. In 2006, the MPS launched an initiative to focus on the 'nature of the places'—called 'the challenged wards initiative'—that focused problem-solving on what gave rise to people's 'need' for policing. Eight wards in London were selected and each local borough[8] was asked to produce an in-depth analysis of the 'problem' as it existed in these wards, with a problem-solving action plan to address these problems. Five of the eight wards were 'town centres', where alcohol-related violence predominated. Three of the wards were areas where there were higher levels of serious violence, and in particular shootings—a relatively rare event in the whole of London.[9] This work has now been extended into a more comprehensive strategic approach to guns, gangs, and youth violence in South London.

The conversation about 'what to do about violence' and 'what to do about offenders' became far more grounded in local information and local needs. In the eight wards, strategic thinking flowed initially from reported crime, and grew to include additional information from intelligence analysts. Each of the ward-level approaches was shared among the participating wards, contributing to a more holistic understanding of the kinds of offending that affected the lives of the public. This approach requires a detailed problem profile of the contexts of violence as reported to the police. A detailed local understanding also sheds light on the offenders and the offending that takes place within discrete local arenas.

The learning from this above is now being taken into proactive challenges of the MPS to gang and gun violence; and such initiatives demand that the MPS approach its understanding of its own information more creatively. The conversation must be grounded in understanding, as best as possible, what people are telling the police in the reporting of crime.

---

[7] Although research had documented the link between alcohol and violence, the translation of the research into an intelligence-led strategic approach to violence-reduction was slow to be adopted. Transforming policing from a reactive to a proactive service requires organizational change and a commitment to follow the 'evidence' located in part in understanding how people use the police to manage the violent crime they experience. For research linking violence in the night-time economy to alcohol, see Finney, A, *Violence in the Night-Time Economy: Key Findings from the Research* (Home Office, 2004) and Hobbs, R et al, *Bouncers: Violence and Governance in the Night Time Economy* (Oxford University Press, 2005).

[8] In London, borough boundaries are contiguous with those of local authorities and Crime and Disorder Reduction Partnerships.

[9] Despite an increase in the level of gun crime reported in London, gun crime across London is rare. Gun crime clusters even more tightly than other kinds of crime, and it is for this reason that clear targeting of police resources to prevent gun and gang crime is aimed at only a few places in London.

EXAMPLE THREE: HARNESSING WHAT LOCAL POLICE KNOW TO PREVENT VIOLENCE IN LOCAL OPEN DRUGS MARKETS

The full roll-out of neighbourhood police teams throughout London heralded a new possibility for local police problem-solving. Teams of police officers and community support officers work together in 630 areas in London.[10] These local teams have the advantage of working—indeed are mandated to work—with local people and locally available resources to address what matters most to communities with what is judged to be most harmful to people's local quality of life. Across London, the five most common priorities of local ward panels are issues of antisocial behaviour involving 'young people', antisocial behaviour in general, burglary, theft from motor vehicles, and drug dealing and using.

This last example of an intelligence-generating methodology describes the way in which a short questionnaire circulated to and completed by one borough's Safer Neighbourhoods teams produced a robust picture of the local availability of illegal drugs, the operation of drugs markets and the impact of illegal drugs on crime, residents and policing. One borough was selected as a research site to explore how the grounded knowledge of local teams might give us a borough-wide view and help inform the debate about the impact of the illegal economy on policing in London. The gathered information sketched out common issues that many of the local teams were facing. The short survey documented the local availability of illegal drugs. It also enabled us to describe the context within which the illegal drugs economy works in one local borough with clear resonances across London, especially for the rise in the violence linked to the illegal economy. And it helped us gain a better understanding of offending. The social networks of those who are dealing drugs are extensive—sometimes relying on kinship, sometimes on contacts cultivated in prison or local schools. Offender network analysis can be built on the back of this local knowledge, and officers' teams—often working in their own areas—can exchange information about offenders and offending that crosses 'ward' boundaries.

Even more important was that the majority of the public ward panels also identified 'drugs' as a key local issue. Local teams are in active dialogue with residents and businesses to address the way in which the illegal drugs economy relies on intimidation to control the spaces where the commodities can be exchanged. Such dialogues are a key to shoring up confidence and communication between local people and the police. Smart use of information is as crucial to community confidence as it is to challenging the harm of offenders.

[10] See Safer Neighbourhoods in the Metropolitan Police, <http://www.met.police.uk/saferneighbourhoods>. 'Safer Neighbourhoods is about local police working with local people and partners to identify and tackle issues of concern in their neighbourhood.'

CONCLUDING DISCUSSION

I argue here that there are ways of being smarter about our intelligence. For most routine policing of local areas, a good deal of information is already 'known'. This information should be used as the foundations for strategic thinking about how to minimise the harm of violence threatening communities. I have used examples of simple methodologies based on routinely recorded police information or routinely available information (by tapping the intelligence of working local teams). There are many questions that have been raised:

- What does police information tell us about the need and use of the public for police?
- How do the police capture what people say to better target criminal activity?
- What does this tell us about who is doing what to whom, where, and why?
- People are talking to police when they report criminal and antisocial incidents, so how do we better reach those who are not speaking to police?
- How do we harness the knowledge of the police themselves?

These forms of wisdom are critical to good intelligence, and a key foundation for any prevention of criminal harm.

I wish to advocate a practical view of thinking strategically about 'intelligence' here. I have seen many analysts trying to document what is *missing* from police information in order to speculate about the 'true' picture of crime (however valuable this is for intelligence about crime). As a consequence, the value of what *is* recorded as criminal incidents is often overlooked and undervalued as intelligence. Essentially we take an array of detail from people about criminal incidents and let this detail languish in an electronic crime record. In my own field of expertise—violence—this is especially true. We know that most incidents of violence take place between people who are known to one another, and this is particularly the case the more serious the offence of violence. We also know that a small proportion of violence is reported to police, particularly in comparison to criminal incidents where insurance claims can help salve the intrusion of a criminal event.

Yet the debates amongst professionals centre largely on whether such violence is up or down, without looking carefully at what we know about the violence and whether its patterns have changed or are changing. While frequency of violence is clearly an important factor in contemporary debate, the frenzy of activity and discussion overlooks its typical—and telling—features, features that recorded violent crime does tell us. In this chapter I am interested primarily in what 'on piste' police-recorded crime information tells us about what kinds of incidents people (primarily) choose to tell the police about, and how the police can use this information as part of their intelligence for the targeting of offenders, the prevention of crime, and ultimately the minimization of harm to communities.

REFERENCES

BRAGA, AA, 'The crime prevention value of hot spots policing', *Psicothema* 18/3 (2006) 630–7.

FINNEY, A, *Violence in the Night-Time Economy: Key Findings from the Research* (London: Home Office, 2004).

HOBBS, R, HADFIELD, P, LISTER, S, and WINLOW, S, *Bouncers: Violence and Governance in the Night Time Economy* (Oxford: Oxford University Press, 2005).

LEGG, S and HUTTER, M, 'A collection of definitions of intelligence' (2007) available at <http://www.idsia.ch/idsiareport/IDSIA-07–07.pdf>.

STANKO, EA, *Intimate Intrusions: Women's Experience of Male Violence* (London: Routledge, 1985).

——, 'Reconceptualising the policing of hatred: Confessions and worrying dilemmas of a Consultant', *Law and Critique* 12/3 (2001a) 309–29.

——, 'The day to count: Reflections on a methodology to raise awareness about the impact of domestic violence in the UK' *Criminal Justice* 1/2 (2001b) 215–26.

——, KIELINGER, V, PATERSON, S, RICHARDS, I, CRISP, D and MARSLAND, L, 'Grounded crime prevention: Responding to and understanding hate crime' in Kury, H and Obergfell-Fuchs, J, *Crime Prevention: New Approaches* (Mainz: Weisser Ring, 2003) 123–152.

——, 'From academia to policymaking: changing police responses to violence against women', *Theoretical Criminology* 11/2 (2007) 209–19.

—— and HALES, G, *Policing Violent People and Violent Places: Reducing the Harm of Violence in Communities* (London: The Police Foundation, forthcoming).

18

INTELLIGENCE, KNOWLEDGE, AND THE RECONFIGURATION OF POLICING

Dr Clive Harfield and Maren Eline Kleiven

INTRODUCTION

Another day, another buzzword? Barely a decade after the first British articulation of intelligence-led policing as the foundation for policing the twenty-first century (HMIC, 1997), a rather similar-sounding phrase is emerging and gaining widespread currency: 'Knowledge-Based Policing'. In Britain the nascent UK Serious Organised Crime Agency (SOCA) is focusing on knowledge, rather than intelligence, as driving the new approaches to tackling organized crime. Also, the Lothian and Borders Police in Scotland assert that 'promotion of a culture of knowledge-based policing through better information management and analysis' will help them achieve their strategic aim of 'making best use of existing and emerging technology' as part of their overall corporate communication strategy which seeks to develop a knowledge-based communication culture (Lothian and Borders Police, 2006: 11). At the time of writing (November, 2007) the late Tom Williamson's edited volume *The Handbook of Knowledge-Based Policing: Current Conceptions and Future Directions* (2008) is four months from publication. The concept is not confined to the UK. The Australian Federal Police draw attention to their 'international role and growing profile as a modern, knowledge-based policing organization with truly global reach' (AFP, 2004: 2). In Norway, the Norwegian Police Service is hosting the seventh annual colloquium of the International Centre for the Prevention of Crime which, amongst other issues, will be highlighting contemporary developments in knowledge-based policing, posited as an overarching philosophy within which should be incorporated intelligence-led policing (ILP), problem-oriented policing (POP), hot-spot policing, and community mobilization. Europol defines intelligence as 'Knowledge (processed information) designed for action (Kleiven, 2007). Meanwhile from the Organization for Security and Cooperation in Europe (OSCE), comes the exhortation that codes of conduct and ethical principles are the 'cornerstones' of knowledge-based policing (2006: para 5.2). All of which discussion echoes business thinking elsewhere and the lexicon of the 'knowledge society' (Ericson and Haggerty, 1997; Hislop, 2005; Scarborough and Swan, 2001).

Already then, there seem to be a number of different perspectives on knowledge-based policing from a variety of organizations. There is a danger that it may already have become a phrase characterized more by assumption than understanding, in the same way that intelligence-led policing, zero tolerance, problem-oriented policing, and community policing (to name but a few) have entered the professional language but do not necessarily enjoy practitioner common understanding (Ratcliffe, 2005: 436). The question therefore arises, what is meant by knowledge-based policing and what does it offer for the future of intelligent policing? Is it a business process such as the UK National Intelligence Model (NIM), a policing model such as POP, a knowledge-management technique based on better use of information technology (IT), or a philosophical foundation for professional standards and so part of the human rights conceptual framework? Is it anything substantively different from what prevails or has gone before? What value does the idea add, if any?

WHATEVER HAPPENED TO INTELLIGENCE-LED POLICING?

As a concept intelligence-led policing itself potentially stumbles at the first hurdle: 'policing' can be variously defined and interpreted. It can mean the coercive enforcement of the criminal law; the moderation of behaviour through the securing of voluntary compliance and problem solving; non-criminal regulation and self-regulation. Policing in its widest sense is an activity undertaken by many agencies and organizations, both in the public and private sector (Johnston, 1992; Dorn and Levi, 2007). So intelligence-led policing begs its own question, intelligence-led what, precisely?

In England and Wales the most recent drive for intelligence-led policing was a product of the 1990s, following the New Public Management public sector reform crusade (Long, 2003: 631; as Grieve points out in Chapter 1 above, intelligence-led policing was being advocated as early as 1881, Vincent, 1881: 202). At the same time senior detectives, the then (later Sir) David Phillips and John Grieve amongst them, were arguing for better use of intelligence in the detection, investigation, and prosecution of crime (Grieve, 2004). In a seminar presentation at the National Police College, Bramshill (March 1998), Phillips called for intelligence-led policing as a way of reclaiming policing for detectives and the prioritization of criminal investigation over community policing, arguing that the latter would inevitably benefit from better-targeted criminal investigation. Military use of intelligence was the inspiration: the cause, the 'fight' against crime. However, it is interesting to note that just as the public police were beginning to think about intelligence, so commercial sector organizations were moving beyond the concept of (commercial) intelligence to knowledge management because having accurate and timely information in and of itself was no longer considered enough (Gordon and Grant 2005: 28).

HM Inspectorate of Constabulary situated intelligence-led policing in the context of the drive for better value for money (HMIC, 1997; see also Audit Commission 1993, 1994, and 1996a and b; Local Government Management Board, 1999). HMIC's review also paved the way for two new manifestations of intelligence-led policing: the National Criminal Intelligence Service (NCIS) and the National Crime Squad (NCS)—significant infrastructure innovations in a country espousing local policing, locally controlled. NCIS devised and published the National Intelligence Model (NIM) (Flood, 2004), intended to drive intelligence-led policing through a uniform business process that would provide the disparate infrastructure of the police service with a common language—it did not initially provide a common definition of intelligence (Kleiven, 2007)—transcending the different levels of local, regional and national policing. The intention was to achieve proactive policing of prolific offenders, although even proactive intelligence-led policing is a response to individual behaviour patterns in order to achieve detections, rather than to influence and alter the behaviour. For the UK, the NIM came to be the definition of intelligence-led policing in practice, almost the Holy Grail of policing, 'The Answer'. It was by no means certain, however, that everyone agreed on the question: there is a 'lack of clarity among many in law enforcement' about what it means, what it is supposed to achieve, and how it is supposed to operate (Ratcliffe, 2003: 1; see also Kleiven, 2007).

The NIM was gradually but inconsistently adopted across the three UK criminal jurisdictions by law enforcement agencies. Despite enjoying the endorsement of the Home Secretary's statutory National Policing Plan for England and Wales which set a target date of 1 April 2004, implementation was anything but uniform (John and Maguire, 2003; Maguire and John, 2006) and subject to a number of systemic weaknesses (Sheptycki, 2004), and design limitations: 'while the NIM provides for the structure, process, and product, it does not explicitly examine the strategies chosen to manage criminality and disorder' (Ratcliffe, 2005: 489).

Significant failures of UK police intelligence, against a background of equally significant failures and misunderstandings within the wider UK intelligence community (the substantial and recent official inquiry literature is summarized in Harfield and Harfield, 2008: Chapter 2), have resulted, at best, in a loss of public and professional confidence in intelligence as a profession; at worst, in the development of cynicism about the political use of intelligence; this at a time when the social context of policing arguably has changed significantly in the aftermath of 9/11 (Kleiven, 2007).

Agency partnership complicates the arena for intelligence-led policing significantly because it introduces organizational motivations (and performance targets, not all of which are necessarily complementary) other than the relatively simplistic measures of crimes detected and convictions obtained. Although the NIM could, theoretically, involve partner agencies and could, theoretically, inform community policing and POP (Ratcliffe, 2003: 3; 2005: 437), through the focus on specific detection targets—even to the extent of ignoring some serious crime-types (Dorn and Levi, 2007: 231)—it has acquired a narrower perception as being 'owned' by detectives and performance managers (Ratcliffe, 2003: 5) so that community policing and POP can be seen as separate, if related, policing models (Tilley, 2003). Simply put, it is as if intelligence-led policing has come to be associated with crime detection whilst POP/problem-solving is reserved for community policing, with no serious attempt to understand how these two equally important models of 'policing' interrelate. There is no general understanding, for instance, about the relationship between relevant NIM 'products' (the Strategic Assessment, the Control Strategy) and the local crime audits undertaken by Crime and Disorder Partnerships (CDRPs) (although see Lewis, Chapter 11 above, for approaches adopted in Manchester). The suggestion that CDRP partners should be represented at police Tasking and Coordination meetings (a key part of the NIM action prioritization process) in order to maximize potential intervention options has, in the personal experience of the authors, met with the standard objection that such meetings deal with sensitive information about criminal investigations and the 'need to know principle' dictates that partner agencies cannot be admitted (on the 'need to know principle' see Harfield and Harfield, 2008: Chapter 9.2.4). A counter-argument to this restrictive stance can be based on the consequences of intelligence 'failures' examined in Laming (2003), Bichard (2004), and HMI Probation (2006; see also Kelly, Chapter 19 below). It is clear from Ratcliffe's 3i model (2003)—in which analysts *interpret* the criminal environment in order to *influence* the decision-makers who can then *impact* upon the criminal environment—that some of the key decision-makers capable of initiating impact will be in organizations outside the police service. Failure to recognize this will lead to a consequential loss of knowledge as the potential is missed and so too, the opportunity for learning through subsequent reflection and results analysis.

The tendency of organizational cultures and professions to exclude the uninitiated (see Butler, 2004: paras 47–52 on the limitations and mythology of intelligence), together with widespread loss of confidence, means that if partnership policing and pluralization are not to degenerate into dysfunctional, isolated, and potentially counterproductive individual enterprises, there needs to be a commonly acceptable and accessible framework of reference through which disparate and plural policing provision is informed and governed, both at the strategic and operational levels. In this context, intelligence-led policing may have outlived its usefulness as a guiding mantra because, in the UK at least, it has come to mean intelligence-led *criminal law enforcement performance management* rather than *policing* in its widest, community-safety sense.

IS 'KNOWLEDGE' MORE THAN 'INTELLIGENCE'?

For one of the architects of intelligence-led policing, John Grieve, intelligence is 'information designed for action' (2004: 25). Does use of the word 'knowledge' signify that knowledge-based policing is actually or is at least intended to be an improvement upon, or an enhancement of, intelligence-led policing?

In the private business sector, Information Age interest in and development of knowledge management has been intense. Gordon and Grant's study of power and knowledge in the academic literature identified 4,235 articles published between 1986 and 2004 just by searching the keywords 'knowledge management' in a single academic database (2005: 28). Only recently, however, has the literature expanded to include consideration of knowledge management in a policing context. Dean and Gottschalk, in their reflections on an appropriate construction for knowledge management in law enforcement, identify a 'hierarchy of police knowledge expressed as a continuum': data—information—intelligence—knowledge. They define *data* as the raw material from which *information* (perceived facts and their relevance/purpose) is developed; *intelligence* is viewed as facts and other data organized 'to characterize or profile a particular situation'; whilst *knowledge*, operating at 'a higher level of abstraction', comprises judgements and assessments informed by belief, (perceived) truths, and expectations (2007: 5–6). Butler provides further, cautionary illumination: 'intelligence merely provides techniques for improving the basis for knowledge. . . .The most important limitation on intelligence is its incompleteness' (2004: paras 47 and 49). Both these commentaries, in characterizing the relationship, privilege the concept of knowledge over that of intelligence.

The provision of security and policing services by private security companies, and also private military companies, includes provision of intelligence services. For example, Control Risks Group offers assistance with or in countering, the following:

Anti-money laundering, asset tracing, business intelligence, construction fraud, counterfeiting, data mining, due diligence, forensic accounting, fraud awareness training, fraud investigations, fraud risk management, information leaks, IT incident response, litigation support, mergers and acquisitions, network forensics, pre-employment screening, procurement fraud and technical investigations (Control Risks, 2004).

Some of these commercial organizations have highly relevant pedigrees. The New York-based company Diligence, which specializes in intelligence and risk management, is staffed by former CIA, MI5, and KGB officers and includes a former British Home Secretary amongst its executive leadership (Murray-Watson, 2006). Securitas asserts 'size is no longer the biggest competitive advantage. The decisive factor will be a critical mass of knowledge . . ." (2005: 17). Eurasia Group, who describe themselves as 'defining the business of politics' and whose clients include the New York Police Department (Piccoli, 2007), analyse political, social, economic, and security developments and the consequential impact on financial markets and business operations. This information is not constrained by centrally imposed performance indictors, nor does it prescribe a list of actions to be prioritized: this (business) intelligence is provided as a tool which should only be used by those with the experience (knowledge) to be able to use it. The clients for such intelligence and professional assessments use this material to develop or protect their own commercial interests: this is the application of intelligence within the wider context of the clients' business knowledge. Again the relationship between intelligence and knowledge is at least sequential and arguably hierarchical.

The implication of these perceptions, and the precise use of language by Dean and Gottschalk and Lord Butler, is that intelligence-led policing must fall short of what might be achieved through knowledge-based policing. That is not to say that intelligence-led policing is inherently flawed, merely that it is limited in its potential achievements, the parameters of the original vision having only been set so far. The distinction that begins to emerge is of intelligence as a tactical tool and of knowledge as a strategic tool. This, in turn, has implications for the interpretation and use of two key NIM products, the Strategic Assessment and the Control Strategy of prioritized actions derived from the assessment.

THE CHANGING CONTEXT OF POLICING

The Keynesian, welfare-service concept of 'policing by consent' no longer enjoys legitimacy amongst a cosmopolitan public, within which significant communities are becoming increasingly radicalized and mistrustful of the police (Home Office, 2004a; O'Malley and Palmer, 1996; HM Government, 2006). The largely secular twentieth century, dominated by the state, is now confronting a global economy, internet culture, and resurgent religion, all of which redefine the environment in which policing, howsoever defined, operates. The current context of policing in the UK is characterized by police reform, an emphasis on partnership, the growing reliance on the private supply of policing functions, and the paradigm progression from law enforcement to harm reduction through managing risk.

The extent to which these factors prevail in other jurisdictions varies but overarching all these factors as they influence policing and regulation in the UK are regional and global influences such as common approaches to justice and home affairs in the EU (Britain picking and choosing which to collaborate upon and which to opt out of), transnational criminality, international law enforcement cooperation, post-conflict reconstruction, and the so-called 'war on terror' (Anderson et al, 1995; McDonald, 1997; Sheptycki, 2000; Mitsilegas et al, 2003; Occhipinti, 2003; Caplan, 2005; Andreas and Nadelmann, 2006).

All of these factors influence policing in the UK and so contribute to the knowledge demands that could inform such policing. Even community policing, in some communities, is assuming a transnational element with immigrant communities in Britain or expatriate communities abroad retaining close communication and regularly travelling between their adopted homeland and their countries of origin. Events overseas or regular visits with extended families and kin groups that reside in different national jurisdictions can influence community interaction and activity within the UK so that certain neighbourhood policing teams may well need to be fully conversant with relevant issues overseas in order to understand properly the community issues they are dealing with daily here. This is a task made none the easier by government's lack of certain knowledge about just how many immigrants there are ('Ministers accused of underestimating number of foreign workers by 400,000', *The Independent*, 31 October 2007; 4). In this sense what constitutes community intelligence is being redefined, and with it the knowledge context within which intelligence must be applied.

POLICE REFORM

Successive British governments since the 1990s have considered, and more often than not enacted, police reform.[1] Nevertheless it has been argued that further reform is required to translate a largely Victorian concept of local policing, locally delivered, into a far from local twenty-first-century policing environment. HMIC (2005) noted a significant lacuna in capacity and capability at the level of policing which falls between local and national: the so-called Level 2 gap. It is legitimate to ask the extent to which such significant policy changes are knowledge-based. If the overarching politics of policing is not sufficiently well-informed, then government and organization policy will have an adverse impact on policing delivery at community level. Policy-makers have a community of expert knowledge to draw upon (for instance HMIC, ACPO, the Audit Commission, Home Office officials) but to what extent do they draw upon the knowledge held within the policed community (Thornton and Mason, 2007; Bhatti, Chapter 13 above) that can help analysts interpret the environment upon which impact is required (Ratcliffe, 2003)?

The government proposals to merge some of the smaller English and Welsh police forces were based on research undertaken by HMIC (2005) as well as on other work previously undertaken by the prime minister's Strategy Unit. There are sound policing-delivery reasons for such mergers, which have occurred episodically for the entire 200-year history of policing in England and Wales. The proposals, which enjoyed support, sometimes public, sometimes private, from the majority of ACPO members, met opposition from Police Authorities (a) because of the perceived tie to local forces within communities and (b) because of precept differential. The former was a red herring: because BCUs deliver community policing, it is they and not police forces that directly influence community perceptions. Indeed, some forces badge their vehicles by BCU rather than by force. The community arguably lacks access to the wider knowledge that would have illuminated this. Knowledge-based policing perhaps should be conceived of as a two-way process in which the policed community is made more aware of issues in order to engage meaningfully in the debate about reasonable expectation and feasible delivery. The relevance of community knowledge in informing policing strategy and tactics is highlighted by the contemporary terrorist threat which has morphed from being a threat of external attack by outsiders to one of radicalized domestic protest and insurgence.

PARTNERSHIP

The second issue, that different police authorities set different local tax thresholds for police funding that could not readily be equalized through merger, was a substantive issue that the Home Office appeared not to have identified when initiating the proposals. The merger project, the research for which was initiated by one Home

---

[1] Relevant documents and statutes include, for instance, Home Office, 1993, 2001, 2004a, 2004b; HMIC, 2005; Northern Ireland Office, 2006; Police and Magistrates' Courts Act 1994; Police Act 1996; Police Act 1997; Crime and Disorder Act 1998; Local Government Act 1999; Police Reform Act 2002; Serious and Organized Crime Act 2005; Police and Justice Act 2006.

Secretary, publicly launched by another, and eventually postponed indefinitely by a third, seems to be an example of strategic policy-development without a sufficient knowledge-base. The short-lived history of the 2005–6 mergers 'debate' also illustrates how instability can undermine any knowledge-based approach. The predisposition for mergers was not abandoned: at national level inter-agency partnership was considered to have failed, thus justifying the creation of the Serious Organised Crime Agency (SOCA) a new, single agency created by merging several existing agencies; although within a year of becoming operational it, too, was briefly considered ripe for being merged into the new Border Immigration Agency (Caroline Flint MP, Home Office Minister, Standing Committee D, *Hansard,* HC, col 35, 11 January 2005; Harfield, 2006: 745; Cabinet Office, 2007: paras 5.68–5.69).

Meanwhile, at the level of local policing, delivery pluralization is promoted (Jones and Newburn, 2006). Government strategies have created an extended police family (Police Community Support Officers, Street Wardens, local authority parking regulation, use of private security to provide preventative patrolling in some public spaces for instance), within the concept of 'partnership policing' under the umbrella of 'homeland security'. This creates new intelligence demands and opportunities, as identified above, and also a need for new knowledge and understanding in order to be able to utilize the intelligence so that, in solving one problem, interventions do not merely create another (for example, ensuring that planning for coercive action includes consideration of measures to minimize community alienation that would otherwise fuel radicalization and ultimately create a spiralling need for further reliance upon coercion perceived by the community as antagonistic). In this environment a significant challenge for knowledge-based policing would seem to be the harnessing of community knowledge as a context within which to use acquired intelligence. The partnership between agencies working for community safety and harm reduction and the community itself, is the most imprecise, but potentially the most important, partnership to be fostered within a concept of knowledge-based policing.

PRIVATE SUPPLY OF PUBLIC POLICING FUNCTIONS

This delicate relationship is further complicated by the private supply of public policing functions. The employment of private security to police public spaces such as shopping centres, typically in the form of preventative patrolling, inevitably reduces the opportunities for non-coercive interaction between public police agencies and the community. This raises three knowledge-based policing issues. The first is how to coordinate the deployment of private provision within the wider harm-reduction framework. The second is how to address the paradoxical outcome that increased use of private provision inevitably distances the public services from opportunities to harvest basic community intelligence that ultimately informs the wider knowledge within which specific criminal intelligence can be applied. The final issue raised by public-sector partnership and private supply is that of governance, which itself can only be truly effective if structured in a knowledge-based context. Currently, community safety is governed by police authorities, whose specific statutory role is to maintain an efficient and effective police service as measured against specified performance criteria for their territorial area (Police Act 1996, s 6, which does rather militate against regional police collaboration); and local authority crime and disorder committees with power to review or scrutinize decisions taken by CDRP responsible authorities and make appropriate recommendations (Police and Justice Act 2006, s 19). Any construction of knowledge-based policing needs to accommodate the relationship between planning and governance of public–private partnerships taking into account that private provision will be supplied only within the context of its own knowledge-based interpretation of the commercial market for security.

PARADIGM PROGRESSION

The final element of the current policing context is the paradigm progression from law enforcement to harm reduction and managing risk (Harfield and Harfield, 2008: Chapter 8), especially evident in the UK response to organized crime and terrorism (Home Office, 2004b; HM Government, 2006, Cabinet Office, 2007) which requires a more sophisticated utilization than has hitherto been apparent in the implementation of the NIM by police forces. Because much harm-reduction activity can fall outside the remit, capacity, and capability of the public police service, there is a self-evident need for partnership and for that partnership to be informed by more than just police-service data (see for instance HMI Probation, 2006; Lewis, Chapter 11 above). A number of commentators have identified and illuminated the role that the public police play as a gateway to data about crime, criminality, and criminals (for instance, Ericson and Haggerty, 1997; Brodeur and Dupont, 2006). Useful though this access to significant crime/incident data is, it is not the only information that can be analysed into intelligence, interpreted within the context of knowledge, and so inform policing activity when defined in terms of harm reduction and community safety.

The rhetoric of risk, particularly in relation to organized crime and terrorism, raises other issues. Intelligence is used to identify risk. It is within the wider context of knowledge that a proportionate response to risk should be judged. On the basis of intelligence alone almost any intervention can be justified, however (*post facto*) justification does not carry the same weight as the authority inherent in considered proportionality.

Knowledge provides the context within which judgements about the proportionality of proposed intelligence-led responses should be considered. Organized crime and terrorism are emotive labels, often conceptualized in terms of wars and battles in which decisive victory is both possible and necessary rather than as socio-political, economic, and cultural issues that can only be managed or negotiated. Academic and professional discourse regularly combines the two labels (Shelley and Picarelli, 2002; Picarelli, 2006; Bratton, 2007; Holmes, 2007; Shanty and Mishra, 2008), which can lead to a 'covert expansion of the categories of case to which they apply' (Ashworth, 2002: 107). Thus, through a form of mission creep, the availability of ever-more coercive powers is extended and, by association, so too the expectation that such powers will be used. This inevitably redefines the relationship between the police and the community as increased reliance is placed on coercion at the expense of consensus and compliance.

CONCLUSION: TOWARDS A CONCEPT OF KNOWLEDGE-BASED POLICING?

So what might knowledge-based policing be? Thinking about knowledge-based polic-ing is currently a work in progress with, it might be added, no obvious coordination of effort (perhaps Williamson, *forthcoming*, will prove to be a significant contribution in this regard). This chapter has sought to summarize why intelligence-led policing has been able to go only so far; it has identified that intelligence, as a concept, can reason-ably be posited as a subset of the wider concept of knowledge; and it has identified keys issues in the changing context of policing that must surely influence and change the knowledge environment within which policing (whether delivered by a public police agency or other public and private partners) operates.

A number of factors are relevant in considering and debating the potential value of a concept of 'knowledge-based policing', and indeed whether such a concept is even desirable. At the conceptual level, if intelligence-led policing, as implemented in the UK through application of the NIM, has been constrained by its formulaic approach, then will knowledge-based policing, articulated in the form of a model, merely replace one formula with another? The Norwegian approach is to regard knowledge-based policing not as a single entity but as a portfolio of options: intelligence-led policing, problem-solving, problem-oriented policing, hot-spot policing, community polic-ing, and crime prevention. Rather than define policing style through one of these approaches, the concept of knowledge-based policing in this context is seen as a broad church that accepts and empowers each approach as appropriate given the circum-stances. It is well defined by Helene Oppen Gundhus, a Norwegian social scientist whose doctoral thesis examined knowledge-work and occupational culture in the Norwegian police:

Knowledge based policing means that the individual police officer cannot base his or hers judgements on just experiential learning anymore. The goal is to combine experiential learning with analytical and scientifically based knowledge. This will make the police better equipped to prevent crime (Gundhus, 2006: 12 (trans Kleiven)).

In the absence of a theoretical dialogue exploring such a defining framework, current debate seems to be focused on practical, ad hoc application and labelling. Is knowledge-based policing, perhaps, a strategic policy-level approach within the context of which intelligence-led policing takes place at a tactical level? Is it, within the UK context, a means of re-engaging intelligence-led policing with community intelligence (Kleiven, 2007)? Harfield and Harfield explore this possibility through the interaction of different modes of intervention (2008: figure 1.1) but above the level of a Basic Command Unit tactical response it does not seem to be the whole answer.

Within a professional and academic discourse dominated by IT solutions to knowl-edge problems (Brown and Brudney, 2003; Gordon and Grant, 2005), is knowledge-based policing perhaps the progeny arising from the marriage of intelligence-led policing to IT-based knowledge management systems? Postulating IT as the solution to knowledge management is a popular response (Dean and Gottschalk. 2007: 21) especially when the failings identified by Bichard (2004) are taken into consideration, but implementing IT-based solutions is rarely straightforward (Home Office, 2007). It seems fairly certain on the basis of the response to the IMPACT programme devised in response to Bichard's recommendations, that IT will never be 'The Answer' to policing problems in the current disparate UK policing infrastructure although within the context of a national police organization there are fewer issues of integration to overcome. Ultimately, IT (rather like intelligence) is only ever a tool, not a solution.

Is knowledge-based policing merely an expression of better coordinated partnership? Just as the NIM is intended to connect different hierarchical tiers of police-force delivery, could a theory of knowledge-based policing be the foundation for defining partnership delivery of harm reduction? Coordination implies management, which implies protocols and procedures: a National Knowledge Model for policing perhaps—or more appropriately, a National Knowledge Model for harm reduction? As Johnson illustrates (2006), successful partnership may be impeded by coordination and prescribed conventional wisdom. Success, instead, may depend on organic, dynamic, spontaneous consilience, which is militated against by a restrictive and exclusionary implementation of intelligence-led policing as intelligence-led criminal law enforcement.

So, could knowledge-based policing instead be viewed in terms of organizational culture, a universal approach to doing business? In the same way that intelligence-led policing came to be implemented in as many different ways as there were police organizations implementing it, the same fate potentially awaits any rigidly-constructed model of knowledge-based policing. The need to apply a wider knowledge in utilizing intelligence seems to be a lesson that is evident from recent experience (Harfield and Harfield, 2008: Chapter 2), but as the NIM experience has shown, the police service can be too-readily tempted to adopt uncritically, and then adapt to ensure it has a local rather than national flavour, something that looks like 'The Answer' because it has the appearance of being formulaic, seductively scientific, and straightforward, particularly if it privileges the role of the police service over that of partners.

As a label, 'knowledge-based policing' would seem to imply a different way of working and thinking from that which prevails: a way of thinking in which creativity and innovation are at least as, if not more, important that partnership processes and protocols that could constrain thinking and the freedom to work creatively together—to which a critic might respond, with some justification, that processes and protocols are the rails which keep the inter-agency partnership train on track. But the discovery that a potential intervention is not possible because of partnership protocols, for instance, should lead to a review of the partnership-working in order to dispose of any impediments.

If intelligence-led policing has proved, de facto, to be exclusive and exclusionary and focused on detection outputs (Kleiven, 2007), even if this was not the original intention, then knowledge-based policing must be constructed in a way that is inclusive and exploratory of all potential interventions in order to achieve harm-reduction outcomes. And this leads to consideration of whether 'knowledge-based policing', as a conceptual term, itself also inherently constrains creative thinking. If a label is required, would 'knowledge-based community safety' or 'knowledge-based harm reduction' be more inclusive?

There is a need for further debate that cannot be satisfied within the constraints of single chapter. As a starting point from which to consider the questions posed at the beginning, it is suggested that a knowledge-based approach to community safety and policing can be broken down into a series of key questions at different levels. The suggested framework is neither exhaustive nor exclusive.

At the level of individual problems these questions include: what are the current threats of harm to community safety; what is the full range of possible interventions; is the existing response-infrastructure capable of responding appropriately or will the infrastructure constrain response options; and which agencies (public or private) are best placed to address the identified threats?

At the level of service delivery, questions include: what are the gaps in community safety and policing provision; why and how should they be filled; which activities can be provided by private suppliers; and which activities are not appropriate for private supply?

At the conceptual level, there can be no knowledge-based policing without the creation of knowledge through learning and understanding. How is the learning from any given intervention going to be captured, considered, and disseminated? How can practitioner, partner, policymaker, and academic narrative better inform harm-reduction, future strategy, and future tactical interventions? Wherein lies the governance and accountability overseeing the management of and access to knowledge, and developments based on acquired knowledge?

If knowledge-based policing is to mean something more substantial than a mere sound-bite, it must communicate a concept that caters for the on-going reconfiguration of policing in the post-9/11 world. It must take community safety, and the role of policing within that, forward. By drawing upon a wider context of knowledge, it could be possible to ensure proportionate responses to the rapidly evolving demands of and context for modern policing, community safety, and harm-reduction. Evolving demands mean continually changing questions and challenges. Perhaps, in constructing a concept and exploring the narrative of knowledge-based policing, the most important consideration is to avoid the seductive illusion of 'certainty' afforded by formulaic models, and to avoid denying creativity and responsiveness by trying to define knowledge-based policing as 'The Answer'.

REFERENCES

ANDERSON, M, DEN BOER, M, CULLEN, P, GILMORE, W, RAAB, C, and WALKER, N, eds, *Policing the European Union* (Oxford: Clarendon Press, 1995).

ANDREAS, P and NADELMANN, E, *Policing the Globe: Criminalization and Crime Control in International Relations* (Oxford: Oxford University Press, 2006).

ASHWORTH, A, *Human Rights, Serious Crime and Criminal Procedure* (London: Sweet & Maxwell, 2002).

AUDIT COMMISSION, *Helping with Enquiries* (London: Audit Commission, 1993).

——, *Tackling Crime Effectively* (Vol 1, London: Audit Commission, 1994).

——, (1996a) *Tackling Crime Effectively* (Vol 2, London: Audit Commission, 1996).

——, (1996b) *Tackling Patrol Effectively* (London: Audit Commission, 1996).

AUSTRALIAN FEDERAL POLICE, (2004) available at <http://www.afp.gov.au/__data/assets/pdf_file/3851/factsheethistoryaustralianfederalpolice.pdf>, accessed 6 December 2007.

BICHARD, M, *The Bichard Inquiry Report* (HC653, London: TSO, 2004).

BRATTON, W, 'The unintended consequences of September 11th' *Policing: A Journal of Policy and Practice* 1/1 (2007) 21–24.

BRODEUR, J-P and DUPONT, B, 'Knowledge workers or "Knowledge" workers?' *Policing and Society* 16/1 (2006) 7–26.

BROWN, M and BRUDNEY, J, 'Learning organizations in the public sector: A study of police agencies employing information and technology to advance knowledge' *Public Administration Review* 63/1 (2003) 30–43.

BUTLER, Lord, *Review of Intelligence on Weapons of Mass Destruction* (HC 898, London: TSO, 2004).

CABINET OFFICE, *Security in a Global Hub: Establishing the UK's New Border Arrangements* (London: Central Office of Information, 2007).

CAPLAN, R, *International Governance of War-Torn Territories: Rule and Reconstruction* (Oxford: Oxford University Press, 2005).

CONTROL RISKS, *Corporate Investigations* (London: Control Risks, 2004) available at <http://www.crg.com/html/service_level3.php?id=409>, accessed 30 October 2007.

DEAN, G and GOTTSCHALK, P, *Knowledge Management in Policing and Law Enforcement* (Oxford: Oxford University Press, 2007).

DORN, N and LEVI, M, 'European private security, corporate investigation and military services: Collective security, market regulation and structuring the public sphere' *Policing and Society* 17/3 (2007) 213–238.

ERICSON, R and HAGGERTY, K, *Policing the Risk Society* (Oxford: Oxford University Press, 1997).

FLOOD, B, 'Strategic aspects of the UK national intelligence model' in Ratcliffe, J, ed, *Strategic Thinking in Criminal Intelligence* (Sydney: Federation Press, 2004) 37–52.

GOLDSTEIN, H, *Problem-Oriented Policing* (New York: McGraw-Hill, 1990).

GORDON, R and GRANT, D, 'Knowledge management or management of knowledge? Why people interested in knowledge management need to consider Foucault and the construct of power' *Tamara: Journal of Critical Post-modern Organizational Science* 3/2 (2005) 27–38.

GRIEVE, J, 'Developments in UK criminal intelligence' in Ratcliffe, J, ed, *Strategic Thinking in Criminal Intelligence* (Sydney: Federation Press (2004) 25–36.

GUNDHUS, HO, 'For sikkerhets skyld'. IKT, kunnskapsarbeid og yrkeskulturer i politiet ['For the Sake of Security'. ICT, Knowledge-work and Occupational Culture in Policing] (Oslo: University of Oslo, 2006).

HARFIELD, C, 'SOCA: A paradigm shift in British policing' *British Journal of Criminology* 46 (2006) 743–761.

—— and HARFIELD, K, *Intelligence: Investigation, Community, and Partnership* (Oxford: Oxford University Press, 2008).

HER MAJESTY'S GOVERNMENT, *Countering International Terrorism: The United Kingdom's Strategy* (Cm 6888, London: TSO, 2006).

HER MAJESTY'S INSPECTORATE OF CONSTABULARY, *Policing with Intelligence* (London: HMIC, 1997).

——, *Beating Crime* (London: HMIC, 1998).

——, *Closing the Gap: A Review of the 'Fitness for Purpose' of the Current Structure of Policing in England and Wales* (London: HMIC, 2005).

HER MAJESTY'S INSPECTORATE OF PROBATION, *An Independent Report of a Serious Further Offence Case: Anthony Rice* (London: HMIP, 2006).

HISLOP, D, *Knowledge Management in Organizations* (Oxford: Oxford University Press, 2005).

HOLMES, L, ed, *Terrorism, Organized Crime and Corruption* (Cheltenham: Edward Elgar, 2007).

HOME OFFICE, *Police Reform: The Government's Proposals for the Police Service* (Cm 2281, London: HMSO, 1993).

——, *Policing a New Century: A Blue-print for Reform* (Cm 5326, London: TSO, 2001).

——, *Building Communities, Beating Crime: A Better Police Service for the 21st Century* (Cm 6360, London: TSO, 2004a).

——, *One Step Ahead: A 21st Century Strategy to Defeat Organized Crime* (Cm 6167, London: TSO, 2004b).

——, *New Powers Against Organized and Financial Crime* (Cm 6875, London: TSO 2006).

——, *Bichard Inquiry Recommendations: Fourth Progress Report* (London: TSO, 2007).

INTELLIGENCE AND SECURITY COMMITTEE, *Report into the London Terrorist Attacks on 7 July 2005* (Cm 6785, London: TSO, 2006).

JOHN, T and MAGUIRE, M, 'Rolling-out the national intelligence model: Key challenges' in Bullock, K and Tilley, N, eds, *Crime Reduction and Problem-Oriented Policing* (Devon: Willan Publishing, 2003) 28–68.

JOHNSON, S, *The Ghost Map: A Street, an Epidemic and the Two Men who Battled to Save Victorian England* (London: Allen Lane, 2006).

JOHNSTON, L, *The Re-birth of Private Policing* (London: Routledge, 1992).

JONES, T and NEWBURN, T, eds, *Plural Policing: A Comparative Perspective* (London: Routledge, 2006).

KLEIVEN, M, 'Where's the intelligence in the National Intelligence Model?' *International Journal of Police Science and Management* 9/3 (2007) 257–273.

LAMING, Lord, *The Victoria Climbié Inquiry* (Cm 5730, London: TSO, 2003).

LOCAL GOVERNMENT MANAGEMENT BOARD, *Best Value: An Introductory Guide* (London: Local Government Association, 1999).

LONG, M, 'Leadership and performance management' in Newburn, T, ed, *Handbook of Policing* (Devon: Willan Publishing, 2003) 628–654.

LOTHIAN & BORDERS POLICE, <http://www.lbp.police.uk/freedom-of-information/consultation/CCStrategy.pdf>, accessed 6 December 2007.

MAGUIRE, M and JOHN, T, 'Intelligence-led policing, managerialism and community engagement: Competing priorities and the role of the National Intelligence Model in the UK' *Policing and Society* 16 (2006) 67–85.

McDONALD, W, ed, *Crime and Law Enforcement in the Global Village* (Cincinnati: Anderson, 1997).

MITSILEGAS, V, MONAR, J and Rees, W, *The European Union and Internal Security: Guardian of the People?* (Basingstoke: Palgrave MacMillan, 2003).

MURRAY-WATSON, A, 'The sleuths who go where investment banks fear to tread' *Daily Telegraph,* 1 October 2006, accessible at <http://www.telegraph.co.uk/money/main.jhtml?xml=/money/2006/10/15/ccsleuth15.xml>, accessed 30 October 2007).

NORTHERN IRELAND OFFICE, *Devolving Policing and Justice in Northern Ireland: A Discussion Paper* (Cm 6963, London: TSO, 2006).

OCCHIPINTI, J, *The Politics of EU Police Co-operation: Toward a European FBI?* (Boulder: Lynne Rienner, 2003).

O'MALLEY, P and PALMER, D, 'Post-Keynesi and Policing' *Economy and Society* 25/2 (1996) 137–155.

OSCE 2006, *Annual Report of the Secretary General on Police-Related Activities in 2005* SEC. DOC/2/06.

PICARELLI, J, 'The turbulent nexus of transnational organized crime and terrorism: A theory of malevolent international relations' *Global Crime* 7/1 (2006) 1–24.

PICCOLI, W, Presentation to ESRC workshop: *The New Economy of Security: Contemporary Insecurities and the Pluralization of Coercive Force*, University of Aberystwyth, 26 October 2007.

RATCLIFFE, J, 'Intelligence-led policing' *Trends and Issues in Crime and Criminal Justice No 248* (Australian Institute of Criminology, 2003).

——, 'The effectiveness of police intelligence management: A New Zealand case study' *Police Practice and Research* 6/5 (2005) 435–451.

SCARBROUGH, H and SWAN, J, 'Explaining the diffusion of knowledge management' *British Journal of Management* 12 (2001) 3–12.

SECURITAS, *Annual Report* 2005, available at <http://www.securitas.de/uploads/tx_annual-rep/annual_report_2005_eng.pdf>.

SHANTY, F and MISHRA, P, eds, *Organized Crime: From Trafficking to Terrorism* (Santa Barbara, Ca: ABC-Clio, 2008).

SHELLEY, L and PICARELLI, J, 'Methods not motives: Implications of the convergence of international organized crime and terrorism' *Police Practice and Research* 3/4 (2002) 305–318.

SHEPTYCKI, J, ed, *Issues in Transnational Policing* (London: Routledge, 2000).

——, 'Organizational pathologies in police intelligence systems: Some contributions to the lexicon of intelligence-led policing' *European Journal of Criminology* 1 (2004) 307–332.

THORNTON, S and MASON, L, 'Community cohesion in High Wycombe: A case study of Operation Overt' *Policing: A Journal of Policy and Practice* 1/1 (2007) 57–60.

TILLEY, N, 'Community policing, problem-oriented policing and intelligence-led policing' in Newburn, T, ed, *Handbook of Policing* (Devon: Willan Publishing, 2003) 311–339.

VINCENT, H, *A Police Code and Manual of Police Law* (London: Cassell, Petter, Galpin & Co, 1881).

WILLIAMSON, T, ed, *The Handbook of Knowledge-Based Policing: Current Conceptions and Future Directions* (Devon: Willan Publishing, 2008).

19

KNOWLEDGE MANAGEMENT AND THE EFFECTIVE WORKING OF CRIME AND DISORDER REDUCTION PARTNERSHIPS

Catherine Kelly

POLICING AND CRIME AND DISORDER REDUCTION PARTNERSHIPS

The management and structuring of the police services has experienced much change in recent years, in an effort to create services which meet the needs of a rapidly changing society. This is at a time when, as Crawford (2006) discusses, there is an increasingly contested debate in the UK focusing on the effective regulation of conduct and the politics of behaviour.

Partly on the premise that crime is a social problem rather than purely a policing problem, police services are now required to work in partnership with a number of different partner organizations. Nigel Fielding (2005) comments that:

... the Police Reform Act 2002 maintained that policing is a function carried out by many agencies of which police are but one ... we must now regard the police as one organization amongst a number required to conduct the policing function. (Fielding, 2005: 22)

The creation of Crime and Disorder Reduction Partnerships (CDRPs) have reflected this changing perception of the policing function. Ellis et al (2007: 35) comment: 'The Crime and Disorder Act 1998 (Stationery Office, 1998) and the Crime Reduction Strategy for England and Wales that followed it in 1999 (Home Office, 1999), stressed the importance of local organizations working in partnership with Local Authorities and the Police to tackle the causes of crime.' CDRPs are described as statutory partnerships, in which responsible authorities have 'a statutory duty to work with other local agencies and organizations to develop and implement strategies to tackle crime and disorder...' (Crime and Disorder Act 1998, s 6 as amended by Police Reform Act 2002, ss 97 and 98 and Clean Neighbourhoods and Environment Act 2005, s 1).

The responsible authorities, as set out in the Crime and Disorder Act 1998, s 5, are as follows:

- Police
- Police authorities
- Local authorities
- Fire and rescue authorities
- Primary Care Trusts (PCTs) in England.

These responsible authorities, including the police service, are required to work in cooperation with a wide range of partner organizations, which include the Probation Boards, Youth Offending Teams, Drug Action Teams, and Local Criminal Justice Boards, as well as parish councils and a range of local private, voluntary and community groups in order to fulfil their statutory duties and work collaboratively in order to 'tackle crime and disorder'.

Special attention needs to be paid to understanding how such diverse organizations can work in partnership where they are predicated on different organizational aims, values, and norms, and consequently sometimes varying professional approaches and professional objectives. Fielding suggests that: 'The police sense of mission and their instinctive preference for action runs at odds with agencies that are less well resourced, deal in deeper long term responses to social problems, and work more closely to local government requirements' (Fielding, 2005: 130).

ACHIEVEMENTS OF THE CDRPS AND ONGOING CHALLENGES IN INFORMATION AND KNOWLEDGE MANAGEMENT

The CDRPs successes include a reduction in the incidence of crime in the UK. Ellis et al (2007: 35) refer to the fact that:

Between 1999 and 2005, the Home Office awarded grants totalling £926.8 million to fund CDRP crime reduction initiatives. A report on crime reduction (National Audit Office, 2004) pointed to a 39% decrease in the number of crimes reported through the British Crime Survey between 1995 and 2003–2004, and credited much of that success to projects delivered by CDRPs.

At the same time, difficulties have been noted in creating effective collaborative working relationships amongst the partner agencies, with the Probation Services and the Health Services receiving particular mention in this regard. The National Audit Office report, for example, comments: 'Crime reduction projects are more likely to be successful when there is commitment and synergy within a Partnership' (National Audit Office, 2004: 9).

The partner agencies of the CDRP need to exchange and share necessary information and knowledge in order to deliver an effective policing presence working for, and alongside, the community. There is added complexity by virtue of the fact that the

partner organizations making up the CDRP have different sets of management structures, value systems, and organizational cultures. The range and size of the organizations involved in the partnerships must also inevitably lead to practical problems
around coordination of effort including the appropriate sharing of information.

This chapter will look a the ways in which effective knowledge management (KM)
practice can contribute to enhanced collaborative working relationships, and thus
more effective policing under the CDRP structures, focusing primarily on the management of tacit knowledge.

Initially, some key definitions and an overview of relevant KM theory will be
offered. This will be followed by an illustration of how knowledge-management practice may be used to improve knowledge sharing between the partners and will also
suggest practical ways of moving organizations forward in this regard.

WHAT IS KNOWLEDGE MANAGEMENT?

A pragmatic definition of knowledge management is as follows: 'The explicit and
systematic management of vital knowledge and its associated processes of creating,
gathering, organising, diffusion, use and exploitation, in pursuit of organizational
objectives' (Skyrme, 2007).

An alternative generic definition in describing knowledge management is 'the
process of creating, capturing and using knowledge to enhance organizational performance' (Collier, 2006: 109).

In order to understand how to manage knowledge, some underpinning definitions
of knowledge are needed. Although this is a topic which could be discussed in much
more detail from an ontological, epistemological, and political point of view, for the
purpose of this article a relatively simple and pragmatic definition is offered distinguishing between tacit and explicit knowledge, taken from Nonaka and Takeuchi
(1995) which draws on Michael Polanyi's (1966) writings: 'Tacit knowledge is personal, context specific and therefore hard to formalise and communicate. Explicit or
codified knowledge, on the other hand, refers to knowledge that is transmittable in
formal, systematic language' (Nonaka and Takeuchi, 1995: 59).

MANAGING EXPLICIT VERSUS TACIT KNOWLEDGE

Explicit Knowledge (Information)

It is proposed here that the management of explicit knowledge is primarily focused on
the effective management of information, whether this is stored utilizing information
technology or in hard copy format.

Regulations and guidance can be successfully imposed on organizations in order
to prescribe practices around collection, storage, and flow of explicit knowledge or
information, and this is already underway within the CDRPs. A recent letter from the
Home Office regarding the CDRP Reform Programme noted that 'The 2006 Act enables the Home Secretary to introduce regulations to provide a framework for CDRPs

to be known as national minimum standards' and that it is believed that 'the provisions devised to strengthen the information sharing between partners would support more effective working within the CDRPs' (Home Office, 2007).

Managing information-flow through the effective use of information technology and through developing good standards of practice around information management processes are fundamental to effective working, especially in service-based organizations such as the police. Developing common standards for information sharing across the police forces, and between the police forces and partner agencies, is a crucial building block for any knowledge-management strategy, and it is clear that this is an ongoing area of focus and concern for management.

Tacit Knowledge

Moving beyond purely a discussion of the management of explicit knowledge or information, it is proposed here that enabling tacit-knowledge flow is an area which also needs particular attention with the CDRP structures. The management of tacit knowledge is commonly ignored in many organizations in favour of strategies focusing on information management utilizing information technology solutions.

Knowledge management is also concerned with the management of this *tacit* knowledge. Tacit knowledge can be defined as that knowledge which is carried around in people's heads and which is estimated to account for around 80 per cent of the available knowledge within an organization.

While it is possible to manage explicit knowledge or information through the development of appropriate processes, tools, and technologies, managing tacit knowledge requires different kinds of intervention. Managing tacit knowledge must be regarded as a key aspect of any knowledge-management programme and it is this issue which will be discussed in depth in this chapter.

In order to manage tacit knowledge flow, it is vital to consider how to manage effectively the environments in which such knowledge is created and shared. The adoption of an appropriate organizational structure and culture is the key to the success of a truly effective knowledge-management strategy. Organizations which manage to incorporate the development of effective communication channels and participatory work practices can speed up this exchange of tacit knowledge.

This is a challenge for many organizations, and especially those seeking to work in partnership with other organizations. For the police service, this challenge to work collaboratively in sharing tacit knowledge operates on a number of levels, both amongst partner agencies within the CDRP and amongst different units within the policing service itself.

THE KNOWLEDGE MANAGEMENT SECI FRAMEWORK

Some of the ways in which the flow and exchange of tacit and explicit knowledge take place within organizations have been illustrated by Nonaka and Takeuchi's SECI framework (1995), one of the most influential models within the knowledge management area (Figure 19.1).

A brief explanation of the model itself is important to set this overall discussion in context. Underlying the development of Nonaka and Takeuchi's SECI framework

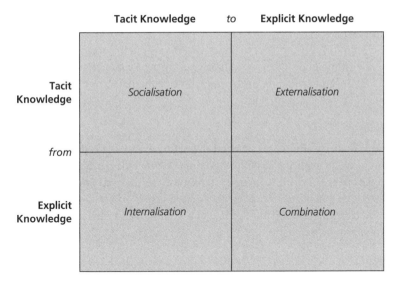

Fig 19.1 Four Models of Knowledge Conversion

Source: Nonaka, I and Takeuchi, H, *The Knowledge-Creating Company* (Oxford: Oxford University Press, 1995) 62.

is an assumption that 'human knowledge is created and expanded through social interaction between tacit knowledge and explicit knowledge' (Nonaka and Takeuchi, 1995: 145). Hence, four different types of knowledge conversion combine in the knowledge cycle, namely socialization, externalization, combination, and internalization as seen in Figure 19.1.

Socialization

Socialization entails working with others on tacit-tacit or face-to-face exchange. This type of exchange might take place through formal meetings at work or, for example, through informal chats around the coffee machine. At a deeper level, junior members of staff working with more senior members of staff will learn, not just through the spoken word but by observation, imitation, and then practice, the mores operating within a professional area of practice. Developing shared experiences and therefore, shared meanings, underpins this tacit-knowledge exchange. It is a very effective means of knowledge creation and sharing, but also limited in its reach by its very nature.

Externalization

The externalization process attempts to capture and/or communicate both explicit and tacit knowledge.

Explicit knowledge may be communicated through written documents including guidance around aspects of service provision. For example, within the CDRP Reform Programme's new regulation around information sharing, it is proposed that 'codifying current practice' will be a key aspect going forward (the Police and Justice Act 2006, Schedule 9(5)).

Communicating tacit knowledge may be achieved through an organization's development of stories, metaphors, analogies, and concepts which impact on the development of the employees mental models or thought processes around work or professional practice.

Making clearer key assumptions or value systems within an organization starts to create amongst members of the organization a sense of cohesiveness, a sense of belonging, and an understanding of the organizations particular modus operandi and the individual's place within this.

Combination

Combination entails combining explicit knowledge for new use, for example combining different pieces of explicit knowledge into a new form or format. Some examples could be trend analysis of crime reduction interventions on the part of the police service, or a new content management system that pulls together information in an easily accessible and coherent fashion, thus leading to new insight and enhanced processes within particular areas of practice.

Internalization

Internalization occurs when individuals within an organization mentally absorb the available explicit information. In other words, the individual begins to incorporate the explicit knowledge available within the organization within their own mental models until it becomes tacit knowledge to that individual.

Internalization can occur without having to 'live' other people's experiences. For example, understanding how problems may have been solved by individuals within the organization will have an impact on the future behaviour and attitude of other employees who may be experiencing similar problems.

KEY ASPECTS OF THE SECI MODEL AS APPLIED WITHIN THE CDRP CONTEXT

The SECI model is useful because it illustrates the importance of having an ongoing interaction and adjustment between tacit knowledge (the 'lived' experience) and explicit knowledge (the formalized or 'book' knowledge). In a world of continuous change, it is no longer possible for any organization to simply follow documented procedures and regulations without ongoing modification and adaptation. Reactivity to changing external circumstances is absolutely crucial to ongoing organizational effectiveness.

The SECI model recognizes and recommends this ongoing interaction and iterative process in knowledge creation and flow which is ultimately designed to ensure greater organizational effectiveness. It also folds the human experience at all levels within the organization firmly into a process to most effectively meet organizational goals on an ongoing basis, and releases the energy and power of workers to innovate in striving to meet organizational objectives.

Knowledge-management practice places human creativity and cognition at the centre of the route to organizational effectiveness, in contrast to the more mechanistic and bureaucratic management style which has been dominant in many public-sector organizations up to now and which has been highly focused on demonstrating 'value for money' through centrally imposed measurable outputs and performance indicators.

This approach to public service management is illustrated by the Audit Commission's remit which is to ensure that 'public money is spent economically, efficiently and effectively in the areas of local government, housing, health and criminal justice services' (Audit Commission, 2003: 1). Although ensuring value for money is key for any organization, the imposition of excessively prescriptive performance indicators to measure effectiveness of public service provision came at a time when, somewhat ironically, the private sector itself has been moving away from these management principles in the face of an increasingly turbulent and rapidly changing business environment. Private sector organizations have recognized a need for greater levels of employee autonomy in decision-making which allows for enhanced flexibility and higher levels of organizational reactivity to environmental changes.

An additional issue now facing organizations in focusing excessively on managing information through the use of technologies relates to the legal framework which now exists within England and Wales. While it can be assumed that the KM information technology tools are generally conducive to the flow of explicit knowledge or information, the application of these tools in a partnership such as the CDRP poses interesting problems under English law. The Data Protection Act (1998), for example, lays down stringent rules on the dissemination and use of personal data. This may adversely affect the communication and knowledge sharing between local police forces and between partner organizations under the CDRP structure. Similarly, the Freedom of Information Act (2000) may at times prevent the conversion of sensitive tacit knowledge into explicit knowledge, if it can then be accessed by third parties at a later date.

It needs to be recognized that in a working environment governed by such laws, it is important to ensure that CDRP organizations also have structures in place to facilitate communications in ways which allow a greater level of informality and holism. Part of the remit of knowledge management is to put such structures in place.

It is really only possible to manage tacit knowledge through managing the environment in which tacit knowledge is created and shared. Key elements impacting on knowledge sharing are, first, the creation of an appropriate organizational structure and, second, the embedding and nurturing of an organizational culture which encourages and rewards collaborative working relationships and, above all, enhances the development of working trust. If trust is established, then the levels of communication of tacit knowledge will increase. The chief concern here is to ensure that tacit knowledge is created, used, and shared in an optimum fashion. How this can be achieved will be discussed in the next four sections.

IMPLEMENTING KNOWLEDGE MANAGEMENT IN CDRPS

ORGANIZATIONAL STRUCTURES AND KNOWLEDGE CONDUCTIVITIES

Mintzberg defines organizational structure as follows: 'The structure of an organization can be defined simply as the sum total of the ways in which it divides its labour into distinct tasks and then achieves co-ordination between them' (1979: 3).

Organizational structures should ideally enable organizational objectives to be achieved effectively and efficiently, and harness the skills of the employees at all levels to best advantage to meet organizational goals. Structures shape and reflect the communication patterns and management style within organizations. They take many shapes, from the hierarchical, to the matrix, to the networked. Many public-sector organizations have typically adopted a hierarchical or tall structure. This results in long lines of vertical communication, and often weak lines of lateral communications between functions and teams. Tall structures are often combined with a commitment to a bureaucratic form of management. Bureaucracy, according to Weber (2003), who first coined the term, is an organization having the following main features:

- a continuous organization of functions bounded by rules;
- specified spheres of competence;
- a hierarchy of offices, where jobs at one level are subject to the authority of jobs at the next highest level;
- all appointments are made on the basis of technical competence;
- the officials of the organization are separated from its ownership;
- rules, decisions, and actions are made explicit and recorded in writing.

The benefits of a bureaucratic organization are clear lines of authority, accountability, and responsibility. These are solid management principles which should underpin any effective organization. However, the ongoing incorporation of incremental changes are not key strengths for excessively bureaucratic organizations, and this can lead to problems of adaptation in an unpredictable operating environment.

NETWORKED ORGANIZATIONS

Knowledge-management practitioners, keenly aware of the need for organizations to be more organic and adaptable, most commonly propose the networked organizational structure as a solution. Alongside the proposals for a networked organizational structure is a tandem commitment to a different relationship between employees and employers, and a different view of the employees' role within the workplace.

Bahrami (1996) suggests that organizations need to structure themselves as a 'federation' or 'constellation' of interdependent units, with both centralized and decentralized aspects. The centre of the organization should provide broad direction and thus ensure the necessary level of cohesion and collaboration among the various interdependent units, while the independent units apply their own judgements as to how to best achieve overall objectives for that unit, all set within a clearly defined overall set of strategic aims and objectives at both a macro and a micro level. In addition, special project teams and core employees may be utilized and seconded to different parts of the organization to address specific key issues at any given point in time. Collaborative partnerships are developed where it can be envisaged that they will contribute to the partner organizations achieving some tangible gain in working towards the achievement of both partner organization goals.

More recently, Bryan and Joyce (2007: 26) suggest that:

The starting point is streamlining the way hierarchy is used so that it can become efficient and effective. Such a design involves creating one simple backbone structure to drive performance and place authority at the front line . . . This approach will require most [organizations] to eliminate the matrix structures that have grown up in their intermediate levels and, at the same time, to replace these with formal network structures that use mutual self interest rather than authority to motivate collaboration.

INTER-ORGANIZATIONAL NETWORKING

Developing effective network structures amongst a range of different organizations which have limited overlaps in terms of organizational goals poses extra challenges. CDRPs incorporate inter-organizational working amongst an extremely large and diverse group of organizations. A very useful paper by Marchington and Vincent (2004) on inter-organizational relations suggests that organizations' and organizational members' ability to work effectively with partner organizations are affected strongly by the nature of the contracts which exist between the organizations.

Drawing on Sako's (1992) work, a distinction is made between obligational contractual relations (OCR) and arms-length contractual relations (ACR). Sako describes ACR relationships as entailing a low dependence on the other party, a short term commitment; the terms and conditions of the contract are written down and are detailed and specific while narrow communication channels exist between partners.

On the other side, OCR relations involve highly dependent relations with the other party: there may be a long-term commitment; terms and conditions of the contract may be oral rather than written; loose performance measures may be in place; and extensive multiple channels of communication can exist at a variety of levels in both organizations, with frequent contact and much socializing. ACR relations involve lower levels of trust, while OCR relations are built on high levels of mutual understanding, commonality, and trust.

CDRPS ACR-TYPE RELATIONSHIPS?

There is evidence that the form of the relationships developed among the CDRP partners have not been consistent across the UK and that variations in practice, and different levels of success in reducing incidences of crime, have existed on a national level in this regard.

Recent communications from the Home Office to the CDRP responsible authorities clearly indicate that a move towards creating formal relationships, which are more defined in contractual terms, is imminent. Regulations around 'national minimum standards' have been introduced. As already outlined, additional requirements around the sharing of depersonalized information have been set out in the regulations. The guidance around the new regulations (published in September 2007) offer the CDRP organizations clearer direction as to how these minimum standards may be met and promise to:

- outline clearly what the law requires of responsible authorities in implementing a strategy to tackle crime and disorder;
- summarize what partnerships need to do in order to meet the new requirements, including examples;
- show how partnerships can go above and beyond these minimum standards, including examples;
- address potential barriers that may be faced by partnerships and possible solutions to these.

It is suggested that these new regulations introduced within the CDRP structure incorporate the development of an ACR type relationship, with clearer expectations laid out as to the nature of the expected interaction between the partners.

However, in terms of building a more effective exchange of tacit knowledge, deeper levels of cooperation between the partner organizations will need to be nurtured. So while the CDRPs are now developing more clearly defined contractual relationships, it is also necessary to consider in the longer term how to develop deeper OCR-type relationships to enable more effective sharing of tacit knowledge.

Tyler (2003: 566) suggests that 'As we enter this new era of co-operation among people, organizations and society, we need to focus on developing new consensual forms of co-operation. These new forms emphasise gaining "buy in" from people rather than seeking to shape their behaviour by changing the contingencies of the situation, via incentives or sanctions.'

In order to create these more committed working relationships amongst partner agencies, there will need to be a greater focus on creating commonality in broad aims, and the development of relationships built on mutual reciprocity and trust. Developing this modus operandi within organizations will thus entail a more active management of organizational culture.

ORGANIZATIONAL CULTURES

Organizational culture is a way of describing how an organization conducts its activities and the standards of behaviour, norms, and values it adopts. It is a deeper level of analysis of behaviour in an organization, as compared to looking at organization structure, as it considers a range of factors which impact on the behaviour of employees within organizations. A simple way of defining organization culture is offered by Handy (1999) as 'the ways in which things are done around here'.

Brooks (2003) cites Jaques (1952) as one of the earliest writers on this subject, who describes the culture of an organization as comprising behaviours, attitudes, customs, values, beliefs, and the 'less conscious conventions and taboos' (Jaques, 1952: 251).

Culture is thus reflected in the visible aspects of the organization, like its stated objectives or mission, and its espoused values. But culture is also embedded in the way people act, what they expect of each other, and how they make sense of each other's actions. Culture is, at base, rooted in an organization's core values and assumptions.

Homa Bahrami (1996), cited in Evans (2003) suggests that the traditional workplace focuses on maintaining external controls over employee behaviour through regulation and monitoring, whereas the knowledge-intensive organization emphasizes the development of internal controls though the development and inculcation of behavioural norms, which then allow greater levels of autonomy for workers resulting in much higher levels of organizational flexibility. Thus, creating a networked organizational structure in place of strongly hierarchical structures, which enable the flow of knowledge, necessitates the embedding of strong values and norms internally within the minds of the employees. In this sense, internal controls come into being, as opposed to the external controls associated with the bureaucratic management model.

In relation to CDRPs, creating organizational cultures which emphasize the importance of knowledge sharing is more complex, as many of the organizations which make up the CDRPs have differing individual organizational norms and values systems. The challenge here is to ensure that goals are negotiated, developed, and communicated at a very broad level for these partner organizations through which the benefits of working together can be made clearer.

Organizations which are working in collaboration with other organizations in this way thus need carefully judged management intervention in order to foster interactions which will help to build cooperative working relations. Whether a trusting relationship emerges between different organizations, such as those within the CDRP structure, is strongly impacted upon by the mechanisms that are developed to facilitate open communication and negotiation around possible common goals and the steps which are taken to encourage coordination and communication between the different organizations. Relationships of trust most often emerge from individuals and organizations who believe that each of the parties' interests will be served through the existence of such relationships.

Evans comments that 'Trust has become a vital ingredient . . . particularly given the shift towards virtual organizations, organizations that do not physically exist but instead consist of a group of companies/people all working in an area of common interest' (Evans, 2003: 44). Trust is also essential for facilitating effective problem solving, because it 'encourages the exchange of relevant information and determines whether team members are willing to allow others to influence their decisions and actions' (Carnevale and Wechsler, 1992: 471) Grandori and Soda (1995: 21) quoted in Newell and Swan (2000) note that 'Trust is one of the most frequently mentioned concepts in connection with inter-firm cooperative relations.' Here, in seeking to understand how to create greater levels of trust, it is helpful to consider how Grandori and Soda deconstruct the different types of networks which develop in, and amongst, individuals and organizations. In so doing, they classify networks as social, bureaucratic, or proprietary.

Proprietary networks, which are concerned with the protection of intellectual property rights, are not relevant to this discussion. However, bureaucratic networks and social networks are relevant and it will be shown that they undoubtedly perform different, and complementary, functions in framing a relationship of trust.

BUREAUCRATIC NETWORKS

Bureaucratic networks are typically underpinned by formal agreements and formally identified roles and coordination mechanisms, and could be likened to an ACR-type relationship as already discussed.

Communicating and clarifying the different parties' duties and responsibilities will ensure that the partnership approach does not result in a diffuse and incoherent understanding of lines of authority, responsibility, and accountability amongst the various service providers.

Establishing the fundamental grounds of a contractual relationship between the parties will allow trusting relationships to emerge at an operational level.

SOCIAL NETWORKS

As a next step, it is important to foster the conditions to allow the different organizations to begin to work collaboratively and start to develop trusting relationships, and thus share and exchange tacit knowledge more freely. Wildridge et al (2004), cited in Ellis et al (2007) found that the effectiveness of partnerships is threatened where individual agencies are unable to see benefits to themselves in collaborative working.

Social networks, built around and beyond the purely contractual networks, will facilitate a development of further understanding amongst the partner organizations, as they allow a stronger level of engagement, based primarily on personal contacts and interpersonal exchange. It is to the development of this so-called 'social capital' that this chapter will now turn.

SOCIAL CAPITAL

According to Putnam, social capital can be defined as the 'connections among individuals—social networks and the norms of reciprocity and trustworthiness that arise from them' (Putnam, 2000: 19).

In discussing social capital in relation to inter-organizational networking, it is useful to refer to Woolcock (2001), drawing on Gittel and Vidal (1998), who specifies three different types of social capital, two of which are of relevance here. As outlined in Crawford (2006), *bonding social capital* refers to strong social ties that typically emerge from groups of people who have similar backgrounds, interests, and value systems. These groups of people are interdependent. An analogy here would be the police service or the fire service where many of the members of the force would have similar value systems and have a loyalty to other members of the organization based on their professional background and experiences.

Bridging social capital, on the other hand, refers to bonds between different social groups, including people with different belief systems or world views, cultural views, or religious views. These are weaker attachments but nonetheless capable of fostering trust and mutual understanding. The partner organizations within the CDRP could be said to fall within this category, where there are not necessarily strongly shared values, but there are enough common goals to enable people to get along and work together in achieving certain 'instrumental' goals.

The ties which exist amongst members within bridging social capital are much weaker than in bonding social capital, but they are nonetheless still capable of ensuring that people can work together effectively. Crawford notes that 'weak ties are often the most useful form of social organization for getting things done' and points out that strong ties, while providing a common sense of identify and a common purpose, can sometimes result in the 'pursuit of narrow sectarian and parochial interests' (Crawford, 2006: 963).

To maintain a balance between bonding and bridging social capital is clearly in the interests of organizations such as the police force in order to ensure a balance between homogeneity and heterogeneity as regards both value systems and instrumental means of achieving certain policing outcomes.

How to work towards greater levels of bonding social capital amongst the CDRP partner organizations is a key challenge for the partner organizations, and it is proposed here that a knowledge-management professional, ideally with a professional background within the partner organizations, may contribute to this in crucial ways, working from a clearly defined professional skill set.

THE ROLE OF THE KNOWLEDGE-MANAGEMENT PROFESSIONAL IN FOSTERING GREATER LEVELS OF SOCIAL CAPITAL IN ORGANIZATIONS

Marchington et al look at the ways in which inter-organizational relations can be 'developed, reinforced or broken [through] day-to-day interactions between boundary-spanning agents' (Marchington et al, 2004: 1036). Boundary-spanning agents are those workforce members who work at the boundaries of an organization. Boundary-spanning individuals have been found to 'play a key role in leveraging inter-organizational relations and in fine-tuning detailed arrangements . . .' (Marchington, 2004: 1032).

Drawing on Marchington, it is suggested that there is a way to formalize this boundary-spanning role and frame it in a different fashion within the CDRPs structure, through appointing particular *link* people or *knowledge agents* to work with the various partner organizations on a more active level. Such boundary-spanning individuals, through such professional roles, could act as conduits for both information and knowledge flows between, and through, the organizations. Within the private sector, and especially within investment banking, management consultancy, and accountancy firms in the UK, such knowledge workers are already utilized to aid the flow of information and knowledge throughout the organizations, and are professionally trained to take on this role. It is suggested that information and knowledge-management professionals in the CDRPs could take on this active role in ensuring that both information and knowledge flow more freely through the individual and the partner organizations. The particular roles such information and knowledge managers would perform would be as follows:

- comprise a dedicated resource to ensure that information management and records management are properly and professionally organized within the partner organizations and that information is up to date and available when required;
- work to ensure greater levels of social interaction amongst the partner organizations, though developing the appropriate fora such as, for example, Communities of Practice or Communities of Interest;
- work with CDRPs partners and relevant IT professionals to ensure that IT systems and intelligence systems are fit for purpose and that staff are trained effectively in utilising these systems;
- provide a professional resource, with an awareness of the responsibilities and duties incumbent upon the partner organizations (in terms of legal requirements including an awareness of Freedom of Information and Data Protection legislation and its impact on public sector organizations), and the ability to guide, direct, and develop information-management policy to ensure necessary levels of compliance;
- develop appropriate circulation lists and email lists in which relevant information is filtered and forwarded to the appropriate groups and individuals, reducing information overload on the partner organizations.

The development of such a role in the CDRP programmes could go some way towards facilitating this ongoing exchange of explicit and tacit knowledge amongst partners, and thereby offer a useful means of ensuring the development and exchange of knowledge and an enhanced ability to fulfil organizational and inter-organizational goals.

SUMMARY AND CONCLUSION

This chapter has discussed and explored the effective management of tacit knowledge in CDRPs, with reference to the ongoing interactions between tacit and explicit knowledge.

Successful management of tacit knowledge is largely predicated on the management of the organizational context in which tacit knowledge is created and shared. As such, creating organizational structures which enhance knowledge flows, and organizational cultures which utilize largely normative methods of control (thus allowing for the emergence of trusting working relationships) is crucial. It has been proposed that the dedicated knowledge-management professional may also have a key role to play in enhancing information and knowledge flow within, and between, partner organizations.

Overall, as proposed by knowledge-management practitioners, it is important that trust is placed in the professionals at the front line of service delivery in judging how best to fulfil their roles, as long as these judgements are based on a clear understanding of organizational objectives, inter-organizational objectives, and underlying norms and value systems.

It is also suggested that if this approach is adopted, it will mean that less effort will need to be directed at fulfilling centrally generated managerial directives, thus allowing rather the CDRP partner organizations to direct the bulk of their efforts on meeting the ongoing expectations to reduce the incidence of crime in the communities served in innovative and effective ways.

REFERENCES

AUDIT COMMISSION, *About Us* (London: Audit Commission, 2003) available at <http://www.audit-commission.gov.uk>.

BAHRAMI, H, 'The emerging flexible organization: Perspectives from Silicon Valley' in Myers, PS, ed, *Knowledge Management and Organizational Design* (Oxford: Butterworth Heinemann, 1996) 55–77.

BROOKS, I, *Organizational Behaviour: Individuals, Groups and Organization* (Harlow: Pearson Education Ltd, 2003).

BRYAN, L and JOYCE, CI, 'Better strategy through organizational design' *The McKinsey Quarterly* 2 (2007) 21–29.

CARNEVALE, D and WECHSLER, B, 'Trust in the public sector' *Administration and Society*, 23/4 (1992) 471–495.

COLLIER, PM, 'Policing and the intelligent application of knowledge' *Public Money and Management* (April 2006) 109–116.

CRAWFORD, A, '"Fixing broken promises?": Neighbourhood Wardens and social capital' *Urban Studies* 43/5 (2006) 957–976.

ELLIS, E, FORTUNE, J and PETERS, G, 'Partnership problems: Analysis and re-design' *Crime Prevention and Community Safety* 9 (2007) 34–51.

EVANS, C, *Managing for Knowledge: HR's Strategic Role* (Oxford: Butterworth Heinemann, 2003).

FIELDING, NG, *The Police and Social Conflict* (2nd edn, London: Glass House Press, 2005).

GITTEL, R and VIDAL, A, *Community Organising: Building Social Capital as a Development Strategy* (Thousand Oaks, California: Sage Publications, 1998).

GRANDORI, A and SODA, G, 'Inter-firm networks: Antecedents, mechanisms and forms' *Organization Studies* 16 (1995) 183–214.

HANDY, C, *Understanding Organizations* (London: Penguin Books, 1999).

HOME OFFICE, 2007, available at <http://www.opsi.gov.uk/si/si2007/em/uksiem_20071830_en.pdf>, accessed on 15 August 2007.

HOME OFFICE CRIME, 2007, available at <http://www.crimereduction.homeoffice.gov.uk/regions/regions00.htm>, accessed on 10 September 2007.

JAQUES, E, *The Changing Culture of a Factory* (New York: Dryden Press, 1952).

MARCHINGTON, M and VINCENT, S, 'Analysing the influence of institutional, organizational and interpersonal forces in shaping inter-organizational relations' *Journal of Management Studies* 41/6 (2004) 1029–1056.

MINTZBERG, H, *The Structuring of Organizations* (Englewood Cliffs, NJ: Prentice-Hall, 1979).

NATIONAL AUDIT OFFICE *Reducing Crime* (London: The Stationery Office, 2004).

NEWBURN, T, *Handbook of Policing* (Devon: Willan Publishing, 2003).

NEWELL, S and SWAN, J, 'Trust and inter-organizational networking' *Human Relations* 53/10 (2000) 1287–1328.

NONAKA, I and TAKEUCHI, H, *The Knowledge-Creating Company* (Oxford: Oxford University Press, 1995).

POLANYI, M, *The Tacit Dimension* (London: Routledge & Kegan Paul, 1996).

PUTNAM, RD, *Bowling Alone: The Collapse and Revival of American Community* (New York: Simon & Schuster, 2000).

SAKO, M, *Prices, Quality and Trust: Inter-firm Relations in Britain and Japan* (Cambridge: Cambridge University Press, 1992).

SKYRME, D, *Knowledge Connections*, available at <http://dev.skyrme.com/resource/glossary. htm>, accessed on 14 November 2007.

TYLER, T, 'Trust Within Organizations' *Personnel Review* 32/5 (2003) 556–568.

WOOLCOCK, M, 'The place of social capital in understanding social and economic outcomes' *Isuma: Canadian Journal of Policy Research* 2/1 (2001) 11–17.

WHIMSTER, S, ed, *The Essential Weber: A Reader* (London: Routledge, 2003).

20

KNOWLEDGE MANAGEMENT AND THE NATIONAL INTELLIGENCE MODEL

FADS OR FUNDAMENTALS, COMPLEMENTING OR CONTRADICTING? WHAT ARE THE OPPORTUNITIES FOR TRANSFERABLE LEARNING?

Adrian Bowers

INTRODUCTION

Contributing to this volume has afforded the present author, a member of the team that devised the National Intelligence Model (NIM) for policing in England and Wales, the opportunity for reflection, a decade on, about the relationship between intelligence-led policing (ILP) and knowledge management (KM): the former, arguably, a framework in search of a theory; the latter, arguably, a theory in search of a framework; and each in need of the appropriate organizational culture in order to flourish. This chapter explores the interaction between the two concepts and how this might characterize their contribution to twenty-first-century policing.

During the 1990s the concept of a 'learning organization' attracted much attention from writers on strategic management and thereby generated a significant amount of literature (for example Stata, 1989; Senge, 1990; Argyris, 1990; Pedler, Burgoyne and Boydell 1991; Garvin, 1993 and 1996; Skyrme and Amidon, 2002). There has been a general recognition that if organizations are to survive and prosper in today's dynamic and complex environment they must learn to change and develop. Senge (1990) predicted that 'the most successful corporation of the 1990s will be something called the learning organization. The ability to learn faster than your competitors may be the only sustainable competitive advantage.' In terms of law enforcement, this is certainly proving to be the case, ranging from the policing of specific crime types such as sophisticated burglary to high-technology crimes, and from policing arenas as diverse as neighbourhood policing and protective services.

At the roots of KM lie the key themes of the 'learning organization', 'intellectual capital' and 'systems thinking' (Seddon, 2005) but, as with all concepts, the emergence of jargon has tended to exclude and deter the uninitiated. What is the link between learning and knowledge and to what extent can models be used to make this relationship explicit? In reality many organizations create knowledge in an indiscriminate, non-strategic way. As a consequence this does not generate organizational learning, nor can that knowledge be viewed as a neutral tool in the learning process. Such has been the corporate fashion for KM and intellectual capital (Stewart, 1997) that the downside has largely been overlooked. Lucier and Torsilieri (1997) conclude, for instance, that KM (or equivalent) programmes often have limited results.

ILP has emerged into the mainstream of UK policing over the last twenty years, but its journey has been one of reactive adaptation, rather than reflection leading to continual learning and more informed strategic decision-making. Its latest, and arguably most sophisticated, reincarnation—the National Intelligence Model (NIM)—was launched in 2000 amid much fanfare and expectation from both government and police forces. After three years, take up was described as patchy, the overall implementation encountering major hurdles that 'pose serious challenges to the long term viability of the model' (Maguire and John, 2003). As of 2007 the government has invested in excess of £20 million in the model and signified its importance by including the NIM in the National Community Safety Plan 2006/09, but as Christopher highlights true cultural change is not yet evident:

Organizational apathy has witnessed forces not making bids for the funding and failing to second officers to the national implementation team. In response the Home Office has resorted to legislation requiring forces to implement the NIM by 2004 (through the Police Reform Act 2002 (UK). This will see chief officers regulated to comply with an exacting standards framework of minimum requirements that will deliver business benefits and ensure effectiveness. Ultimately, therefore, the government intends to engineer intelligence into policing centrality through legislative coercion (Christopher, 2004: 185).

To date, compliance with the 2004 published minimum standards at the local level on the whole has been achieved but, with the exception of isolated case studies (Maguire and John, 2006), empirical evidence linking this to organizational business benefits and greater effectiveness is not readily accessible. There are strong inferences linking better-performing forces to the use of the NIM as one of a number of key business approaches, but there remains a dearth of empirical research published or commissioned to support or develop this hypothesis.

Current law enforcement approaches rely on the production of doctrine (known within the NIM as a 'Knowledge Asset') through professional practice guidance, with support for its implementation, review, and inspection provided by the recently formed National Police Improvement Agency (NPIA) and Her Majesty's Inspectorate of Constabulary (HMIC) respectively. The focus is now directed on reviewing the role of the NIM in police forces' responses to major criminality (such as serious and organized crime) linked to the regional and national picture.

There is a need to understand better why this situation arose and identify how future projects such as this could be implemented more successfully and looking to

KM, lessons from the commercial enterprise are a logical way forward. This requires in the first instance some empirical exploration of both concepts to identify if sufficient parallels existed to make any comparison viable as a basis for transferable learning.

THE NATIONAL INTELLIGENCE MODEL (NIM)

In 1999 the National Intelligence Model (NIM) was developed by the National Criminal Intelligence Service (NCIS) in response to some of the challenging problems surrounding the concept of intelligence-led policing, attempting to pull all the learning and existing knowledge together. It represented a major effort both to promote effective ILP on a national basis and begin to standardize intelligence-related structures, processes, and practices across all forces. Importantly, too, it aimed to improve the flow and use of intelligence between the local, cross-border, and international levels (labelled respectively Levels 1, 2 and 3). The key aim was to address the 'regional void' at Level 2 that had increasingly been recognized as a serious hiatus in the effective control of serious crime and major offenders.

The NIM provided, for the first time, a cohesive intelligence framework across the full range of levels of criminality and disorder. As its principal architect, Brian Flood, puts it:

The model is, therefore, very ambitious, for in describing the links between the levels it offers for the first time the realisable goal of integrated intelligence in which all forces might play a part in a system bigger than themselves. How can we have a sound crime strategy if we cannot paint the picture of crime and criminality from top to bottom? (Flood, 1999)

More significant was the emphasiz placed on the crucial role of the strategic process, accessing closed and open data-sources to map out the long-term risks and threats to an organization from local through to international levels. Inadequate investment in this process, we have since learnt, inevitably leads to a serious disconnect between prioritized demands and organizational structures, systems, staffing levels, and skill sets.

Under the stewardship of Chief Constable Sara Thornton (on behalf of the Association of Chief Police Officers), *Guidance on the National Intelligence Model* was published in 2005 (ACPO, 2005). This saw the NIM 'front end' maturing considerably, evolving from its creation at Figure 20.1, into its current form as highlighted at Figure 20.2.

Space here does not permit detailed exploration of the NIM, so basic familiarity is assumed in the discussion that follows. An introduction to the model and the rationale underpinning it will be at <http://www.police.homeoffice.gov.uk/operational-policing>.

Since the beginning of roll-out across the police forces of the UK in 2002, it has become apparent that the NIM is something more than an integrated approach to 'intelligence-led policing':

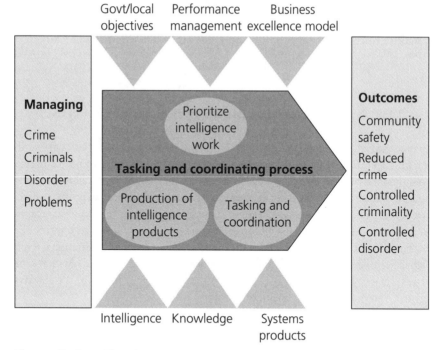

Fig 20.1 Business Planning

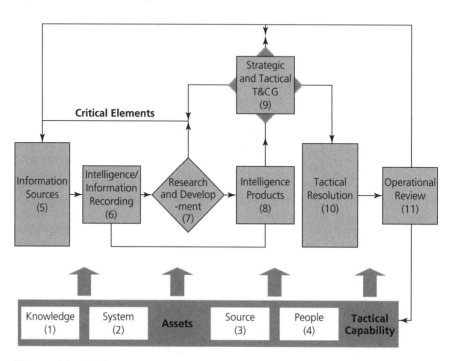

Fig 20.2 The NIM—A Model for Policing

Despite many misapprehensions both inside and outside the police the NIM is not simply about the use of criminal intelligence. It is in essence a *business model*—a *means of organising knowledge* and information in such a way that the best possible decisions can be made about how to deploy resources, that actions can be coordinated within and between different levels of policing and that lessons are continually learnt and fed back into the system (Maguire and John, 2003).

Maguire and John revisited their 2003 findings three years later (Maguire and John, 2006). This took into account the 2003-5 National Reassurance Policing Programme, the reinvigoration of Neighbourhood Policing, changes in the Crime and Disorder Partnership (CDRP) strategy (Home Office, 2004), together with the pressure for performance metrics involving Volume Crime Management and the 'Narrowing the Justice Gap' framework (Home Office, 2000). Is the NIM fit for purpose in meeting the challenges of these competing priorities? John and Maguire confirmed their original findings concluding that the NIM is essentially a business model, and so a means of organising knowledge, as well as offering a framework of business processes for the management of policing priorities of all kinds.

The word 'knowledge' here has particular significance within the NIM lexicon. Knowledge products/assets (as shown in Figures 20.1 and 20.2 above), in NIM terms, relate to law, policy, and procedure. This is a type of knowledge known as *explicit* knowledge and largely ignores the *tacit* knowledge produced through interactions between policing practitioners, producing hunches and insights based often on many years' experiences. Capturing and maximizing tacit knowledge, to which this discussion returns below, is key to successful intelligence/knowledge creation.

The NIM is also described as a complete or holistic business model, originally focusing on the police service but equally applicable in other public-sector domains. The Police and Justice Act 2006 contained a number of changes to partnership provisions intended to enhance CDRPs, introducing a regulatory framework and national minimum standards including the Assessment of Police and Community Safety (APACS). In force from the 1 August 2007, the minimum standards set out six hallmarks of effective practice:

- Empowered and effective leadership;
- Intelligence-led business processes;
- Effective and responsive delivery structures;
- Community engagement;
- Visible and constructive accountability;
- Appropriate skills and knowledge.

In the first instance, intelligence-led business processes will see the relevant authorities and responsible bodies triennial audit (Crime and Disorder Act 1998) being replaced by a strategic assessment, the intention being that as learning and knowledge of good practice develops, innovative approaches will fuel the refreshing of this guidance and reflect the landscape in which partnerships operate, linking to other areas of work such as Local Area Agreements and Offender Management Teams working with prolific and priority offenders.

KNOWLEDGE MANAGEMENT
AND INTELLIGENCE-LED POLICING

KM has attracted many definitions that have not yet become manifest in practical models or frameworks for implementation. Skyrme proposes a generic approximation as definition (1999): 'Knowledge management is the explicit and systematic management of vital knowledge and its associated processes of creation, organization, diffusion, use, and exploitation.' This creates the juxtaposition of ILP, with no generally accepted definition yet a very robust framework/model in the form of the NIM within which to operate, against KM with a definition but lacking any such framework or model.

At this juncture, consideration of the definitions of 'knowledge' and 'intelligence' is helpful. The Concise Oxford Dictionary (1991) describes knowledge as:

1. 'A theoretical or practical understanding of a subject, language etc. The sum of what is known'.
2. 'Awareness or familiarity gained by experience. A person's range of information'.
3. 'True, justified belief'.

And intelligence as:

1. 'The capacity for understanding; ability to perceive and comprehend meaning'.
2. 'Military information about enemies spies etc'.
3. 'A group or department that gathers or deals with such information'.
4. 'Good mental capacity: a person of intelligence'.

A simple comparison of the two sets of definitions suggests a correlation between a 'capacity for understanding' (intelligence) and 'theoretical or practical understanding' (knowledge). A person's range of information (knowledge) could include military information (intelligence). A person of 'good mental capacity' (intelligent) would be able to 'perceive and comprehend meaning' and arguably seek to establish 'true justified belief' (knowledge). So, there is parity in raw dictionary definitions but further reflection is necessary in relation to the practicalities inherent in using Skyrme's definition above—'the explicit and systematic management of vital knowledge/intelligence and its associated processes of creation, organization, diffusion, use and exploitation'.

The preceding paragraphs outline in brief the NIM approach, but the reality is that the NIM does not articulate or explain in great depth the actual processes involved in *creating* intelligence. It focuses instead primarily on outputs: the four intelligence products, namely Strategic Assessment, Tactical Assessment, Subject Profiles, and Problem Profiles (ACPO, 2005: Appendix 1). So what about knowledge management? For KM, albeit there is no one overarching or holistic model, what does exist are a number of processes, the creation of knowledge being the one process that has attracted the most academic interest as developed by the Japanese academics Nonaka and Tackeuchi (1995) and shown here in Figure 20.3.

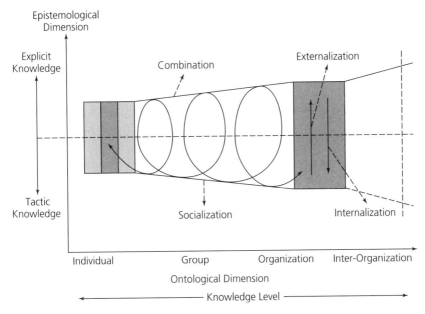

Fig 20.3 Knowledge Creation from a Two-Dimensional Perspective

This model looks at knowledge creation from a two dimensional perspective: its creation through informal (*tacit*) and formal (*explicit*) means and four interlinked conversion processes, some explanations for which now follow. Nonaka and Tackeuchi describe *tacit* knowledge as that which is 'highly personalized and hard to formalize. Subjective insights, intuitions and hunches fall into this category of knowledge'. They contrast it with *explicit* knowledge which 'can be expressed in words and numbers and can be easily communicated and shared in the form of hard data, scientific formulae, codified procedures or universal principles'.

THE CONVERSION PROCESSES—THE 'SECI' MODEL

The assumption that knowledge is created through the interaction between tacit and explicit knowledge allows us to postulate four different modes of knowledge conversion. These are described as:

- Tacit-to- tacit (*socialization*)—Socialization is the process of sharing experiences and thereby creating tacit knowledge such as shared mental models and technical skills where individuals acquire new knowledge directly from others. This can be found within communities of practice (Wenger, 1997) which, for example in a policing environment, could include daily patrol talk between officers on a particular shift.
- Tacit-to-explicit (*externalization*)—the articulation of knowledge into tangible form through dialogue. This can be found within formal meetings which, within

a policing environment, would include the Tasking and Coordinating meetings in accordance with the NIM.

- Explicit-to-explicit (*combination*)—combining differing forms of explicit knowledge, such as that in documents or on databases. This includes the development of a marketing strategy: for example, the development of the four intelligence products.

- Explicit–to tacit (*internalization*)—such as learning by doing, where individuals internalize knowledge from documents into their own body of experience. In practical terms this may include the implementation of a commercial marketing strategy or a control strategy under the NIM. Following such implementation, the processes of socialization tacitly exploring the outcomes should 'kick start' the process again, creating (within for example a 'learning organization') the potential for continual innovation and improvement.

The process of knowledge creation as outlined above is central to a complete account of knowledge management. For all organizations the ability to create knowledge must be regarded as a core capability.

This model was compared to the processes that occur within the NIM at its three levels of local, national, and international. As previously stated the NIM does not explicitly explore the processes of knowledge creation. However, using the examples above, they are obviously implicit within it. This is evident in everything, from the production and use of NIM products to the tasking and coordinating process and the implementation of control strategies. Operational debriefing coupled with results analysis offers the opportunity to close the learning loop and the potential for continual innovation and improvement. So the NIM not only fulfils the *epistemological* dimension but also the *ontological* dimension of the 'SECI' model, as the three levels of the NIM move knowledge from the individual through the group to organizational and inter-organizational levels.

Thus, the NIM creates knowledge in two dimensions, but how does it fare in terms of the processes of organization, diffusion, and exploitation as outlined in the definition of KM? The role of information systems, particularly within commercial enterprise, has prompted conceptualization of technology-driven knowledge management. However within the NIM the use of standardized products and the formalized tasking and coordinating groups at both a tactical and strategic level provide very solid frameworks for the organization, diffusion, and exploitation of vital intelligence/knowledge. Furthermore they bring a focused human decision-making element to the process, ensuring debate focuses on what is 'vital knowledge'.

The role of KM within the NIM can therefore identify, create, and exploit vital knowledge/intelligence needs and so a competitive advantage for an organization. Both approaches also require a supporting structure—formal ways of turning the intangible, in the form of a definition or description, into competitive advantage, organizational learning, and continual improvement—in effect to create organizations that permanently re-invent themselves. The NIM achieves this and can be described as 'knowledge management in action'.

Albeit both concepts are identified as fundamental to future sustained success, they are still very much an emerging field. In similar vein, both are described as experiencing limited success. An early hypothesis held that implementing knowledge-based initiatives using conventional approaches to strategy formulation within current organizational structures will not be effective. This would appear to be linked to the fact that knowledge management is chiefly concerned with human behaviour, namely the interactions and the social processes that surround knowledge creation and use—in other words a people-approach rather than a process-approach to change.

CURRENT KNOWLEDGE-BASED INITIATIVES AND THE LINK TO PERFORMANCE

By 1997 the KM bandwagon was being adopted and considered throughout Europe and America, but early evidence indicated that many knowledge management (or equivalent programmes) had limited results with up to one-third having little business impact at all. Common problems included little support from senior managers and an insufficient focus on strategic priorities, leading to limited aspirations and a piecemeal approach (Lucier and Torsilieri, 1997). Even some five years on, 'the phrase "knowledge management" describes an aspiration rather than a reality for the majority of organizations.' (Quintas, 2002). The numerous drivers prompted a variety of responses from different organizations in various countries. Nonetheless, for the majority of Western organizations the priorities are the capture of employees' knowledge, exploitation of existing knowledge resources or assets, and improved access to expertise (know-how).

This approach, however, entirely misses the point as the primary role of KM and the NIM as knowledge initiatives is to continually create new knowledge/intelligence in order to:

- cope with rapid and unexpected changes where existing 'programmed' responses are inadequate;
- provide flexibility to cope with dynamically changing situations;
- allow front-line staff to respond with initiative, based on situational needs.

Quintas identified a number of emerging themes relative to the implementation of knowledge initiatives (2002). Firstly, it is clear that managers and organizations have to develop understanding of knowledge itself. Secondly, and probably more importantly, is how knowledge is created. Thirdly, communication is fundamental to all knowledge-management processes. Finally, a fourth theme focuses on people and the management of human resources. Maguire and John were commissioned to evaluate the NIM roll-out, and produced an interim report in 2003 under the heading 'key challenges'. It draws attention to some major implementation hurdles described as posing serious challenges to the long-term viability of the model as the nationally favoured means of conducting police business. The gap between theoretical rationale of the model and successful practical application is dependent upon a number of factors, some of which bear direct comparison to the situation with KM. These included committed leadership, thorough training for participants at all levels, better support structures for analysts, better communication and understanding of roles between analytical and operational staff, and efforts to increase the standardization of products and systems. There is a need to create a greater sense of ownership and understanding: in essence a culture of intelligence. The report continues to identify that until these hurdles are successfully negotiated and the model is operating much more as its designers envisaged, linking the intangible to tangible outcomes (for example crime reduction and community safety) will remain extremely difficult.

The interdisciplinary nature of KM means that there is currently no definitive agreement on what successful implementation looks like. Interest is currently converging on knowledge from a number of different perspectives, including information management, organizational learning, strategic management, change management, human resource management, management of innovation, and the measurement and management of intangible assets (Carlisle, 2002).

Overall strong correlations are evident in the approaches of both KM and the NIM in that the identification of vital knowledge and its creation and exploitation for competitive advantage sit at the core of both approaches. These are approaches used in the implementation of *knowledge initiatives*. In addition, however, the NIM sets these processes in the context of its environment, linked to specific business areas and outcomes, in an attempt to be a *complete business model*.

Understanding of the generic term 'knowledge initiatives' is critical to making it happen. Current understanding was explored in two ways: firstly in a series of seven semi-structured interviews with skilled practitioners from the NIM and KM fields, and then followed by a 'Focus Group' (Bowers, 2004).

MAKING IT HAPPEN—CRITICAL SUCCESS FACTORS (CSFS)

Through this study seven generic CSFs were identified. Prioritized on the basis of interviewee response these are:

1. Change management/buy in/roles and responsibilities
2. Organizational culture
3. New skill sets/recognition and reward
4. Traditional leadership approaches
5. Measurement and the link to performance
6. Incompatible technology
7. Impact of external environment.

Notwithstanding the subjective nature of the data, the fact that both NIM and KM initiatives are significant change programmes linked to organizational culture prompted significantly more debate than the other six areas. This is linked to skill sets required within a knowledge environment and the role of leadership. Interestingly, explicit references to the phrase 'change programme' were rare, albeit implicit in many of the responses.

Focus Group

A focus group was then convened, comprising seven individuals: three members from a KM background and four from a NIM background. Their experience ranged from product development and project management through to consultancy and operational delivery. All individuals had experience in developing and implementing strategy. The aim of the group was to take the research findings to date and through an iterative process prioritize the critical elements of a knowledge initiative. What are the opportunities for transferable learning from the commercial world? Is it possible to outline a generic change management programme that will see knowledge projects in the police/public sector environment not only engage stakeholders but prove to be successful initiatives?

Each member of the focus group was provided with a table of the interview-stage findings and was asked to identify and rate the top three issues they would action to implement successfully a knowledge initiative. These could either be taken from the list or from their own knowledge and experience. They were further asked to outline how each element contributes to the successful implementation of a knowledge initiative. Those identified were analysed and thematically grouped in Table 20.1 below.

It is immediately obvious that there was a distinct difference in approach. The KM members saw the supply-demand relationship as fundamental, whereas the NIM members saw the role of senior leadership as the top priority. The supply-demand issue was further debated and there was general consensus that creating a culture that had a 'craving for demand' was fundamental to a successful knowledge initiative. Establishing that benchmark led to identifying that a 'bottom up' approach to this

Table 20.1 Focus Group Analysis of Interview-Stage Findings

Participant 1 NIM	Participant 2 KM	Participant 3 NIM
The issue of demand.	Get demand side right.	Understanding what NIM seeks to achieve and how.
No history of strategic planning within policing.	Historical mindset around KM.	Sense of leadership.
Culture stemming from the structure. The difference between strategy and doctrine.	The change management programme is very people related.	Spreading the sense of ownership.
Participant 4 NIM Leadership.	Participant 5 NIM Leadership and drive.	Participant 6 NIM The supply chain.
Role of business manager.	Effective top-down Communication.	Implementation. Infrastructure requirements.
Focus on information management, not knowledge management.	Infrastructure.	Craving demand.

type of change (in contrast to the NIM traditional top down approach to implementation) is much the preferred approach.

The following quotes (preceded by the relevant pneumonic) highlight these differences:

KM—'. . . the concept of demand is simply saying that those people who are going to use this knowledge in an effective and useful manner ultimately, if the plan is a success, can often be those who are best able to specify how it is generated and how it is supplied and it's a little bit like asking customers what you want.'

And continued . . .

this is the sort of analogy to supply and demand from a marketing product development related environment and experience says that if you can incentivise your customers, in this case your front line officers, let's say to recognise the value of this information and therefore create desire in them to obtain it, they will push back on the organization, they will demand it and they will help you on an incredibly broad front to figure out how best to deliver it

This continued expanding on the need to major on a 'bottom up' approach to change:

. . . so it's a bit like a 'bottom up' design process rather than top down which is very much about doing it to people . . . so the double benefit of incentivising the users of information is not only do they use it, which is your ambition, but they tell you how to give it to them and often very inventive in the way they go about getting it because they have a culture of doing things in—pardon the expression—on the cheap, and you'll find you often get a very efficient design out of your front line, which you won't get necessarily when you do top down, that's certainly our experience.

NIM—One of the things that we try to do at the outset was to get in, get more buy-in from chief officers . . . when it became clear that the team's not going to be resourced to the level that we thought was necessary, we actually had to do that kind of thinking and ask ourselves what alternative routes to investment in demand we could actually provide or we could take . . . we decided that our first responsibility would be to produce the intelligence-training package which could be delivered to the people at the grass roots, at the lowest-level operative on the basis that if we couldn't push implementation from the top we try and pull it from the bottom.

Once each member of the group had outlined their priorities, the discussion organically developed around the following themes set out in Table 20.2.

Table 20.2 Themes of Discussion

The supply/demand chain and the role of a performance culture and performance metrics within it.

Leadership from a strategic level through to 'behavioural role models' and knowledge teams.

The change process—evolutionary or revolutionary, and project methodology—real world thinking.

The human dimension of knowledge programmes—the stakeholder mix.

Performance metrics for the project and the organizations outcomes.

All of the themes were sometimes explicitly, more often implicitly, linked to existing organizational cultural paradigms and the influence of the cultural web.

The implications for senior leadership is that their role needs to be less traditional, focusing upon articulating the project vision, but understanding this is a people- not process-centred initiative. To that end, a bottom up process was seen as key, engaging advocates described as 'behavioural role models', or game changers based upon their credibility within the organization. The aim then, is to take a sympathetic element of the organization, using prototypes to demonstrate its capability, and initiate a culture of demand prior to expanding the concept across the organization. The role of technology was identified as an enabler, the creation of knowledge remaining primarily a human function.

The role of organizational culture cannot be underestimated, and because knowledge initiatives are described as revolutionary change, this becomes even more significant. Culture can be very hard to change, so establishing a baseline position is crucial. A number of models exist to assist in this process and it is considered a critical prerequisite to the commencement of any project. This revolutionary change needs to be undertaken in an evolutionary way: those whom it will primarily effect having control and deciding on the route, with senior management guiding them towards the agreed vision. Knowledge initiatives are long-term projects in which senior executives may have to accept that this may affect short-term performance, and in the main only produce a series of outputs. These initiatives identify the need for bespoke 'knowledge workers' whose skill sets need developing, recognizing and rewarding, possibly based upon behaviours. This model challenges a hard metrics culture and for some senior executives may be seen as too risky. Therefore a mix of hard and soft measures may be more palatable, perhaps using trend analysis to start the process of linking the project to actual outcomes. Senior executives need to be aware that there are distinct demands on knowledge-project teams and greater risk factors for the reason outlined above. Knowledge initiatives are considered fundamental to organizational success but the difficulties lie in the need to make people recognize the need to work in a different way. Changing behaviour requires innovative project management and the courage to complete the journey.

So what conclusions can be reached about considering and implementing knowledge initiatives? The following are some facts about them:

- There are many types.
- These often mean revolutionary change.
- There are distinct demands on Knowledge-Project Teams.
- They are people-centred not process-centred change.
- They have long-term implications/You are operating in a short-term culture.
- Performance may dip in the short term.
- Traditional leadership approaches and structures can be barriers .
- They require a cultural shift throughout the whole organization/organizations.

Greater access to information will continue to lead to more knowledge opportunities. This will require greater sophistication and continual learning within the intelligence environment to ensure that a competitive advantage is maintained. We are all knowledge workers with specific roles—but do we all realize it and know what those roles are? Most importantly, do we realize this project we have just been given, however large or small, is actually a knowledge initiative with all its added complications?

Considerations when planning and preparing for a Knowledge Initiative are as follows:

- Adopt an evolutionary approach.
- Start with an analysis/risk assessment of internal/external cultural influences.
- Remember the importance of 'creating demand'—gain the commitment of the people first.
- Identify and engage behavioural role models.
- Remember the benefits of a 'bottom up' design process.
- Consider the importance of a 'non traditional' leadership role.
- Design a tapestry of hard and soft metrics.
- Technology is just an enabler.
- Importance of prototyping and benchmarks
- Focus on rewarding the outputs of group activity in the short term.
- Recognize and reward behaviours.
- Make it real for people.
- Recognize the need for rewarding knowledge workers.

In relation to this, Senge argues that:

In a learning organization, leaders are designers, stewards and teachers. They are responsible for building organizations where people continually expand their capabilities to understand complexity, clarify vision, and improve shared mental models—that is they are responsible for learning. . . Learning organizations will remain a 'good idea' . . . until people take a stand for building such organizations. Taking this stand is the first leadership act, the start of inspiring (literally 'to breathe life into') the vision of the learning organization (Senge, 1990: 340).

CONCLUSION AND IMPLICATIONS FOR LAW ENFORCEMENT AND THE UK PUBLIC SECTOR

With the increasing ability of technological systems to communicate with each other, the potential for knowledge creation and exploitation is exponential. In addition, the government's drive for totally joined-up public-sector working, in particular the CDRP reform programme and a recent drive to reduce police bureaucracy,[1] means

---

[1] The interim report of the Independent Review of policing (Flanagan, 2007) commissioned by The Home Secretary and conducted by Sir Ronnie Flanagan seeks to examine, in a targeted way, four areas of particular importance which have the potential to deliver key improvements to the delivery of policing. These four specific 'workstreams', are 'Reducing Bureaucracy'; 'Mainstreaming Neighbourhood Policing'; 'Making Most Effective Use of Resources'; and 'Enhancing Local Accountability'.

that knowledge projects will dominate the public sector for the foreseeable future. To a degree they already have, dominated by technological approaches which have often proved expensive failures. The learning to date indicates that we should be focusing on creating something that facilitates the effective interaction between people and not try to replace that interaction. Technology is purely an enabler.

Organizational risk-management is now at the heart of the human element of knowledge management and arguably is the cornerstone of public sector responsibility to protect the public. This is tragically evident in the events leading to the murders of Holly Wells and Jessica Chapman in Soham in 2002 and the death of Victoria Climbié. Inquiries into these and other similar episodes highlighted clearly and painfully the areas for improvement needed in the safeguarding systems at the time (Harfield and Harfield, 2008: Chapter 2). In response to the Soham murders the government commissioned an inquiry chaired by Sir Michael Bichard to investigate those areas, welcoming the publication of his report in 2004 and accepting all of its recommendations which in turn have led to a number of measures to protect vulnerable people.[2]

Not surprisingly, events such as those above have reinforced our culture of compliance, everything requiring to be recorded in great detail. The opening recommendation by Sir Ronnie Flanagan in his recently published interim report states:

The Home Office, the Association of Chief Police Officers (ACPO) and the Association of Police Authorities (APA) must demonstrate clear national leadership on the issue of risk aversion and commit themselves to genuinely new ways of working to foster a culture in which officers and staff can rediscover their discretion to exercise professional judgement...(Flanagan, 2007: 10, Recommendation 1)

These recommendations, whether presented as policy, procedure, legislation, or guidance are all in fact knowledge initiatives the implementation of which can benefit from our continued learning, learning in the private sector and empirically supported research. They require a totally different approach to implementation and leadership.

Managing our knowledge effectively within business models (the present author currently uses six or seven, including the NIM, in different combinations) to paint accurate strategic pictures of organizational risks, performance demands, and the needs of the public is going to be a critical success factor for the future. Confidence in your knowledge processes facilitates confident decision-making and I suggest allows for that embracement of risk often needed to deliver real outcomes.

However, the NIM is now some eight years old and by a somewhat tortuous route will no doubt eventually be signed off as implemented across the police forces of the UK. The author's view is that this is a focus on compliance with policy rather than a change of culture and the move to a learning organization. The three key questions that need to be considered are:

- What are the three greatest risks your organization faces which if not addressed will undermine your delivery of core business?

[2] The Protection of Children Act 2000, the Protection of Vulnerable Adults scheme 2004, the Criminal Records Bureau 2002,the Sexual Offences Act 2003, the Children Act 2004, and Guidance on the Management of Police Information 2006.

- For each of those risks what are the three things that will most effectively manage that risk?
- If the answer to the first question is not immediately to hand—are the knowledge levels what they should be, are all your information assets (including for example human resource and financial data) providing you accurate pictures—are they being correctly tasked—do you really understand your business?

It is possibly too late now to influence the knowledge project that began life as the NIM, but sufficient learning now exists to ensure we do better next time. It needs to be clearly stated that these projects albeit a form of change management will seriously challenge many of our existing views on how we should run our organizations in the future. Textbooks on strategic management may look very different in 10 years' time: a whole new area of research is just opening up in front of us.

REFERENCES

ACPO, *Guidance on the National Intelligence Model* (Wyboston: Centrex, 2005).

ARGYRIS, C, *Overcoming Organizational Defences* (Allyn and Bacon, 1990).

BOWERS, A, *An Analysis of Intelligence Led Policing and Knowledge Management to Identify Opportunities for Transferable Learning* (Reading University Business School, 2004).

CARLISLE, Y, *Strategic Thinking and Knowledge Management* (Milton Keynes: Open University Business School, 2002).

CHRISTOPHER, S, 'A practitioner's perspective of UK strategic intelligence' in Ratcliffe, J, ed, *Strategic Thinking in Criminal Intelligence* (Sydney: The Federation Press, 2004).

FLANAGAN, R, *The Review of Policing: Interim Report* (London: HMIC, 2007).

FLOOD, B, 'Know your business. NCIS has brought together the best practice in intelligence-led policing' *Nexus* 7 (Winter 1999) 8–9.

GARVIN, DA, 'Building a learning organization' *Harvard Business Review* (July-Aug 1993) 78-88.

——, 'Learning from experience' (paper presented at Knowledge Management 96 Conference, Business Intelligence, December 1996).

HARFIELD, C and HARFIELD, K, *Intelligence: Investigation, Community, and Partnership* (Oxford: Oxford University Press, 2008).

HOME OFFICE, *Narrowing the Justice Gap Framework* (London: Crown Prosecution Service, 2000).

——, *Building Communities, Beating Crime* (London: TSO, 2004).

——, *The National Reassurance Policing Project* (London: Home Office, 2005).

JOHN, T and MAGUIRE, M, 'Rolling-out the National Intelligence Model: Key challenges' in Bullock, K and Tilley, N, eds, *Crime Reduction and Problem-Oriented Policing* (Devon: Willan Publishing, 2003).

LUCIER, C and TORSERILIER, J, *Why Knowledge Programmes Fail. A C.E.O.'s Guide to Managing Learning* (Cleveland: Booz-Allen and Hamilton, 1997).

MAGUIRE, M and JOHN, T, 'Intelligence led policing, managerialism and community engagement: Competing priorities and the role of the National Intelligence Model in the UK' *Policing and Society* 16/1 (2006) 67–85.

NONAKA, I and TAKEUCHI, H, *The Knowledge-Creating Company* (New York: Oxford University Press, 1995).

PEDLER, M, BURGOYNE, J and BOYDELL, T, *The Learning Company: A Strategy for Sustainable Development* (London: McGraw-Hill, 1991).

SEDDON, J, *Freedom from Command and Control: A Better Way to Make the Work Work* (New York: Vanguard Press, 2005).

SENGE, P, *The Fifth Discipline: The Art and Practice of the Learning Organization* (New York: Doubleday, 1990).

SKYRME, DJ, *Knowledge Management: Making Sense of an Oxymoron*, available at <http://www.skyrme.com/insights/22km.htm>, first published 1997, revised 2003. Accessed on 2 July 2008.

—— and AMIDON, DM, 'The learning organization' in Little, S, Quintas, P and Ray, T, eds, *Managing Knowledge an Essential Reader* (London: Sage 2002).

STATA, R, 'Organizational learning the key to management innovation' *Sloan Management Review* (Spring 1989) 63-73.

QUINTAS, P, *Managing Knowledge in a New Century* (Milton Keynes: Open University Business School, 2002).

WENGER, E, *Communities of Practice: Learning, Meaning and Identity* (Cambridge: Cambridge University Press, 1997).

21

PERFORMANCE VERSUS INTELLIGENCE: THE UNINTENDED CONSEQUENCES

Sir Paul Scott-Lee, Esther Martin, and Andrew Shipman

Performance driven or intelligence led? These two perspectives and styles of policing have historically been seen as mutually exclusive and diametrically opposed and as such have provided fertile ground for division and conflict amongst intelligence and performance professionals; but is this really the case? Performance management and intelligence analysis in policing can be viewed as two competing principles. They often occur in separate departments with different senior managers with a language and associated tools that can result in them being viewed as competitive processes seeking to influence priorities and the allocation of resources. But as ACC Nick Gargan, ACPO portfolio lead for intelligence argued in October 2007, intelligence and performance are doing largely the same things and the police service should move forward with intelligence and performance as a single function: 'The intelligence versus performance debate must come to an end and we must view intelligence as part of performance or performance as part of intelligence'.[1]

This chapter will examine the key features of intelligence analysis and performance management. It will consider if this tension exists due to them being fundamentally different processes with different objectives or whether they are just different approaches seeking to deliver effective policing. The analysis will conclude that while they are distinctive disciplines they are not in conflict. Conflict, however, can emerge if neither are fully integrated into the strategic planning and tactical implementation process. This will be amplified if the performance regime has developed with a focus on counting outputs rather than outcomes.

Having discussed the general issues, the experience of West Midlands Police will be used to illustrate the processes that have been developed to achieve continuously improving performance through robust implementation of NIM and performance management techniques.

---

[1] Nick Gargon, ACC Thames Valley Police, conference presentation: 'Tackling Organized Crime in Partnership', London, 30–31 October 2007.

THE REALITY BEHIND THE CONFLICT?

Table 21.1 summarizes the key characteristics of the National Intelligence Model (NIM) and performance management with the potential tensions that can exist between the approaches. Performance management is still a developing concept in the police service and, as it does not have the structure of NIM, it will have greater variety between forces. There are some general characteristics and labels that are applied, but their implementation can vary considerably.

But how real is the tension? Do we as intelligence and performance specialists perpetrate a myth that we are striving towards different goals, when in reality we are all working towards achieving a single vision? The vision of West Midlands Police is 'reducing crime and disorder and making our communities feel safer'. By understanding the risks we face and managing those risks through effective and efficient processes we can determine a strategic direction and tactical solutions. Failure to keep these principles at the forefront of thinking and the absence of clear lines of communication can lead to parallel or divergent intelligence and performance processes. This will transfer into the products delivered and relationships between professionals within these functions.

Whilst there can be no argument that police forces must have a robust performance management process to ensure that Home Office targets can be met, it is vital that we can understand and manage the risk from terrorism, serious, organized, and volume crime through the application of intelligence processes.

According to Marilyn Peterson of the US Department of Justice, 'Intelligence is critical for decision making, planning, strategic targeting, and crime prevention. Law

Table 21.1 Traditional Perspective of Performance and NIM Tensions

National Intelligence Model	Tensions	Performance Management
Strategic Assessment	Differing ACPO portfolio leads	Strategic planning
Intelligence Silo		Performance silo
Conformity and Compliance (prescriptive products and process)	Convergent and divergent thinking	No set product or framework
Focus on External Environment (community/ partnership and problem solving)	Problem solving versus process analysis	Focus on internal environment (systems and process)
Identification of Risk and Harm	Differing priorities	Ingrained performance culture to reduce/detect volume
Tangible Risks	Differing focus	Softer issues—customer satisfaction surveys
Threat from Crime and Disorder	Differing perspectives	Threat from Government targets

enforcement agencies depend on intelligence operations on all levels; they cannot function effectively without collecting, processing, and using intelligence' (Peterson, 2005).

Notwithstanding two decades of debate about police performance (starting with Home Office Circular 114/83 promoting economy, efficiency, and effectiveness within the context of New Public Management: see Long, 2003), a defined concept of performance management in the police service is less developed than the doctrine of intelligence underpinning the NIM. Other than a Police Crime and Standards Directorate (PCSD) manual, first published in 2004, there is not the same written doctrine or mandated codes of practice which promote a standardized approach to performance management. An assessment of performance management forms part of the Police Performance Assessment Framework (PPAF) based on a qualitative assessment completed by Her Majesty's Inspectorate of Constabulary.

Performance management activity will usually be defined by the following methods, discussed in detail below, that a force uses to deliver performance:

- strategic planning process;
- its framework of accountability and performance monitoring;
- use of data and analytical techniques;
- approaches to improving key business processes.

STRATEGIC PLANNING PROCESS

The strategic planning process of forces has been defined by the requirement to produce a three-year strategic plan that is linked into the Public Service Agreements (PSAs) timescale and the annual National Community Safety Plan. The process of community consultation, budget setting and publication of the government's plans tend to define the time frame in which planning takes place. The NIM Strategic Assessment Process also has its own timeline based around its underpinning processes.

In addition to these processes, the development of the Police Performance Assessments Framework (PPAF), soon to be replaced by Assessment of Police and Community Safety (APACS), has further defined the external performance culture that has been applied by central government to police authorities and forces. The move from PPAF to APACS is being heralded as a relaxation by central government of the centrally driven indicators to one where forces in consultation with their communities set targets for performance that better reflect local need. This strategic context for the delivery of policing helps to shape the regimes that are constructed by forces to deliver better performance. Straight away, it is easy to see how tensions can develop between NIM and the performance regime if centrally set targets do not align with the priorities identified locally through the Strategic Assessment process conducted in force.

Probably the best illustration of this process that assists in understanding the need to manage the process of performance analysis with NIM has been the response to Public Service Agreement 1 (PSA1). PSA1 was the main performance target to be set following the last Comprehensive Spending Review; it required forces to reduce crime by either 15 or 20 per cent by March 2008 based on a baseline year of 2003/4.

PSA1 comprises a basket of offences that ranges from burglary to theft of a pedal cycle. It represents a significant volume of all recorded crime and is a key measure of police performance. CDRPs set local stretch targets, Local Public Service Agreements (LPSAs), which have financial incentives attached to their achievement.

The response of performance analysis to the challenge of PSA1 has been one of identifying leverage, that is to say crimes that have the greatest volume which, if reduced, can provide the biggest contribution towards achieving the target. While this has included relatively minor assaults it has also brought into focus an emphasis on criminal damage, vehicle crime, and other thefts. Reduction in these crime types has provided the greatest opportunity to impact on overall crime reduction. Associated with the target of crime reduction was the requirement to increase the number of Offences Brought to Justice (OBTJs). PSA1 has therefore resulted in a focus on volume crime.

NIM has traditionally focused on the risk of harm from the perspective of victims and this has led to threat assessments that would seek to prioritize resources in the direction of other types of more serious crime. If the external environmental scanning process in support of the Strategic Assessment did not robustly identify a failure to meet PSA1 targets as a threat to the force it will have looked as if there was a misalignment between the performance targets of the force and the suggested priorities derived by intelligence analysis.

FRAMEWORK OF ACCOUNTABILITY AND PERFORMANCE MONITORING

Forces now have at their disposal a significant volume of data on performance which has allowed the development of monitoring regimes that provide timely information that can be disaggregated from force level to Basic Command Unit (BCU), team, and individual officer.

How this data is used to measure performance and hold people to account directly affects operational behaviour. Addressing the requirement to reduce overall crime has led to the development of performance targets that in many instances will cascade from force and BCU level to sector, neighbourhood, and personal targets. An assessment of how you are performing will be predicated on whether you are meeting the target. Activities such as numbers of intelligence reports submitted, arrests made, driving document production requests (HORT1) issued, and stop and search forms submitted become proxy measures for activity that is assessed as contributing to crime reduction—so an officer's time is focused on meeting these targets in order to avoid adverse comment. Targets and measures are sometimes introduced as the data is freely available without any understanding of how these activities actually support delivery of force priorities. In fact what often happens is 'hitting the target but missing the point'. It is therefore no surprise that the interim report from Sir Ronnie Flannigan on bureaucracy in policing contains examples of excessive activity to detect the minor shop theft, or the heavy handed response to a playground fight. Each provides easy, sanctioned detection and Offences Brought To Justice!

There is no doubt that the focus of PSA1 has resulted in impressive crime reduction across forces but this has not been matched by similar improvements in communities' feelings of safety. Neighbourhood policing has been introduced to reduce the gap in reassurance with an emphasis on the delivery of local policing to meet community needs. The types of issues that are frequently raised by communities are not measured in recorded crime, for example antisocial behaviour. To create capacity to meet these needs while still dealing with issues of risk and harm requires a more evolved performance-management framework.

Effective performance frameworks need to be built around a detailed understanding of risk and opportunity as identified through the NIM process together with a framework of accountability that focuses effort away from 'low-hanging fruit' to the more complex and persistent issues that require a depth of analysis and understanding.

USE OF DATA AND ANALYTICAL TECHNIQUES

Forces now exist in data-rich environments that provide opportunities for the provision of timely and detailed performance information from force level to individual officer. This access to data, if used to support the performance management culture of the force, can again create the tensions outlined above if not used intelligently. It is here that the analytical techniques used to present and interpret performance can affect the allocation of resources and determine operational behaviour.

One of the most frequent and simplistic tools used to judge performance is the comparison of the current level of crime with the level last week, last month, or last year. This approach fails to take into account the context of the data. What if the month you are comparing against was the lowest recorded ever? Or what happens if this month last year had major disorder with hundreds of extra offences being recorded? This approach to monitoring performance persists and is a key element of PPAF and the iQuanta police performance information portal. This crude measure of performance has prevailed for too long and yet can be used to make a judgement on the performance of Basic Command Units (BCUs), their senior managers, and staff. As an approach to performance analysis, it can also create tensions with NIM—for instance when this short-term view of performance can persuade senior managers to depart from their control strategy to move resources to respond to this perceived adverse 'trend' in performance. Responding to this 'trend' then provides an opportunity for strong 'leadership', holding staff to account, and the introduction of force-wide operations to stimulate activity. However, senior managers who are convinced about the benefits of NIM confidently 'hold their nerve' when performance 'blips' appear and avoid the compulsion to move resources to chase crime.

Good performance analysis requires a more sophisticated understanding of patterns in data, an organizational memory to capture the learning from previous patterns, and robust results analysis to know what works so that sustainable approaches to improvement can be achieved. Techniques are needed that enable a proper understanding of crime data recognizing that BCUs can experience different crime patterns at different times of the year across different offence types. When this level of sophistication is applied to data and it forms a common language of understanding between intelligence and performance analysis, the opportunities for improvement start to emerge.

The relationship between the tools and techniques adopted for both performance and intelligence analysis are further explained through the application of the Strategic Threat and Risk Assessment Index (STRATi), designed and used by West Midlands Police to prioritize strategic risk. The future achievement of improved performance therefore lies in a collaborative strategic assessment process produced by a team which includes both intelligence and performance professionals. This should not only identify the threat and risk from crime and disorder but also encompass the organizational capability, risks, and opportunities. It is through this joint working that a combined response can provide the necessary direction to enable a command team to construct a comprehensive strategic plan and related performance framework.

APPROACHES TO IMPROVING KEY BUSINESS PROCESSES

The title National *Intelligence* Model masks the fact that this is a versatile model that applies across all policing and translates into business planning; its attachment to Intelligence has limited its application into other areas of business. Equally, the narrow interpretation of performance management has focusedHome Office submissions and counting of activity.

Figure 21.1 illustrates how NIM seeks to provide a mechanism to identify crime and disorder risks together with organizational capabilities required to address these

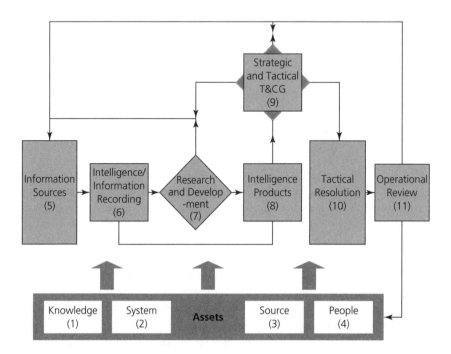

Fig 21.1 NIM Business Process

risks. The language of process improvement is not that apparent in NIM, yet NIM is a business-improvement model which has products such as problem profiles and results analysis. It has the potential to be even more effective if continuous improvement techniques form part of its repertoire.[2]

Understanding whether internal systems and processes are working effectively and efficiently may not have an obvious link to operational policing but it does offer the opportunity to realize significant performance improvement.

There are examples where business-process improvement techniques such as Lean Systems Thinking[3] and Six Sigma[4] have provided methodologies that cross over with minimal adaptation from the private-sector world of manufacturing and service delivery. Some of the transformation in call handling that has taken place in recent years is based on understanding how demand flows through forces and how mapping this process can illuminate waste and blockages. Working on these areas can reduce effort and free up resources enabling greater effort to be focused on priorities. In order to exploit the opportunities that this approach presents to forces, it is vital that they are able to reconcile the identification of both crime and organizational threats through effective communication and collaboration. It also requires clear leadership from senior managers to set this context.

RESOLUTION OF TENSIONS WITHIN WEST MIDLANDS

West Midlands Police has a reputation for innovation in its application of NIM principles and has recently been awarded beacon status by HMIC[5] for its approach to performance management. This recognition would count for nothing though, if these awards were granted without strong performance. The rest of this chapter will look at the development of performance management in the force and how it has integrated this approach with NIM so that the tensions identified at the start of the chapter have in fact become opportunities to improve performance. Within West Midlands it has been possible to marry these two thought processes and work streams to deliver performance intelligently and. whilst it can be acknowledged that performance and intelligence are still walking parallel paths. We are following the same road signs.

NIM furnishes police forces with a mechanism to identify and address the threats and risks presented by crime and disorder, breakdowns in community cohesion, public perceptions, and organizational capability through robust strategic planning and an effective tactical response. Performance management provides a mechanism for

---

[2] For more information on National Intelligence Model see <http://www.acpo.police.uk/asp/policies/Data/nim2005.pdf>.

[3] Seddon, John, *Freedom from Command and Control—A better way to make the work work.* (Vanguard Eductation Limited, 2003).

[4] For information on Six Sigma see <http://www.pmi.co.uk>.

[5] <http://police.homeoffice.gov.uk/performance-andmeasurement/performance-assessment/assessments-2006–2007/>.

continual improvement of systems, processes, and their measurement. Of course, a combined response to threat and performance relies upon a collective understanding of each others' roles and focus. This understanding would mean that whilst each team may be located within separate functional silos, both at ACPO and practitioner level, the barriers between these are transparent and breachable. It would be naive to suggest to the reader that West Midlands have overcome all tensions between the two professions simply by raising awareness of each other's role. However, the position is an improving one. More important has been the active management of relationships between individuals and across both departments.

HEADWAY

Operation Headway was a key turning point for West Midlands Police bringing together intelligence and performance analysis techniques to inform a new force-wide approach to crime reduction.

The traditional response to rising levels of crime was to have force-wide initiatives themed around crime types. All Operational Command Units (OCU, the equivalent of Basic Command Units in other police forces) were expected to divert resources to these initiatives irrespective of their control strategies or localised crime patterns that may have suggested different crime types or time periods of offending. During the initiative, OCUs were empowered to identify the crime types that provided the greatest leverage to contribute to overall crime reduction. This was done through their local knowledge and understanding of crime patterns and risk. Whilst this operation provided the required step-change down in crime, its success lay in the combined efforts of performance and intelligence through the interpretation of localized data. Similar initiatives, which have met with success, since this turning point, have seen an overt marriage of NIM and performance management.

A key element of NIM is the reliance upon results analysis to evaluate effectively the success or otherwise of the tactics which are deployed to manage crime. In reality NIM does not provide a strong set of tools to analyse results, but this can be effective when it draws on some of the tools utilized by performance analysts—especially through the mapping and measurement of processes. Therefore, it has been vital to take a cohesive position towards results analysis as part of the relationship between the two teams. It resulted in the agreement to terms of reference[6] for every OCU co-produced by practitioners from both departments. Results analysis was completed by each OCU to outline intended actions, whether these were undertaken, the outcome, and the effect. These products were then collectively reviewed by a Performance Inspector and the Senior Analyst for the force to identify and herald the most rounded results analysis produced. Access to funding to cover expenditure during the operation was dependant on the submission of robust and honest results analysis.

This integration of the two disciplines at both a strategic and tactical level has proved effective in breaking down barriers and raising awareness. The performance review function contributes to NIM products and processes, providing the foundation

---

[6] An outline of the scope and purpose of the product for customer agreement prior to commencement.

for one of the key strands within both the strategic and tactical assessments. It is then developed through the application of intelligence and analytical techniques to provide context and direction. The product of this analysis can then be used to help direct the strategic planning process and tactical response.

The experience of Operation Headway and subsequent initiatives has ensured that both departments now take a collective responsibility in identifying effective practice and business benefits together with the potential for transferability across the force.

Performance Framework

The force now has a developed performance-management framework that is led by chief officers. It is supported by a comprehensive balanced scorecard that monitors the delivery of the force strategic vision of 'Reducing crime and disorder and making communities feel safer'. The scorecard presents data on key processes or enablers that are identified as being key to achieving performance outcomes.

Control Charts

Underpinning the success of the force has been the development of a sophisticated approach to analysing performance that has supported improvement of performance. This approach to analysing data has influenced an approach to performance management that has moved away from transactional compstat[7] methods of holding staff to account for performance to one that places an emphasis on learning, improving key work processes, and looking at data to provide leverage for improved performance.

The use of statistical-process control charts[8] (SPC) has become the defining analytical tool for the force that now supports both performance and intelligence analysis. SPC charts allow the distinction to be made between naturally occurring variations in crime levels, which are contained within upper and lower control limits, and special causes or significant variations where something unusual is occurring in a crime area. This is represented by a breach of either the upper or lower control limit.

The force uses software that allows the construction of SPC charts by crime types: at CDRP, force, BCU, and neighbourhood level; and by day, week, month, and year. The charts, using some simple rules, allow a detailed understanding of crime patterns and trends. It brings into focus the effect of seasonality and significant events. More significantly it has supported the move from simplistic analysis of whether crime is up this week or this month into an intelligent application which allows analysts to make predictions about seasonality and performance risks.

The SPC chart below (Figure 21.2) shows the movement of total recorded crime in the force since 2002. The changes in the upper and lower control limits have occurred when there have been eight data points above or below the mean. This represents a statistically significant change in the process. The change as a result of Operation Headway is annotated. The learning from this operation led to a change in the way performance was driven and was sustained. A further step-change in

---

[7] 'COMPSTAT': This system, introduced in New York by the then Police Commissioner William Bratton, entailed divisional commanders attending a monthly meeting of their peers and managers where they would face often hostile questions about their performance on local objectives. See Moore, 2003.

[8] Wheeler, Donald J and Chambers, David S, *Understanding Statistical Process Control* (SPC Press, 1992).

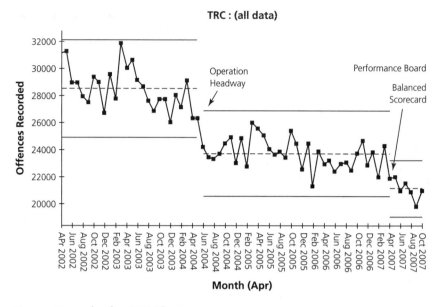

Fig 21.2 Example of an SPC Chart

performance has occurred from April 2007 when the force introduced a revised approach to performance management.

The use of control charts on their own will not result in improvements in performance; they form part of a way of thinking about continuous improvement together the use of a variety of tools and techniques.

The framework for performance management that has developed in force is based on these foundations.

STRATI (STRATEGIC THREAT AND RISK ASSESSMENT INDEX)

Intrinsic to the successful management of risk is the introduction into the process of an effective strategic risk assessment model. There already existed a plethora of risk models from the complex and convoluted 3PLEM to the simpler IMPACT versus PROBABILITY. However, none of the existing models available explained clearly and simply what we were trying to achieve, and so it was with some trepidation that West Midlands Police branched out to design its own way of prioritizing risk. The West Midlands National Intelligence Model Development Unit developed STRATi, the Strategic Threat and Risk Assessment Index. The process relies upon empirically based analysis overlaid with the expertise of policing professionals. This ensures a transparent process for the identification of critical risk which is transferable to all levels of policing from protective services to neighbourhood policing.

It was important to revisit the overall purpose of policing. Whilst the vision statement was an effective reflection of our desired outcomes, this needed to be further refined to enable an effective risk assessment model to be applied with the same rigour and equality of focus to each aspect of the vision, which would provide strategic direction throughout all aspects of the forces overall aim and purpose. With this in mind the three key strands of the strategic vision were identified as:

- *Protecting the public from death and serious physical/psychological harm*: this considers the risk presented by crime that falls into the categories of major and serious and organized (Organized Crime Groups, Urban Street Gangs, Public Protection).
- *Promoting community stability and trust and confidence*: this considers risks presented by the potential for a breakdown in community cohesion, and to address the softer issues that have historically rested with the performance department in respect of antisocial behaviour, criminal damage, and environmental signals that indicate a potential dislocate.
- *Reducing Victimization*: this considers volume crime and PSA targets.

The basic ethos of STRATi relies upon our understanding of the nature of a threat to the effectiveness of the force, within the context of these three key strands these threats are then assessed in terms of:

- levels of control currently achieved over a threat;
- organizational levels of knowledge based on professional judgement;
- organizational impact should the threat be realized.

Each area is scored and the overall score contributes to the assessed level of risk, which then enables resource prioritisation at both a strategic and tactical level.

A key element of STRATi is its reliance upon statistical modelling—not least the contribution made by a collective understanding across the force of control charts (SPC). However good the model for identification of risks, unless these are translated into measurables within the Strategic Plan with an associated performance regime, their impact on the culture of an organization will be limited. The strategic planning process and the externally set targets will inevitably determine the framework of performance monitoring.

Though a well-worn cliché, 'What gets measured gets done' is the reality of modern policing performance cultures. Fully understanding the implications of this mindset and how it affects behaviour of all ranks and grades of staff is critical. If the performance regime of the force is seen as transactional and punitive then the resulting behaviours can, if not properly managed, appear to undermine the aim of NIM to reduce harm.

Performance Management Board (PMB)

The PMB is the strategic forum for performance management and improvement. The board is chaired by the Deputy Chief Constable (DCC) and attended by the other chief officers who have both functional portfolios and responsibility for the performance of at least four Operational Command Units (OCUs). The defining feature of this board is that its operation is based on facilitating improvement and learning rather than simply 'holding to account' OCU senior managers.

The board meets during the second week of each month and has a detailed briefing by the head of the Performance Review Department. The performance briefing is built around a balanced scorecard that provides information on the attainment of force priorities and key processes. Use of the balanced scorecard means that decisions by PMB are not based simply on whether crime is up or down but a more sophisticated and rounded view of the key drivers of performance. This can range from the effectiveness of custody processes through to budgetary and attendance management.

The meeting will identify those OCUs that the board considers would benefit from assistance to improve performance. The assistant chief constables (ACCs) will then meet with their OCU commanders after the meeting to have a more detailed review of performance. Again, the balanced scorecard provides the context for this review. Those OCUs identified for support will work with their ACC and the Performance Review Department to identify key processes for improvement. From this discussion an Agreed Structured Action Plan (ASAP) will be drafted. The performance review department have staff, trained in continuous improvement tools and techniques, who work with OCU staff on the areas of business they are looking to improve. Other headquarters' departments support this process through the provision of additional analysis or deployment of specialist staff. This has provided an opportunity to build relationships between both intelligence and performance practitioners and provide a united intelligence and performance team-approach to all visits to the identified OCU. Whilst performance practitioners apply their lean-systems training they are supported by intelligence professionals with specialist knowledge of the systems and processes such as Tasking and Coordination and Intelligence management. This specialist support enables the collective team to recommend process improvements and identify effective practice. Figure 21.3 illustrates this relationship between NIM and

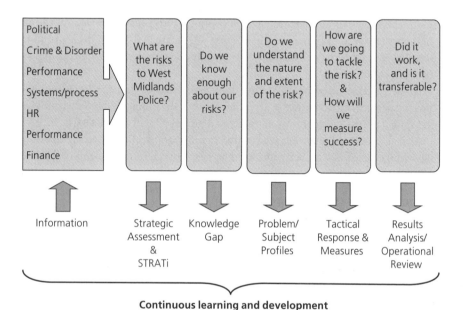

**Continuous learning and development
& Organizational capabilities**

Fig 21.3 Links Between a Performance-Management and Intelligence-Led Approach

Continuous improvement. Built into the ASAP process are opportunities for OCU senior management teams to attend a three-day course based around Six Sigma and Lean Systems improvement methodologies delivered by an external company. Staff on the OCU who will be tasked with improvement activity are offered a place on a five-day improvement course run by staff from the Performance Review Department. The ASAP process has a robust post-implementation review.

This change of mindset and combined response to risk, harm, and performance has not been achieved by a single action or policy which brings NIM and performance analysis together, but through a combined harm and systems approach to the delivery of continuous improvement and the management of risk.

CONCLUSION

For forces to move towards a more intelligent performance-management process, the conflict between performance and intelligence professionals must be recognized and managed. This should not mean that the disciplines are merged, as each area has a unique contribution to make in the identification and management of force strategic and tactical priorities. Senior managers need to acknowledge that they have different functions and manage the relationship to exploit the opportunities both provide to improve performance and manage risk. Each discipline contributes valuable tools and techniques to deliver against these priorities. For example, it would seem bizarre for an intelligence analyst to process-map the offender management processes or for a performance analyst to timeline a murder.

In WMP, the use of SPC, as the common approach to understanding and interpreting data, was the starting point for improved working relationships. The journey has resulted in a mature performance framework, where NIM is being used to identify risk and opportunity, and performance management to improve the efficiency and effectiveness of the processes. Integration of the two into the planning framework has helped to create a greater alignment between the many external priorities set by government with those issues faced by local communities. The practical application of this joint framework enables the force to respond quickly to changes in the policing environment. Key to the success of this performance framework has been the depth of understanding and leadership provided by the force Command Team. The knowledge of intelligence and improvement is not confined to a small team of practitioners but is a language understood and used by senior managers across the force to deliver improved performance.

REFERENCES

GARGON, N, ACC Thames Valley Police, conference presentation: 'Tackling organized crime in partnership' (London, 30–31 October 2007).

LONG, M, 'Leadership and performance management' in Newburn, T, ed, *Handbook of Policing* (Devon: Willan Publishing, 2003) 628–654.

MOORE, M, 'Sizing up Compstat: An important administrative innovation in policing' *Criminology and Public Policy* 2/3 (2003) 469–494.

NATIONAL INTELLIGENCE MODEL DEVELOPMENT UNIT West Midlands Police, *Strategic Threat and Risk Assessment Index Practitioners Manual* (2006).

NATIONAL POLICE IMPROVEMENT AGENCY, *Guidance on The National Intelligence Mode: CENTREX* (2005) 4.

NORTON, DP, 'The balanced scorecard: Measures that drive performance' *Harvard Business Review* (January-February 1992).

PETERSON, MB, *Intelligence-Led Policing: The New Intelligence Architecture* (USA: US Department of Justice, 2005).

SEDDON, J, *Freedom from Command and Control—A Better Way to Make the Work Work* (New York: Vanguard Education Limited, 2003).

SIX SIGMA, <http://www.pmi.co.uk>.

WHEELER, DJ and CHAMBERS, DS, *Understanding Statistical Process Control* (Knoxville: SPC Press, 1992).

22

THE HOME OFFICE AND THE POLICE: THE CASE OF THE POLICE FUNDING FORMULA[1]

Professor Ken Pease OBE

Those of my former students who have become community safety practitioners, and seek references from me to support their case for promotion, give prominence in their CVs to central government cash attracted to their Crime and Disorder Reduction Partnerships, not to any crime reductive impact to which such funding may have led (Pease, 2007). This oddity led me to the realization that in one guise or another, funding arrangements reveal the exercise of power in relationships and distinguish the essential from the incidental purposes of those involved. From the parental allocation of pocket money to subsidies under the European Common Agricultural Policy, the basis on which money is disbursed and the form which objections to that disbursement take tell one much about how individuals and groups relate to each other. In 1948, the bulk of the public supported the notion of a National Health Service, but the medical profession, especially its most senior members, did not. Aneurin Bevan's method for their conversion, famously, was to 'stuff their mouths with gold' (see Foot, 1975; Tobias, 1994). Senior consultants in medicine perhaps were (and remain) in a particularly powerful position to open their mouths and expect riches to be available for ingestion. Medical consultants, by dint of their professional prestige and political influence, can make life difficult for governments wishing to constrain their earning power. Other public-sector workers are, to a greater or lesser extent, not so fortunate. At the time of writing, a dispute about police pay is brewing, centring upon the non-backdating of a 2.5 per cent pay rise. Lying at its core is the police eschewal of the right to strike, in exchange for implementation of long-term pay arrangements. The dispute comes some 30 years after the government of James Callaghan hived off the police remuneration issue to a commission chaired by Lord Edmund-Davies, which yielded the formula by which police pay was subsequently assessed. The issue was already hoary. The Desborough Committee, which sat in 1919, said that, as an officer of the Crown, 'a policeman has responsibilities and obligations which are peculiar to

[1] Thanks to Aiden Sidebottom and Andromachi Tseloni for most helpful comments and advice on this chapter.

his calling and distinguish him from other public servants'. In 1962, the Royal Commission said 'the constable is unique among subordinates in the nature and degree of the responsibility he is required to exercise'. Edmund-Davies, in 1978, concurred and recommended a 45 per cent pay rise, implemented in full by the incoming Conservative government as one of Prime Minister Thatcher's first decisions. The indexation that underpinned the deal remained in place for 27 years until the present government decided to scrap it.

While the issue of police pay is of interest in its own right, and the disputes about such pay illustrate some of the subtleties of the relationship which separates the police from other public-sector workers, it is less revealing than the distribution of money from the Home Office across places. After all, once a police officer's pay is determined, it is (with some minor tweaks) the same from Cumbria to Cornwall. The motif running through the chapter concerns the allocation of police resources so as to be commensurate with need. After a preamble seeking to make a case that resourcing within forces is generally not proportionate to need, attention will turn to distribution at the force level from the Home Office via the Police Funding Formula (hereinafter PFF). This will encompass its imperfections, police objections to it, and what all this might tell us about the relationship between police and Home Office, and what might be done to achieve a more equitable distribution of resources both within and between forces.

ALLOCATION WITHIN FORCES: WINTER IN FLORIDA, SUMMER IN ALASKA, AND OTHER MATTERS

In a recently published analysis (Ross and Pease, 2008), the association between crime and number of police officers allocated to an area was calculated. At the crudest level, number of crimes stands proxy for policing need. First, it was shown that at the force level, doubling the number of crimes to be dealt with is associated with approximately a 62 per cent increase in the number of police officers available to deal with them. So, at the force level, doubling the problem does not double the resource to deal with it. Next, Basic Command Units within one large force were examined in the same way. It shows that a doubling of crime is associated with a mere 23 per cent increase in police strength. So even more than is the case at force level, policing resource does not keep pace with the problem. Finally, analysis by beats within one Basic Command Unit of a different force showed, on the face of it, that a doubling of crime corresponds with roughly a 36 per cent increase in the number of dedicated officers. These analyses are crude. The most crime-challenged areas will suck police resources in via response to emergency calls, and these additional interventions are not taken account of. Factors other than crime clearly impact on police work. This rough and ready demonstration of the mismatch between crime and police strength is nonetheless important, as will be outlined in the next paragraph.

The first reaction of police commanders to the admittedly crude analysis, suggesting that police resourcing is systematically distorted relative to the presenting crime problem, tends to be criticism on one of the following lines:

- that the balance is made fairer by the disproportionate reactive attention given to crime-challenged areas;
- key performance indicators for the police do reflect extent and type of crime, so that the present distribution of resources is experience-based in a more refined way than is reflected in the analysis;
- that the force area has special features (Rumanians in Knightsbridge, hosting many motorway miles) which drive resourcing patterns and practices.

The first argument is true if one regards proactive and reactive policing as equivalent. Reactive policing cannot offset inadequate levels of proactive policing, so the notion of balance is spurious in this context. One might as well say that good treatment of those suffering heart attacks makes up for inadequate resourcing of the prevention of cardio-vascular problems. The second argument is relevant only insofar as the amount of crime in an area varies inversely with its seriousness. While the necessary tedious and lengthy analyses of BCS data have not yet been undertaken (but should be), the writer is confident that crime-challenged areas suffer both more, and more *serious,* crime. If this is the case, the truth would be the precise opposite of that contended in the objection. The third objection is perfectly valid, and points towards a different way of coming at the issue of police funding, which will be touched upon later in the present chapter.

ALLOCATION VERSUS NEED

The writer's attendance at many fortnightly Tasking and Coordinating meetings in one urban police station suggests another powerful driver of the distortion in police resourcing demonstrated by the crude analyses mentioned above. My erstwhile colleague Michael Townsley and I came to refer to this as the 'winter in Florida, summer in Alaska' problem. It refers to the phenomenon whereby policing attention is given to crime spates in areas of traditionally low crime, when such levels are well below those in areas which suffer a large amount of crime, even when these are at their minimum. The soubriquet derives from the notion that Florida residents, accustomed to warm days, complain when the weather is merely mild. Alaskan residents bask in weather which is just cold[2] rather than glacial. Since areas of low crime are inhabited by many citizens who are locally influential and vociferous, concern about 'blips' in low crime areas will be communicated to the police, even when such blips take local crime to a level that would be the envy of those in more hard-pressed places. In the writer's view, the 'winter in Florida' perception accounts for much of the distortion in policing levels relative to the presenting problem at the intra-force level.

The conclusion the reader is invited to reach on the basis of this section is that there is no universal within-force rationale for 'resourcing proportionate to need' which

---

[2] The writer remembers weather forecasters during his time in Saskatoon reporting -8 as mild during winter.

could act as a touchstone for the process whereby the Home Office distributes money among forces via the PFF. Indeed, if the observed mismatch survives more extensive analysis, it merits action. Cynicism born of long experience suggests that funding for such analysis is not likely to be forthcoming. Attention moves now to the means whereby the Home Office seeks to make need commensurate with funding.

THE POLICE FUNDING FORMULA

This formula is used to determine the distribution of money from central government among police forces in England and Wales. The formula was introduced following the Police and Magistrates' Courts Act 1994. Its underpinning assumption is that the policing need of an area can be inferred from the characteristics of the area and its population, that these characteristics are capable of measurement, and that the relationships are sufficiently precise to form an equitable basis for the allocation of funding. The process whereby the PFF was constructed was very sophisticated, and like many sophisticated measuring devices, it easily diverts attention from the essence of its function.

The Catch 22 of the formula is that while it seeks to resource forces in proportion to the problems which they face, received wisdom suggests that it must not do this in any way which makes use of measures of crime and disorder, lest the police become exposed to perverse incentives. The reason for this is obvious and hitherto uncontested. If recorded crime and disorder were the indices on the basis of which funds were disbursed, organisational self-interest would dictate that a force would seek to maximize the amount of crime and disorder it came to record. Recorded crime figures would increase, with predictable political consequences, not least opposition outrage at unprecedented levels of crime. The forces rewarded would be those which showed greatest ingenuity in boosting their crime figures. The easiest way to boost figures is to target so-called victimless crimes, and one could anticipate crackdowns, inter alia, on drug use and prostitution, whose identification flows directly from police presence. Put colloquially, detecting such crimes is like shooting fish in a barrel. The officer does not have to detect anyone, merely be at a place where criminal transactions take place.

The writer takes the position that it would not be such a bad thing if more crimes (albeit mostly 'victimless') came to light and more criminals officially processed. The National Crime Recording Standard sought to realize the position whereby crimes reported to the police were appropriately recorded. This went some way towards ensuring that recorded crime more accurately reflects citizen experience, but only in respect of crimes with victims who (in greater or lesser numbers) reported to the police what had happened to them. If victimless crimes deserve their status as crimes (a different debate), their prevalence needs to be more accurately reflected, since the National Recording Standard has little effect.

To reiterate, the approach whereby crime data is used in whole or part as the basis on which money is disbursed by central government is defensible insofar as it would bring more of the crime which occurs to official attention. However it is currently unfeasible for two reasons, one political and one of principle. The consequential increased volume of recorded crime would prove politically unacceptable. The reason of principle presents itself insofar as the different crime and disorder levels are a function of variations in the quality of police service. If better policing means less crime, better forces would be penalized. It will emerge in what follows that the key question is how one interprets variation between forces which remains beyond that accounted for by the PFF. That interpretation is crucial to a decision about the formula's fairness. This residual variation may either be an indication of policing quality or the consequence of socio-demographic factors not taken into account by the PFF.

CALCULATION OF THE PFF

The statistical technique of multiple regression analysis was used to derive the PFF. The version of the 'principal formula' discussed here is that included in The Police Grant Report (England and Wales) 2007/8, setting out the disbursement of the £4.4 billion to police forces. The grant offers a basic sum per resident of the area to be policed plus a basic sum per person projected to be in an area during a twenty-four hour period (such as commuters and clubbers). This is supplemented by 11 top-up factors, seven of which relate to crime. Others introduce weightings on the basis of fear of crime, traffic, and population sparsity. The indicators used to derive the top-up factors include:

- the number of claimants of unemployment-related benefits with a duration of unemployment more than one year;
- the proportion of terraced households;
- the proportion of student households;
- the proportion of lone-parent households;
- the number of overcrowded households; [3]
- the number of bars per 100 hectares.

The working through of the relationships which justify the top-up factors is not included in the 2007/8 report, so the writer had to make use of a more dated alternative.[4] Nonetheless scrutiny of this, together with the awareness of other relevant research, leads one to suppose that the relationship between the factors incorporated in the top-up measures and the presenting crime problem are so approximate as to allow only the crudest allocation. In short, the assumption that the various kinds of policing need in an area can be related to the characteristics of the area and its population is unjustified. Three arguments are advanced in support of this view.

1. Evidence from the Earlier, More Detailed, Account of the Formula's Use

The key statistic reported is R^2, the coefficient of determination. This shows how much of the variation in the item of interest is accounted for by the factors in the equation.

---

[3] Actually, the natural logarithm of that number. Logarithmic transformations are sometimes used, as they are here, to make data sets more consistent with the assumptions underpinning the statistics used.

[4] <http://www.nationalarchives.gov.uk/ERORecords/HO/415/1/afwg/afwgap3.htm>.

For example, the amount of auto-crime was predictable from the demographic factors used in the equation with $R^2 = 0.49$, so that half of the variability in auto-crime is not captured by the formula then in use. Property crime had $R^2 = 0.60$, and other coefficients were likewise less than impressive. At first blush, the PFF captures 60 per cent of the variation in policing need, the rest being random. Or is it? The alternative is that the 40 per cent 'random' element is to some degree a measure of force efficiency. The interpretation of the variance in crime and disorder not accounted for in the PFF is a crucial issue for understanding the evaluation of police performance generally.

2. Evidence from Other Research

Substantial research has been carried out on the link between socio-demographic variables and crime. Its inescapable conclusion is that the links are complex in nature and surprisingly modest in size. Recent work advancing the issue was carried out by Andromachi Tseloni and Chris Kershaw, the latter a senior Home Office researcher, (Kershaw and Tseloni, 2005). Their information on crime, fear of crime, and disorder was drawn from the 2000 British Crime Survey. The local census variables (relating to postcode sectors) were drawn from the 1991 England and Wales Census. The modelling of measures of fear and disorder proved more robust than the modelling of crime. It appeared to be more possible to predict types of area where concern about crime and problems of disorder are likely to be highest than those areas most at risk of crime. Their R^2 figures are even lower than those reported in the technical documentation on the PFF, and are more in line with those of Osborn, Trickett and Elder (1992). The general thrust of the work by Tseloni and her collaborators is consistent with scepticism that socio-demographic variables are predictive enough to form a reasonable basis for the allocation of funds (see for example Tseloni, Osborn, Trickett and Pease, 2002; Osborn and Tseloni, 1998).

One twist on the use of socio-demographic information to establish policing need is the reality of the ecological fallacy, whereby judgements about individuals are made on the basis of facts about groups (Robinson, 1950). The individual citizen in the same area fares differently on the basis of her local context. In another analysis of the British Crime Survey, Tseloni showed that the between-household variability is 9.5 to 19 times greater than the between-area variability of total household crime, thefts, and burglaries (Tseloni, 2004). Bowers, Johnson and Pease (2005) divided areas of Liverpool by affluence (using the Index of Multiple Deprivation) into quintiles. Table 22.1 shows the prevalence rate of burglary for each housing type by quintile. It will be seen that the risks associated with each dwelling type varies according to the affluence of the area in which it is located. Detached homes, for example, have a prevalence of burglary in the least affluent areas which is some seven times that of the most affluent areas. The moral of this is clear. Area and individuals interact to yield crime risks. This is most clearly and elaborately demonstrated by Tseloni (2006), in a publication of crucial importance to the topic. Relying on area characteristics is unsatisfactory.

THE HOME OFFICE AND THE POLICE

Table 22.1 Burglary Prevalence Per 100 Households by Area Affluence and
Dwelling Type

April 95–00		Dwelling Type		
Prevalence Rate	Semi	Detached	Terraced	Flat
Quintile 1	16.37	10.32	18.87	12.29
Quintile 2	20.39	17.85	18.44	15.87
Quintile 3	29.56	27.46	21.31	20.26
Quintile 4	44.16	57.83	21.95	25.69
Quintile 5	53.21	71.29	25.91	27.31

Note: Modified from Bowers et al 2005. The prevalence rates are high because of the long period over which data were summed.

3. Intrinsic Implausibilities

There are a number of terms in the formula which beg to be scrutinized more closely, for example the number of residents. The police grant for a particular police authority consists of a basic amount per projected resident, and a basic amount per person projected to be present in the authority during a 24-hour period (ie residents plus commuters) for special events. One can think of a range of mixes of visitors to an area with different crime potential (clubbers versus commuters, for example), a range of types of special event (embroidery exhibitions or Prodigy concerts) with different plausible criminogenicity. The number of bars per 100 hectares will have different implications according to the area from which they draw clientele, the opening hours and management practices of the pubs, and their concentration or more even distribution throughout the area. In short, the measures available to the analysts, and with which they have dealt skilfully, are intrinsically implausible as measures of policing need across contexts.

IMPLICATIONS

Taking the evidence that some 60 per cent of the variation in crime can be ascribed to variations in the factors incorporated in the PFF, to what do we ascribe the remaining 40 per cent?[5] The two simplest alternatives are:

1. Socio-demographic or other variation not captured by the PFF.
2. Differences in quality of policing performance.

What are the implications of settling on one or other of these explanations (acknowledging that the truth is more likely to be a mixture of the two)? If the first alternative is correct, the PFF does indeed dispense a very rough form of justice. It may also be taken to mean that the quality of policing at the force level makes no difference

[5] In fact this is an oversimplification. If policing talent is distributed non-randomly across areas differing in crime, the residual variation having taken account of the factors in the formula will be more or less than 40 per cent, depending upon the nature of the non-randomness.

to the crime rate beyond that implicit in area characteristics. If the second alternative is correct, it means that good-quality forces are being over-resourced for their presenting problems, which they have succeeded in suppressing below the expected level. Poor forces are under-resourced for the (partly self-caused) level of crime which they experience.

There are ways in which the two alternatives may be distinguished and, in the light of the implications, it seems important to do so. If the variation in crime not captured in the PFF is random, forces should find themselves on one or other sides of the line of best fit randomly from year to year. If the unexplained variation is attributable to enduring socio-demographic factors not captured by the PFF, forces would find themselves on the same side of the line of best fit over time. If the unexplained variation is attributable to force competence, it should vary with (for example) the tenure of particular chief constables (or at the BCU level, particular commanders). To the best of the writer's knowledge, the PFF has not been explored along these lines.

CONCLUSION

At the beginning of this chapter, it was asserted that financial arrangements are telling indicators of relationships between public-sector actors. The allocation of funds was described and the unexplored implications set out. To recognize what the PFF says about Home Office–police relationships, one also needs to know that a wholly separate Home Office exercise is in place to establish police force efficiency (see Drake and Simper, 2005, for a review and critique). This means that when it comes to doling out money via the PFF, the tacit Home Office assumption is that policing does not impact on crime to the extent of measurably changing it. When it comes to doling out bouquets and brickbats, the assumption is that it does. The political advantages of this schizoid attitude to policing may be substantial, but they come at the cost of a good, integrated method of assessing and rewarding police performance. The sad footnote to this is that police force remonstrations against the iniquities of the PFF focus on specific force needs (Menhinnet, 2007), neglecting the necessary attention to the assumptions built into the PFF outlined in this chapter.

REFERENCES

Bowers, KJ, Johnson, SD and Pease, K, 'Victimisation risk, housing type and area: The ecological fallacy lives!' *Crime Prevention and Community Safety: An International Journal* 7 (2005) 7–18.

Drake, L and Simper, R, 'The measurement of police force efficiency: An assessment of UK Home Office policy' *Contemporary Economic Policy* 23 (2005) 465–482.

Foot, M, *Aneurin Bevan* (London: Paladin, 1975).

JOHNSON, SD, BOWERS, KJ, BIRKS, D and PEASE, K, 'Predictive mapping of crime by ProMap: Accuracy, units of analysis and the environmental backcloth' in Weisburd, D, Bernasco, W and Bruinsma, G, eds, *Putting Crime in its Place: Units of Analysis in Spatial Crime Research* (New York: Springer, 2008).

KERSHAW, C and TSELONI, A, 'Predicting crime rates, fear and disorder using area information: Evidence from the 2000 British Crime Survey' *International Review of Victimology* 12 (2005) 295–313.

MENHINNET, D, 'Police funding branded crippling' *Surrey Comet* (23 December 2007).

OSBORN, DR, TRICKETT, A and ELDER, R, 'Area characteristics and regional variates as determinants of area crime levels' *Journal of Quantitative Criminology* 8 (1992) 265–285.

—— and TSELONI, A, 'The distribution of household property crimes' *Journal of Quantitative Criminology* 14 (1998) 307–330.

PEASE, K, 'Mindsets, set minds and implementation' in Knuttson, J and Clarke, RV, eds, *Implementing Crime Prevention* (Devon: Willan Publishing, 2007).

POLICE GRANT REPORT (England and Wales) 2007/8 (HOC 207, London: The Stationery Office, 2007).

ROBINSON, WS, 'Ecological correlations and the behavior of individuals' *American Sociological Review* 15 (1995) 351–57.

ROSS, N and PEASE, K, 'Community policing and prediction' in Williamson, T, ed, *Knowledge Based Policing* (Chichester: Wiley, 2008).

TOBIAS, J, 'In defence of merit awards' *British Medical Journal* 308 (1994) 974–975.

TSELONI, A, *Multilevel Modelling of the Number of Property Crimes: Household and Area Effect* (Working Paper Series No 5, Department of International and European Economic and Political Studies, Thessaloniki: University of Macedonia, 2004).

——, 'Multilevel modelling of the number of property crimes: Area and household effects' *J R Statist Soc: Series A* 169 (2006) 205–233.

——, OSBORN, DR, TRICKETT, A and Pease, K, 'Modelling property crime using the British Crime Survey: What have we learned?' *British Journal of Criminology* 42 (2002) 89–108.

INDEX